Design and Layout
of Foodservice Facilities

Design and Layout of Foodservice Facilities

SECOND EDITION

John C. Birchfield

Raymond T. Sparrowe

John Wiley & Sons, Inc.

Copyright © 2003 by John Wiley & Sons, Inc. All rights reserved

Published by John Wiley & Sons, Inc., Hoboken, New Jersey
Published simultaneously in Canada

For general information on our other products and services or for technical support, please contact our Customer Care Department within the United States at (800) 762-2974, outside the United States at (317) 572-3993 or fax (317) 572-4002.

Wiley also publishes its books in a variety of electronic formats. Some content that appears in print may not be available in electronic books.

Library of Congress Cataloging-in-Publication Data

Birchfield, John C.
    Design and layout of foodservice facilities / John C. Birchfield, Raymond T. Sparrowe.—2nd. ed.
        p. cm.
Includes bibliographical references and index
    ISBN 0-471-29209-5 (alk. paper)
    1. Food service management. 2. Food service—Equipment and supplies. Restaurants—Design and construction. I. Sparrowe, Raymond T., 1949– II. Title.
    TX911.3.M27 B57 2002
    647.95'068—dc21

                                            2002000628

Printed in the United States of America
10   9

Gourmet meals at the Sparrowe home, crab fests on Kent Island, long discussions with appropriate beverages, and many trips between Chicago and Annapolis have resulted in the revision of *Design and Layout of Foodservice Facilities*. Our work was eased by the patience and understanding of our spouses, Josalee Birchfield and Patricia Sparrowe. We lovingly dedicate this book to them.

CONTENTS

PREFACE

The foodservice industry is evolving rapidly to keep pace with changes in consumer needs and expectations. In the commercial sector, new restaurant concepts are emerging to satisfy an increasingly discriminating market. In the off-site sectors of the industry (formerly known as non-commercial sectors), such as health care, education, and business and industry, foodservice is becoming increasingly market driven. These changes occurring throughout the industry call for the creation of new foodservice facilities as well as the renovation of existing foodservice facilities. The professional foodservice manager is likely to be involved in the design of a new or renovated facility several times during his or her career.

Design and Layout of Foodservice Facilities is intended to be a resource for hospitality professionals involved in a design project, for college and university students preparing for careers in foodservice management, and for design professionals who wish to know more about the foodservice design process. It offers a step-by-step introduction to the design process, beginning with market research and financial feasibility studies, and following with design principles, equipment selection, and engineering.

NEW IN THE SECOND EDITION

The following updates and changes have been made to the Second Edition:

Market and Financial Feasibility. These essential parts of the planning process for a new foodservice facility have been given more in-depth coverage in Chapter 1. This greater coverage is a response to the increased emphasis on market and financial justification for investment in new and renovated facilities among investors, bankers, trustees, and other constituencies.

The Project Team. Many foodservice design projects involve the work of teams, including the owner's representative, the architects, engineers, foodservice consultant, interior designer, general contractor, and foodservice equipment contractor. Chapter 2 of this edition describes the roles and responsibilities of each member of the project team in greater detail than the First Edition. This enhanced coverage is designed to assist hospitality professionals to participate effectively in the design process as owners or owners' representatives.

ix

Planning and Programming. Additional emphasis is given to the essential planning activities that precede actual design, including the development of an architectural program statement for foodservices. This emphasis reflects the importance of the program statement for later design decisions.

Revised Treatment of the Design Sequence. The sequence of steps described in Chapter 2 is now closely aligned with the "phasing" of a project followed by design professionals. By coordinating the foodservice design sequence with the phasing followed by architects and engineers, this edition enables the hospitality manager to know what to expect as the project moves forward.

Separate Chapters for Design Principles and Space Analysis. The First Edition combined discussions of space analysis and design principles in a single chapter. In the Second Edition, each of these important topics receives its own chapter.

Expanded Coverage of Foodservice Equipment. Two chapters are now devoted to foodservice equipment. Chapter 6 deals with the materials and standards for construction of fabricated equipment, and Chapter 7 covers manufactured equipment. This expanded coverage of custom-fabricated equipment is especially useful to hospitality professionals involved in a large foodservice design project.

Innovations in Foodservice Equipment. Sections have been added to the coverage of foodservice equipment for new items now popular in the industry, including espresso machines, power potwashing systems, and combi oven/steamers.

A New Chapter on Architecture and Engineering. The First Edition featured separate chapters on interior design and foodservice engineering. This edition has a single chapter dealing with architecture and engineering for foodservice facilities. In order to afford greater depth in coverage of foodservice design, much of the material specifically devoted to the work of interior design professionals was omitted in the Second Edition.

INSTRUCTOR'S MATERIALS

The authors have created tools to assist instructors in preparing their college and university courses, including:

Instructor's Manual (0-471-34956-9). The *Instructor's Manual* includes:
- ❑ Suggestions for using the textbook in a 15-week semester
- ❑ Background information for each chapter that is useful in preparing lectures
- ❑ Student homework assignments for each chapter, many using Internet resources
- ❑ Examination questions and answers for each chapter
- ❑ Guidelines for assigning and evaluating a student design exercise as a major project

Web Site (www.wiley.com/college). The web site offers:

❏ PowerPoint slides for download

❏ Examination questions in Microsoft Word format for downloading

❏ Links to foodservice equipment manufacturers' web sites

❏ Visio and Autocad files of representative foodservice equipment for use by students in completing assignments and the design exercise

ACKNOWLEDGMENTS

The authors wish to recognize and thank Alexander Schneider and Daniel Takemori, the technical/CAD operators of Birchfield Jacobs Foodsystems, Inc., for their work and enthusiasm in preparing CAD illustrations for this book. We also are grateful for the assistance of Mihoko Hosoi, hospitality information specialist, at Cornell University's School of Hotel Administration. At John Wiley & Sons, JoAnna Turtletaub, Eileen Chetti, and Tzviya Siegman have been exceptionally helpful and patient editors.

The authors would also like to acknowledge the following reviewers for their insight and recommendations throughout the manuscript preparation process: Kimberle A. Badinelli, Virginia Polytechnic Institute and State University; Ricardo Fredricks, University of New Orleans; R. Thomas George, The Ohio State University; Glenn S. Lemaire, Manchester Community Technical College; Douglas C. Santoro, Morrisons Health Care Division; and J. Thomas Welding, Kent State University

The foodservice facility plans in this book are provided courtesy of Birchfield Jacobs Foodsystems, Inc., or Sparrowe Foodservice Consulting Design unless otherwise noted.

ABOUT THE AUTHORS

John C. Birchfield is the founder of Birchfield Foodsystems, Inc., a food-service consulting and design firm with offices in Annapolis, Maryland. Mr. Birchfield was an Associate Professor of Hotel, Restaurant, and Institutional Management at Michigan State University, and has had operational experience in hotels, clubs, restaurants, and colleges. In 1973, Mr. Birchfield won the International Foodservice Manufacturer's Association Silver Plate Award as Foodservice Operator of the year. He is a past president of the National Association of College and University Food Services and of the Foodservice Consultants Society International. A graduate of Cornell University's School of Hotel and Restaurant Management, Mr. Birchfield also holds a master's degree from Rutgers University in the field of Institutional Management and Nutrition.

Mr. Birchfield is the author of many articles and two books on food-service and management, *The Contemporary Quantity Recipe File*, published by Cahners Books, and the comprehensive *Foodservice Operations Manual,* published by Van Nostrand Reinhold. He served on the advisory board of Cahners Publishing Company for three years and has been a guest columnist for *Food Management Magazine*.

Mr. Birchfield has designed numerous foodservice facilities and has served as an operations consultant to many institutions, hotels, and clubs in the United States and Europe.

* * *

Raymond T. Sparrowe, Ph.D., is the co-author of the Second Edition of *Design and Layout of Foodservice Facilities*. He has been involved in foodservice facilities design and management consulting since 1985, both as an associate at Birchfield Foodsystems, Inc., and in his own practice. Dr. Sparrowe has designed foodservice facilities for education, healthcare, and cultural institutions, and has consulted with many organizations in foodservice operations. He is the co-author (with Kaye Chon, Ph.D.) of *Welcome to Hospitality: An Introduction*. Dr. Sparrowe also was a member of the team that developed the USDA's highly successful videotape and training package entitled *Food Safety Is No Mystery*. In 1996, with Pamela Popielarz, Ph.D., he was awarded the Van Nostrand Reinhold award for excellence in hospitality management research for his study on the career progression of hotel and restaurant managers.

Dr. Sparrowe has taught in the Manfred Steinfeld Program in Hospitality Management at Roosevelt University in Chicago, and at Cleveland State University. He is now on the faculty of the John M. Olin School of Business at Washington University in St. Louis, where he teaches courses in leadership and organizational behavior. Dr. Sparrowe's scholarly research has been published in the *Academy of Management Review*, the *Academy of Management Journal*, and the *Journal of Applied Psychology*. He holds a bachelor's degree from the University of California at Santa Barbara, a master's degree from Michigan State University, and his doctorate in organizational behavior is from the University of Illinois at Chicago.

CHAPTER 1

PRELIMINARY PLANNING

(handwritten margin notes: "or replace single peice of equipment" / "4 Levels — v. small" / "① Renovate part of existing FSF" / "② Total renovation significant portion of existing FSF" / "③ New construct / complete renov." / "④ Prototype for chain")

THIS CHAPTER

- ☑ Assists the reader in determining the scope of a project, which will in turn determine the complexity of the planning process
- ☑ Explains the process of concept development for hotels, chains, restaurants, and institutions
- ☑ Guides the person who is contemplating a design or equipment replacement project through the decision-making process regarding menu, market, management, money, and method of execution
- ☑ Introduces the elements of a feasibility study and outlines the different kinds of feasibility research that are necessary before designing a foodservice facility

THE SCOPE OF A PROJECT

Scope refers to the size and complexity of a foodservice facility design project. The scope of the project influences the design approach taken by the owner or manager. If the project involves only the layout of a new hot-food production area for an existing restaurant, the approach used and the planning process will be fairly simple. If the project entails the construction of a new restaurant or the complete renovation of an existing facility, the planning process becomes more difficult. And if the project includes the construction of a new facility that is to serve as the prototype for a chain or franchise, the planning process is even more complex.

Scope can be divided into four levels of complexity, each of which requires the involvement of different individuals and different amounts of planning time. Determining the scope of the project is an important first step before the planning begins.

Level I Scope

Projects of level I scope involve no more than the selection of a major piece of equipment or the replacement of a small area of a foodservice facility. Examples of level I projects include:

❏ Replacement of a dish machine and dish tables in a school cafeteria
❏ Replacement of the display refrigerator and service counter in a deli-catessen
❏ Purchase and installation of an outdoor walk-in freezer in a nursing home
❏ Replacement of the range section in a country club

Projects of level I scope typically can be carried out under the leadership of the owner or manager, assuming that he or she is familiar with foodservice equipment and has a good grasp of the workings of the food facility. If the owner does not have a working knowledge of equipment, a food facilities design consultant may be needed. The owner also will require the assistance of the kitchen equipment dealer and/or manufacturer's repre-sentatives in selecting and installing the equipment. Figure 1-1 compares the professionals involved in projects with different levels of size and com-plexity.

Level I scope projects usually can be completed in a period of six to twelve weeks. Figure 1-2 compares the time requirements of typical proj-ects at each of the four levels of scope.

Level II Scope

Level II scope projects involve the renovation of a significant portion of an existing foodservice facility. Examples of level II scope projects include:

❏ Renovation of the entire service area in a university foodservice facility
❏ Replacement of all of the walk-in coolers and freezers in a country club
❏ Replacement and relocation of the warewashing system in a hospital
❏ Addition of banquet rooms and serving kitchens in a hotel

The professionals likely to be involved in level II scope projects include the owner, an architect, mechanical and electrical engineers, a foodservice

	Level			
	I	II	III	IV
Owner	☑	☑	☑	☑
Foodservice Design Consultant	☑	☑	☑	☑
Architect		☑	☑	☑
Engineer	☑	☑	☑	☑
Interior Designer		☑	☑	☑
General Contractor		☑	☑	☑
Subcontractor		☑	☑	☑
Equipment Dealer	☑	☑	☑	☑
Manufacturer's Representative	☑			
Banker			☑	☑
Lawyer			☑	☑
Accountant			☑	☑
Realtor			☑	☑

Figure 1-1. Professionals involved in projects of different levels of scope.

Task	Level I	Level II	Level III	Level IV
Planning	1 week	4 weeks	6 weeks	3 months
Equipment Selection	1 week	2 weeks	1 month	2 months
Design and Engineering	1 week	4 weeks	2 months	4 months
Preparing Bid Documents	2 days	4 weeks	2 months	2 months
Equipment Delivery	4–6 weeks	2–3 months	4–6 months	4–6 months
Installation	3–5 days	2–6 weeks	1–3 months	1–3 months

Figure 1-2. Time lines for projects of different levels of scope.

facility design consultant, and a kitchen equipment contractor. (The roles of these individuals are described in Chapter 2.) A full complement of professionals is necessary at level II because such projects are complex and require expertise in construction, engineering, and foodservice equipment layout and design.

Level II scope projects require a much longer time to complete than do level I projects. Figure 1-2 shows a typical time line for a level II renovation project.

Level III Scope

Level III scope projects involve the complete renovation of an existing foodservice facility or the design and construction of a new foodservice facility. Examples of level III scope projects include:

❏ Renovation of the dietary department of a hospital
❏ Construction of a new theme restaurant
❏ Renovation of the kitchen, service, and dining areas in a country club
❏ The development of foodservices for a new hotel

The planning process for the renovation of a foodservice facility often is even more complex than designing a new facility because of the difficulty of dealing with existing walls, structural members, utilities, and space, and the demolition of parts of the existing structure. Moreover, in renovation projects decisions must be made about which pieces of existing equipment should or could be used in the newly renovated facility.

The professionals likely to be involved in level III scope projects include the owner, an architect, mechanical and electrical engineers, a foodservice facility design consultant, an interior designer, a general contractor, and a kitchen equipment contractor.

Level III scope projects may take from one to three years from design to completion. Figure 1-2 shows a typical time line for a level III renovation project.

Level IV Scope

Level IV scope projects involve the development of a chain or franchise prototype. Chain or prototype foodservice facilities require intense planning and design efforts because they will be constructed in multiple locations. Inefficiencies in design or inadequacies in equipment could be repeated hundreds of times, and thus will be exceptionally expensive to correct. Such projects, in addition to the requirements of level III scope projects, involve a corporate strategy, a well-researched marketing plan, complex financial planning, and a strong management team. The food facility design at level IV must fit the needs of the menu, market, strategy, and financial package that is being developed by the corporation.

Professionals likely to be involved in level IV projects include investors and/or owners of the corporation, marketing consultants, financial planners, bankers, and corporate staff specialists as well as the design team, consisting of an architect, engineers, a foodservice design consultant, an interior designer, and contractors.

The time required for a level IV scope project is longer than for a level III project in the design phases but may be shorter in the construction phases. Figure 1-2 shows the typical amount of time required for level IV scope projects.

Once the scope has been determined, the owner can move forward with the project. In level I and level II scope projects, moving forward means going directly to the design process. However, when the scope of the project involves the renovation of an existing facility or the development and construction of a new foodservice facility, the next step in the process is concept development.

CONCEPT DEVELOPMENT

The *concept* of a foodservice operation is the overall plan for how it will meet the needs and expectations of its intended market. A foodservice operation's concept is expressed in many ways, including its menu, decor, form of service, pricing, and location. *Concept development* means developing a plan for the success of the operation in its market in advance of actually designing—let alone building—the facility.

It is not unusual for a person to consider a new restaurant or, in fact, to open a new restaurant without knowing what type of food facility will have the best chance of succeeding. The potential entrepreneur may have some investment money, a location or a theme in mind, and a great amount of enthusiasm for the food business, but has not really thought through the total concept of the operation. Unfortunately, enthusiasm and great food products are only half of the success equation. The other half of the equation is the market.

Concept development precedes the actual design of a foodservice facility because the foodservice design team must know what the menu, demand, hours of operation, and mode of service will be.

Single-Unit Restaurant Concept Development

The client who most frequently comes to the food facilities design consultant for help with concept development is the individual restaurant owner. The restaurant owner typically organizes a corporation comprised of a small number of local businesspeople and then begins to develop a concept that will eventually become a freestanding restaurant. The success or failure of the venture often depends on how well the concept was planned and how well the plan was followed.

Numerous concepts are possible for single-unit restaurants. Commonly found concepts often are described in terms of the following general categories:*

❑ *Fine-dining restaurants.* Fine-dining restaurants are distinguished by fine cuisine prepared by celebrity chefs, attentive service, stylish decor, and high prices.

❑ *Theme restaurants.* Theme restaurants offer a dining experience that evokes special times, places, or events, such as English pubs, restaurants owned by sports celebrities, and re-creations of diners from the 1950s.

❑ *Casual dinner houses.* Casual dinner houses emphasize a comfortable and contemporary decor, as well as high value. Well-known casual dinner houses are not single-unit restaurants, but chains such as Bennigan's, T.G.I. Friday's, and Max & Erma's.

❑ *Ethnic restaurants.* Ethnic restaurants are closely tied to the cultures or foodways from which they originated. They include Mexican, Italian, French, German, Thai, and Indian restaurants, to name but a few.

❑ *Family restaurants.* Family restaurants specialize in relatively inexpensive fare and are kid-friendly.

❑ *Quick-service restaurants.* Quick-service restaurants specialize in convenience and fast service and include fast-food operations as well as delis, bagel shops, and sandwich shops.

Each of these categories of foodservice concept involves differences in menu, decor, mode of service, and price. However, not all of these factors are equally important within a given concept. Price is a critical factor in the success of quick-service, family, and casual dinner restaurants, where customers are value-conscious. However, price may not be as important in fine-dining restaurants, where customers expect to pay top dollar. Similarly, location is crucial for quick-service restaurants because their clientele depend upon convenient access. But for some fine-dining and theme restaurants, location is not critical. Concept development for a single-unit restaurant is thus a complex process.

Chain Restaurant Concept Development

When Dave Thomas, the late chairman of the board of Wendy's, traveled around the country with Colonel Sanders in the mid-1950s trying to promote a chicken franchise, he learned many of the dos and don'ts of food franchise marketing. Thomas certainly picked up good ideas about concept development for chain restaurants and franchises, as the success of Kentucky Fried Chicken (known as "KFC") and then Wendy's demonstrates. The basic objectives he developed, which led to the formation of Wendy's, were the following:

❑ Produce a "Cadillac" hamburger with a large number of available condiments.

❑ Limit the menu to the smallest number of items possible, as most restaurants can prepare only a few food items extremely well.

* Adapted from K.-S. Chon and R. T. Sparrowe, *Welcome to Hospitality: An Introduction,* 2nd ed. (Albany, NY: Delmar, 2000), 210–15.

❏ Create an image different from major competitors. In the case of Wendy's, distinctive features included an old-fashioned, nostalgic theme, carpet on the floor, marketing directed at adults, and a larger hamburger than the competition's.

Concept development for Wendy's was more comprehensive than that for a single-unit restaurant. The franchise strategy was carefully thought out to create a balance between company-owned stores and franchised stores. In 1970, only two stores were open, both of them owned and operated by the company. By 1975, 83 company-owned stores and 169 franchised stores were in operation. A ratio of 30 to 40 percent company-owned stores to 60 to 70 percent franchised stores permitted a balance of control and greater financial return. The strategy entailed rapid expansion of the franchise and heavy promotion of the Wendy's name through national advertising. Wendy's now has over 5,400 stores worldwide.

Multiunit casual dinner houses and theme restaurants, such as Chili's, Bennigan's, and the Olive Garden, follow a similar pattern in concept development. Their emphasis is on identifying the key characteristics of their target markets and then locating restaurants where there is a high concentration of individuals who have those characteristics. Key characteristics may include income, age, education, and home ownership.

What gives multiunit restaurants a competitive advantage over single-unit restaurants is the opportunity to learn from experience with multiple examples of the same concept. When a chain restaurant firm has five hundred virtually identical restaurants, it can analyze the factors that differentiate its high-performing restaurants from its low-performing restaurants, and make changes as necessary before opening additional units.

Multitheme Restaurant Concept Development

A particular form of multiunit restaurant for which concept development is critical to success is the restaurant organization that opens and operates restaurants whose concepts are not identical but different. The Levi Organization and Lettuce Entertain You are two examples of successful restaurant chains that have developed multitheme restaurant concepts. These two companies each use several different themes, and each restaurant is promoted with its theme rather than by using the corporate name. Lettuce Entertain You, for example, operates Papagus (a Greek concept), Maggiano's (an Italian concept), Ben Pao (an Asian concept), Cafe Ba-Ba-Reeba! (a tapas bar), and the Corner Bakery. The development of these restaurant concepts through excellent marketing, well-planned menus, and good design comes about through the efforts of a very sophisticated management team.

Hotel Food and Beverage Concept Development

The development of foodservice concepts for hotels has evolved in recent years from the traditional view that considered the food and beverage department as a necessary evil to the modern idea that the food and beverage department is an important profit center. Some large hotels have food and beverage sales of over $35 million per year, an amount that exceeds room sales and creates in management a high expectation of profit from these two departments.

The Hilton Hotel in Atlanta, Georgia, has developed a concept for its first-class rooftop restaurant that goes beyond the idea of a foodservice facility as a profit center. The restaurant, called Nikolai's Roof, was conceived as a luxury dining room and is marketed to the city of Atlanta as well as to hotel guests. The decor is exquisite, the food is served with flair and showmanship, and the entire theme captures the imagination of the city's residents. The concept was developed with such success that the hotel's own guests had great difficulty getting reservations to dine. A hotel restaurant so overcrowded that it could not serve the guests of the hotel would have been unthinkable in earlier days of hotel keeping in the United States. Nikolai's Roof is an excellent example of the execution of a hotel dining concept that complements the hotel itself as well as drawing a significant number of guests from the community.

Hotel managers have known for many years that hotel restaurants must have certain desirable features if they are to be successful. These features include:

❏ Availability of parking

❏ Unique theme or decor (differing from the decor of the hotel itself)

❏ Strong promotion to the community

❏ A menu and a method of service that are distinctive

The developers of hotel properties, and in some cases hotel chains, have used outside foodservice facilities and interior design consultants to create unique specialty restaurants that can be successfully marketed to both hotel guests and the community.

Institutional (Noncommercial) Foodservice Concept Development

Institutional foodservice is usually conceived as a service to an organization, and most often has a not-for-profit philosophy. Most institutional food operations are expected to break even, and all are expected to budget and operate within well-defined ranges of costs so that they do not become a financial burden on the organization they serve. In some cases, the institutional food operation is expected to make a profit and to pay for all of its direct and indirect operational costs.

The development of an operational concept for the institution is often ignored, and this is usually a serious mistake. The institution must accurately interpret its market and must "sell" its products, even when the food is indirectly paid for by the customer. For instance, in hospital foodservice, an unattractive meal presentation will cause dissatisfaction and complaining on the part of the patient and possibly adverse health effects as well if he or she does not eat a meal and thus does not get sufficient nourishment. In a college or university dining hall, a comprehensive concept of service and decor can greatly influence financial success. Attractive food court service or a scramble design, for example, can increase the popularity of a college foodservice operation and generate additional profit. A dining facility operated by a corporation for its employees should also have a well-planned concept and decor. The ability of corporate foodservice operations to attract employees may influence the degree of subsidy that a company is willing to contribute to the operation.

THE FIVE M'S OF CONCEPT DEVELOPMENT

The successful foodservice operation combines the following elements of concept development: market, menu, money, management, and method of execution (Figure 1-3).

Market   The importance of conducting market studies before proceeding with the construction of a food facility cannot be too heavily stressed. The basic marketing questions that must be answered are:

❑ To whom is the food operation being marketed?

❑ Is the market large enough to generate sales and produce a profit?

❑ How will the market be identified?

❑ What method will be used to communicate to this market?

❑ Will the potential customer want or need the food product?

❑ Will a quality assurance plan be developed that will encourage the customer to return because of superior service and/or product quality?

❑ Will internal marketing successfully sell the customer additional services or products after he or she arrives at the food facility?

A classic mistake made by both large corporations and individual restaurant operators is to conduct the market analysis and then fail to act on the basis of the information obtained. There are several cases in which extensive marketing feasibility studies were conducted by outside market-

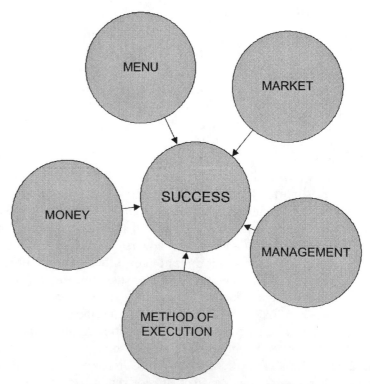

Figure 1-3. The five M's of concept development.

ing firms, but the owners and managers made their decisions on gut feelings rather than from the hard data derived from the study.

Even owners (or potential owners) of food operations who have no marketing background can conduct their own market research, with a small amount of guidance and a large amount of energy and common sense. Do-it-yourself marketing and the limitations of this approach are discussed later in this chapter.

Menu

The importance of the menu to the design of the food facility cannot be overemphasized. The subject of menu writing is too broad to be addressed adequately in a book on foodservice facilities design. The owner or manager is encouraged to seek additional sources of information as a part of the process of developing a menu for a new or renovated food operation.

The menu has a tremendous influence on the design and success of a food operation. From a design and layout perspective, these are just some of the factors determined by the menu:

- ❏ *Amount of space required.* A complex menu requires more space to prepare than a limited or simple menu does, because separate workstations and additional equipment are necessary.
- ❏ *Service area size and design.* The greater the number of menu items, the more area required for service. For example, in a cafeteria each beverage requires a dispenser and each entree a point of service.
- ❏ *Dishwashing area size and dish machine capacity.* Complex menus often require multiple plates, dishes, and utensils, and so the dishwashing area and machine capacity will need to be greater than in the case of simple menus.
- ❏ *Types of cooking equipment.* Complex menus require multiple types of equipment, especially in the final preparation area, where it may be necessary to steam, fry, bake, broil, and sauté.
- ❏ *Equipment capacity.* Limited menus may require relatively few pieces of equipment but need large capacities of each. Complex menus may require many different types of equipment with relatively small capacities.
- ❏ *Size of dry and refrigerated storage areas.* Complex menus may require larger storage areas to maintain the par stocks necessary to meet demand.
- ❏ *Number of employees.* Simple menus require fewer employees than do complex menus.
- ❏ *Amount of investment required.* When large or complex menus require more equipment, space, and employees, costs rise.

Money

Successful capitalization of a food facility includes funds for:
- ❏ Planning costs
- ❏ Building construction or renovation
- ❏ Equipment (fixed)
- ❏ China, glassware, utensils

❏ Furniture and fixtures

❏ Decor

❏ Operating costs

These funds must be identified and committed before serious planning can begin. Yet, in concept development, the commitments may not be made in the early planning stage because the costs are not yet known. Therefore, planning for capital funds is a two-step process: First the financial needs are estimated and sources of financial support are contacted to determine the possibility of obtaining investment funds; then, after concept development has taken place, preliminary designs and construction estimates have been made, and market research is completed, financial commitments are made by lenders and investors.

Management

The quality of the management of the foodservice operation will be the most important element in achieving success. Following are typical questions to be addressed by the owners:

❏ Who will operate the foodservice facility?

❏ What kind of food experience and educational background must this person have?

❏ Who will assist this person in covering the long hours that are usually required to operate a foodservice facility?

❏ What level of pay will this person receive?

❏ Will this person be rewarded in some way for excellent sales and profit results?

❏ How will the owners set operational policies and communicate these to the management staff?

The answers to these questions will determine the organizational structure and the kind of management team that will be used to operate the food facility. The successful restaurant often is owned and operated by one individual whose personality becomes a part of the guests' dining experience. On the other hand, the management of the food and beverage department of a hotel may be under the control of more than one person and usually is part of a more complex organizational team. In this case, the policies and procedures of the food facility should be described in an operations manual to ensure consistent implementation of management policy. From the point of view of the investor or the institutional administration, the management of a food facility must follow traditional management principles of good communication, strong controls, and sound personnel relations regardless of the number of people operating the facility. The operational philosophy and specific management guidelines to be used in foodservice operations must be carefully considered by the investors in a foodservice facility. Failure to develop management guidelines will very likely lead to the financial failure of the operation.

Method of Execution

The last step in concept development involves operational matters. Although the opening date might seem to be in the distant future to the person planning a food facility, decisions about operating methods must be made during the concept development phase on matters such as production methods, control systems, and personnel.

Will convenience foods or traditional "from scratch" cookery be used? This decision will have a great influence on the size of refrigerated and dry storage areas and on the size of the kitchen. Production methods will also determine the number of employees in the kitchen and the skill level of these employees.

PRODUCTION METHODS

Food and beverage controls involve many different parts of the facility, and planning for these controls before the project is under construction is strongly recommended. The following areas of control should be carefully considered:

CONTROL SYSTEMS

- ❏ Cash control
- ❏ Sales analysis
- ❏ Guest check control
- ❏ Food production forecasting
- ❏ Storeroom and refrigeration control
- ❏ Back door security
- ❏ Labor control
- ❏ Purchasing and receiving control
- ❏ Quality control
- ❏ Portion control

The development of financial feasibility studies cannot begin until the amount of labor required is known. The employee schedules, hours of operation, staffing patterns, staff benefits, skill levels, and level of supervision of employees must all be determined before serious development of the food facility begins. As part of its concept development, the fast-food industry based its low labor costs on the use of hourly unskilled labor, scheduled to work short periods of time. When the food operation is busy, part-time employees are scheduled to work. The traditional eight-hour day is seldom used in the fast-food industry, except for supervisors and managers. The use of part-time employees in fast-food restaurants has also significantly reduced the cost of benefits. The use of part-time employees was an important part of concept development in the fast-food industry.

PERSONNEL

FEASIBILITY

Many terms are commonly used in the hospitality industry to describe the process of determining whether or not a food facility is likely to return a profit to its owners. The following is a partial list of these terms:

- ❏ Market or marketability study
- ❏ Market segmentation analysis
- ❏ Market and operations analysis

- ❏ Appraisal report
- ❏ Economic study
- ❏ Time-share feasibility study
- ❏ Feasibility study, report, or analysis
- ❏ Financial feasibility study
- ❏ ROI (return on investment) analysis
- ❏ Sales/performance study

Although each term has a slightly different meaning or involves a slightly different approach, they all share the goal of determining the potential of a facility to generate sales and a profit. In the case of the financial feasibility or ROI (return on investment) analysis, the emphasis is on financial matters such as capital needs, operating funds, cash flow, and return on investment. However, even financial feasibility reports have as their primary focus the determination of whether or not a facility under good management can give investors or owners a return on their investment. For purposes of explaining the feasibility studies and of guiding the owner, manager, or student into a commonsense approach to these studies, they are classified here into two general categories: those that deal with market feasibility and those that attempt to determine financial feasibility. The two forms of feasibility study can be understood in relation to the financial statements for the operation. The *market feasibility study* focuses on the income statement and is conducted to determine whether revenues are sufficient to generate a profit. The *financial feasibility study* focuses on the balance sheet and is conducted to determine whether retained earnings (derived from net income) will be sufficient to satisfy the owners' expectations for a return on their investment.

The Market Feasibility Study

The primary question addressed in the market feasibility study is: What level of sales revenues can the operation be expected to generate? The answer to this question really cannot be known until the operation has opened; however, building a new restaurant only to find that the sales are insufficient to generate a profit is an expensive lesson. The market feasibility study attempts to project the sales level for the operation before the investors have committed their funds to purchase property, construct a building, and hire a team of employees.

The sales revenue for a foodservice facility is a function of two factors over an appropriate period of time: the number of customers and the price they paid.

$$\text{Sales} = \text{Price} \times \text{Quantity}$$

Market feasibility studies thus have to formulate sales estimates from two separate projections: How many customers will there be? How much will each customer spend? These two estimates are interrelated through the simple economic principle that demand (quantity sold) is more or less a function of price.*

---

* "More or less" refers to the price elasticity of demand, a concept that goes beyond the scope of this book.

Market feasibility studies can be conducted either to test the feasibility of an established foodservice concept or to develop new foodservice concepts that would be appropriate for a given market. Chain restaurant organizations interested in expansion usually want to determine whether, or where, in a given market area their concept would enjoy the greatest opportunity for success. Independent restaurateurs, as well as chain restaurant organizations, who are interested in developing a new restaurant use the market feasibility study to develop and refine the concept.

Because the market feasibility process is complex and time-consuming, it is often conducted by specialized consultants. Independent restaurateurs may find that the cost of engaging a market feasibility consultant is prohibitive. However, it is possible—and certainly advisable—for entrepreneurs to conduct an abbreviated market feasibility study. Resources and guidelines for conducting a restaurant feasibility study are available from the National Restaurant Association. (Consult Appendix 1 for information on contacting the National Restaurant Association.)

Market feasibility studies generally follow the process presented—in simplified and shortened form—in Figure 1-4. *Demographic data* and *economic factors* for the community are analyzed to determine the potential market for the restaurant. *Traffic counts* and proximity to *demand generators* are used to assess the viability of possible sites for the restaurant. A *competitive analysis* is performed to determine whether the market can sustain another restaurant at each potential site. Based on these analyses, sales projections are formulated. Each of these steps in the market feasibility study is described in greater detail below.

Demographic data include information about the population near the proposed location of the restaurant, including age, income, gender, occupation, number of children at home, home ownership, the use of automobiles, and similar information. These data about individuals are relevant because

DEMOGRAPHIC DATA

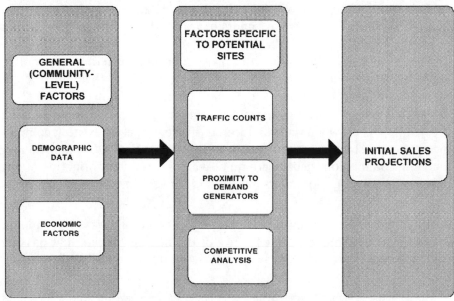

Figure 1-4. The market feasibility process.

target market segments for restaurants are often described in terms of the same factors. Demographics thus are known to predict restaurant behavior. For example, the developers of a casual dinner house may believe that their concept will attract young, single professionals between the ages of twenty-six and thirty-four who have incomes in the $35,000–$50,000 range and who pay monthly rents between $1,000 and $1,600. Obviously, the dinner house should be located where there is a high concentration of individuals who fit the profile of the target market. Gathering demographic data enables the developers to detect the presence of the proposed restaurant's target market segment.

The most comprehensive demographic data are gathered in the decennial U.S. Census. Until recently, using census data involved either extensive library research or access to a mainframe computer. Now, however, detailed census data are available to the public on CD-ROM at a reasonable cost. Also, in the interest of promoting economic growth, many local municipalities have developed extensive databases combining demographic data with information about businesses, organized on detailed maps of the area. This kind of database, called a GIS (geographic information system), gives restaurant developers immediate access to information about the market and the competition.* GIS software and databases also are increasingly available for desktop computers and so bring the resources of high-priced market consultants to the fingertips of entrepreneurs.

ECONOMIC FACTORS   The prevailing economic climate in a community has a significant impact on the market feasibility of a foodservice operation. The health of the restaurant industry in a local area is closely related to the disposable income of its residents. Generally, when disposable income rises in boom times, restaurants prosper. In bust times, disposable income falls and restaurants suffer. However, the effects of economic prosperity and depression affect various restaurant concepts differently. Concepts that offer a high degree of perceived value for the price will suffer less than restaurants with high prices. Also, restaurants that draw customers from a particular industry or from a few large, nearby firms may be protected from broader economic fluctuations if the industry or the large firms prosper during down times. Economic projections for a local area often are available from the chamber of commerce or the local economic development council.

New housing developments are an important indicator of economic growth, especially when they are located on the fringes of existing communities. New restaurants often follow new housing developments. County planning commissions usually are quite willing to share information about planned housing developments, new roads, and zoning issues.

TRAFFIC COUNTS   Restaurants are usually developed along major thoroughfares. Determining market feasibility requires an estimate of the number of cars that pass by each potential location, which is used in determining which site is optimal.

* C. Muller and C. Inman, "The Geodemographics of Restaurant Development," *Cornell Hotel and Restaurant Administration Quarterly, 35 (3)* (1994): 88–95.

Traffic counts can usually be obtained free of charge from the local chamber of commerce, highway department, mayor's office, tourism agency, or other municipal offices.

Some fast-food chains have developed very exact specifications for locating a good site for the foodservice facilities. For instance, one of the guidelines for placement of a Kentucky Fried Chicken (KFC) outlet is that it be located on the "going-home side of the street," for obvious reasons. Other chains have minimum community size, minimum traffic count, and minimum average income standards that must be met before consideration will be given to building or franchising on a particular site.

DEMAND GENERATORS

Demand generators are destinations that draw extensive traffic, such as shopping malls, recreation and sports facilities, and public facilities such as museums, zoos, and parks. Restaurants located near demand generators benefit from the traffic they produce—as, for example, when shoppers have lunch after visiting the local mall.

For some foodservice concepts, proximity to other restaurants enhances rather than hurts market feasibility. Fast-food concepts, for example, often locate in clusters along interstate highway interchanges. Similarly, cities and suburbs often have a "restaurant row" in commercial areas.

COMPETITIVE ANALYSIS

A competitive analysis is crucial to the market feasibility study because the local market potential for a given concept must be shared among all of the competitors. If demographic research identifies an area that has a sales potential of $6 million to $8 million for casual dinner houses, it is important to know how many already are in operation. Moreover, when the restaurateur identifies an area that appears to be ripe for development, he or she should assume that the competition will soon arrive. Most chain restaurant organizations have access to GIS market data, and many of them use those data extensively to identify prime development opportunities.

An independent restaurant entrepreneur who is conducting a market feasibility analysis should identify all the similar concepts within the geographic area, compare menus and prices, and count seats. More importantly, he or she should count customers at various times during the week at the restaurants that would be the closest competition. If patrons are lined up outside the doors to get a seat on Monday or Tuesday night, that is good news. However, if there is no waiting at the competition on Friday or Saturday night, the independent restaurateur should look elsewhere. It is also important to take seasonal factors into account. Counting cars and customers at the competition during the summer months will bias estimates upward, just as counts taken during the winter when two feet (610 millimeters) of snow are on the ground may bias estimates downward.

SALES PROJECTIONS

Sales projections are informed by the information gathered about demographics, economic factors, traffic patterns, demand generators, and competitive analysis. Recall that sales projections are composed of estimates about quantity (number of customers) and price. Demographic data indicate the relative size of the local population and thus are useful in projecting the number of customers (quantity). Income information may also be found in demographic data and may thus assist in estimating the price range that people are willing to accept. Economic factors are especially important in projecting price. Entrepreneurs often make the mistake of basing their sales estimates on data gathered during boom times and thus find themselves suffering during bust times. Traffic pattern data are crucial in estimating customer counts, as is the presence of demand generators. Competitive analysis helps the entrepreneur determine his or her share of the customer market and predict price points against the competition.

The weakness in many market feasibility studies can be found within the sales projection section. This part of the feasibility report is often the first place that a banker will look to determine the accuracy of the financial forecast. Bankers always appreciate conservative sales projections that reflect the restaurateur's planning for sales fluctuations during difficult periods. Restaurant entrepreneurs also often overestimate the dining patterns and price sensitivities of the local market. Sometimes this is the result of wishful thinking, but other times it is the result of insufficient planning and preparation. A valuable way for the entrepreneur to check his or her assumptions about the market is to develop a questionnaire and distribute it to those who reside or work in the area. A questionnaire is helpful in determining such things as:

❏ Detailed demographic data about age, income, and family size
❏ Eating-out patterns (frequency, meal preferences)
❏ Price sensitivity and the average price paid for lunch and dinner at competing establishments
❏ Favorite eating places for various occasions

For a hotel, the sales pattern would be influenced by the house count (number of persons who occupy the guest rooms). The calculation, therefore, should be based on the projected occupancy. Data on hotel occupancy levels are available from leading hospitality industry accounting firms. Price Waterhouse Coopers, Smith Travel Research, and Pannell, Kerr, Foster, for example, regularly publish hotel operations data from all parts of the country and different segments of the hotel field (resorts, transient hotels, and motels).

By utilizing these resources, one should be able to make accurate sales projections that will be credible to the lending institution or investor.

Projections for hospitals and nursing homes are based on patient room occupancy data, but in the health care field a feasibility study usually does not include any data on sales. Foodservice in hospitals and other health care institutions is a service and support arm of the facility, with the primary management and financial considerations focused on the quality of the service and cost containment of the operation.

Once relevant market data have been gathered, a complete sales forecast should be prepared. Figure 1-5 describes the basic steps involved in preparing the sales forecast and illustrates how it is done in a hypothetical college foodservice operation.

This overview of marketing feasibility studies should give the manager, owner, investor, or student a basic understanding of the process, as well as the confidence to conduct such a study if the project is not too large in

The projected sales revenue for a foodservice facility is a function of customer count and the average check for a given period of time. Sales equal customer count multiplied by average check.

Step 1: Customer Counts (Projected)

The market research should indicate the total number of seats necessary for the new or renovated facility. During any meal period, each seat is likely to turn over, or be used by more than one customer. How often a seat turns over is a function of several factors, including how long the meal period is and how long it takes a customer to finish his or her meal. Seat turnover between 11:30 A.M. and 1:30 P.M. in a fast-food restaurant may be relatively high compared to that in a fine-dining restaurant.

To determine the total potential customer count, the number of anticipated seats is multiplied by the seat turnover to determine the customer count for each meal during a given period of time, such as a week. It is essential to make separate calculations for each meal during the week, because the total number of seats needed for the new or renovated facility derived from market research should represent the optimal capacity during peak demand periods—for example, Friday and Saturday evenings in a fine-dining restaurant. Other meal periods are likely to have a lower demand (expected customer count). The example below shows projected customer counts for a college dining facility.

	Sun.	Mon.	Tues.	Wed.	Thurs.	Fri.	Sat.	Total
Breakfast	Closed	200	225	250	250	220	100	1,245
Lunch	Closed	300	350	375	375	300	200	1,900
Dinner	Closed	320	350	350	300	200	150	1,670

Step 2: Average Check (Estimated)

Determine the average check by using the actual average check if the operation already exists, or the prices from the new menu if one is anticipated. If a new operation is being planned, check the questionnaire results and the average check for similar operations or restaurants in the area. Check averages will be different for breakfast, lunch, and dinner. In the college dining facility example below, the estimates are in the far right column.

	Sun.	Mon.	Tues.	Wed.	Thurs.	Fri.	Sat.	Total	Price
Breakfast	Closed	200	225	250	250	220	100	1,245	$2.75
Lunch	Closed	300	350	375	375	300	200	1,900	$4.00
Dinner	Closed	320	350	350	300	200	150	1,670	$5.00

Step 3: Multiply Projected Customer Count by Estimated Average Checks

The sales estimate for a week is the sum of the project sales for each meal period (far right column).

	Sun.	Mon.	Tues.	Wed.	Thurs.	Fri.	Sat.	Total	Price	Sales
Breakfast	Closed	200	225	250	250	220	100	1,245	$2.75	$ 3,423.75
Lunch	Closed	300	350	375	375	300	200	1,900	$4.00	$ 7,600.00
Dinner	Closed	320	350	350	300	200	150	1,670	$5.00	$ 8,350.00
										$19,373.75

Step 4: Prepare a Sales Projection for the Year

Sales projections for an entire year are computed by multiplying the weekly sales estimate by the number of weeks the operation is open during the year. It is necessary, however, to correct for seasonal fluctuations in demand. A restaurant with an outdoor patio seating seventy-five is likely to have greater sales during the summer months. For the college dining example, the yearly sales are calculated as follows: 30 weeks of full operation @ $19,373.75 = $581,212.50, plus 10 weeks of summer school (50 percent sales potential) @ $9,686.88 = $96,868.75, for a total of $678,081.25.

Figure 1-5. Calculation of projected sales.

scope. Excellent sources of more detailed information on the subject are the associations that represent segments of the foodservice industry.

The Financial Feasibility Study

The lending institution, investor, owner, and manager will all want to know the financial projections for the planned new or renovated food facility. Each of these persons will, of course, have a different set of reasons for seeking the projections, and each will want data from the projections presented in a different manner. For instance, the banker will be looking in part for the ratio of invested capital to borrowed capital. The banker may also want to know the amount of operating cash and the cash flow from sales that will be involved in the operation. The manager needs to know what his or her budget is and what the expectation of the owner is concerning profit and loss. The manager and the banker probably will not be using the same

JOE'S GRILL PROJECTED COMPARATIVE BALANCE SHEET		
	January 1, 2003	*January 1, 2004*
ASSETS		
Current assets		
Cash	$ 12,000	$ 14,000
Food inventory	6,000	7,000
Total	$ 18,000	$ 21,000
Fixed assets		
Building	$220,000	$220,000
Furniture and fixtures	60,000	65,000
Land improvements	10,000	10,000
Total	$290,000	$295,000
Total assets	$308,000	$316,000
LIABILITIES		
Current liabilities		
Accounts payable	$ 8,000	$ 13,000
Note to bank	40,000	35,000
Total	$ 48,000	$ 48,000
Long-term liabilities		
Mortgage, building	$180,000	$175,000
OWNER'S EQUITY		
Capitalization	$ 80,000	$ 93,000
Total liabilities and equity	$308,000	$316,000

Figure 1-6. Example of a projected balance sheet.

financial reports and projections, but they certainly will be getting their information from the same original source, which will probably be the financial feasibility study. Usually in the financial feasibility study two basic documents—the projected balance sheet and the pro forma profit-and-loss statement—are prepared, along with other supporting reports and schedules. A good outline of the kind of information that must be projected can be made by examining the line items on each of these documents.

A simple comparative balance sheet, like that shown in Figure 1-6, illustrates the kind of data that must be determined. This balance sheet is a simplification of the projected comparative balance sheet that should be developed under the guidance of the firm's accountant. Note that the balance sheet shows a projected comparison between the assets, liabilities, and capital for a twelve-month period. The balance sheet illustrates a number of projections that must be made by the person or firm preparing the financial feasibility study.

PROJECTED BALANCE SHEET

On the asset side of the balance sheet:

❑ The amount of cash needed as operating funds
❑ The amount of cash tied up in food inventory
❑ The investment in land and building
❑ The cash needed for a down payment on land and building
❑ The cost of furniture, fixtures, equipment, and utensils
❑ The cost of parking lots, driveways, lighting, and other improvements to the property

On the liabilities and equity side of the balance sheet:

❑ Necessary short-term funds that must be borrowed
❑ The amount of payables
❑ The amount of long-term mortgages on building and land
❑ The amount of funds that will represent the owner's equity (capitalization)

Decisions regarding the type of business organization (proprietorship, partnership, corporation, and so forth) and control of ownership (closely held, limited number of investors, the sale of common stock, and so forth) are made prior to preparing the projected balance sheet.

The pro forma profit-and-loss (P&L) statement should be prepared by the owner, manager, or other persons who will be involved in the management of the food facility. This statement projects the income and expense for a particular period of time. For the financial feasibility study, a three-to-five-year projection would be considered sufficient. The format for the P&L should follow the Uniform System of Accounts developed for hotels and restaurants for income and expense categories that fit the needs of the food operation. An example of a pro forma P&L is found in Figure 1-7.

PRO FORMA PROFIT-AND-LOSS STATEMENT (INCOME STATEMENT)

Several supporting schedules are prepared to supplement the P&L statement. Because food and labor costs combined typically run between 60 and 80 percent of sales revenue, schedules providing detailed information

**JOE'S GRILL
PRO FORMA STATEMENT OF PROFIT AND LOSS**

	2003	2004	2005
REVENUE			
Food sales	$400,000	$500,000	$600,000
Cost of food sales (40%)	(160,000)	(200,000)	(240,000)
Beverage sales	200,000	300,000	400,000
Cost of beverage sales (30%)	(60,000)	(90,000)	(120,000)
Gross profit on sales	$380,000	$510,000	$640,000
CONTROLLABLE EXPENSES			
Salaries	$ 60,000	$ 70,000	$ 80,000
Wages	120,000	140,000	160,000
Benefits	3,600	5,200	6,000
Supplies	2,000	3,000	4,000
Insurance	3,000	3,500	4,000
Entertainment	4,000	4,500	5,000
Utilities	30,000	32,000	34,000
Maintenance	10,000	15,000	20,000
Replacement, china and glass	3,000	7,000	8,000
General	2,000	3,000	4,000
Total	$237,600	$283,200	$325,000
FIXED EXPENSES			
Real estate taxes	$ 15,000	$ 15,000	$ 15,000
Lease on land	12,000	12,000	12,000
Total	$ 27,000	$ 27,000	$ 27,000
Total controllable and fixed expenses	$264,600	$310,200	$352,000
Net Profit Before Taxes	$115,400	$199,800	$288,000

Figure 1-7. Pro forma statement of profit and loss.

on how the cost of food sales and the cost of personnel and related expenses were calculated are often provided.

Cost of Sales　A schedule detailing how the amount shown on the cost-of-sales line of the P&L statement was calculated is often prepared. Because the cost of sales for the menu equals the selling price minus the cost of the ingredients used in preparation, two closely related steps are involved in preparing the schedule: determining the portion cost for each menu item and estimating the price for each menu item.

Menu Item: Ham and Cheese Sandwich

Ingredients	Portion Size	Cost ($)	Total ($)
Ham	2 oz.	2.00 lb.	.25
Swiss cheese	2 oz.	2.40/lb.	.30
Rye bread	2 slices	.80/loaf, 20 slices/loaf	.08
Mustard	¼ oz.	3.60/gal.	.01
Mayonnaise	½ oz.	4.80/gal.	.02
Lettuce	1/20 head	.80/head	.04
Pickle chips	2 slices	4.00/gal.	.02
		Total	.72

Figure 1-8. Calculating standard recipe cost.

The portion cost for each menu item is determined by examining the recipe and costs for each ingredient. Figure 1-8 illustrates the costing process for a menu item. The form provides the following information:

❏ A list of all food ingredients
❏ The portion size of each ingredient
❏ The cost of each ingredient
❏ The total portion cost

If the menu price includes the meat, vegetable, dessert, and beverage, then the above example would necessarily include a complete list of all foods that are a part of this meal. A small amount ($.05) might be added to cover the cost of seasonings and other condiments.

The two traditional methods for determining the selling price for menu items are (a) to divide the portion cost by a set percentage (the desired food cost percentage for the operation), and (b) to add a set dollar amount to the cost. Using the first pricing approach, a manager who seeks to have a 32 percent food cost percentage would divide the food cost of a menu item by the desired percentage. For example, a food cost for a ham sandwich of $.72 would be divided by .32, and the selling price would be $2.25. Using the second approach, the manager would add a fixed amount to the cost of each menu item. Adding $2 to the cost of the ham sandwich would result in a selling price of $2.72.

A third approach to setting prices involves looking not at each item but at the menu and *menu mix* (the quantity sold of each menu item) as a whole. The goal of this approach is to set prices so that the *contribution margin* (the amount of revenue remaining when the cost of sales has been subtracted from revenue) is sufficient to pay all expected fixed expenses and satisfy the owner's expectations for a return on investment.

A spreadsheet like that shown in Figure 1-9 can be used to estimate the overall cost of sales by building from the cost of each menu item.* It shows

---

* The spreadsheet is based on the "menu engineering" process developed by Kasavana and Smith. For further information, see M. Kasavana and D. Smith, *Menu Engineering: A Practical Guide to Menu Analysis* (Lansing, MI: Hospitality Publications, 1981).

	Selling Price ($)	Portion Cost ($)	Contribution Margin ($)	Item Cost (%)	Item Quantity	Total Sales ($)	Total Cost ($)	Total Item Contribution ($)
Menu Item 1	8.95	3.11	5.84	34.75	240	2,148.00	746.40	1,401.60
Menu Item 2	7.95	2.74	5.21	34.47	225	1,788.75	616.50	1,172.25
Menu Item 3	11.95	3.88	8.07	32.47	85	1,015.75	329.80	685.95
Menu Item 4	6.95	3.05	3.90	43.88	280	1,946.00	854.00	1,092.00
Menu Item 5	9.95	3.18	6.77	31.96	160	1,592.00	508.80	1,083.20
Menu Item 6	11.95	4.01	7.94	33.56	110	1,314.50	441.10	873.40
Menu Item 7	8.95	2.77	6.18	30.95	220	1,969.00	609.40	1,359.60
Menu Item 8	5.95	2.43	3.52	40.84	315	1,874.25	765.45	1,108.80
						13,648.25	4,871.45	8,776.80
					Food Cost Percent	35.69%		

Figure 1-9. Spreadsheet for determining cost of sales.

columns for the projected price, the portion cost, the contribution margin (price minus cost), the menu item cost percentage (cost divided by price), the projected quantity sold (the menu mix), the total sales (price multiplied by quantity), the total cost (portion cost multiplied by quantity), the total cost (cost multiplied by quantity), and the total contribution (contribution multiplied by quantity) for each menu item. The total cost, $4,871.45, when divided into $13,648.25, the total sales, gives an overall cost percentage of 35.69 percent given the projected prices, costs, and menu mix.

Using a spreadsheet like that shown in Figure 1-9 allows the owner to evaluate the effects of different pricing strategies on the overall food cost percentage for the operation. The advantage of the spreadsheet approach over traditional strategies to pricing, such as simply marking up the cost by a given percentage or dollar amount, is that prices can be set to generate the maximum contribution margin. In foodservice, profits come not from minimizing the food cost percentage but from maximizing the contribution margin. However, for the purposes of preparing the pro forma profit-and-loss statement, the overall food cost percentage derived from the spreadsheet can be used to estimate the cost of sales.

Finally, it is essential to check the competition in setting prices for each menu item, because an operation that is not competitively priced will suffer.

Once the menu pricing and preferred menu mix have been established, the calculation of the cost of food sales is simple: The projected sales revenue is multiplied by the overall food cost factor, and the result is shown on the pro forma P&L statement. In Figure 1-9, the cost factor is 40 percent of food sales. For the years shown, the cost of food sales is estimated to be 40 percent of the sales revenue.

Cost of Personnel and Related Expenses The method of projecting the total labor costs for the pro forma P&L statement is to decide on the number of persons needed in each job category and then prepare an employee sched-

Position	Number of Persons	Hours per Week	Weekly Cost ($)
Manager	1	40–50	800.00
Assistant manager	1	40–50	600.00
Chef	1	40	600.00
Cook	2	80	960.00
Cook's helper	1	40	400.00
Dishwasher	3	120	840.00
Waitress	4	160	960.00
Total weekly cost			$5,160.00
Weekly labor	$5,160 × 52 Weeks		$268,320
Overtime at 10%			26,832
Benefits at 25%			73,788
Total Labor and Benefits			$368,940

Figure 1-10. Calculating the cost of personnel and related expenses.

ule. Salary and wage levels should be estimated, and the annual cost of labor computed. A small amount, perhaps 10 to 12 percent, should be added for overtime. The labor schedule might appear as shown in Figure 1-10.

The examples illustrated are very simple to construct and take a commonsense approach to providing the backup data that are often required for a financial feasibility study. Other major costs, such as utilities and taxes, should be obtained from local utility and government agencies, to be sure of accurate projections. The estimates of other expense categories should be made by using comparative data from the National Restaurant Association or any of the professional associations shown in Appendix 1.

The Go/No-Go Decision

After completing the market and financial feasibility studies and presenting these to bankers and potential investors, the owners can make a good judgment as to the potential success of the food facility project. Further contacts with zoning boards, liquor license agencies, and other municipal groups will bring the project to a point of decision. The accumulation of the data contained in the feasibility studies together with encouragement or discouragement from lenders, investors, and municipal agencies will lead the owner to the first go/no-go decision. In other words, if the project looks financially sound, the market is identified, a need for the foodservice exists, and the capital is obtainable, the decision to go ahead can be made. If one or more elements of the go/no-go decision are uncertain, there are three alternative courses to explore. The first is to correct the problem area that has been identified. Is the facility too large? Are the labor costs too high? Is the menu wrong for the market? Is the competition too strong in the immediate trading area?

The second option is to abandon the project and look for another place to invest the funds. The third alternative is to delay the decision until the final go/no-go decision point. This alternative is financially risky, because to progress from this point means incurring costs for foodservice facilities design consultants, architects, lawyers, accountants, and other professionals.

Chapter 2 describes some of the outside assistance that will be needed to ensure a successful foodservice project. The biggest mistake that could be made at this point in the process is to try to do the planning without the help of professionals.

SITE SELECTION AND PLANNING

E. M. Statler's famous quote, "The three most important things for the success of a hotel are location, location, and location," is certainly true for many foodservice facilities. A poorly located restaurant will certainly experience a low level of sales, and a coffee shop in a hotel may miss a significant amount of business unless it has easy access both to the hotel guests and to street traffic. On a college campus, students will typically select convenience as the primary reason for eating in a particular food facility. Avoiding high rent by selecting a location that is inconvenient or out of the mainstream of foot or automobile traffic is usually a bad decision. The location of a food facility on the immediate left or right of an entrance to a shopping mall is often considered a poor location, because the typical mall customer needs first to enter the mall and then look around for interesting places to shop and/or eat.

Site selection has been discussed in the feasibility section of this chapter, in which foot traffic, automobile counts, and distance to travel are calculated as a part of the feasibility study process. Other considerations for site selection are:

❑ *Visual recognition.* Can the food facility be easily seen by potential customers? Will the appearance of the outside of the facility communicate the character and concept of the dining experience inside?

❑ *Convenience.* The developers of a destination restaurant, in which the customer has previously made a decision to dine, must consider parking, an attractive entrance, valet parking, and safe surroundings as important site selection criteria. Coffee shop, deli, and fast-food entrepreneurs must depend on impulse buying as the primary market, and therefore site selection must focus on signage, ease of entry, and drive-in windows and/or take-out service.

❑ *Code restrictions.* Site selection may involve local code requirements for setback from the street, parking capacity, street access, or the acceptability of a food facility in a particular neighborhood. Usually these code requirements are available from the engineering or city planning office of the municipality where the food facility will be located.

❑ *Environmental issues.* In suburban areas, the development of an attractive site for a foodservice facility may encroach upon wetlands or adversely affect water runoff in nearby neighborhoods. In older, urban areas, sites may have previously been used for industrial and manufacturing processes that left dangerous materials in the ground. Environmental factors such as these are increasingly important to the site selection process because they present additional costs.

OBTAINING NECESSARY APPROVALS FROM AGENCIES

The approval process for a new or renovated foodservice facility is typically long and complicated, involving many different agencies. Developers often experience the approval process—and the inevitable delays that occur—as frustrating because they are eager to get the facility open and operating so that it can generate a positive cash flow. In defense of those agencies and departments who must be satisfied before proceeding, it is worthwhile to recall that the project needs to be controlled so that it does not create an unsanitary, unsafe, or unattractive addition to the community. Each municipality has a different group of agencies who must approve the food facility, and each has a definite sequence in which the approvals are given. For example, a health department may require preliminary approval of the equipment layout before construction begins and a final inspection after the facility is built and the equipment is in place.

The way to obtain necessary approvals for a complex project (new construction or major renovation) is to develop a comprehensive checklist, in which each member of the planning team (architect, engineers, foodservice consultant, financial advisors, lawyers, etc.) submits a list of necessary agencies and deadlines. After dates are recorded, one person (usually the architect) serves as the coordinator of the approval process.

Typical approval agencies involved in foodservice projects include:

❑ Zoning board
❑ Health department
❑ Municipal engineers (water, sewer, gas, and electrical)
❑ City planner
❑ Fire marshal
❑ Liquor control board
❑ Telephone company
❑ State or federal agencies (on state or federal projects)

SUMMARY

A food facilities design project, regardless of its scope and complexity, must start with a preliminary plan. If the owner or manager follows the planning method suggested in this chapter, a successful food facility is not necessarily guaranteed, but the chances of its success are greatly enhanced. The preliminary planning process should include:

❑ *Scope.* Careful consideration of the scope and complexity of the project. This will enable the selection of an appropriate planning team. If the project is simply a replacement of equipment, the team will be small or perhaps consist of only the food facilities design consultant and the owner or manager. If the scope involves major renovation or construction, a larger group of professional people would be drawn into the project.

❑ *Concept development.* For hotels, restaurants, and institutions, this is now recognized as an important planning stage. It includes consideration of menu, market, money, management, and the method of execution of the plan.

❑ *Feasibility studies.* Marketing and financial feasibility studies are often requested by bankers, investors, and others before financial commitments can be made. For large projects these may be conducted by professional accounting firms; in other instances the owner or manager may want to undertake it him- or herself. A go/no-go decision on the project should be made only after the marketing and feasibility studies have been completed.

❑ *Site selection.* Site selection will have much to do with the success of the facility. The best location may have higher rent or capital costs, but these costs will be covered through increased sales.

❑ *Agency approvals.* Agency approvals are often long in coming and frustrating to obtain, but they are helpful in avoiding safety or architectural problems for the protection of the community.

CHAPTER 2

FOODSERVICE DESIGN

THIS CHAPTER

- ☑ Explains the role of each member of the foodservice facility design team
- ☑ Describes the sequence of steps involved in the design of a foodservice facility
- ☑ Illustrates the work typically done by a food facilities design consultant
- ☑ Describes the method of compiling a cost estimate for a food facility project

THE PROJECT TEAM

The development of a new foodservice facility is guided by a project team consisting of the owner and various design and construction professionals. The size and composition of the project team depend upon the complexity of the project, but the team typically includes the owner (or owner's representative), an architect, engineers, a foodservice design consultant, an interior designer, a general contractor, and a foodservice equipment dealer.

Smaller projects (level II in scope), such as a forty-seat delicatessen built in a space leased in a strip mall, may require only the services of an architect, engineers, and a general contractor. Large projects (level III or IV in scope), such as a university cafeteria serving twenty-five hundred students at each meal, may require the services of all the members of the design team.

The Owner's Representative

In small projects, the owner's interests are represented on the project team by the owner him- or herself. Thus independent restaurateurs are usually deeply involved with the project team throughout the design and construction process. In most larger projects, however, the owner is not a single individual but is instead a corporate entity. Or the owner may be a single individual, but that person chooses not to be directly involved in the project. In such cases the owner's interests will be represented by a person or persons who have been assigned to the project team.

27

The use of an owner's representative is common in large and institutional foodservice design and construction projects. When a hospital renovates its foodservice operation, the hospital's board of directors may be represented on the project team by the director of dietary services. When a new hotel is built, the corporate director of food and beverage services may represent the owner's interests with respect to the foodservice facilities, and the corporate director of rooms may represent the owner's interests with respect to guest rooms.

Although the foodservice operator entrusts the design process to professionals trained in architecture, engineering, and construction, the role of the owner's representative is crucial to the overall success of the project. Design professionals rely on the owner's representative for the information they need to develop a facility that meets its intended objectives. Architects, engineers, and foodservice design consultants do not create masterpieces out of thin air; instead, they rely upon the owner's representative for direction and guidance throughout the project.

The specific responsibilities of the owner's representative vary from organization to organization and from project to project. Depending on the scope of the project, the responsibilities of the owner's representative are likely to include the following:

❏ Selecting design professionals (architect, engineers, etc.), establishing the scope of their services, and negotiating fees

❏ Determining the operational objectives of the project, to guide the design

❏ Setting the budget for the project

❏ Evaluating the designs prepared by the project team in light of the operational objectives for the project

❏ Accepting (or rejecting) the selections of furniture, fixtures, and finishes recommended by the design professionals

When the owner's representative plays an active role on the project team by fulfilling these responsibilities, the outcome is likely to be a successful project that fulfills the owner's expectations. If, however, the owner's representative plays a passive role in the process, the design team is forced to make assumptions based on their professional experience about what the owner requires. Their assumptions may be good ones, but they may not be the right ones for the owner's unique needs.

The Architect   On most building projects, the architect serves as the overall leader of the design and construction process. The architect coordinates the work of all of the design professionals on the project team and supervises the work of the contractors who build and equip the facility. Because of the leadership role played by the architect, she or he often is the first member of the design team to be selected by the owner. Once selected, the architect identifies the other design professionals to serve on the project team, including, as necessary, the engineers, interior designer, and foodservice consultant. Foodservice facility design projects often are an exception to this practice, as the foodservice design consultant may be retained before the architect.

We explain this exception in the section below describing the role of the foodservice design consultant.

The architect guides the design process through a sequence of steps (described later in this chapter) that begins with planning and ends when the owner's representative has accepted the new facility. The architectural work for small projects may be performed by a single individual.

Most projects generally involve several architects from a single firm. The *principal in charge* of the project is usually the person who presents the qualifications of his or her firm to the owner's representative and, if awarded the project, negotiates the terms and conditions of the contract. The principal in charge is ultimately responsible for successful completion of the project. The *project manager* is responsible for the day-to-day workings of the design and construction process. She or he identifies the other members of the team (engineers, consultants) and coordinates their work, schedules the sequence of design activities necessary to complete the project, and keeps the project within the budget. The *design architect* works closely with the owner's representative in the early stages of the project, guiding the planning and schematic design process. The design architect is primarily responsible for taking the owner's operational objectives and designing functional spaces through which those objectives can be fulfilled. The *site architect* sets up a temporary office (often in a trailer) at the construction site. She or he coordinates the work of the contractors and their tradespeople throughout the construction process. The site architect inspects the progress of the work and resolves problems before they become expensive to correct.

The selection of the architectural firm for the project is an important decision because of the key role the architect plays in coordinating the entire project. Several important factors, outlined below, should be involved in the selection process.

EXPERIENCE WITH SIMILAR PROJECTS

Most, though not all, architecture firms specialize in certain building types, such as educational facilities, health care facilities, or hospitality facilities. Selecting an architectural firm with experience designing similar buildings brings the benefit of their experience to the project.

EXPERIENCE WITH FOODSERVICE FACILITIES

Although an architectural firm may have experience with a specific type of project, such as educational or health care facilities, that does not mean that the firm has experience designing the foodservice facilities found in hospitals, schools, or colleges. Experience designing foodservice facilities in similar buildings is an important factor in the success of the project. The foodservice facilities in large institutions (hospitals, colleges, large corporate buildings) are complex and present a number of design and engineering challenges. Architectural firms lacking experience in comparable foodservice facilities may not be as well prepared as experienced firms are to anticipate the needs of complex food production systems.

PERFORMANCE ON PAST PROJECTS

Architectural firms provide prospective clients with lists of past projects. It is a good idea to contact past clients and ask for a frank assessment of the architectural firm's performance. Important questions include the following: Did the firm understand the needs of the operation? Was the project completed on schedule? Were there many changes to the design after construction had begun? Did the architect overlook anything or fail to follow through? How did the final cost of the project compare with the architect's estimates?

EXPERIENCE OF THE ARCHITECT'S TEAM
The success of the project depends not only on the skill and experience of the architectural firm but also on the abilities and experience of the engineers, interior designer, and consultants. In larger projects it is important to evaluate the credentials of everyone on the team.

CHEMISTRY
Large projects (level III or IV in scope) require extensive teamwork between the owner and the architect. Face-to-face interviews are essential to determine whether the members of the architectural firm are the people the owner wants to work closely with throughout the duration of the project. The ways in which the architect and members of his or her team interact during the interview with the owner's representative indicate how things will go in the future. Does the architect listen to the owner? Does the architect seem willing to challenge the owner with a different perspective? Does the architect have a clear idea of how the design process will flow and how the owner will be involved? Chemistry, although it is a vague term, is an important factor in selecting an architect.

Many architects belong to the American Institute of Architects (AIA), a professional organization that provides a number of resources as well as professional development opportunities to its members. Architects who are members of the AIA subscribe to a code of professional ethics that protect and serve the rights and interests of clients.

Engineers

Which engineering disciplines will be represented on the project team depends upon the scope and requirements of the project. Foodservice facilities are often engineering-intensive because commercial kitchen equipment requires extensive electrical and mechanical services. This is why virtually all foodservice projects require the assistance of electrical and mechanical engineers. Depending on the scope of the project, however, civil and/or structural engineers may also be required.

Structural engineers design systems to support the structure of the building and to protect its integrity. They determine how floors will support the fixtures that are required, and they ensure that the roof system will withstand the weight of equipment located there. *Electrical engineers* design the systems that supply electricity as needed in the facility. They determine the overall electrical load in the building, assign circuits, locate panels and receptacles, and determine the route wiring will take throughout the building. *Mechanical engineers* design the plumbing, heating, ventilation, and air-conditioning systems within the facility. Plumbing systems supply hot and cold water and remove waste through drains. Heating and air-conditioning systems temper the air within the facility so that the occupants are comfortable. Ventilation systems circulate air; in the kitchen, specialized ventilators located above cooking equipment remove grease, vapor, and heat from the kitchen. Mechanical engineers also design systems that supply energy in the form of natural gas or steam to the facility. Both gas and steam are frequently used sources of energy in commercial kitchen equipment. *Civil engineers* typically design roads, bridges, and similar structures. They are involved in foodservice projects only when the building site must be developed and made ready for new construction. For example, a restaurant built on an undeveloped site may need the services of a civil engineer to prepare site plans showing what grading must be done and how access to the site will be gained from adjoining roadways.

Foodservice Facilities Design Consultant

Owners and architects often call upon the specialized expertise of a foodservice facility design consultant to assist in the design of foodservice facilities. This is done because an effective design for a foodservice facility demands knowledge of operations, layout and design, engineering, and equipment. Few architects possess the in-depth knowledge of foodservice systems necessary to design complex kitchens. Most owners, while experienced in operations and knowledgeable about equipment, rarely have sufficient in-depth knowledge of layout, engineering, and equipment to design a complex foodservice facility without professional assistance. There are more than seven hundred established manufacturers of foodservice equipment, and each manufacturer offers multiple products, models, and options. Knowing which products and options are best for a specific application is not a simple matter. The owner of a poorly designed foodservice facility suffers for years: initially by having to pay the heavy investment required in equipping a facility that fails to meet his or her needs, and year after year through higher labor, utility, and maintenance costs.

Certain kinds of projects may not require the specialized expertise possessed by a foodservice facility design consultant. Small facilities, such as independent sandwich shops, quick-service diners, or family restaurants, often are simple and straightforward in operation, so that specialized design expertise may be unnecessary. Small, independent restaurateurs often seek the assistance of their foodservice equipment dealer for layout and equipment selection. Chain restaurant firms and large foodservice management companies may not retain a foodservice facility design consultant because they possess the necessary expertise in design, layout, engineering, and equipment in-house.

The architect may select his or her own foodservice consultant, or the client may need assistance for early planning before naming the architect. The food facilities design consultant should become involved with the project at the beginning—ideally, even before the architect is named. The reason for the early selection of a design consultant is to seek assistance with concept development and feasibility studies.

The services most often provided by foodservice consultants are discussed below.

FOODSERVICE MASTER PLANNING AND PROGRAMMING

Master planning and programming are services often provided by foodservice consultants to noncommercial (institutional) foodservice operations. Hospitals, colleges and universities, corporations, schools, correctional institutions, and the military all provide foodservice, but foodservice is not their primary mission. Approaching the development of a foodservice facility haphazardly, without making a careful study of the long-range objectives, can lead to inefficient operations and waste capital funds. Noncommercial foodservice operations also often are large and far more complex than typical restaurants. A university foodservice operation, for example, may feed thousands of students three times per day from as many as twenty different foodservice facilities, maintain a commissary (central production facility), and operate a warehouse. These two factors lead institutions to seek expert assistance in determining what kinds of foodservice concepts, systems, and technologies will best serve their markets prior to the actual design and construction of new food facilities.

Some colleges and universities, for example, found themselves entering the 2000s with foodservice facilities that were designed to meet the menu preferences and dining habits of students thirty years ago. Through the foodservice master planning process, the consultant assists the university by determining, using market research, what combination of new foodservice concepts would best meet the needs of the students, faculty, and staff. The master plan indicates where on campus new facilities should be located and estimates the amount of space required for each. The foodservice master plan also describes the production, storage, and service systems that would be necessary to support the new foodservice facilities.

PROGRAM A foodservice facility program, often called an architectural program, translates the operational objectives of the master plan into a description of the functional spaces required in each foodservice facility. A program is a narrative presentation of the way a particular projected foodservice facility is intended to operate. The consultant's specific objective is to highlight space and room usage and to define the flow of people and material through the proposed facility. The form and content of an architectural program for foodservice are described in detail in Chapter 4.

SYSTEMS ANALYSIS AND RECOMMENDATIONS Systems are defined as a series of interacting parts (subsystems) that must be evaluated to achieve the most satisfactory and efficient result. The decisions that foodservice operators make about how to store food, clean vegetables, cook hamburgers, serve guests, and wash dishes all involve systems. Both small and large foodservice operations rely upon systems. A small deli may serve food on disposable plates, just as a hospital might use specialized trays and a fine-dining restaurant bone china. The difference between small and large lies in the complexity of the system. A warewashing system in a deli may involve no more than running trays, pots and pans, and utensils through a small dish machine and returning them, when clean, to their proper storage places. In a hospital, however, warewashing may involve transporting soiled dishes back from patient rooms on large carts, scraping food waste into a disposer that recirculates water, separating out dishware and placing it in the appropriate washing racks, soaking silver, feeding dish racks through a dish machine, stacking clean dishes in specialized carts, and returning the carts filled with clean dishes and silver to the tray makeup line to be used again at the next meal. Pots may be washed separately in a dedicated machine. Transport carts are moved into a cart washing area, where they are cleaned and sanitized using a high-pressure system; when dry, they are returned for use during the next meal.

A formal systems analysis conducted by a consultant is appropriate where a foodservice operation faces a decision among several alternatives, each with differing investment costs and potential returns. Tray delivery systems for hospitals, fast-food production systems, cook-chill/inventory systems, and warehouse/food-delivery systems are examples of complex foodservice systems that are likely to benefit from the analysis and recommendations provided by a foodservice facilities consultant.

FOODSERVICE FACILITY EVALUATIONS

A service often provided by foodservice consultants in conjunction with planning and design services is the evaluation of an operation's existing facilities and equipment. A facilities evaluation assesses the strengths and weaknesses of an operation in relation to its intended objectives. Facilities evaluations frequently are conducted when an owner suspects that the existing facility no longer is adequate to the needs of a changing market.

Master planning and programming, systems analysis, and facilities evaluations are services provided by foodservice consultants that are closely related to the actual design process and often are provided in preparation for the construction of a new facility or the renovation of an existing facility.

Foodservice consultants, like other design professionals, may belong to a professional organization, the Foodservice Consultants Society International (FCSI). Consultants who are members of FCSI subscribe to a code of ethics that ensures a high level of professional service and integrity in client relations. FCSI consultant members receive payment for their services and do not sell foodservice equipment, materials, or supplies. In contrast to foodservice designers who are employed by equipment dealers or manufacturers, FCSI consultant members are prohibited from receiving "any monetary benefit or other consideration from the sale of equipment or other product" (FCSI By-Laws, Section IVa).

Interior Designer

Working with the owner's representative and the other members of the design team, the interior designer gives the foodservice operation its distinctive visual character and theme through the design of interior spaces, the selection of colors, and the specification of furniture and finishes. The interior designer thus focuses on the public or customer parts of the facility, rather than on the kitchen or storage areas.

In competitive markets, the success of a restaurant depends upon a distinct identity or theme that shapes the customer's expectations and contributes to a memorable dining experience. The guest's perceptions of the dining facility itself—apart from the quality and presentation of the food—create the environment in which the food and service are experienced. How the light falls and the colors, textures, and shapes within the dining area all affect customer perceptions. Many restaurants use interior design to create a dining experience that transports the guest to another place or time, such as a French café or a 1950s diner. Interior designers are often involved in projects of this kind, where the success of the concept depends upon the execution of a distinct dining experience.

General Contractor   When the architect, engineers, foodservice consultant, and interior designer have completed the work of drawing up plans and specifications for the foodservice facility, the project is put out for bid to general contractors. The general contractor who is awarded the contract then becomes a member of the project team. The general contractor's role is to build the facility as it was designed by the architect, engineers, foodservice consultant, and interior designer. The general contractor works with a series of building tradespeople including, for example, plumbers, electricians, roofers, and tile setters. These firms, working for the general contractor, are subcontractors (often referred to simply as "subs"). The general contractor schedules, coordinates, and oversees the work of his or her subs and thus is accountable for building, equipping, and furnishing the facility in accord with the intentions of the owner and designers.

Although the general contractor is a member of the project team, he or she has a somewhat different relationship with the owner than do the architect, engineers, or foodservice consultant. The general contractor's relationship with the owner is set by the terms of the contract, and his or her progress in completing the facility is strictly monitored by the architect. This means, in theory, that the general contractor does not participate in the planning process or in the decisions made by the project team about the design, materials, or techniques to be used in the foodservice facility. In point of fact, however, the general contractor often is involved in decision making through his or her suggestions regarding alternative construction methods or materials for achieving the intent of the owner and designers.

Two other approaches to organizing the project team for the construction of the facility are common in the building industry. The first involves using a construction manager rather than a general contractor. In this approach, the construction manager becomes involved much earlier in the design process and gives input into design decisions based on potential construction costs. The construction manager, unlike the general contractor, is involved in the preparation of the contract documents. Like the general contractor, however, the construction manager coordinates the work of the building trades.

The second approach involves using a design-build firm that has architectural, engineering, and construction capabilities all within one organization. The design-build approach has been used by governmental organizations to develop large public works projects where strict adherence to the budget is essential. Several large restaurant chains also use the design-build approach by employing in-house architects, engineers, designers, and contractors.

Foodservice Equipment Contractor   The foodservice equipment contractor, often known in the industry as the KEC (kitchen equipment contractor), is the firm that provides the foodservice equipment for the project. The KEC may be involved in the project through a contract directly with the owner or as a subcontractor under the general contractor. The foodservice equipment contractor, like the general contractor, typically is selected through a competitive bidding process for large projects. On smaller projects, the foodservice equipment contractor may be engaged through negotiation with the owner.

The qualifications of the foodservice equipment contractor have a direct and immediate effect on the overall quality of the equipment installation. Foodservice facilities, large or small, often require custom-fabricated equipment (dish tables, chef's counters) that require precise manufacture and installation, as well as complex systems (ventilation hoods, walk-in coolers and freezers, conveyor systems) that are built for the project and must be assembled at the job site. Not all restaurant suppliers have the experience and expertise necessary to complete a large foodservice installation. The experience of a foodservice design consultant on multiple previous installations often proves helpful in identifying and evaluating the qualifications of potential foodservice equipment contractors.

THE DESIGN SEQUENCE

The overall development of a new or renovated foodservice facility proceeds through a series of steps, one leading to the next. The design sequence used by both architects and food facilities design consultants is an integral part of the overall process of developing a new or renovated foodservice facility. The overall foodservice facility development process follows ten steps, which are illustrated in Figure 2-1.

Step 1, concept development, and step 2, market and feasibility, often are referred to as predesign planning processes. These steps may not require the services of architects and engineers; however, owners often retain a foodservice consultant for assistance in these functions. Step 10, implementation and training, is a postdesign service often important in foodservice facilities where the employees need training in using new equipment and new production processes. This function is often provided by foodservice consultants.

Steps 3 through 9 define the sequence of the design process itself, through which the new or renovated facility moves from idea to reality. Architects and other designers often reduce these seven steps into five phases:

Phase I: Schematic design (which includes programming and space analysis)

Phase II: Design development

Phase III: Construction documents

Phase IV: Bidding and contract award

Phase V: Construction administration (which includes inspection and acceptance)

Chapter 1 discusses concept development and market and feasibility, the predesign steps in the development process.

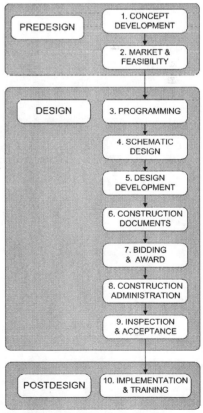

Figure 2-1. The foodservice facility design sequence.

Space Analysis and Programming

The objectives of space analysis are to determine the size of each functional area and the relationships among functional areas according to the owner's operational objectives.

The analysis of the space required for each of the functional areas in a facility is based both on the particular needs of the owner and on generally accepted standards. For example, the space needed for the dining area is computed by multiplying the number of seats needed to generate adequate revenues by a factor reflecting the square footage needed for each seat. That factor may range from 11 square feet (1.0 square meters) per seat for banquet seating to 16 square feet (1.5 square meters) per seat (or more) for a fine-dining restaurant; the actual factor selected is determined by the concept and the owner's preferences. If a restaurant requires 160 seats, at 15 square feet (1.4 square meters) per seat, then the dining room would require 2,400 net square feet (224 net square meters) exclusive of support areas. Space analysis proceeds to identify each of the necessary areas, and the space required by each, for the foodservice facility. Chapter 4 discusses space analysis in greater detail and provides guidelines for each of the primary functional areas in a foodservice facility.

Space analysis also involves establishing the physical relationships among each of the functional areas in the facility. One technique used to determine physical relationships, the adjacency matrix, is illustrated in Figure 2-2. The cells in the matrix are evaluated pair by pair by the owner's representative and the foodservice design consultant. The importance of any two areas being located adjacent to each other is determined by assign-

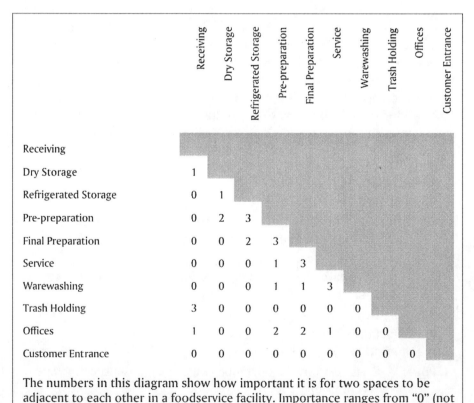

The numbers in this diagram show how important it is for two spaces to be adjacent to each other in a foodservice facility. Importance ranges from "0" (not at all important) to "3" (extremely important).

Figure 2-2. Adjacency diagram (simplified).

ing a priority from 0 (unnecessary) to 3 (essential). Figure 2-2 shows a 3 in the cell where "Refrigerated Storage" and "Pre-preparation Area" intersect, indicating that it is essential for the coolers to be in close proximity to the pre-preparation area. There is a 0 in the cell where "Customer Entrance" and "Trash Holding" intersect, showing that it is unnecessary—indeed, undesirable—for these areas to be located next to each other.

In completing the adjacency matrix, the owner and the design team evaluate the relationship between every one of the functional areas in the planned facility. This process helps ensure that all members of the project team are working from the same set of fundamental assumptions about the owner's objectives and needs.

A related approach in space analysis is the bubble diagram, such as the relatively simple example shown in Figure 2-3. Designers sketch bubble diagrams to show the relative sizes and relationships among functional areas early in the design process. These diagrams are particularly helpful to the owner's representative in identifying design problems. In Figure 2-3, the position of the ballroom—between the preparation area, the dining room, and the warewashing area—clearly must be changed. The preparation area should conveniently serve the main dining room, and being adjacent to the ballroom should be viewed as a secondary consideration.

Space analysis provides the data necessary for the preparation of the architectural program for the facility. Among design professionals, an architectural program or program statement is a specific kind of document that describes in a narrative the requirements of each functional area. It states the function of each space in a building, how that space will be most frequently used, and the number of square feet needed to serve these needs. A

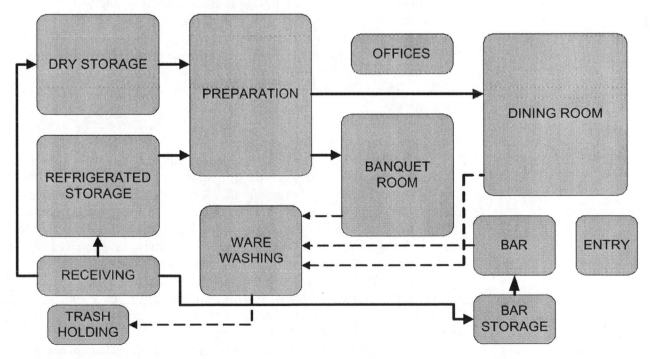

Figure 2-3. Example of a bubble diagram (arrows show the flow of food products).

Figure 2-4. Example of a section of a foodservice facility program statement.

Room Number: 103

Room Name: Dishroom

Relationship to Other Rooms:

Near dining room, for self-busing of dishes, and adjacent to kitchen. Easy access to service lines, so that clean dishes can be returned to serving area.

Description of Use:

This room will be used to wash all utensils, serving pans, china, glassware, and cafeteria trays. The space must be well ventilated but need not be air-conditioned. The pot sink will be located in this room, as well as space for the storage of utensils and dishes on portable carts. Utility requirements will include provision for drains, hot and cold water, electrical power in single and three phase, and a high level of ventilation (air turnover).

Square Footage Needed: 420 (39 square meters)

Finishes:

Walls must be structural glazed tile for ease of cleaning and resistance to wear. Floors must be quarry tile with slip-resistant qualities. Ceiling should be moisture-resistant and approved for use in commercial foodservice establishments. Lighting should be at 50–60 foot-candles, or at a level acceptable to the local health department.

program statement for a foodservice facility is the same as an architectural program, except that the focus is on specific functional areas such as receiving, storage, pre-preparation, final preparation, service, and warewashing. An example of a program for a dishroom is found in Figure 2-4.

Space analysis and programming make it possible for the design team to estimate the total size, the basic construction approach, and the kinds of finishes necessary for the building. This information is essential before the architect, engineers, and foodservice consultant begin the process of actually generating plans for the facility. Figure 2-5 shows an example of a summary program statement that identifies the total space required for a restaurant.

The total space required for the facility is calculated first, by summing all of the space requirements for the functional areas as determined through space analysis and programming. That figure, however, is only the net amount of square feet required for the facility. The estimates reflected in the program statement frequently do not include the space required for walls and wall thickness, chases for pipes and other utility services, stairwells, corridors, fire escapes, or rooms for mechanical equipment such as elevator machinery or telephone equipment. The square footage calculated from the program statement is increased to reflect the space required for these functions, and the resulting estimate is the gross square footage required for the facility.

The gross square footage can be used by the design team in preparing a preliminary estimate of the cost of construction for the facility. Industry ref-

Functional Area	Net Square Feet (Net Square Meters)
Receiving Dock	64 (5.9)
Receiving Area	80 (7.4)
Trash Holding	60 (5.6)
Cleaning Supplies Storage	80 (7.4)
Dry Storage	240 (22.3)
Cold Storage (Walk-in Cooler)	160 (14.9)
Frozen Storage (Walk-in Refrigerator)	120 (11.1)
Liquor/Beverage Storage	80 (7.4)
Pre-preparation	320 (29.7)
Final Preparation	280 (26.0)
Bakery	120 (11.1)
Servers' Stations	160 (14.9)
Bar Service	200 (18.6)
Bar Seating	320 (29.7)
Maitre d' Station	40 (3.7)
Dining Seating	2600 (241.5)
Table/Chair Storage (Dining Area)	160 (14.9)
Warewashing	220 (20.4)
Foodservice Offices	180 (16.7)
Foodservice Rest Rooms/Lockers	240 (22.3)
Total Foodservice	5724 (531.8)

Figure 2-5. Example of summary of space estimates from a program statement.

erence publications provide data on current costs for various types of construction on a per-square-foot basis. These data can be used to generate a rough estimate of the construction cost of the project. It is not uncommon to discover that the amount of space and the quality of construction necessary to create a facility that fulfills the owner's objectives exceeds the resources he or she has to invest. The owner's representative and the design team then must evaluate their previous work in concept development, feasibility, space analysis, and programming to determine how the requirements of the program can be reduced without adversely affecting the financial feasibility of the project. This is usually a difficult process, because those involved may feel very strongly about the size or function of a given space. For example, the chef may be committed to a large receiving dock, the owner to the maximum number of seats in the dining room, and the architect to a particular configuration for the entry, coat check, and host/hostess station. The following are examples of the kinds of questions and issues that often are raised at this point.

❑ *Can the number of seats in the dining room be reduced?* This is generally an undesirable option in commercial restaurants because sales revenue is a function of the number of available seats.

❑ *Can the size of the walk-in refrigerators be reduced?* This option may be feasible if fresh meats, produce, and dairy items can be delivered daily.

❑ *Is it necessary to have a room dedicated to washing garbage cans?* Perhaps this space is not necessary for the long-term success of the facility.

❑ *Is there a less expensive alternative to finishing the kitchen walls in ceramic tile?* Other materials may offer a lower initial investment cost, but they may be less durable and more difficult to keep clean and sanitary.

The one word that describes this space and cost-cutting exercise is *compromise*. After the program is approved in writing by the client, then and only then should the design process begin.

Schematic Design

The primary purpose of the schematic design is to show the shape of the building, the entrances and flow patterns, and the location of the dining rooms, kitchen, and other major components of the foodservice facility. The architect's drawings at this stage will show elevations of the outside of the building, site plans for the building lot, and the location of roads, sidewalks, and parking lots. The foodservice design consultant's drawings show the shape, size, arrangement, and major equipment items for all of the foodservice and related areas. Schematic designs are often used to gain preliminary approval from zoning officials, or for public relations purposes in selling stock to potential investors. For institutions, schematic designs would be used to seek approval from the board of trustees or other governing board.

The architect and foodservice design consultant typically revise and present schematic designs several times before gaining the approval of the owner's representative. In some cases, they may present several schematic designs, each illustrating a different approach to the program.

The architect's schematic designs for the entire building are usually presented in small scale ($\frac{1}{16}$ inch or $\frac{1}{32}$ inch = 1 foot), so that the entire facility and the surrounding property will fit on a single large sheet of paper (often 42 inches long by 30 inches high). The foodservice design consultant's schematic designs are usually prepared at a scale of $\frac{1}{8}$ inch = 1 foot so as to fit the storage, preparation, service, and dining areas of a large facility on a single sheet. Figure 2-6 is a schematic design for a small production kitchen in an institution.

A cost estimate for the project is prepared at the end of the schematic design phase. This estimate, in contrast to the rough estimate prepared with the program statement, is based on more-specific information about the project. This estimate will often be a joint effort by the architect, engineers, and foodservice design consultant. The architect will gather information from the building program (step 3) as to the quality of finish of each space and will then use more detailed price-per-square-foot data that are available from outside commercial publications. The engineers will examine

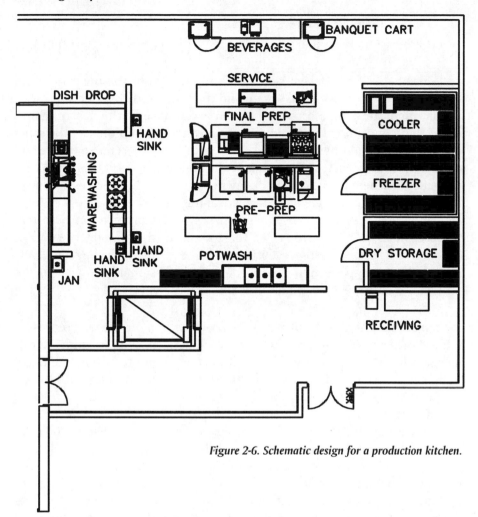

Figure 2-6. Schematic design for a production kitchen.

the size of the space, the type of HVAC (heating, ventilation, and air-conditioning) system needed, and the amount and kind of equipment needed in the foodservice areas. The foodservice design consultant will determine the general kinds of foodservice equipment needed in the project and prepare a cost estimate, even though the actual equipment items have not yet been selected. The consultant relies on his or her experience with projects of similar size and scope in generating estimates at the schematic design phase of the project. The foodservice design consultant submits to the engineers an estimate of the electrical load, steam requirements, and special ventilation needs for the foodservice equipment so that the cost of all utilities for the foodservice area can be calculated. The final cost estimate, compiled by the architect, includes:

❏ Land acquisition
❏ Site preparation
❏ Building construction
❏ Electrical, plumbing, and other mechanical systems
❏ Foodservice equipment
❏ Interior design and furnishings

❏ Construction loan interest costs

❏ Professional fees and other costs that will occur during planning and construction

This phase of the design sequence continues until the owner's representative is satisfied with the design and the projected cost of the project. At that point, he or she provides written acceptance of the design team's work, thus concluding the schematic design phase. Acceptance of the schematic design should be made in writing by the owner's representative and the architect on an actual floor plan of the building or food facility. Acceptance of the schematic design by the owner's representative does not mean that changes in the design of the facility cannot be made. Changes can be—and often are—made in subsequent phases of the project. On occasion, those changes take the project all the way back to the point of concept development. The owner's acceptance does not prevent changes; it only provides fair compensation for the design professionals involved in the project if their work must be done again.

Design Development

Design development is the phase of the project when the owner's representative, architect, engineers, foodservice design consultant, and interior designer flesh out the design of the project through increasingly detailed drawings. The design development phase leads up to, but does not include, the preparation of actual working drawings from which general contractors will bid the project.

The design development phase of the design sequence allows the project team to investigate different approaches and alternative systems for meeting the owner's functional needs. This phase thus involves what is called value engineering, in which the project team evaluates the projected operational costs of major equipment systems over their expected lifetimes. For example, the owner may be interested in a power potwashing system that circulates hot water and detergent over soiled pots and pans in a large wash tank rather than relying on an employee to scrub them clean. However, the power system might cost $12,500 to purchase and install, compared to $2,500 for a traditional three-compartment pot sink. Applying value engineering to this decision, the labor savings for the power system over its life expectancy would be evaluated against its higher purchase price as well as its greater utility and maintenance costs.* It is possible that the long-term savings from reduced labor requirements of the power potwashing system would make up for its higher purchase price and utility and maintenance costs.

In the design development phase of the project, the foodservice design consultant typically prepares the following:

❏ *Detailed floor plans showing the location of each piece of equipment.* This work is done in close coordination with the architect to ensure that, for example, equipment will fit as shown on the plan, columns will not interfere with production processes, and ceiling heights will be

---

* The actual financial calculations used in value engineering are more complex than is suggested in this simple example because they take into account factors such as the cost of capital and the reinvestment of cash flows.

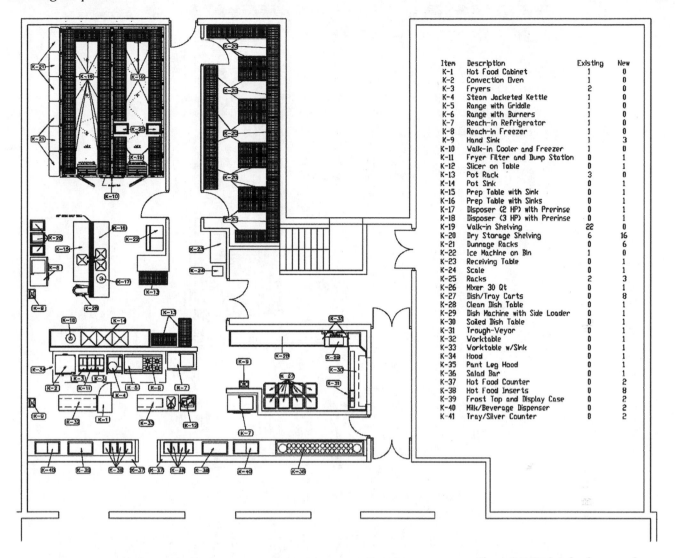

Figure 2-7. Design development for a conference center kitchen.

Item	Description	Existing	New
K-1	Hot Food Cabinet	1	0
K-2	Convection Oven	1	0
K-3	Fryers	2	0
K-4	Steam Jacketed Kettle	1	0
K-5	Range with Griddle	1	0
K-6	Range with Burners	1	0
K-7	Reach-in Refrigerator	1	0
K-8	Reach-in Freezer	1	0
K-9	Hand Sink	1	3
K-10	Walk-in Cooler and Freezer	1	0
K-11	Fryer Filter and Dump Station	0	1
K-12	Slicer on Table	0	1
K-13	Pot Rack	3	0
K-14	Pot Sink	0	1
K-15	Prep Table with Sink	0	1
K-16	Prep Table with Sinks	0	1
K-17	Disposer (2 HP) with Prerinse	0	1
K-18	Disposer (3 HP) with Prerinse	0	1
K-19	Walk-in Shelving	22	0
K-20	Dry Storage Shelving	6	16
K-21	Dunnage Racks	0	6
K-22	Ice Machine on Bin	1	0
K-23	Receiving Table	0	1
K-24	Scale	0	1
K-25	Racks	2	3
K-26	Mixer 30 Qt	0	1
K-27	Dish/Tray Carts	0	8
K-28	Clean Dish Table	0	1
K-29	Dish Machine with Side Loader	0	1
K-30	Soiled Dish Table	0	1
K-31	Trough-Veyor	0	1
K-32	Worktable	0	1
K-33	Worktable w/Sink	0	1
K-34	Hood	0	1
K-35	Pant Leg Hood	0	1
K-36	Salad Bar	0	1
K-37	Hot Food Counter	0	2
K-38	Hot Food Inserts	0	8
K-39	Frost Top and Display Case	0	2
K-40	Milk/Beverage Dispenser	0	2
K-41	Tray/Silver Counter	0	2

adequate for ventilation systems. Figure 2-7 is an example of a detailed floor plan for a conference center foodservice facility.

❑ *Utility plans (electrical, plumbing, ventilation) showing the location of each utility connection and the load imposed by each piece of equipment.* This work is done in close coordination with the engineers to ensure that, for example, the dish machines have adequate hot water, drains flow freely, electrical circuits do not fail when a banquet cart is plugged into a nearby wall outlet, and ventilation hoods do not pour cold air on the head of the chef during cold winter weather. Figures 2-8 and 2-9 show examples of electrical and mechanical utility connection drawings like those prepared during design development.

❑ *A book of catalog sheets (often called cut sheets or buyout brochures) for each equipment item to be purchased from a manufacturer.* This work is done in close coordination with the owner's representative to ensure that, for example, each piece of equipment will have the kind of features, accessories, and controls desired by the owner; each manufacturer selected offers the quality and durability necessary for long-

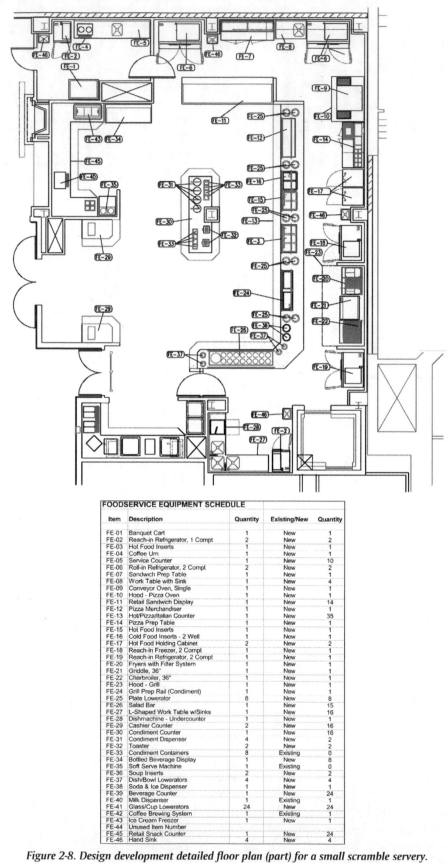

FOODSERVICE EQUIPMENT SCHEDULE				
Item	Description	Quantity	Existing/New	Quantity
FE-01	Banquet Cart	1	New	1
FE-02	Reach-in Refrigerator, 1 Compt	2	New	2
FE-03	Hot Food Inserts	1	New	1
FE-04	Coffee Urn	1	New	1
FE-05	Service Counter	1	New	10
FE-06	Roll-in Refrigerator, 2 Compt	2	New	2
FE-07	Sandwich Prep Table	1	New	1
FE-08	Work Table with Sink	1	New	4
FE-09	Conveyor Oven, Single	1	New	1
FE-10	Hood - Pizza Oven	1	New	1
FE-11	Retail Sandwich Display	1	New	14
FE-12	Pizza Merchandiser	1	New	1
FE-13	Hot/Pizza/Italian Counter	1	New	35
FE-14	Pizza Prep Table	1	New	1
FE-15	Hot Food Inserts	1	New	1
FE-16	Cold Food Inserts - 2 Well	1	New	1
FE-17	Hot Food Holding Cabinet	2	New	2
FE-18	Reach-in Freezer, 2 Compt	1	New	1
FE-19	Reach-in Refrigerator, 2 Compt	1	New	1
FE-20	Fryers with Filter System	1	New	1
FE-21	Griddle, 36"	1	New	1
FE-22	Charbroiler, 36"	1	New	1
FE-23	Hood - Grill	1	New	1
FE-24	Grill Prep Rail (Condiment)	1	New	1
FE-25	Plate Lowerator	8	New	8
FE-26	Salad Bar	1	New	15
FE-27	L-Shaped Work Table w/Sinks	1	New	16
FE-28	Dishmachine - Undercounter	1	New	1
FE-29	Cashier Counter	2	New	16
FE-30	Condiment Counter	1	New	16
FE-31	Condiment Dispenser	4	New	2
FE-32	Toaster	2	New	2
FE-33	Condiment Containers	8	Existing	0
FE-34	Bottled Beverage Display	1	New	8
FE-35	Soft Serve Machine	1	Existing	0
FE-36	Soup Inserts	2	New	2
FE-37	Dish/Bowl Lowerators	4	New	4
FE-38	Soda & Ice Dispenser	1	New	1
FE-39	Beverage Counter	1	New	24
FE-40	Milk Dispenser	1	Existing	1
FE-41	Glass/Cup Lowerators	24	New	24
FE-42	Coffee Brewing System	1	Existing	1
FE-43	Ice Cream Freezer	1	New	1
FE-44	Unused Item Number			
FE-45	Retail Snack Counter	1	New	24
FE-46	Hand Sink	4	New	4

Figure 2-8. Design development detailed floor plan (part) for a small scramble servery.

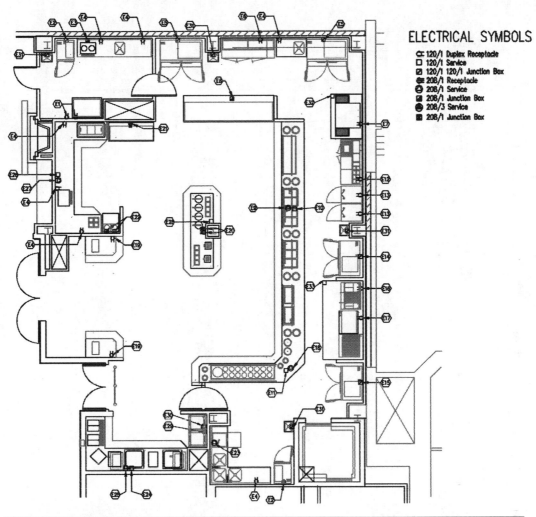

ELECTRICAL SYMBOLS

- ⊏ 120/1 Duplex Receptacle
- ☐ 120/1 Service
- ☑ 120/1 120/1 Junction Box
- ⊕ 208/1 Receptacle
- ⊕ 208/1 Service
- ☑ 208/1 Junction Box
- ⊕ 208/3 Service
- ▦ 208/1 Junction Box

FOODSERVICE EQUIPMENT ELECTRICAL REQUIREMENTS

Conn	Item	Description	Volts	Phase	Amps	KW	HP	AFF	Connection
E1	FE-01	Banquet Cart	120	1	10.4	1.25		60	NEMA 5-15
E2	FE-02	Reach-In Refrigerator	120	1	8.6	0.87	1/4	72	Wire to JB on Unit
E3	FE-04	Coffee Urn	208	1	18	3.8		24	Bring service to JB under counter
E4	n.a.		120	1	15			52	DR in wall above counter
E5	FE-06	Roll-in Refrigerator	120	1	16.2	1.04	1/2	72	Wire to JB on Unit
E6	FE-07	Sandwich Prep Table	120	1	20		1/2	18	NEMA 5-20
E7	FE-09	Conveyor Oven	120	1	15		1/12	36	NEMA 5-15
E8	FE-11	Retail Sandwich Display	208	1	10		1		
E9	FE-13	Hot/Pizza/Italian Counter	208	1				6	Stub service up from base to JB in Counter
	FE-15	Hot Food Inserts	208	1		2.4			Connect to JB (E8) in Counter
	FE-03	Hot Food Inserts	208	1		3.2			Connect to JB (E8) in Counter
E10	FE-13	Hot/Pizza/Italian Counter	120	1				6	Stub service up from base to JB in Counter
	FE-12	Pizza Merchandiser	120	1	10.2				Connect to JB (E10) in Counter
	FE-16	Cold Food Inserts	120	1	2.3		1/5		Connect to JB (E10) in Counter
E11	FE-13	Hot/Pizza/Italian Counter	120	1				6	Stub service up from base to JB in Counter
	FE-24	Grill Prep Rail (Condiment)	120	1	2.4		1/5		Connect to JB (E11) in Counter
	FE-26	Salad Bar	120	1	15				Connect to JB (E11) in Counter
E12	FE-14	Pizza Prep Table	120	1	20		1/2	18	NEMA 5-20
E13	FE-17	Hot Food Holding Cabinet	120	1	17.6	2.11		60	NEMA 5-20
E14	FE-18	Reach-in Freezer	120	1	11	1.26	3/4	72	Wire to JB on Unit
E15	FE-19	Reach-In Refrigerator	120	1	8.1		1/3	72	Wire to JB on Unit
E16	FE-20	Fryers w/Filter System	120	1	4.8	0.55		48	DR for food warmer
	FE-20	Fryers w/Filter System	120	1			1/2	48	and for filter motor
E17	FE-21	Griddle. 36"	120	1	15			48	Power for electronic burner ignition
E18	FE-13	Hot/Pizza/Italian Counter	208	1				6	Stub service up from base to JB in Counter
	FE-36	Soup Inserts	208	1		1.2 (2)			Connect to JB (E18) in Counter
E19	FE-29	Cashier Counter	120	1	15			12	Dedicated circuits for cash computers
E20	FE-32	Toaster	208	1	9.62	2		52	Mount two (2) receps in wall above Counter
E21	FE-34	Bottled Beverage Display	208	1	11.5		1		NEMA L14-30
E22 (2)	FE-35	Soft Serve Machine	208	1	9 (2)		1 1/2 (2)	60	Two circuits: 22 Ampacity each
E23	FE-44	Dishmachine Undercounter	208	1	43.6			30	Connect to Dishmachine
E24	FE-39	Beverage Counter	120	1				6	Stub service up from base to JB in Counter
	FE-38	Soda & Ice Dispenser	120	1	11				Icemaker (1)
	FE-38	Soda & Ice Dispenser	120	1	11				Icemaker (2)
	FE-38	Soda & Ice Dispenser	120	1	7				Soft Drink Dispenser
	FE-40	Milk Dispenser	120	1	6				Milk Dispenser
E25	FE-39	Beverage Counter	208	1				6	Stub service up from base to JB in Counter
E26	FE-45	Retail Snack Counter	120	1				6	Stub service up from base to JB in Counter
E27	FE-45	Retail Snack Counter	208	1				6	Stub service up from base to JB in Counter

Figure 2-9A. Design development utility drawing (electrical) for a small scramble servery.

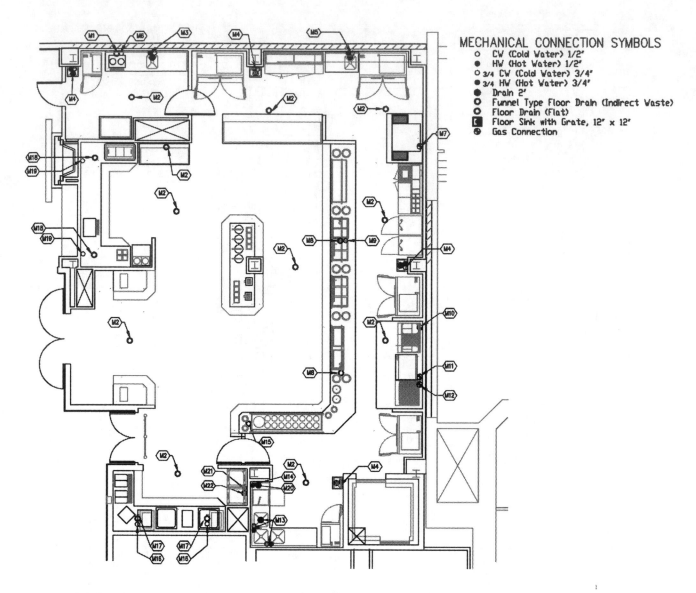

MECHANICAL CONNECTION SYMBOLS
○ CW (Cold Water) 1/2"
● HW (Hot Water) 1/2"
○¾ CW (Cold Water) 3/4"
●¾ HW (Hot Water) 3/4"
● Drain 2"
◉ Funnel Type Floor Drain (Indirect Waste)
◉ Floor Drain (Flat)
▣ Floor Sink with Grate, 12" x 12"
⊕ Gas Connection

FOODSERVICE EQUIPMENT
MECHANICAL CONNECTION SCHEDULE

Conn	Item	Description	Water	Drain	Gas	Steam	AFF	Notes
M1	FE-04	Coffee Urn		FTFD			6	Stub up in base.
M2		Varies		FD				
M3	FE-05	Work Table w/Sink	1/2" HW, CW	2"			24	
M4	FE-46	Hand Sink	1/2" HW, CW	2"			24	
M5	FE-08	Work Table w/Sink	1/2" HW, CW	2"			24	
M6	FE-04	Coffee Urn	1/2" CW				6	Stub up from base into Counter
M7	FE-09	Conveyor Oven			80,000 BTU		24	
M8	FE-13	Hot/Pizza/Italian Counter		FTFD			6	Stub up from base into Pedestal
M9	FE-13	Hot/Pizza/Italian Counter	1/2" CW				6	Stub up from base into Pedestal
M10	FE-20	Fryers w/Filter System			165,000 BTU		24	
M11	FE-21	Griddle			40,000 BTU		24	
M12	FE-22	Charbroiler			105,000 BTU		24	
M13	FE-27	L-Shaped Table w/Sinks	1/2" HW, CW	4"			24	
M14	FE-28	Dishmachine, Undercounter	3/4" HW 140 D				4"	Hose Bib Connection
M15	FE-26	Salad Bar		FTFD			6	Stub up in Base
M16	FE-39	Beverage Counter	1/2" CW				6	Stub up in Base
M17	FE-38	Soda & Ice Dispenser		FTFD				Set in Notch in Base
M18	FE-45	Retail Snack Counter		FTFD			6	Stub up in Base
M19	FE-45	Retail Snack Counter	1/2" CW				6	Stub up in Base
M20	FE-44	Dishmachine, Undercounter		2"			6	
M21	FE-39	Beverage Counter	1/2" CW				6	Stub up in Base

Figure 2-9B. Design development utility drawing (mechanical) for a small scramble servery.

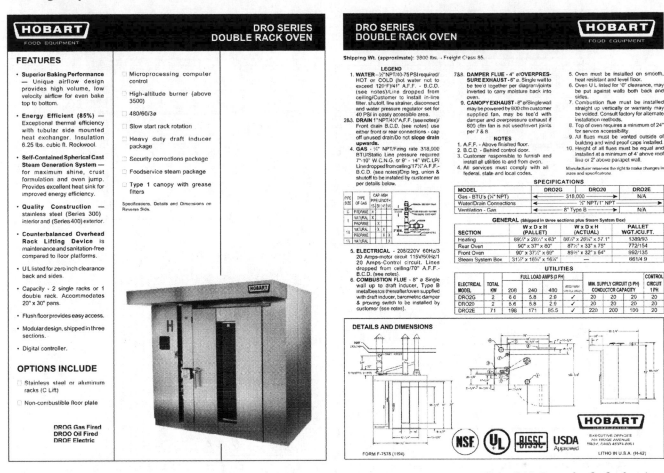

term value; and no important items will be overlooked. Figure 2-10 shows an example of a foodservice equipment catalog sheet.

❏ *Elevations, sections, and/or detail drawings for each piece of custom-fabricated equipment.* This work is done in close coordination with the owner's representative to ensure that, for example, worktables, chef's counter, scrapping and dish tables, service counters, and bars all meet the owner's functional needs. Figure 2-11 shows examples of foodservice equipment elevation drawings.

❏ *Detail drawings of any special construction required for foodservice equipment.* The foodservice design consultant may prepare detail drawings showing, for example, how walk-in coolers and freezers are constructed in depressions in the floor, or how trench drains for kettles and braising pans are to be fabricated.

❏ *Preliminary specifications.* Written specifications describe in narrative form the general conditions, quality standards, materials, products, and execution of the installation. The foodservice design consultant prepares a preliminary set of specifications for review by the owner's representative and other members of the project team so that they can be revised and refined.

Near the conclusion of the design development phase of the project another cost estimate is prepared. This estimate will be more accurate than

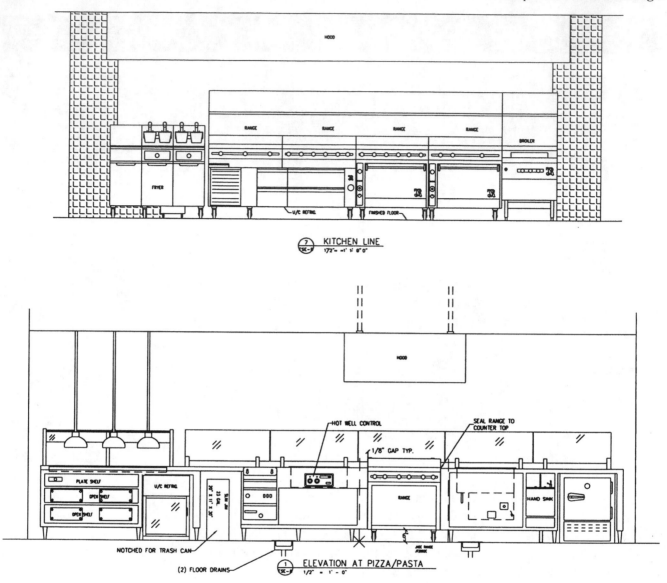

Figure 2-11. Examples of elevation drawings.

previous estimates because the architect, engineers, and design consultant will have substantially completed the design of the entire project. All of the materials and products will have been selected, and the techniques for construction of the project will have been identified. The actual cost of new construction projects should vary from the design development cost estimate by only a small amount due to changes in prices, labor costs, or other conditions.

The design development phase of the sequence concludes with the owner's acceptance of all the materials prepared by the design team. The owner's acceptance of this phase of the design work authorizes the design team to proceed to the preparation of actual construction documents. Changes made from this point forward are relatively time-consuming to incorporate into the plans and specifications because a single change may have to be reflected on multiple drawings as well as at several points in the specifications.

The construction documents phase of the design sequence involves the *Construction Documents* preparation, in final form, of the following:

❑ *Drawings* showing construction of the new or renovated facility, including all site work, structural systems, rooms and other spaces, utility systems, equipment, finishes, and details

❑ *Specifications* describing the materials and products, the standards of workmanship, the methods of fabrication and construction, the applicable code requirements, and the methods of installation, cleaning, and testing

❑ *General conditions of the contract* defining terms, assigning responsibility, establishing payment schedules, describing how changes are to be handled, and listing the specific project conditions

The specifications and general conditions are bound together to form the project manual, which, combined with the drawings, comprises the contract documents for the project.

A large building project, such as a hotel or hospital, may require a stack of drawings two inches (51 millimeters) thick and a nine-hundred-page project manual. To prevent misunderstanding of the designers' intent, construction documents follow specific standards and a uniform format. Drawings are prepared in accord with architectural standards that describe the organization, appearance, and annotation of graphic materials. Specifications are written according to guidelines and organized into divisions in accord with the format recommended by the Construction Specification Institute. The standards for drawings and specifications are widely accepted in the construction industry and so prevent costly misunderstandings by the general contractor.

There are three basic types of specifications:

❑ *Descriptive specifications*. Descriptive specifications completely identify all the important characteristics of the material or product.

❑ *Proprietary specifications*. Proprietary specifications identify the product by reference to a manufacturer and model number, and require the contractor to provide that item and no other.

❑ *Performance specifications*. Performance specifications establish performance criteria that are relatively independent of the specific description of the item.

Foodservice equipment specifications usually are descriptive and include the materials, construction, components, utility requirements, dimensions, features, and options necessary to identify the product completely and unambiguously to the bidder. Figure 2-12 provides an example of a foodservice equipment item specification for manufactured equipment, and Figure 2-13 provides an example of an item specification for fabricated equipment.

Specifications for manufactured equipment also usually include a reference to a specific manufacturer and model number. The purpose of naming a specific manufacturer and model is to establish, by way of example, the quality of workmanship, materials, and features desired by the owner. Reference to a specific make and model is not intended, in most cases, to

Item D-2	Dish machine, carousel type

Quantity:	One (1)
Dimensions:	14' 8" long
Manufacturer:	Stero of Petaluma, CA
Model:	SCT-94
Utility Requirements:	208/3/1 125 amps/45 KW one 3-wire feed for booster heater
	208/3/1 3-wire feeder to machine panel for:

Scrapper motor	2 HP/5.9 amps
Wash pump motor	2 HP/5.9 amps
Rinse pump motor	2 HP/5.9 amps
Conveyor motor	¼ HP 1.1 amps
208 to 115 control circuit	5 amps
Wash tank heat	20 KW/55.6 amps
Rinse tank heat	20 KW/55.6 amps
Disposer	3 HP/8.9 amps

CW, HW ½" to hand sink and cleaning hose

HW 1" 140ºF 20 PSI to booster heater

CW ¾"

Drain, floor sink for machine waste

Drain, 2" for scrapper waste

Drain, 2" for disposer waste

Drain, 2" for sink waste

Vent: 1,000 CFM exhaust to 11⅞" × 17⅞" duct at 69" AFF

Features:

1. Stainless-steel construction
2. Automatic fill with water level control
3. Door safety switches
4. Cleanup hose (25')
5. Interplumbed
6. Interwired with circuit breaker panel with breakers for each motor
7. Kit 55
8. Isolated final rinse with inspection door; final rinse saver
9. Stainless-steel conveyor drive with reversing switch
10. Thermostatically controlled electric tank heat
11. C-45 booster heater
12. Oval 12-gauge stainless-steel tables
13. Scrap trough 12-gauge stainless steel; provide disposer (item D-4) and interwire
14. Glass rack shelf 3' 6"
15. All-purpose overhead shelf 6'
16. Richlite stacking shelf 12' 0"
17. Drying hood (90 degree) with vent and inspection door
18. Mount doors in-facing
19. Hand sink with hardware
20. 14-gauge stainless-steel wheeled interconnected carriers with all-purpose racks
21. Cold-water aquastat
22. Bus box that supports two remote start/stop stations
23. Two-rack rotating rack shelf
24. Supervision of installation by factory-approved representative

Figure 2-12. Foodservice equipment specification for manufactured equipment.

D-5	**Clean-dish table**	
	Quantity:	One (1)
	Dimensions:	As shown on detail drawings
	Manufacturer:	Fabricated
	Model:	
	Features:	

1. Construct in conformance to Part 2.03 and as shown on plans and detail drawings
2. Provide 10" backsplash joining dish rack unloader
3. Close end of backsplash at end opposite dish rack unloader
4. Provide table limit switch and connect to dish machine
5. Understructure of cross members and spreaders as shown on detail drawings (omit front cross member and spreaders for placement of hot-water booster heater)
6. Provide overshelves of length shown on detail drawings and attach securely to wall at height selected by owner's representative at time of installation
7. Table and rolled edge (1¼" radius) to be of 12-gauge stainless steel polished to a #4 finish

Figure 2-13. Foodservice equipment specification for fabricated equipment.

exclude comparable products manufactured by other companies. However, the burden of proof that another product is equal to or better than what was named in the reference specification lies with the foodservice equipment contractor.

In some cases, the owner will not accept anything but the manufacturer and model named in the specification. This form of specification is called *proprietary* because it requires the foodservice equipment contractor to furnish a product manufactured by a single firm (a proprietary product). Proprietary specifications are thought to reduce competition during the bidding phase of the project because they specifically permit one manufacturer and exclude all others. When named in a proprietary specification, the manufacturer has little incentive to bargain. For this reason, most public works (government-funded) construction projects allow proprietary specifications only after a stringent set of requirements has been fulfilled.

Privately funded foodservice projects may—and often do—use proprietary specifications for manufactured equipment. This may be done for a number of reasons:

❑ The owner may have had an exceptionally positive experience with the manufacturer named in the specification.

❑ The item named in the proprietary specification may be the only one available with the precise combination of features desired by the owner.

❑ There may be advantages in maintenance and service with a particular manufacturer, as when the owner already possesses several units from the named manufacturer

Complex equipment systems, such as ventilation hoods, conveyor systems, or walk-in refrigerators and freezers, require significant coordination among the architect, engineers, and foodservice design consultant. These systems are often designed and engineered around a specific manufacturer's components. Changing to a different manufacturer would entail significant redesign and reengineering that would cost more than any price advantage.

Performance specifications are rarely used in the foodservice industry. Performance specification wording, however, does frequently appear in equipment catalog materials. For instance, to specify that a fryer "must be capable of preparing 100 pounds of french fries per hour" clearly sets a performance criterion. The problem with performance specifications is that the criteria often are very difficult to measure or judge. When the fryer is installed, how can the consultant or owner measure the actual results? Frying 100 pounds of french fries in one hour might be possible, but to what degree of doneness? Are the french fries frozen or fresh? How large is each fry? A specification that explicitly describes the materials or products to be furnished is less likely to be misinterpreted.

Although foodservice equipment specifications can be written in several different ways, the most important consideration is whether or not the exact requirements for the equipment are clearly described.

Bidding and Contract Award

When the contract documents are complete, they are made available to interested bidders. This process is colloquially referred to as "putting the project on the street." The architect (or construction manager, if there is one on the project) coordinates this process. Small foodservice projects involving equipment only, with little or no architectural work, may be bid by the owner.

Bid packages (copies of the contract documents) may be mailed directly to interested bidders identified by the project team. Bid packages also may be made available by construction industry organizations that have "reading rooms" where contractors can review and order bid packages. The foodservice design consultant often identifies foodservice equipment contractors who, on the basis of previous project experience, are qualified to bid.

Contractors are given a set period of time (usually between two and six weeks) to prepare their bids. On large renovation projects, the architect may schedule a mandatory site visit, during which time interested bidders can examine the existing facility and obtain clarification on project conditions.

The bidding process often raises questions that require clarification or necessitate changes to the contract documents. Such clarifications and changes are communicated to the bidders in the form of an addendum. All of the addenda become part of the formal contract.

At the time specified, the bids are opened. In some cases, such as public works projects, the bids are opened in the presence of the bidders and their quotations are read aloud. Private bid openings are not attended by the bidders.

The foodservice design consultant also evaluates any substitutions or alternates proposed by the bidders and included with their bids.

❑ *Substitutions* are proposals to provide materials, products, equipment, or systems from a manufacturer other than the one named in the specifications (the base bid). In proposing a substitution, the foodservice equipment contractor is claiming that what he or she proposes to furnish and install is equal to or better than what was specified in the contract documents. The bidder may propose to offer the substitution at a lesser price. However, it is more common for the bidder simply to seek approval for the substitution at the same price as the base bid.

❏ *Alternates* are proposals to provide materials, products, equipment, or systems different from what was described in the specifications, generally at a significantly lower price. The project team may have included several alternates in the contract documents that it required contractors to bid. Or the foodservice equipment contractor may have voluntarily proposed one or more alternates. In proposing an alternate, the bidder claims that the alternate performs comparably (provides similar results), but does not claim that it is equal to or better than what was originally specified as would be the case for a substitution.

Proposals for substitute or alternate engineered systems, including kitchen ventilation, walk-in refrigeration, and conveyors, are especially problematic. Although there is a large variation in both the cost and quality of these systems, the differences in quality are more difficult for operators to see than the differences in cost. One manufacturer's ventilation system may cost only 60 percent of what another manufacturer's system costs, but both systems are made of shiny stainless steel and both move air around over the cooking equipment. The engineering and performance differences may appear only in the winter months, when cold air supplied to the inexpensive hood meets hot air rising from the cooking equipment and it begins to "rain" (drip condensation) over the range section.

The evaluation of bids determines the *lowest qualified bidder,* who is then awarded the contract. After the contract has been awarded, and necessary permits and approvals obtained, construction can begin.

Construction Coordination

The actual work of construction is performed by the general contractor and his or her subcontractors from the building trades. During this phase of the design sequence, the architect assumes primary responsibility for monitoring the progress and quality of the work. On large building projects, this responsibility is carried out by a field architect, who establishes an office at the job site and works closely with the trades.

During the construction phase, the foodservice design consultant does the following:

❏ *Submittal review.* The foodservice equipment contractor prepares plans of the foodservice facility, obtains shop drawings for all custom equipment from the fabricator, and assembles a book of catalog sheets showing all the equipment to be provided. These submittals are reviewed by the foodservice design consultant to ensure that they conform to the contract documents. Deviations from the requirements of the contract are noted directly on the submittals. When there are substantial errors or omissions in the submittals, the foodservice design consultant will require that they be redone and resubmitted. Small deficiencies may be accepted as noted.

❑ *Coordination.* Questions about the foodservice equipment installation may arise from the foodservice equipment contractor, the general contractor, or the plumbing, electrical, or HVAC contractor. The foodservice design consultant responds to these questions, keeping a written record of the questions and responses.

❑ *Review changes to the work.* Project conditions or other factors may require a change in the work from what originally was specified. For example, a foodservice equipment manufacturer may discontinue the specified model after the bid was awarded but before the item was ordered by the foodservice equipment contractor. The foodservice design consultant reviews the rationale for such changes and, if acceptable, communicates his or her acceptance to the architect. The architect, in turn, prepares a *change order,* a formal contract document that authorizes the foodservice equipment contractor to proceed with the change.

❑ *Attend job site meetings.* On some projects, the foodservice design consultant may attend job site meetings, especially at crucial points in the installation of the foodservice equipment. Participation in job site meetings can be effective in preventing problems in execution of the installation. Not all subcontractors read the entire project manual carefully, and so some may overlook important points affecting their work. For example, tile-setting contractors remove excess grout from tiles using muriatic acid. Unfortunately, using muriatic acid on quarry tile installed on the floor of a walk-in cooler can damage the finish on its walls unless proper precautions are taken. The consultant's participation in job site meetings can reinforce important provisions of the specifications that affect various trades.

Inspection/Acceptance

During construction, the facility is under the possession and control of the general contractor, and he or she is responsible for the progress of the work as well as for protection of the building and its contents. Prior to turning the completed facility over to the owner, the architect, engineers, foodservice design consultant, and interior designer examine their parts of the project to determine whether the work meets the requirements of the contract documents. A punch list is prepared, describing all work that remains to be done to complete the project according to the plans and specifications. The foodservice consultant prepares the punch list for the foodservice equipment installation and submits it to the KEC and to the owner. The completed facility is turned over to the owner only when the project team is satisfied that the work is complete and fulfills the requirements of the contract.

Because the installation of the foodservice equipment is complex, the foodservice design consultant will review the progress of the work several times during the final phase of construction. The first site visit may occur when the walk-in systems have been erected, the hoods have been hung from the ceiling, and the rough-in connections for utility services are complete. The purpose of this visit is to check the installation of the hoods and the walk-ins, since any rework of these systems will surely be time-consuming. Checking the locations of the utility rough-ins may pinpoint a problem when it is relatively easy to make corrections.

The second visit may occur after all the equipment has been set in place and most of the pieces are connected to their respective utility services. This site visit usually is arranged so that the foodservice design consultant, the foodservice equipment contractor, and the architect can go over the progress of the installation in detail. Any problems observed during this site visit are noted and compiled into what is termed a preliminary punch list. The items on the list must be corrected by the foodservice equipment contractor before the final site visit is made. Figure 2-14 is an example of part of a punch list.

The final site visit is made after all equipment has been connected and tested and is ready for food preparation. A second punch list is prepared, usually much shorter than the first. A letter to the owner's representative

---

PROJECT MEMO

Date: February 5, 2003

To: David West, AIA
             Design Space International
             6400 Tuttle Road
             Dublin, Ohio 43017

From: John Birchfield, FCSI
             Foodservice Consultant

CC: Richard Albright, Dublin Center Retirement Village
             Bill Davis, Davis Foodservice Equipment

Project: Kitchen renovation
             Dublin Center Retirement Village
             Phase I

On February 2, 2003, we examined the work on the foodservice equipment for this project. Items needing correction are as follows:

All stainless-steel tables and pot sink: Grind and polish rough welds on understructure joints to a smooth #4 finish.

Item D-11	Spray system remote stations: Furnish and install on the wall a bracket to hang the spray wand when not in use.
Item H-1	Hoods: Furnish extractor wand for hood cartridges.
Item K-3	Refrigerator: Gauge shows 41.4°F. Verify that unit is holding temperatures below 38°F. Adjust or repair as necessary.
Item K-5	Existing mixer: Relocate where shown on plan.
Item K-9	Proofer cabinet: Specified unit was FWE PHU-1826. Unit delivered is FWE P-72-XL. Replace unit with item as specified.
Item K-10	Hand sink: Provide HW to sink in pot wash area.
Items K-11, K-12, and K-13	Range, charbroiler, griddle: Locate these items under hood where shown on plan to ensure proper operation of fire suppression system.

Figure 2-14. Part of a punch list.

and the architect is prepared by the foodservice design consultant in which he or she recommends acceptance of the food facility.

The submission of the letter recommending acceptance of the project by the owner is often the final step in the design sequence.

Implementation and Training

In foodservice facilities projects, equipment demonstration and training sessions often provide immense benefit to the employees. If the proper use of new equipment is demonstrated to the kitchen staff at the outset, they will be far better prepared to come up to speed in the new facility quickly. Equally important is an explanation of how the design and layout are intended to work. Employees often do not have the opportunity to participate in planning and design sessions and so find themselves in a new facility whose operating principles and design rationale they may not fully understand. In outmoded and poorly designed kitchens, the staff had to find ways to work around the problems. Over time, their work-arounds became habits, and the habits become the accepted way of doing things. When the old kitchen is replaced by a new one, the accepted and habitual ways of doing things no longer make sense. Employees need guidance and support in learning how to use the new kitchen and its equipment efficiently.

One approach that was taken by a successful director of foodservice in training employees for opening a new food court utilized teams of employees. A detailed description of each of the food concepts that was to be in the new facility was prepared. The first team to be established was the menu team, who developed the menus for each station. They researched and tested standard recipes and suggested ways of merchandising the products. Then an equipment team was created, with a head cook as leader and with other cooks, a maintenance person, a dishwasher, and a salad prep person as team members. This team evaluated equipment descriptions and catalog sheets and determined ideal production techniques, cleanup procedures, and maintenance schedules for each of the food stations. A third team was charged with public relations and marketing. This team recommended the decor for each station, researched menu board systems, and prepared a plan and budget for advertising in the local paper.

When each team completed its work, the foodservice director held meetings in which the team leaders presented their reports to the entire staff of the operation. As a result, employees were well prepared to operate the new facility. They knew what to expect.

The approach described above is, of course, only one of many that are possible. The key to successful training for a new facility is employee involvement. Employees who are involved in the planning process gain a sense of ownership, and ownership leads to commitment to the success of the new facility.

Opening Day

The key to a successful opening day is *planning*. The first impressions guests have of a new facility are critical. Preopening planning is so important that many restaurant chains and hotels employ specialists who spend weeks or months preparing a new facility for opening day. After the facility has been in operation for several weeks, they turn over the reins to the regular management and go on to the next facility.

A good discipline for opening-day planning is to list everything that has to be in place when the first guest arrives. One way to make that list is to go through an existing operation, noting everything that is there: silver, napkins, menus, employee uniforms, telephones, etc. Then determine what has to be done to get that item in place in the new facility. It's a good idea to work backward on a calendar. For example, if opening day is August 1 and menus take two weeks for printing and laminating, with another two weeks added for safety, when must the menus be ordered? If menus must be ordered by July 1, and the graphic designer needs six weeks to prepare camera-ready copy, when must prices be finalized? Working backward in time through each item that must be prepared before opening day will result in a schedule that lists each critical deadline.

SUMMARY

The project team for the development of a foodservice facility can work together most effectively if each member understands the roles of the others. This chapter clarifies the functions of the various team members, including the owner's representative, architect, engineers, foodservice design consultant, interior designer, general contractor, and foodservice equipment contractor. The chronology of events that typically occur when a project is being planned and constructed is described as the design sequence. The architect and food facilities design consultant work together during many stages in this sequence. Two of the steps, however—feasibility, and implementation and training—are frequently the sole responsibility of the design consultant. Contract documents establish the legal relationship between the client and the contractor and are frequently used to interpret the quality of work that must be accomplished by the contractor. Specifications that are a part of the contract documents must be carefully written so that the quantity and quality of each piece of equipment is clearly understood. A standard format for writing the specifications provides clarity and assists all persons who must read and interpret the contract documents.

The manager or other foodservice professionals can obtain maximum benefit from the food facilities design consultant if the role of the consultant is clearly understood.

CHAPTER 3

THE PRINCIPLES OF DESIGN

THIS CHAPTER

☑ Explains the impact of design on efficiency and safety

☑ Describes the basic principles of design for all food facilities

☑ Focuses on human engineering in design

THE IMPACT OF DESIGN ON EFFICIENCY AND SAFETY

Labor costs and food costs will consume between 60 percent and 80 percent of the income of most food operations, and the control of these two costs will determine the difference between profit and loss. It follows, then, that the efficiency of a food facility can be judged by how well the design limits the cost of labor.

Designing a food facility to achieve maximum labor productivity must be a collaboration between the foodservice consultant, the owner (operator), and the architect. In other words, doing the design right, and using the best professional talent available, will pay significant dividends. For example, consider the savings of one second cook (or cook's helper) and one server, accomplished by good design.

Cook's helper @ $21,000/year	$ 21,000
Server @ $6.50/hour × 40 hours × 50 weeks	13,000
Total	$ 34,000
Benefits @ 18%	$ 6,120
Uniforms, 2 persons @ $4/day each	2,000
Employee meals @ $5/meal	1,500
Total annual cost of two employees	$ 43,620
Three-year savings	$130,860

The savings from good design that made unnecessary two low-to-medium-wage employees over a three-year period ($130,860) would more than pay for the services of highly skilled design professionals.

A good design incorporates certain principles, described in this chapter. These principles can be applied to any food operation, with the ultimate goal of satisfying the customer and achieving a profit. If the food operation is designed with the safety of the guests and employees as a major consideration, then high food quality, good sanitation, the smooth flow of materials and people, and good supervision will follow. Poor standards of design will of course yield cross traffic patterns for guests and employees, backtracking that results in wasted effort, difficult-to-clean surfaces, and poorly thought-out work and dining spaces. Employee safety is likely to be compromised in poorly conceived designs, bringing the risk of higher insurance costs and exposure to litigation.

BASIC DESIGN PRINCIPLES

Although there are significant differences in the physical layout, menu, and method of service of various foodservice facilities, there are underlying design principles that are followed by food facilities designers in virtually all situations. These principles lead to efficiency and a pleasant environment for the worker and customer but do not result in one particular layout. Prototype restaurants of the three leading hamburger chains are quite different in layout, each for its own reasons, but all follow a common set of design principles.

A common misconception about design is that there is only one "right" way to lay out the equipment and arrange the space. There are, in fact, many design solutions that would be acceptable and workable for the same facility. A competent designer will approach a facilities design project knowing that in each project a different set of variables will prevail. Each foodservice facility is treated as unique, with its own design problems to be solved.

The reader should understand the difference between design and layout. Design encompasses the entire facility, with all the considerations that were discussed in Chapter 1 on concept development. Layout involves a consideration of each small unit or work space in a foodservice facility. In the fields of architecture and foodservice facilities design we speak of "designing" a building or a foodservice operation and of "laying out" a range section or a bakery.

Each design professional has a set of guidelines that he or she has found helpful in approaching the design of a food facility. Thus while certain principles are universally accepted, there is no standard set of design rules for all professionals working in the foodservice field. The following principles, which are based on the authors' experience as foodservice facilities design professionals, are intended to provide a general framework for approaching the design process.

Efficient and effective designs should:

❏ Be flexible and modular
❏ Show simplicity
❏ Create an efficient flow of materials and personnel
❏ Facilitate ease of sanitation
❏ Create ease of supervision
❏ Use space efficiently

Menus change to respond to changes in consumers' tastes and preferences. New preparation techniques and new equipment may be necessary if an operation is to keep abreast of consumer trends. If changes in preparation and equipment require substantial modifications to the facility, they are likely to be very expensive—perhaps prohibitively so.

The use of heavy-gauge stainless steel in the construction of kitchen equipment is almost universally accepted by the foodservice industry. Stainless steel does not rust, is easy to clean, is not porous, and does not easily wear out. However, stainless steel has the major fault of being very inflexible. A stainless-steel table in the kitchen cannot be modified easily to accommodate a change in the design. If, for instance, a work area 14 feet (4.27 meters) in length is required, the principle of flexibility would lead the designer to specify two tables, one 6 feet (1.83 meters) long and one 8 feet (2.44 meters) long. These two lengths would permit rearrangement of the kitchen without the necessity of buying new tables to accommodate a new design.

Foodservice operators often find that a new menu item requires an additional piece of cooking equipment. However, the total cost of the installation may be as much as two or three times greater than the purchase price of the equipment because another hood has to be added and new utility services provided. Adding an additional few feet of ventilation hood when a foodservice facility is built is relatively inexpensive when compared to the cost of extending the hood three years after the operation has opened.

Another inflexible construction method that was popular in the past was the construction of concrete pads as a base for kitchen equipment. These bases were used in place of legs for refrigerators, ovens, or other heavy pieces of equipment because they eliminate the difficult chore of cleaning under the equipment. The problem with concrete bases is that when the equipment requires replacement or needs to be rearranged, the bases may then be the wrong shape or in the wrong location. A concrete base is difficult to eliminate and almost impossible to move. Concrete bases are now infrequently seen in commercial kitchens.

The principle of flexibility requires components that can be rearranged to meet changing conditions, such as new management, different methods of service, a new menu, or a new preparation method. Designing for change is the primary means of achieving flexibility.

In the dining area, flexibility can be achieved by the use of movable walls (room dividers) as well as other partitions such as planters or screens. In the service area, the space can be divided to accommodate both table service and buffet service.

Modularity in design provides standardized sizes and functions of space and equipment. For example, in the construction industry, doors are modular because they are sized according to an industry standard. Modularity means that a given equipment item can easily be replaced with a comparable item from the same or another manufacturer, rather than having to rely on a custom design available from only a single manufacturer. Much of the equipment manufactured for use in commercial kitchens, such as ranges, refrigerators, carts, and racks, is modular.

Flexibility and Modularity

In a free-flow or scramble cafeteria, the service components should be modular, so that the service lines can be easily shifted as the menu and customer tastes change. Modular range sections, which are commonly used, permit the designer to select from many types of equipment and to arrange these in a smooth and continuous lineup. Quick-disconnect utility lines that allow inexpensive changes of equipment are an excellent example of flexibility and modularity. The modular pieces can be designed for off-the-floor installation, with the entire range section mounted on legs for ease in cleaning. In future years, if a piece of equipment needs to be replaced, the modular unit can be removed without disturbing other pieces of equipment.

Simplicity   In the designing of a foodservice facility, striving for simplicity offers a great many advantages. Food facilities seem to invite clutter, and clutter leads to poor sanitation, confusion, and inefficiency in the work areas, as well as to an environment that customers may find uncomfortable and overcrowded.

The principle of simplicity can be incorporated into the design of foodservice components and systems in various ways. Several examples of simplicity are:

❏ Clean, uncluttered lines for range sections
❏ Simple wall-hung tables in areas where a heavy grease' or soil condition exists
❏ The use of modular or drop-in cooking equipment that eliminates corners, edges, and unnecessary undershelves or overshelves
❏ The elimination of wheels on equipment that will seldom be moved
❏ The elimination of utility connections that penetrate the floor (rather than the wall behind the equipment), creating dirt pockets and clutter
❏ The selection of a piece of equipment without unnecessary accessories
❏ Convenient server stations near the serving area in the dining room
❏ The arrangement of tables in the dining room to create natural and comfortable aisle space for servers and guests

Examples of the violation of the principle of simplicity exist in many restaurant kitchens. For instance, the large stainless-steel equipment stands for fryers and grills are very expensive and difficult to clean. A better solution is a simple, flat stainless-steel surface with drop-in fryers and grills. This approach would save thousands of dollars in the original installation and make the cleaning process much simpler for the employees.

Flow of Materials and Personnel   The movement of food through a foodservice facility should follow a logical sequence beginning with receiving and ending with waste disposal. Since both receiving and waste disposal usually occur at the back dock of a foodservice operation, the food moves through the facility in a circle, as illustrated in Figure 3-1.

If the food does not move through the production cycle in the order shown, then backtracking by the personnel will occur, resulting in lower productivity and wasted labor.

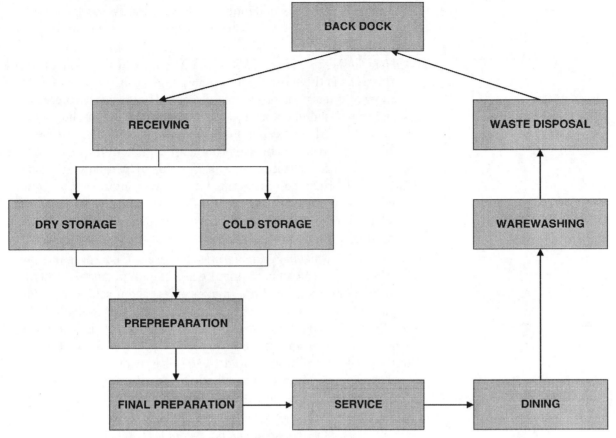

Figure 3-1. The flow of materials and personnel in a foodservice operation.

Flow is an important consideration in efficient design throughout a foodservice facility. The following are examples of some flow considerations in design:

❏ The movement of employees from one section of the kitchen to another

❏ The flow of dishes through the dishwashing system and back to the service area.

❏ In a restaurant, the flow of customers from the entrance to the cocktail lounge and/or to the main dining room

❏ In a cafeteria, the flow of customers from the entrance through the service cafeteria to the dish drop-off point

❏ The flow of raw food ingredients through the main traffic aisles of the kitchen to the preparation area

It is helpful for the designer to diagram the flow patterns on the preliminary floor plan, showing the movement of customers, food, dishes, trash, and garbage. Color-coding the flow lines makes the patterns easier to distinguish and assists the designer in arriving at a design solution that accommodates the proper flow of materials and personnel.

Ease of Sanitation

In virtually every type of foodservice facility, more employee labor hours are spent cleaning than are spent preparing the food. A facility designed with sanitation in mind can be cleaned more quickly and easily and thus requires fewer labor hours for this aspect of the operation. Some examples of sanitation design considerations:

❏ *Building finishes that are durable and easy to clean.* Structural glazed tile on the walls is the most desirable building finish because of ease of cleaning and resistance to damage. Ceramic tile is easy to clean and can be purchased in colorful patterns that make the kitchen a pleasant place to work. Epoxy paint on cement block is the least expensive wall finish but will turn brown around areas that are exposed to high heat. The painted surface is also easily chipped by rolling equipment. The use of bright colors in the kitchen will improve the general appearance of the space and encourage cleanliness. Quarry tile is the standard floor finish for the industry because it does not wear, is grease-resistant, and is less slippery than other floors when wet.

❏ *Utilization of wall-hung equipment.* The use of equipment that is attached to the wall, eliminating the use of legs, pedestals, and other supports rising from the floor, makes an excellent sanitation design. A space is created under the equipment, allowing for ease of cleaning. Figure 3-2 illustrates this principle. On the left is a traditional pedestal-mount steam-jacketed kettle. On the right is the same kettle designed to be mounted to the wall. A metal frame called a chair carrier is built into the wall and floor to support the weight of the kettle. Notice how much easier it is to mop under the wall-hung kettle than under the pedestal-mount kettle.

❏ *Equipment racks with a minimum number of legs.*

❏ *Garbage disposals in work areas to facilitate waste disposal.*

❏ *Shelf storage design.* Portable storage shelving systems and open shelving under tables can be cleaned easily.

Ease of Supervision   Many hotels and foodservice institutions built during the 1920s and 1930s had vegetable preparation areas that were remote from the main kitchen or separated by partitions and were therefore difficult to supervise. The open type of design, which is now preferred, allows the supervisor to oversee the

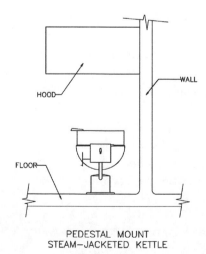

Figure 3-2. Methods of mounting equipment.

PEDESTAL MOUNT
STEAM–JACKETED KETTLE

WALL MOUNT
STEAM–JACKETED KETTLE

production areas more efficiently. The elimination of walls and partitions also permits workers to move and communicate with each other more easily and tends to reduce the number of people needed.

The separation of production areas by floor level not only violates the ease-of-supervision principle by increasing the amount of supervision needed but also creates cumbersome flow patterns between the floors. The designer should avoid separating the production areas by floor whenever possible.

It is often desirable to put a half wall under hoods and between work departments. A 4-foot half wall provides separation and defines work space but does not block the view of the supervisor, who needs to maintain contact with production workers. A half wall is also very useful as:

- ❑ A place to attach wall-hung equipment
- ❑ A sanitary site for utility connections
- ❑ A containment device for spilled water (around stock kettles)

Space Efficiency

As costs of building construction and maintenance rise, designers are constantly striving to incorporate space-saving ideas into their work. In this case, necessity can be turned to advantage—space saving is translated into space efficiency in the design of a small, well-equipped work area.

The principle of space efficiency can, of course, be carried to the extreme. Small, efficient kitchens are a pleasure to use, but kitchens that are too small can be most unpleasant for cooks and other kitchen workers. How can the designer know the difference between small and efficient, on one hand, and too small, on the other? Providing the following components will help ensure that each section of the kitchen has the necessary equipment and storage space to enable employees to work efficiently:

- ❑ A work surface (table)
- ❑ A sink
- ❑ A cutting surface
- ❑ Storage for utensils
- ❑ Storage for pans
- ❑ Storage for raw ingredients
- ❑ Storage for the finished product
- ❑ Proper aisle space for movement

If each work area includes the above features, and the work area is arranged efficiently and is adequate for their utilization, the food facility will be space-efficient. (Space efficiency and the proper layout of work areas will be developed more fully in later chapters of this book.)

Lifetime Value

Commercial foodservice equipment can be expensive and certainly represents a significant part of the cost of a construction project. The foodservice operator is often faced with a limited budget for the purchase of equipment, and it is therefore understandable that price becomes a primary factor in the selection process. In the not-for-profit sector of the food industry (hospitals, schools, the military, colleges), selecting the low bid is often required; for projects funded by federal, state, and local governments, this is often written into the law.

With carefully written specifications for the purchase of a piece of equipment, it is possible to consider the lifetime value of equipment rather than its initial purchase price. For example, a basic exhaust hood can be purchased for a typical cooking battery for $8,000 to $10,000. A more efficient hood designed to operate effectively with far less exhaust would cost more—perhaps $14,000 to $16,000. However, the more efficient design would dramatically cut down on heating and air-conditioning costs for the building. The savings in energy in this example would easily pay for the more expensive hood in two years or less.

The true cost of any foodservice equipment item is not the purchase price alone; rather, it is the purchase price plus the following:

❏ Operational costs

❏ Maintenance costs

❏ How long it will last

❏ Labor efficiency

A piece of equipment that is attractive because of its lower purchase price may, in the long run, prove to be a very expensive investment if it requires more maintenance or more labor or is not energy-efficient.

Compromise   In every design project, conflicting needs will give rise to a series of compromise conditions that the owner and design team must resolve. Ideally, if the conceptual design and planning phases of the project are conducted thoroughly, the number of compromises should be minimal. However, the need to compromise at some points in the design process is virtually inevitable. For example, in the design of a dining area, it might be highly desirable to include a private dining room that could be closed off for special groups. Should this room be near the customer entrance for easy public access or near the kitchen for convenience to the hot-food production area? The answer might be both. However, if placing the private dining room near both the entrance and the kitchen interferes with other major components of the design, the best alternative may be to move it to another part of the facility. Conflicting needs always arise in the design process, and only the skilled and experienced person will be able to balance priorities so that the resulting compromises are logical and defensible. Since the owner's priorities may not be the same as the designer's, frank discussion and give-and-take by all parties are often needed to create a satisfactory working relationship.

The designer will be basing his or her work on a set of principles that should be clearly described to the client before the project begins. If the client insists on making choices that depart from principles of good design, the designer has three choices:

❏ Resign and bill the client for the work completed as of the day of the disagreement.

❏ Formally protest the change and give in to the client's demand. The change should be put in writing for all to see, but not in such a way that the client would be embarrassed.

❑ Resubmit the design, hoping that an agreement can be reached that will satisfy the client and will preserve the principles of good design.

Resubmission is quite common, and it is not unusual to resubmit at least four to six times for the design of a major project. Resubmission should be viewed as a healthy approach to the idea that a good design represents the best thinking of many people.

HUMAN ENGINEERING

A work environment that is designed with the comfort and safety of the workers in mind will have a tremendous effect on worker productivity. If workers have a pleasant place to work, with the proper equipment and tools at hand, they will be likely to enjoy the job and function more efficiently.

Human engineering (or industrial engineering) is a discipline that studies how working conditions affect employee satisfaction, safety, and productivity. The primary factors that influence the quality of the workplace are:

❑ Efficient work space

❑ Sufficient aisle space

❑ Construction, height, and arrangement of work surfaces

❑ Equipment properly designed for the range of motion of the human body

❑ Materials-handling tools and utensils

❑ Temperature and humidity

❑ Control of noise levels

❑ Adequate lighting to perform the task

Each of these factors is described in greater detail in the sections that follow.

Efficient Work Space

There are many different work spaces that must be considered in the overall design of a food facility. The amount of space needed by a dishwasher is far different from that needed by a server at a beverage station. In the dishwasher's situation, the worker needs to move back and forth, stooping, gathering carts and racks, and performing other tasks that require a considerable amount of space. The server may need only enough room to pass by a beverage station and pick up a coffeepot or glass of milk en route to the dining room.

The information provided below on work space can be used as a general guideline. It is no substitute, however, for a commonsense evaluation of the unique requirements of any given foodservice facility. The amount of space that an individual worker needs is influenced by:

❑ The number of people working in the space

❑ The amount and type of equipment

❑ The clearance required for equipment doors

❑ The type of food being processed

❑ The amount of space needed for storage

Adequate Aisle Space   The aisle space needed for different types of work areas is listed below:

Description of the space	Aisle width needed
Single aisle with limited equipment	2 feet 6 inches to 3 feet 0 inches (.76 to .91 meter)
Double aisle with limited equipment	3 feet 6 inches to 4 feet 6 inches (1.1 to 1.4 meters)
Single aisle with protruding equipment	3 feet 6 inches to 4 feet 6 inches (1.1 to 1.4 meters)
Double aisle with protruding equipment	4 feet 6 inches to 6 feet (1.4 to 1.8 meters)
Aisle with little traffic	3 feet 0 inches to 4 feet 0 inches (.9 to 1.2 meters)
Aisle with major traffic	4 feet 0 inches to 6 feet 0 inches (1.2 to 1.8 meters)

An example of a double aisle with protruding equipment is shown in Figure 3-3.

As noted in the preceding list, the width of major traffic aisles should range between 4 and 6 feet (1.2 and 1.8 meters). A major traffic aisle is used for the movement of people and material from storage to production areas, or from production areas to the point of service. A piece of equipment with a protruding door should never be located in a major traffic aisle that is only 4 feet (1.22 meters) wide. An aisle 6 feet (1.83 meters) wide can accommodate a refrigerator door or other protruding equipment.

It is important that aisles be the proper size, because they have a significant influence on the total size of the food facility and on operating efficiency. If the aisle is too narrow, employees will have a difficult time working in the space. If the aisle is too wide, the employees will be required to take many extra steps during the day, and fatigue and low productivity will result.

Work Surfaces   Work surfaces should be arranged within easy reach of the worker. Table tops are often 30 inches (760 millimeters) wide in production areas, because the average worker can reach out only 30 inches (760 millimeters) from a standing position. The height of the work surface should permit the worker to chop or to do other hand work without stooping over. The height of a work surface must be adjusted for the height of the worker and the type

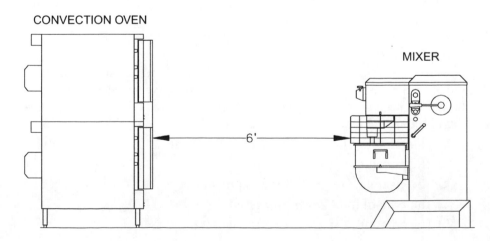

CONVECTION OVEN

MIXER

6'

Figure 3-3. Double aisle with protruding equipment.

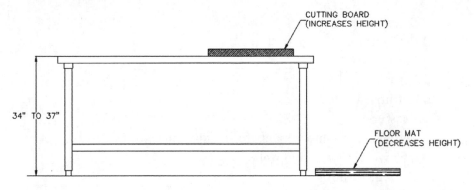

Figure 3-4. Worktable surface height.

of material that is placed on the work surface. A thick cutting board, for instance, will raise the surface height by 1¾ to 3 inches (45 to 76 millimeters).

The standard used by most designers for the height of a work surface is 34 to 37 inches (864 to 940 millimeters) (Figure 3-4). If a work area will be used for heavy, bulky objects, a lower height should be selected. Some height variations can be created for the worker by the use of mats on the floor, cutting boards on the table, or adjustable table feet.

The amount of space needed from one side of a work surface to the other will depend on the size of the materials used and the layout of the work area. For example, if standard 18-by-26-inch sheet pans (460 by 660 millimeters) are used as trays for holding individual tossed salads, space would be needed for:

❏ Empty bowls
❏ Bulk tossed salad
❏ Empty sheet pans
❏ Sheet pans filled with salads

In this example, 6 linear feet of space is provided, even though the worker cannot reach that far from one position (Figure 3-5).

The most important guideline for good workplace layout is to think through the steps in a process and provide a space for the food and equipment needed to carry out these steps. For instance, a sandwich makeup table in a cold-food production area needs:

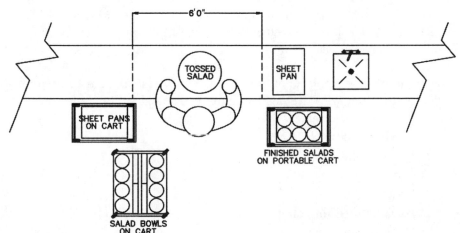

Figure 3-5. Adequate work space for salad preparation.

❏ Storage for plates
❏ Refrigerated storage for food
❏ Storage for bread
❏ Utensil drawer or rack
❏ Cutting surface
❏ Toaster
❏ Refrigerated compartments for condiments
❏ Sink with hot and cold water
❏ Garbage disposal or can
❏ Pickup area for servers

Work Surface Materials   In its Standard Number 1 (revised June 1984), the National Sanitation Foundation (NSF) lists three types of surfaces used for foodservice equipment: food contact surfaces, splash contact surfaces, and nonfood contact surfaces. NSF describes the materials that may be used as follows:

Food contact surfaces: Surface materials in the food zone shall be smooth, corrosion resistant, non-toxic, stable, and nonabsorbent under use condition. They shall not impart an odor, color, taste, or contribute to the adulteration of food.

Splash contact surfaces: shall be smooth, easily changeable, and corrosion resistant or rendered corrosion resistant with a material which is non-cracking and non-chipping.

Nonfood contact surfaces: shall be smooth, corrosion resistant or rendered corrosion resistant.

Properly Designed Equipment   The design of equipment from the human engineering point of view is also a consideration of the professional food facilities design consultant.

The National Sanitation Foundation has established standards for constructing foodservice equipment that are primarily concerned with safety and sanitation. The reader can consult NSF publications, which are available at a small cost from NSF in Ann Arbor, Michigan.

A checklist (Figure 3-6) can be used as a guide to human engineering in equipment design. Although it is not intended as a comprehensive guide to all design features that should be in a food facility, the list does contain items that are often overlooked in designing a foodservice facility. The use of the checklist will help ensure a food operation that is engineered for comfort, safety, and sanitation.

Appropriate Tools and Utensils   The lifting of heavy objects by foodservice workers can lead to accidents and personal injury. Materials-handling tools and equipment that can greatly reduce or eliminate worker injury include:
❏ Forklift trucks
❏ Hand forklift trucks (mules)
❏ Carts
❏ Hand trucks
❏ Portable receiving ramps
❏ Skate wheel conveyors

Floors

❑ Adequate number of floor drains to keep floors dry
❑ Carborundum chips in quarry tile in slippery or wet areas
❑ Slip-resistant wax on vinyl floors
❑ Ramps and handrails in receiving area and storage space for carts and hand trucks
❑ Floor mats for comfort of workers who must stand in one place for long periods of time
❑ Kitchen floor level with walk-in refrigerator floor
❑ Heavy slope of floor around steam-jacketed kettles to encourage quick drain-off of hot liquids to floor drains
❑ Coved corners of floors where they meet the wall, for ease of cleaning

Materials Handling

❑ Hand trucks and carts for moving all foods
❑ Strong, easy-to-clean shelving
❑ Portable shelving
❑ Ladders for reaching stored goods on high shelves
❑ Carts for the movement of processed foods from production area to refrigeration and then to service area

Utensil Handling

❑ Knife racks
❑ Easy-to-clean utensil drawers with removable inserts
❑ Utensil drawers at every workstation and table
❑ Overhead utensil racks

Food Production Equipment

❑ Compliance with NSF standards
❑ Compliance with ADA requirements
❑ Portable equipment, if needed in more than one department
❑ Portable bins for flour, sugar, and salt
❑ Wall-hung or mounted on legs for ease of cleaning
❑ Free of burrs, sharp edges, or difficult-to-reach areas
❑ Safety equipment and guards on equipment, such as shields for mixing machine
❑ Disposals in all production areas (if permitted by local codes)
❑ Open rail-type undershelving that will permit crumbs and small particles of food to fall to the floor
❑ Marine edge on all tables with sinks (to prevent water from spilling on floor)
❑ Adequate space for parking equipment from other departments (bread racks, raw ingredients from stores, etc.)

Warewashing Equipment

❑ Pot storage racks beside potwashing station and in or near each work area
❑ Storage containers for soiled linen
❑ Box, glass, and metal can container in each major work area
❑ Utensil sorting table
❑ Paper and bone container at dishwashing station
❑ Prerinse, power or hand
❑ Cleaning supply storage
❑ Hose reel
❑ Cart wash-down area

Service and Dining

❑ Condiments and support service equipment available near the point of service
❑ Convenient dish drop-off
❑ Easy-to-clean chairs with absence of cracks that accumulate crumbs
❑ Minimum number of steps from food pickup to point of service

Figure 3-6. Human engineering checklist for foodservice facilities design.

The materials-handling tool most frequently used for assembling ingredients in the kitchen is a simple cart. The cart is often abused by the worker, through heavy use and the dropping of full cases of food onto the top shelf. The designer should specify the heaviest capacity cart possible (600–1,000-pound capacity) to prevent damage and abuse.

Forklift trucks are normally reserved for large foodservice warehouses, but the hand-operated forklift is frequently used in the storerooms and kitchens of medium-sized and large foodservice operations. Hand-operated forklifts raise pallets of food a few inches off the floor, permitting easy transport to a freezer or storeroom. Hand trucks are simple L-shaped two-wheeled devices that permit the worker to balance a stack of case goods on two wheels and to move it in or out of storage.

Receiving ramps and skate wheel conveyors permit the movement of materials from one level to the next without lifting. Receiving docks are the wrong height for many of the different types of delivery truck that bring goods to the receiving area. A portable receiving ramp, constructed of light-weight aluminum, is very helpful in solving the height variation problem. Motorized load leveler devices are often designed into the ramp to solve this same problem. Motor-driven belts, dumbwaiters, and elevators are also used to transport materials from one level to the next.

Adequate Lighting

Adequate lighting is essential in food preparation and service. Employees need sufficient light to observe the quality of the food products they are handling and to monitor the cleanliness of their work areas. The standard measure of light is the foot-candle, which is equivalent to the amount of light from a standard candle that strikes a 1-foot-square surface from a distance of 1 foot. The farther away a light is placed from the surface to be lighted, the lower the number of foot-candles. For this reason, lighting needs to be spaced at frequent intervals in a food production area. Figure 3-7 can be used as a guide in selecting the proper light levels for food facilities.

Space	Foot Candles
Kitchen Work Area	30–40
Storeroom	10–20
Cashier	50–60
Loading Platform	20–25
Building Entrance	10–20
Rest Room	20–30
Hotel: General Guest Areas	10–20
Accounting and Bookkeeping Offices	100–150
Dining Rooms	
Quick Service	40–50
Casual Dining	10–20
White Tablecloth	5–15

Figure 3-7. Lighting standards for foodservice facilities.

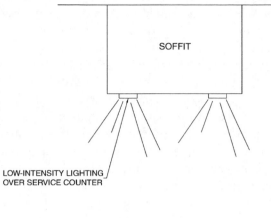

LOW-INTENSITY LIGHTING
OVER SERVICE COUNTER

SOFFIT

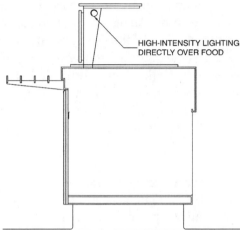

HIGH-INTENSITY LIGHTING
DIRECTLY OVER FOOD

Figure 3-8. Lighting for food display.

In service areas that will be seen by the public, one very effective means of lighting is to provide a high intensity of light on the food and low intensity for the main part of the room. Low- and high-intensity lighting for food display is illustrated in Figure 3-8.

The relationship between temperature, humidity, and air movement is a technical subject that is the responsibility of the engineer on the design project. However, the food facilities design consultant needs to be aware of this aspect of environmental design, which affects the comfort of building occupants. The range of temperature and humidity in which most of the people who use the building will be comfortable is referred to as the comfort zone. In the winter, if the temperature is too high and the humidity too low, an unpleasant dryness results. In winter, outside air usually contains very little moisture. When this air is drawn into a building and heated to 70°F (21.1°C), the humidity drops to a very low level. In the summer, the reverse condition often exists. Moist air from the outside is drawn in and cooled, resulting in high humidity. Air-conditioning reduces the amount of moisture in the hot, humid air and provides a comfortable combination of lower temperature and lower humidity in the summer.

In foodservice facilities, very few kitchens or dishwashing rooms are air-conditioned. Air movement is therefore essential for comfort. If the temper-

Temperature and Humidity

ature is slightly high but air movement is rapid, skin evaporation will usually keep the body cool enough for comfort. Dishwashing rooms and range sections of a food facility are usually the most difficult areas to keep comfortable. In the dishroom, the high humidity produced by the moisture from the automatic dishwashing equipment creates two problems: The workers are uncomfortable, and the dishes do not air-dry. The designer must work closely with the engineers to be sure that air movement is sufficient and that ventilation ducts are provided for both the feed (entrance) and discharge ends of the dish machine. Typical vent requirements recommended by commercial dishwasher manufacturers are 200 CFM (cubic feet per minute/5.66 cubic meters per minute) at the entrance to the machine and 400 CFM (11.32 cubic meters per minute) at the discharge of the machine. It is suggested that air movement be increased slightly above the recommended levels, since dishwashing rooms themselves often do not have enough room exhaust. The additional exhaust will keep the room more comfortable.

The range section of a kitchen is often uncomfortable for the cooks because of the heat generated by broilers, ranges, and other pieces of equipment that produce (and waste) large amounts of energy. The high heat condition is usually the result of inadequate exhaust ventilation by the hood equipment.

Noise Control

High noise levels are very unpleasant for the worker in a foodservice facility. It has been demonstrated in industrial settings that excessive noise causes fatigue, accidents, and low productivity in direct relationship to the volume of the noise. Some techniques that will help to reduce noise in a foodservice facility are:

❏ Sound-deadening materials sprayed onto the underside of all tables and counters.

❏ The separation of areas (other than production) in the food facility department, especially warewashing. The construction of walls between the kitchen and the warewashing area will restrict noise transmission.

❏ Designing conveyors to create a sound barrier between dish drop-off points and warewashing. A sound barrier that might be used in a self-busing application for a restaurant or cafeteria is illustrated in Figure 3-9.

❏ Acoustic ceilings that are grease- or moisture-resistant.

❏ Carpeting in dining rooms in the seating areas.

❏ Carpeting on the walls in dining areas. This is an excellent wall finish because it not only absorbs sound but will take the punishment of chairs and tables that often scar wooden, papered, or painted wall finishes.

❏ Double doors between the dining room and the kitchen.

❏ Background music in both the public areas and the back of the establishment (kitchen, warewashing area, service areas).

❏ Remote refrigeration compressors.

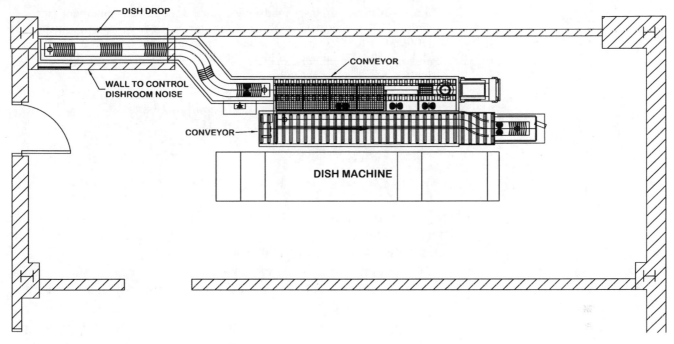

Figure 3-9. Controlling sound using wall construction to create a barrier.

FOODSERVICE DESIGN AND TITLES II AND III OF THE AMERICANS WITH DISABILITIES ACT

The Americans with Disabilities Act became law on July 26, 1991. After January 26, 1992, alterations to existing places of public accommodation and commercial facilities must be accessible to the maximum extent feasible, and new construction must be accessible to individuals with disabilities to the extent that it is not structurally impracticable. Title II covers any state or local government and any of its departments, agencies, or other instrumentalities. Title III covers public accommodations, commercial facilities, and private entities that offer certain examinations and courses related to educational and occupational certification. Public accommodations include over five million private establishments, such as restaurants, hotels, and theaters. Sections 5.1 through 5.9 of Part III of the *Federal Register* (pages 35665–6) deal specifically with restaurants and cafeterias. Section 4.2 of Part III (pages 35620–1) and the corresponding charts deal with the heights of counters and the reach of customers with disabilities. For copies of the act, call the office of the Americans with Disabilities Act at (202) 514-0301.

Following are some general provisions of the act, taken from the *Federal Register* (page 35665), that may be helpful in the planning process.

5.3   Aisle Width: All accessible fixed tables shall be accessible by means of an access aisle at least 36 inches (915 mm) clear between paralleled edges of tables or between a wall and the table.

5.4   Dining Areas: In new construction all dining areas, including raised or sunken dining areas, loggias, and outdoor seating areas shall be accessible.

5.5   Foodservice Lines: foodservice lines shall have a minimum clear width of 36 inches (915 mm), with a preferred clear width of 42 inches (1065 mm) to allow passage around a person using a wheelchair. Tray slides shall be mounted no higher than 34 inches (865 mm) above the floor.

Entrance requirements and ramping are discussed and detailed in the *Federal Register*, and the reader is encouraged to review this material so that full compliance is achieved.

SUMMARY

The design of a foodservice facility will have a significant impact on its safety, efficiency, ease of maintenance, and long-term operating costs. Principles of design include the following:

❏ Flexibility and modularity make it feasible to change the design as consumer demand requires new and different menu items and preparation techniques.

❏ Simplicity in design leads to efficiency and long-term labor savings.

❏ A design that arranges work areas to facilitate the flow of products saves steps and therefore saves labor costs.

❏ A design that makes sanitation a simple process leads to greater food safety, thereby protecting the health of guests as well as the business.

❏ A design in which the manager can easily supervise and assist the employees facilitates communication and coordination and leads to better employee relations.

❏ A design that maximizes lifetime value, rather than minimizing initial capital investment, leads to the long-term financial health and viability of the operation.

❏ All designs reflect some degree of compromise. The more informed the design team can be about the costs and benefits of each alternative, the better the outcome will be.

❏ Human engineering specifies the design factors that lead to efficient work as well as the prevention of work-related injuries.

❏ The Americans with Disabilities Act requires that foodservice facilities be designed to meet the needs of individuals with disabilities to the maximum extent feasible.

CHAPTER 4

SPACE ANALYSIS

THIS CHAPTER

☑ Describes the Space Analysis Process for the Following Functional Areas of a Foodservice Facility:

+ Receiving
+ Storage
+ Office
+ Pre-preparation
+ Hot-food preparation, cold-food preparation, and final preparation
+ Bakery
+ Employee locker room and toilet
+ Service areas
+ Dining
+ Bar
+ Warewashing

CONDUCTING A SPACE ANALYSIS

How large should a food facility be? Should the kitchen be half the size of the dining room? How much space will be needed for warewashing and storage? These and related questions must be answered during the early phase of the design project, since the answers will determine the size and thus the total cost of the facility. By knowing space requirements in advance, the owner or architect can make realistic preliminary estimates of construction costs.

It is the foodservice design consultant's job to determine the space requirements for each section of the foodservice facility before the actual design can begin. This early but difficult estimate is achieved by gathering basic data about the nature of the planned food operation. Figure 4-1 shows the type of data that should be collected to determine space needs. Once this information has been obtained, the space requirements of each functional part of a foodservice facility are analyzed.

77

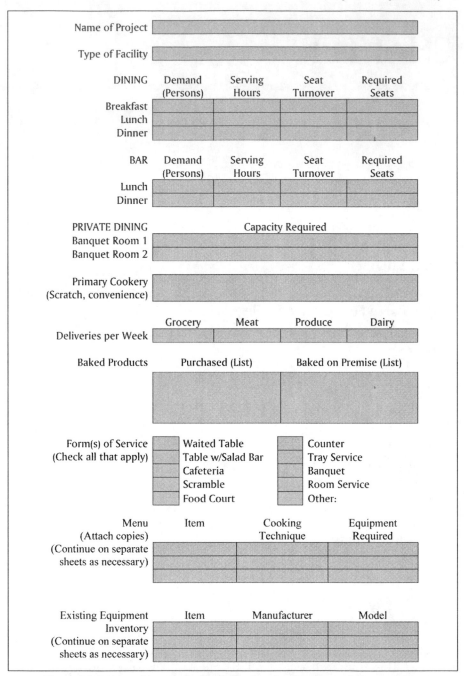

Figure 4-1. Data used in preparation for foodservice planning and programming.

This chapter is devoted to discussing the space requirements of each of the functional areas of a foodservice facility. For purposes of easy reference, the description of each of these functional foodservice areas is divided into four sections:

❑ General description of the space

❑ Relationship to other areas

❑ Amount of space needed

❑ Special design features

The receiving area is located with easy access to driveways and street entrances to the property. Usually the architect decides where major ingress/egress for people, delivery trucks, and service vehicles will be located. The food facilities design consultant must work with the architect to be sure that sufficient space is allocated for the movement of large tractor-trailer trucks and other vehicles that need access to the receiving area. Consideration must be given to proper screening of the receiving dock and especially to trash and garbage storage containers so that persons looking out of the building windows or walking along the street will not have a full view of the receiving dock and garbage containers.

General Description of the Space

The primary relationship of receiving is to the storage areas, which are often scattered and may in fact be located at different building levels. Regardless of the location of storage, easy access must be available for the movement of heavy materials from the receiving dock. The receiving dock must also be accessible to the kitchen for the following reasons:

Relationship to Other Areas

- ❏ Many food products will go directly from receiving to the production areas in the kitchen.
- ❏ Refrigerated storage areas are often located adjacent to the kitchen and will be stocked directly from the receiving dock.
- ❏ Since in small or medium-sized foodservice facilities, supervisory personnel such as the chef, manager, or assistant managers will personally be responsible for receiving the food, easy access from the kitchen to the dock is highly desirable.

Other important relationships for the receiving area include access to trash containers, wash-down rooms, and cleaning equipment.

Space needs in the receiving area vary with the volume of food to be received, the frequency of delivery, and the distance between the receiving area and the storage spaces. If the receiving clerk must transport food products great distances before placing them in storage, the need to temporarily store a quantity of food products on the back dock may require the allocation of additional space. Often, too much space is provided for the receiving dock, resulting in the accumulation of clutter. Figure 4-2 provides general guidelines for allocating the proper amount of space for the receiving area.

Amount of Space Needed

The receiving dock can be designed as an elevated platform for tractor-trailer trucks, at street level, or at any level in between these two heights. The decision on receiving dock height will probably be determined by the architect based on site development and the placement of the building on the property. The depth of the dock (distance from front to back) should permit a person to walk back and forth, with space for goods stored temporarily on wooden pallets. Usually 8 or 10 feet (2.4 to 3.0 meters) is sufficient. The length of the dock should accommodate the number of delivery trucks that are likely to be unloading at one time. For most foodservice operations, a receiving clerk can check in only one or two trucks at a time, and a single

Special Design Features

Type of Food Operation	Space Needed Square Feet (Square Meters)	Number of Trucks
Fast food	40–60 (3.72–5.58)	1
Small restaurant (under 75 seats)	60–80 (5.58–7.44)	1
Medium restaurant (75–150 seats) *or* Small institution (300–1,000 meals per day)	80–100 (7.44–9.30)	1
Large restaurant (150–400 seats) *or* Medium institution (1,000–2,000 meals per day)	120–150 (11.16–13.95)	2
Large institution (over 2,000 meals per day)	150–175 (13.95–16.28)	2
Large hotel, restaurant, or institution with complex menu, catering facilities, snack bars	175–200 (16.28–18.60)	3

Note: Space needed does not include room for trash removal truck or trash container. Space for this equipment (approximately 40–60 sq. ft. [3.72–5.58 sq. m.]) should be added to the receiving dock.

Figure 4.2. Space required for receiving.

or at the most a double truck width is usually sufficient. A third truck width for a trash/garbage vehicle is also desirable. A range of 10 to 15 feet (3.0 to 4.6 meters) per truck should be used as a standard, depending on the angle for backing to the dock.

CONTROL OF FOOD AND SUPPLIES   The control of food and supplies moving in and out of the receiving area will be of concern to the foodservice management staff. Visibility of the receiving area from an office window is highly desirable if the food facility is large enough to justify a receiving office. For a small food facility that does not have a receiving office, visual control from the kitchen or manager's office should be a design consideration. It is often necessary to construct a stairway at the back dock for the use of employees coming and going from the workplace. This presents a serious control problem because it permits easy access to food and supplies by employees as they enter or exit the building. If possible, a separately controlled entrance for employees should be incorporated into the building design. If this is not possible, the next best solution is to design a separate door and corridor from the receiving area to the interior of the building.

PROTECTION FROM THE WEATHER   Receiving personnel must be protected from rain, cold, and excessive heat as they perform their duties on the back dock. Typical architectural solutions include a simple roof overhang, placement of the receiving dock in a recess behind the exterior wall of the building, or the enclosure of the entire receiving area with a heavy-duty folding door. Unless weather conditions are extremely severe, the enclosure of the entire receiving area is excessively expensive. The door from the receiving area should be 5 feet (1.5 meters) wide when two doors are used and a minimum of 4 feet (1.2 meters) wide for a single door entrance. Double entry doors should be used for proper screening to prevent flies and other insects from entering the food production area. Air curtains, which are simple centrifugal fans located over the door entrances, are somewhat effective in discouraging the entry of flies.

The importance of scales adjacent to the receiving dock is often overlooked by many foodservice managers. Many products are prepackaged and weighed, with the weights clearly marked on the containers. It is often assumed—falsely—that these weights are always accurate. All foodservice facilities should have a scale for use by the receiving clerk to verify the weights of foods that are purchased by the pound or kilogram. The location of the scale should be in the breakout area (a small space just inside the receiving doors for checking in and separating foods before putting them into storage) inside the building, so that the scale is protected from the weather.

SCALES

Several types of materials-handling equipment are commonly used in foodservice receiving areas for efficient transport and to avoid stress and injury to employees. Hand trucks (two-wheeled vehicles for moving small stacks of case goods), platform hand trucks (four-wheeled flat vehicles) that are strong enough to hold the weight of ten or fifteen cases of food goods, and wooden or steel pallets are all part of the equipment needs for the receiving clerk. Large numbers of wooden pallets (skids) often accumulate in the receiving area because they are commonly used in the food distribution industry for holding and moving large quantities of case goods. Large foodservice operations may want to consider the design of storeroom spaces to hold these pallets, which must be moved with either a hand-operated forklift device or a forklift truck.

MATERIALS-HANDLING EQUIPMENT

The need for a separate receiving office, breakout area, wash-down room, or garbage room will depend on the size and complexity of the foodservice operation. These functions are usually carried out in the receiving area, and if space is not provided, they may encroach on other space. Office space should be small (50 square feet/4.6 square meters), and the wash-down area and garbage room should be limited in size (50 to 80 square feet [4.6 to 7.4 square meters] should be sufficient). A small area just inside the receiving door can be allotted for breakout space. Figure 4-3 can be used as a guideline in deciding whether or not special rooms are needed.

STORAGE

The amount of storage in a foodservice facility is primarily influenced by the number of meals per day served, the number of items that appear on the menu, the frequency of delivery, and the operating policies of the manage-

General Description of the Space

Number of Seats	Approximate Space Needed (Net)		
	Office	Wash-down	Garbage
Under 50 or fast food	None	None	60 sq. ft.
50–100	None	None	60 sq. ft.
100–175	80 sq. ft. (7.43 sq. m.)	80 sq. ft. (7.43 sq. m.)	80 sq. ft. (7.43 sq. m.)
175–250	100 sq. ft. (9.29 sq. m.)	80 sq. ft. (7.43 sq. m.)	80 sq. ft. (7.43 sq. m.)
250–500	160 sq. ft. (14.86 sq. m.)	80 sq. ft. (7.43 sq. m.)	120 sq. ft. (11.15 sq. m.)
More than 500	240 sq. ft. (22.30 sq. m.)	120 sq. ft. (11.15 sq. m.)	120 sq. ft. (11.15 sq. m.)

Figure 4-3. Support spaces for receiving/dock area.

ment. It is considered good management practice to turn the inventory over twelve times per year (once a month). Turnover for perishable products should, of course, be at least twice a week, and turnover for such items as paper and cleaning supplies may be infrequent. The attitude of management toward inventory turnover should always be discussed prior to beginning the design. A canned-goods storeroom, for instance, might be viewed by one manager as too small because he or she likes the idea of keeping a large par stock on hand. Another manager who prefers to keep the par stock very low, so that cash is not tied up in inventory, might see the same storeroom as too large. The use of computers in the foodservice industry has greatly enhanced the ability of managers to forecast the precise amount of food needed for each meal and, therefore, decrease the amount of food that must be kept on hand at any one time. Computers, more efficient distribution of food products by vendors, and high interest rates have all contributed to a trend toward smaller storage spaces.

The four categories of storage that must be available in all food facilities are:

❏ Dry or canned food storage
❏ Paper and cleaning supplies storage
❏ Refrigerated storage
❏ Utensil and cleaning equipment storage

Relationship to Other Areas

Storage areas should be well ventilated, dry, and constructed of easy-to-clean surfaces. Concrete or tile floors, cement block walls with epoxy paint, and acoustic ceilings are common for all storage areas except those that are refrigerated. Large access doors and a high level of security must be included as part of the design. The most important relationship in the design is easy access from the storage area to both food production and receiving. The number of trips that will be made to the production area from the storage area will far exceed the number made from the receiving dock. It is therefore important to be sure that the staff in food production areas have short distances to travel to refrigerated storage and canned-goods storage spaces. It is often possible to locate a walk-in refrigerator in the immediate vicinity of the cold-food preparation department, so that few steps are necessary to procure salad materials and other frequently used perishable items.

Type of Food Operation	Dry Storage Square Feet (Square Meters)
Fast food	50–125 (4.65–11.63)
Small restaurant	100–150 (9.30–3.95)
Medium restaurant or small institution	200–300 (18.60–27.90)
Large restaurant or medium institution	400–1,000 (37.20–93.00)
Large institution with simple menu	1,000–2,500 (93.00–232.50)
Large hotel, restaurant, or institution with complex menu, catering facilities, snack bars	3,000+ (279.00+)

Figure 4-4. Dry storage space requirements.

Amount of Space Needed and Special Design Features

DRY STORAGE

Calculating a standard amount of dry storage space is difficult because of the many variables that affect the need. The method that is often used is to consider the many variables that cause fluctuations in the quantity of food to be stored and simply make an educated guess. It is usually better to estimate space needs on the basis of the industry's experience with different types of facilities. Figure 4-4 provides guidelines for determining dry storage needs (assuming that deliveries are made twice per week and that cleaning supplies and paper are stored separately).

PAPER AND CLEANING SUPPLIES STORAGE

The storage of paper supplies can be a major space problem for food operations that use a large quantity of disposable cups, plates, napkins, and plastic ware. No standard space requirement is possible because the extent of the use of disposables and the frequency of delivery are different for each food operation. Paper supply companies tend to give significant price breaks for larger orders of paper goods, and the food operator is therefore forced to accept large quantities in order to purchase economically.

Cleaning supplies must be stored separately from food supplies to prevent contamination and accidental mixing of cleaning products with foods. A separate storeroom for cleaning supplies should be large enough to handle 55-gallon drums, cases of dish machine detergent, and other cleaning items. A space 6 to 10 feet (1.8 to 3.0 meters) wide and 10 to 15 feet (3.0 to 4.6 meters) deep will handle the storage needs of most small and medium-sized operations. Figure 4-5 provides a guide for estimating the storage space required by cleaning supplies.

Type of Food Operation	Storage Area Square Feet (Square Meters)
Fast food	60–100 (5.58–9.3)
Small restaurant	75–120 (6.98–11.16)
Medium restaurant or small institution	120–175 (11.16–16.28)
Large restaurant or medium institution	175–250 (16.28–23.25)
Large institution with simple menu	250–300 (23.25–27.90)
Large hotel, restaurant, or institution with complex menu, catering facilities, snack bars	300+ (27.90+)

Figure 4-5. Space required for paper and cleaning supplies storage.

REFRIGERATED AND
FROZEN STORAGE

Space needed for bulk storage of frozen and refrigerated foods should be determined at this stage.

A bulk freezer should be selected based on the menu and frequency of delivery. For instance, if the menu contains a large number of items prepared from frozen food products, the need for freezer space will obviously increase. A fast-food restaurant or college cafeteria will usually use a significant amount of frozen french fries, and the college may also use large quantities of frozen vegetables. A seafood restaurant may use large quantities of frozen fish, french fries, and onion rings, but perhaps no frozen vegetables at all. A hotel or large catering operation may use smaller quantities but might stock a wide variety of frozen foods.

Frozen foods are usually shipped in rectangular cartons that are easily stacked, and the height of the freezer is therefore an important part of the calculation. The size of a freezer should be determined based on cubic feet of space needed. The following is an example of freezer size calculations based on the following assumptions:

❑ The facility is a small restaurant with delivery of frozen foods once per week.

❑ Frozen hamburgers, french fries, and onion rings are a significant part of the volume of the business.

❑ The menu contains five or six additional items that are purchased frozen.

❑ Ice cream, in six flavors, is a popular dessert.

Walk-in refrigerated storage space is very expensive because of the amount of building space that walk-ins occupy, and because of the high cost of the equipment. A careful calculation of the amount of space needed is therefore strongly recommended.

Assuming a standard-sized walk-in (7 feet 4 inches/2.2 meters high) is used, it can be filled only to a height of 6 feet (1.8 meters). In fact, less than 50 percent of the space in the walk-in is usable, as shown in Figure 4-7.

Food Item	Pack	Volume Cubic Feet (Cubic Meters)	Quantity	Total Volume Cubic Feet (Cubic Meters)
French fries	case	1.8 (.050)	25	45.0 (1.260)
Hamburgers	case	1.2 (.033)	30	36.0 (1.008)
Onion rings	case	2.0 (.056)	20	40.0 (1.120)
Vegetables	case	1.5 (.042)	15	22.5 (0.630)
Hot dogs	package	.2 (.006)	35	7.0 (0.196)
Roast beef	12 to 15 lbs.	1.0 (.028)	30	30.0 (0.840)
Ice cream	3 gal.	1.5 (.042)	45	67.5 (1.890)
Miscellaneous	case	1.0 (.028)	35	35.0 (0.980)

Figure 4-6. Calculating volume required for refrigerated and frozen storage.

Therefore, the total number of cubic feet (meters) of storage per linear foot (meter) of walk-in freezer is:

6 feet (height) × 2-foot shelves × 2 (one on each side)
= 24 cubic feet per linear foot

1.8 meters (height) × .6 meter shelves × 2 (one on each side)
= 2.16 cubic meters per linear meter

To determine the necessary length, divide the total cubic feet needed by 24. In the example shown, the length of the walk-in would be:

283 cubic feet ÷ 24 = 11.79 linear feet

8 cubic meters ÷ 2.16 = 3.7 meters

The walk-in should be 12 feet (3.7 meters) long by 9 feet (2.75 meters) wide in this example. The 9-foot (2.75 meter) width provides space on both sides for shelving and an aisle space of 3½ to 4 feet (1.0 to 1.2 meters).

The size of a walk-in refrigerator is determined in a similar manner but is more difficult to calculate because the products stored are not in rectangular boxes. Milk, produce, fresh meats, foods that have been prepared, and other miscellaneous items that need to be stored under refrigeration are difficult to measure in cubic footage (meters).

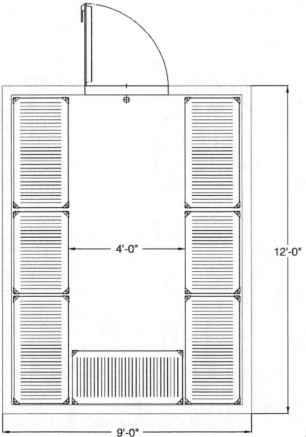

Figure 4-7. Walk-in freezer size determined by volume calculations.

Type of Food Operation	Walk-ins	Square Feet (Square Meters)
Fast food	1	90–120 (8.4–11.2)
Small restaurant	1	120–150 (11.2–14.0)
Medium restaurant or small institution	2	180–240 (16.7–22.3)
Large restaurant or medium institution	3	240–400 (22.3–37.2)
Large institution with simple menu	3	400–600 (37.2–55.8)
Large hotel, restaurant, or institution with complex menu, catering facilities, snack bars	4	600–900 (55.8–83.7)

Figure 4-8. Walk-in refrigerator requirements.

Small fast-food operations or restaurants with very limited menus may need only one walk-in refrigerator. Medium-sized operations may wish to separate meat, produce, and dairy products. Large hotels, restaurants, or institutions may need three or four large walk-in refrigerators, located in different sections of the kitchen. The chart in Figure 4-8 may be used as a general guide for determining the amount of space needed for walk-in coolers.

UTENSIL AND CLEANING EQUIPMENT STORAGE

Food facilities that do not include a storage space for infrequently used utensils, backup supplies of utensils such as knives and serving spoons, and cleaning equipment such as buffing machines and steam cleaners often are plagued with a considerable amount of clutter in the work areas. For instance, a restaurant that occasionally serves buffets for private parties may want to keep chafing dishes, punch bowls, and serving platters in a utensil storage room.

The amount of space needed is so variable that a standard cannot be easily established. For the small or medium-sized foodservice facility, a closet with built-in shelving that can be easily secured provides a sufficient amount of space. Country clubs that hold private functions, buffets, and receptions and need to store substantial quantities of Christmas decorations and other special-events materials may require an extremely large storeroom with movable metal shelving. For the large food facility, the separation of cleaning equipment storage from utensil storage is recommended for reasons of security.

OFFICE

General Description of the Space

Offices are needed for the manager, assistant managers, chef or food production manager, and clerical staff. The justification for these spaces is to provide a private environment for talking with employees, vendors, and other businesspeople and to be sure that the management staff has a reasonably quiet place to work.

The offices of the general manager and catering manager should be accessible to the public without the necessity of having customers walk through the kitchen. Office space for managers and assistant managers who have infrequent contact with the public outside the dining room should be located in a highly visible and easily accessible part of the food facility. Small foodservice operations often have the office located near the receiving area so that the movement of employees and of food in and out of storage areas and the building can be observed. Office space for receiving clerks, storeroom supervisors, and service supervisors should obviously be located in their respective work areas. Often these office areas are simple enclosures or spaces set aside without doors or four walls.

Relationship to Other Areas

Small office areas usually range from 60 to 80 square feet (5.6 to 7.4 square meters) and can be increased from this size as space and funds permit. Combination offices in which the clerical staff are adjacent to a manager's office and separated by a partition require additional space to accommodate door swings and extra office equipment such as computers, copy machines, and word processors.

Amount of Space Needed

The number of office spaces that may be needed for supervisory and management personnel will depend on the complexity of the organization. For instance, in a fairly complex operation, office space may be needed for:

❑ Accounting and payroll personnel
❑ Catering manager
❑ Sales manager
❑ Executive chef
❑ Production manager
❑ Dietitian
❑ Assistant manager
❑ Purchasing manager
❑ Receiving supervisor
❑ Maître d'hôtel

Carpeted floors, light-colored walls with chair rails, and acoustical ceilings with fluorescent lighting are desirable surfaces in an office. The location of telephone and electrical outlets on all four walls will permit maximum flexibility as personnel and space needs change. Management and supervisory personnel often prefer an office with many windows for purposes of supervisory control. Clerical employees, on the other hand, often dislike windows that create distractions from their work or that do not provide a sufficient amount of privacy.

Special Design Features

PREPARATION AREAS

In a well-designed kitchen, the food preparation area is divided into four general areas. Although in a small kitchen these areas are often combined, recognition of each of the areas is an important part of the design. The four working areas of a kitchen are:

General Description of the Space

❏ Pre-preparation
❏ Hot-food preparation
❏ Cold-food preparation
❏ Final preparation

PRE-PREPARATION   The pre-preparation area of the kitchen is where foods are processed, mixed, combined, held, cleaned, or otherwise worked with before the meal period begins. Chopping celery, mixing meatloaf, simmering broth, peeling potatoes, and making salad dressing are all pre-preparation activities. Sinks, large work surfaces, and all of the other equipment necessary to accomplish food pre-preparation tasks are a part of this area of the kitchen.

The pre-preparation area usually includes all of the equipment needed to process foods before the meal begins. Typical equipment located in the pre-preparation area includes:

❏ Worktables with sinks
❏ Racks for storage of pots and pans
❏ Utensil storage (drawers, hanging racks)
❏ Choppers, vertical cutter-mixers, and food processors
❏ Mixers
❏ Ovens
❏ Steam-jacketed kettles
❏ Tilting braising pans

The amount of equipment in this area, and especially the amount of worktable surface needed, will be determined by the amount of hand preparation that is dictated by the menu and by the volume of food being processed. The layout and dimensions of a pre-preparation area for a small restaurant are illustrated in Figure 4-9. Note in the figure that the total space for pre-preparation is 13 feet by 17 feet 6 inches (4.0 by 5.3 meters), or 227.5 square feet (21.2 square meters). The addition of an aisle on two sides of this would increase the amount of space needed by approximately 90 square feet (8.4 square meters), to a total of 317.5 square feet (rounded to 320), or 29.6 square meters (rounded to 30 square meters).

HOT-FOOD PREPARATION   The range section of a kitchen is usually considered the hot-food preparation area. Since this is where heat is applied to the food product, the space must be extremely resistant to soiling from grease and able to withstand high heat. Also necessary are elaborate (and expensive) ventilation systems above the cooking surfaces. The area must be designed to meet the demands of the menu, and equipment should be selected accordingly. The most frequent design error in the kitchen is to select generic equipment that is manufactured to cook all foods under all circumstances rather than pieces best suited to preparing the foods served in the particular facility.

COLD-FOOD PREPARATION   In small and medium-sized kitchens this area is where salads are assembled, desserts are dished up, and appetizers are made ready for service. For a large restaurant or hotel, a separate garde-manger department may be required for the preparation of cold appetizers, entrees, and beautifully

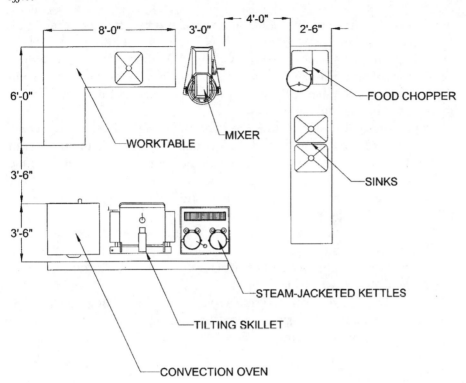

Figure 4-9. Preparation area for a small restaurant.

decorated items for buffets. Typically most of the pre-preparation and final preparation for cold foods will occur in the same general area. Worktables and refrigerated storage should be accessible to all food preparation personnel located in this area. A pickup station designed as part of cold-food preparation allows the servers easy access. In European kitchens, the traditional layout included a cold-food kitchen as a separate area.

FINAL PREPARATION

The final preparation area is the space in which foods are prepared very close to and during the meal period. It is important in the design to define this space carefully and to be sure that all equipment located within it has to do with final preparation. Foods usually cooked in this area include steak, seafood, french fries, fried eggs, toast, hamburgers, frozen vegetables, and other similar items that can be prepared quickly and will deteriorate rapidly if cooked ahead of time. In a successful restaurant the final food preparation area is the most carefully attended and supervised part of the entire kitchen. Foods prepared in this area can be held only a very short period of time before being presented to the guest. Successful fast-food chains have designed elaborate means to be sure that foods are not held more than five to six minutes in the final preparation area before being served. The final preparation area typically includes a range, grills, fryers, steamers, and broilers. Obviously, some small amount of pre-preparation also occurs in this area, but in an efficient operation it is kept to a minimum.

Relationship to Other Areas

The flow of people and materials from storage to pre-preparation to final preparation can best be illustrated by a simple diagram (Figure 4-10). Although this diagram seems very simplistic, the concept that it illustrates is

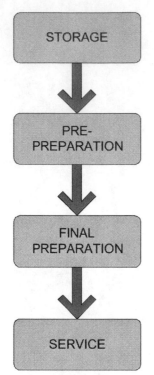

Figure 4-10. The relationships among storage, pre-preparation, final preparation, and service.

extremely important if good kitchen design is to be achieved. Frequently kitchens are laid out with steam-jacketed kettles (used in pre-preparation) in the final preparation area or fryers (used in final preparation) located in the pre-preparation area. Although these arrangements may save some duplication in equipment, they tend to cause congestion in the flow of materials and personnel.

Figure 4-10 also shows how preparation spaces relate to the service components of a food facility. The reader should also bear in mind the comprehensive picture of a facility, with the kitchen at the center of all the functional spaces. The design should always reflect these relationships and facilitate the movement of employees and food between functionally related areas. For instance, the distance between the final preparation area and the customer should be short because the time that it takes to move the food is critical. On the other hand, the relationship of the preparation area to the employee locker room is not critical, and these spaces could be a considerable distance away from each other.

Vertical as well as horizontal space relationships must be considered. As a general guideline, when spaces must be located on different floors, the following functional areas may be at a different level from the kitchen:

❏ Bulk dry storage
❏ Bulk frozen storage
❏ Paper and utensil storage
❏ Employee locker rooms
❏ Receiving

Warewashing, service areas, and dining areas should never be located on a different level from the kitchen. This guideline is often violated in large hotels and institutional kitchens, where it is quite common to see dishwashing located on a different level from the dining room. Architectural limitations at times make it necessary to violate this rule, but there is always a cost in labor, efficiency, and effectiveness of supervision.

Amount of Space Needed

A question frequently asked by the owner or architect at the beginning of a project is: What is the ratio of kitchen space to dining room space? The food facilities design consultant will usually answer that it depends. First of all, no clear standards exist for a ratio between dining room and kitchen space, and second, different types of operations have different requirements. Space needs depend on:

❏ The number of items on the menu
❏ The number of different forms of final preparation required by the menu items (e.g., fry, sauté, steam)
❏ The use of convenience foods versus scratch cookery
❏ The complexity of the preparation required (e.g., fast food versus the cuisine found in expensive table service restaurants)
❏ The number of foodservice functions supported by a single kitchen, which may include banquet service, coffee shop service, and main dining room foodservice

Type of Food Operation	Meals per Day	Dining Room Size Square Feet (Square Meters)	Kitchen Size Square Feet (Square Meters)
Restaurant, table service, 100 seats	1,000	1,400 (130.20)	1,300 (120.90)
Restaurant, table service, 175 seats	1,800	2,625 (244.13)	2,000 (186.00)
Country club, 200 seats	600	3,400 (316.20)	1,288 (119.78)
Hospital, cafeteria, and 200-bed tray service	1,400	2,250 (209.25)	2,300 (213.90)
College cafeteria, 350 seats	2,400	4,200 (390.60)	1,500 (139.50)
University cafeteria and catering department	4,000	5,625 (523.13)	2,530 (235.29)
Coffee shop, 100 seats	800	1,225 (113.96)	850 (79.05)

Figure 4-11. Kitchen size in relation to dining room size.

Although there are "rules of thumb" regarding the size of the preparation areas relative to the size of the dining areas—such as 60 percent dining and 40 percent kitchen—such recommendations fail to take into account many important factors. On one hand, where the menu is simple, the kitchen might be only 25 or 30 percent of the size of the dining area. On the other hand, a restaurant with a complex menu and significant take-out business might need a kitchen as large as or larger than the dining area.

A comparison of kitchen sizes and dining room capacity can be made from Figure 4-11, which indicates the range of space requirements in different types of food facilities.

Because of the extreme variability in space needs, the owner or manager should look to the design consultant for professional advice before deciding on the amount of space to allot to the food production area.

The equipment in the final preparation areas of the kitchen is determined by the production requirements of the various menu items. Final preparation equipment often includes many of the following items (see Chapters 6 and 7 for information on equipment):

- ❏ Convection, deck, and conveyor ovens
- ❏ Fryers
- ❏ Grills
- ❏ Tabletop steam-jacketed kettles
- ❏ Steamers
- ❏ Charbroilers
- ❏ Ranges with open burners or hot tops
- ❏ Reach-in refrigerators and freezers
- ❏ Worktables and "chef's tables"

Special Design Features

Since food production areas are continually subjected to heat as well as soiling from grease and spilled foods, damage-resistant, easy-to-clean surfaces are essential. Equipment surfaces of stainless steel are the most practical. Floors of quarry tile with Carborundum chips provide a slip-resistant, easy-to-clean surface. When made of ceramic tile or structural glazed tile, walls behind the equipment will withstand the combination of heat and grease. Ordinary epoxy paint on cement block is not recommended because the high heat will discolor the painted surface. To avoid sanitation problems, careful attention should be given to eliminating cracks and spaces around equipment.

Ventilation over final preparation equipment is a key consideration in the design of this area. The increased use in recent years of compensating hoods that bring a large percentage of makeup air (air that replaces exhausted air) into the hood itself does not eliminate the need for independent ventilation in the kitchen area. The kitchen must be well ventilated without complete dependence on the hood system to exhaust the air.

BAKERY

General Description of the Space

The bakery remains a popular production area in the foodservice facility in spite of the availability of a wide variety of fresh and frozen bakery products. The foodservice manager or owner must give the food facilities design consultant complete details concerning the volume of baking that is to be done on the premises.

A small or medium-sized restaurant (under 150 seats) that plans to make only rolls, cobblers, sheet cakes from a mix, and a few specialty desserts may require only a small worktable, ingredient bins, a mixer, and access to an oven. On the other hand, a large institution planning to bake pies, cakes, rolls, loaf breads, Danish pastries, doughnuts, and extensive specialty products may require a very large bakery space and a sizable equipment budget. The long-range plans for the food facility need to be carefully considered. If the owner plans to have a bakery, the following questions need to be addressed during the planning process:

❑ What products will be baked on the premises (versus bought from vendors)?

❑ Will the bakery products be made from scratch or from mixes?

❑ Will the products be delivered fresh from the bake shop to the service area, or will they be frozen and stored until needed?

❑ Will the bakery make products to be sold on a retail basis in addition to supplying all bakery products to the foodservice area?

Relationship to Other Areas

The bakery is one food production area that can be separate from the main activity of the foodservice facility. If sufficient space exists, however, the bakery should be near the main food production areas so that supervision is easier, equipment can be shared occasionally, and common storage spaces can be used. If the bakery is located at a remote point in the food facility, it should have easy access to receiving, and depending on size, it may need its own separate dry storage and walk-in refrigerator/freezer.

The movement of finished bakery products to the kitchen or service area should be accomplished in rolling closed cabinets. Ramping or the use

Number of Seats in the Facility	Limited Baking Square Feet (Square Meters)	Extensive Baking Square Feet (Square Meters)
Under 50	40 (3.72)	80 (7.44)
50–100	100 (9.30)	150 (13.95)
100–175	250 (23.25)	400 (37.20)
175–250	300 (27.90)	600 (55.80)
250–500	400 (37.20)	800 (74.40)
More than 500	600 (55.80)	1,400 (130.20)

Note: Storage not included.

Figure 4-12. Bakery size guidelines.

of elevators should be planned if the bakery is not on the same level as the area where the product will be served or sold. The planning of central bakeries serving multiple dining facilities must include well-thought-out food transportation systems to ensure that the product is not damaged in transit and that the proper temperature (hot, cold, or room temperature) is maintained.

Amount of Space Needed

The information found in Figure 4-12 can be used to make a rough estimate of the amount of space needed in a bakery, keeping in mind the many variables that can affect this determination.

Special Design Features

The floors of most bakeries quickly become covered with flour and other dry ingredients that are used in large quantities in the baking process. The flour sticks to the floor of the work area, especially when the area becomes damp, and is difficult to remove at the end of the work day. The floor should be constructed of quarry tile or other smooth masonry material (marble, tile, or terrazzo) that will not be damaged by frequent scrubbing and occasional scraping.

The mechanical engineers will need to provide an air supply and exhaust for the bakery, usually in the form of simple oven vents. From thirty to forty-five air changes per hour should be sufficient for this space, exclusive of the air ventilated by the oven exhaust.

EMPLOYEE LOCKER ROOM AND TOILET

General Description of the Space

The employee locker room and rest rooms are too often given minimal consideration by those who are involved in the total design of a food facility. These facilities deserve careful attention because they affect sanitation, security, and employee attitude. The space, if properly planned, can be clean, orderly, and have a bright appearance that sets the tone for management's expectations of cleanliness and orderliness in other areas of the building.

Number of Employees	Space Required Square Feet (Square Meters)
5 or under	60 (5.58)
5–10	100 (9.30)
10–20	150 (13.95)
20–40	225 (20.93)
40–75	250 (23.25)
75–100	350 (32.55)

Note: Number of employees refers to the peak number on duty at one time, not the total number of employees on the payroll.

Figure 4-13. Space required for employee locker room and toilet

Relationship to Other Areas

The locker rooms and rest rooms can be designed together so that space is efficiently used and control over uniforms is maintained. The area can be remote from the main food production areas, but the entrance and exit to the space should be arranged so that employees can be observed as they move from the work area to the locker room. Locker rooms can create food and utensil control problems if they are located near exits or are in remote locations that are difficult to supervise.

Amount of Space Needed

The space needed for a combined locker room and rest room area is estimated in Figure 4-13.

Space requirements for rest room facilities should be checked with local codes to be sure that they comply with requirements for the handicapped and for the minimum number of employee toilet facilities.

Special Design Features

An employee locker room and rest room area can easily be made too large, which encourages loitering. The purpose of the space is to provide a place for changing clothes, using the toilet, and washing the hands before reporting for work. It should not be used for coffee breaks, card games, eating, and so on. The design should include locker room benches, double stacked lockers to save space, and, for the larger food facility, a linen control system for exchanging soiled uniforms for clean uniforms.

Foodservice managers often disagree whether an employee dining room or coffee area is necessary. Some managers feel that these employee rooms encourage long breaks and that employees should eat in the main dining room before the meal period for customers. Large hotels and food operations, on the other hand, usually provide an employee lounge.

SERVICE AREAS

There are almost as many different types of service areas as there are types of foodservice establishments. Each of the following types of food operations has a different kind of service area, and the list is certainly not complete: fine-dining restaurant, snack bar, lunch counter, fast-food restaurant, diner, cafeteria, and delicatessen.

The service area and the type of service planned for a food facility will be among the first decisions made during the concept development phase of the design process. For a small table service restaurant, the service area might be very limited because only a pickup station at the hot- and cold-food areas in the kitchen and a server station in the dining room are needed. A large institutional food facility using the scramble form of cafeteria service may need extremely large service areas in the range of 2,000 to 3,000 square feet (186 to 279 square meters). The service area in a table service restaurant provides an efficient means for the food production staff to get the food to the service staff, while the service area in self-service food operations offers a means for the food production staff to get the food to the customer. In both of these circumstances the time that it takes for the food to be delivered to the customer is critical and obviously should be as short as possible. The method for accomplishing this task is often referred to as a food delivery system.

The simplest food delivery system may involve holding a short-order meal for a few moments under a quartz heater at the server pickup station. A complex food delivery system in a large hospital might involve numerous employees and hundreds of thousands of dollars' worth of equipment. Regardless of the size of the food operation or its method of service, the importance of planning an efficient food delivery system cannot be overemphasized. As an illustration of the typical delivery systems used in foodservices facilities, the following chart is a partial list of several types of service areas.

Type of Operation	Type of Delivery System
Table service restaurant	Kitchen pickup station
Snack bar	Service counter direct to customer
Fast food	Service counter direct to customer
Cafeteria	Straight-line cafeteria
Delicatessen	Deli counter
Buffet	Buffet line
Scramble	Separate food stations
Food court	Separate food locations around a common dining area
Tray service (health care)	Cold and hot carts rolled to patient room or dining area

Figure 4-14. Type of foodservice operation and typical delivery system.

Relationship to Other Areas   The most important connection of the service area is to the hot- and cold-food production part of the foodservices. A small distance between these two functional areas will provide a reduced labor cost and a higher quality food product. Conversely, a long distance between these two areas will increase the cost of labor and equipment significantly and make it much more difficult to keep foods at the proper serving temperature. Service areas also have a primary relationship to the following spaces in the food facility:

❑ Warewashing

❑ Dining room

❑ Private dining rooms

❑ Customer entrances and exits

❑ Cashiers or other control systems

Other facilities that must be accessible to service areas are:

❑ Storerooms

❑ Refrigeration

❑ Bakery

❑ Office areas

❑ Cleaning supplies

Amount of Space Needed   Variations in the size and type of foodservice facilities make it extremely difficult to develop a standard space requirement. As a guideline to the foodservice planning team, several types of service areas and their space requirements are listed in Figures 4-15a through 4-15d.

The charts for service area space needed indicate that as the level of service changes from table service to self-service scramble or food court,* the amount of space needed increases dramatically. The scramble cafeteria or food court requires the greatest amount of space of any of the forms of service because of the need for good circulation within the space. It is assumed that the cost of constructing the service area will be more than offset by the potential volume of customers who can be served and by an increase in the speed of service. The scramble cafeteria or food court also allows a wide range of menu items to be merchandised to the customer.

Special Design Features   Figures 4-16 through 4-19 show typical service area design features of several common types of foodservice facilities: a table service restaurant with bar, a fast-food counter, a scramble/food court cafeteria, and a health care tray-makeup system.

---

* The terms "scramble" and "food court" are often used interchangeably to refer to a large area in which customers freely circulate from one point of service to another. There is, however, a slight difference. Commercial "food courts" typically have a cash register at each point of service, whereas "scramble cafeterias" typically have central cashier stations where customers pay for everything on their trays.

Number of Seats	Meals per Day*	Service Area† Square Feet (Square Meters)
Under 50	300	75 (6.9)
50–100	500	100 (9.2)
100–175	750	140 (12.9)
175–250	1,000	160 (14.7)
250–500	1,600	175 (16.1)
More than 500	2,400	200 (18.4)

* Breakfast not included.

† Includes chef's pickup station (excluding range and aisle spaces) and a server station.

Figure 4-15a. Service area space requirements for table service restaurants—limited menu.

Number of Seats	Meals per Day*	Service Area† Square Feet (Square Meters)
Under 50	200	100 (9.2)
50–100	300	120 (11.0)
100–175	600	160 (14.7)
175–250	700	200 (18.4)
250–500	1,000	250 (23.0)
More than 500	1,500	300 (27.6)

* Breakfast not included.

† Includes server stations, pickup stations for hot and cold food, and separate beverage stations.

Figure 4-15b. Service area space requirements for luxury table service restaurants—extensive menu.

Number of Seats	Meals per Day*	Service Area† Square Feet (Square Meters)
100–175	800	350 (32.2)
175–250		
One Line	1,250	475 (43.7)
Two Lines	1,500	900 (82.8)
250–500	2,000	1,600 (147.2)
More than 500	5,000	2,000 (184.0)

* Breakfast not included.

† Size of the cafeteria line and aisle space in front of and behind the line.

Figure 4-15c. Service area space requirements for straight-line cafeterias.

Number of Seats	Meals per Day*	Service Area† Square Feet (Square Meters)
175–250	1,500	1,800 (165.6)
250–350	1,800	2,000 (184.0)
350–500	2,250	2,400 (220.8)
More than 500	5,000	3,000 (276.0)

* Breakfast not included.

† The service area of the scramble, including interior circulation space. Condiment and beverage stations located outside of the service area are not included.

Figure 4-15d. Service area space requirements for scramble or food court cafeterias.

DINING ROOMS

The architect and interior designer typically give the appearance of the dining space the highest priority.

General Description of the Space

Obviously, an environment that is pleasant for the guests and that lends itself to an enjoyable dining experience should be a goal in designing the facility. The ease of cleaning floors, walls, and furnishings as well as the potential for food spillage must also be considered. Coverings such as carpeting, for example, are popular in table service restaurants but are

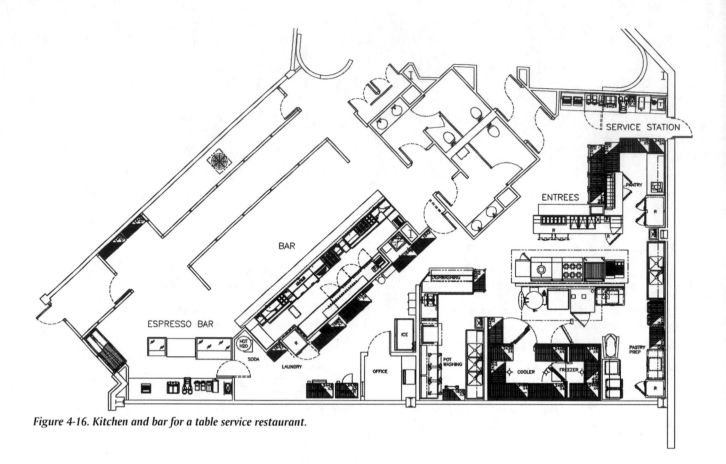

Figure 4-16. Kitchen and bar for a table service restaurant.

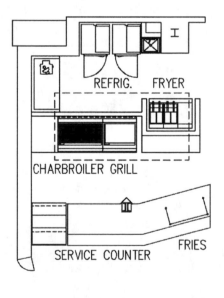

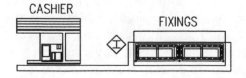

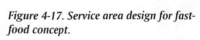

Figure 4-17. Service area design for fast-food concept.

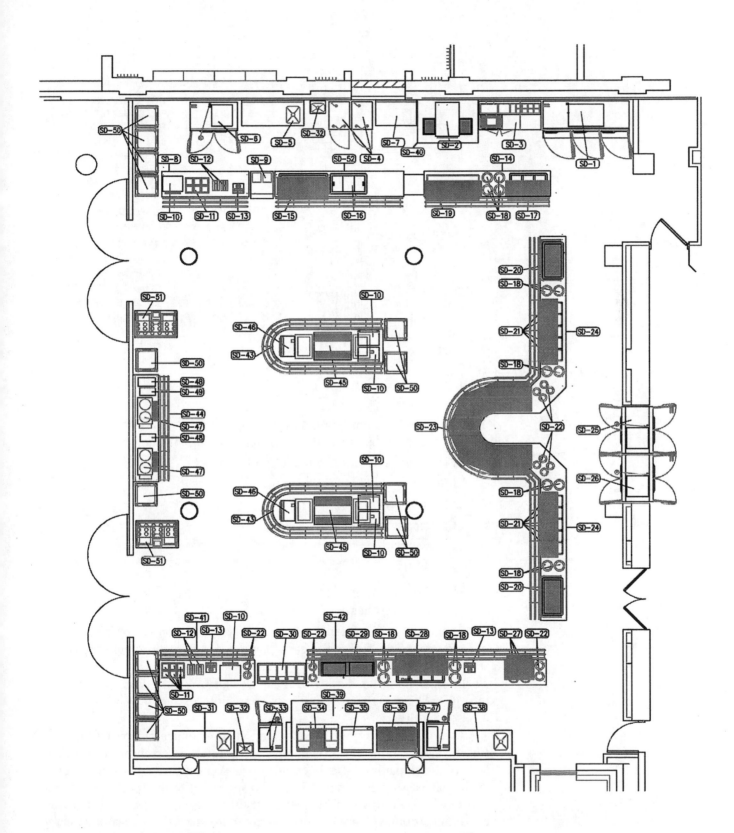

Figure 4-18. Scramble cafeteria.

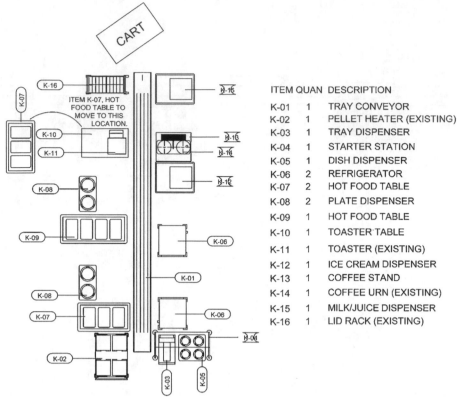

ITEM	QUAN	DESCRIPTION
K-01	1	TRAY CONVEYOR
K-02	1	PELLET HEATER (EXISTING)
K-03	1	TRAY DISPENSER
K-04	1	STARTER STATION
K-05	1	DISH DISPENSER
K-06	2	REFRIGERATOR
K-07	2	HOT FOOD TABLE
K-08	2	PLATE DISPENSER
K-09	1	HOT FOOD TABLE
K-10	1	TOASTER TABLE
K-11	1	TOASTER (EXISTING)
K-12	1	ICE CREAM DISPENSER
K-13	1	COFFEE STAND
K-14	1	COFFEE URN (EXISTING)
K-15	1	MILK/JUICE DISPENSER
K-16	1	LID RACK (EXISTING)

Figure 4-19. Health care tray makeup design.

inappropriate for dining rooms with a higher risk of soil from spilled foods and debris. Other factors in dining room planning include:

- ❏ Heating, ventilation, and air-conditioning
- ❏ View
- ❏ Sound control
- ❏ Seating arrangement
- ❏ Server stations
- ❏ Sanitation
- ❏ Lighting
- ❏ Cashier or other control systems

The owner or manager of a food facility is encouraged to visit a variety of food operations during the early planning stage of a project and to consult some of the illustrated trade journals and reference volumes that are available. Gaining familiarity with the design of a variety of dining room interiors will aid in the selection of mood, color, texture, lighting, and other interior features.

As the number of meals consumed at foodservice chain facilities and franchise operations has grown, hotel corporations, restaurant chains, and fast-food companies have become more sophisticated in their interior design plans. The restaurant owner who succumbs to the temptation of do-it-yourself decorating or who spends insufficient funds to create an attractive dining room will lose business to the more attractive and sophisticated chain operations. Similarly, the institutional cafeteria owner or manager who installs vinyl tile floors and "institutional-looking" chairs and tables will experience a loss of customers to dining facilities that offer a more pleasant setting.

The dining room must be directly connected to service areas and to the kitchen. Remote dining rooms, such as hotel banqueting rooms or private meeting rooms that are located away from the kitchen, may require special equipment for food delivery. One solution for the remote banquet dining room is the use of specially designed service kitchens.

Relationship to Other Areas

Vertical space relationships can be solved in part by the use of elevators or dumbwaiters. In one London eating establishment, an entire building of banquet rooms is serviced by a bank of dumbwaiters from a central kitchen on the first floor. The building is seven stories high and the communication system is controlled by a series of hollow pipes that permit the staff to shout their needs back and forth through the pipes. The system is over a hundred years old and continues to operate smoothly without the need for an electronic speaker. In spite of the success of this English banqueting hall, dumbwaiters are usually not a good solution for the vertical movement of food. Dumbwaiters do not transport people, and they must be attended by two persons. They are also difficult to clean, can cause excessive breakage of dishes, and create communication problems. Budget and space considerations permitting, service elevators are much preferred to dumbwaiters.

The proper size of the dining room can be calculated once it is decided how many customers the food facility will seat. Determining the proper number of seats is easy in an institutional foodservice operation if the number of persons to be fed is known. For a restaurant or commercial cafeteria project, however, where the number of customers is uncertain, determining the number of seats needed can be quite difficult. Forecasting the volume of business that might be anticipated for a commercial restaurant is often no more than an educated guess. In other instances, the number of seats planned into a restaurant is decided based on the available space or funds. The number of seats to be included in the design is a basic investment question and should be given careful consideration. Dining room size, kitchen size, rest room capacities, parking lot size, and many other features of the building are affected by seating capacity.

Amount of Space Needed

The number of persons who can be accommodated during a meal period is determined by the space occupied by the chairs and tables and by the seat turnover rate. Each type of service requires a different amount of space for tables and chairs. For instance, a snack bar that uses disposable ware can be designed with very small tables and utilitarian chairs without arms. On the other hand, a luxury table service restaurant would require a large dining room table with sufficient space for flowers, condiments, a variety of crystal glasses, and side dishes to accompany the main course. Chairs in luxury restaurants are often large because they are padded and have arms. Space in the aisles of such a restaurant needs to be sufficient to accommodate ice buckets for wine and the waiter's tray stand. The space requirements listed in Figure 4-20 are generally accepted industry standards for the various forms of service in the industry.

Form of Service	Service Area per 100 Seats	Square Feet (Square Meters) per Chair
Table service, moderate price	100 sq. ft. (9.3 sq. m.) of server station	12–14 (1.1–1.3 sq. m.)
Table service, high price	150 sq. ft. (13.9 sq. m.) of server station	13–16 (1.2–1.5 sq. m.)
Table service, luxury	200 sq. ft (18.6 sq. m.) of server station	16–20 (1.5–1.9 sq. m.)
Cafeteria service	500 sq. ft. (46.5 sq. m.) of straight–line cafeteria	12–14 (1.1–1.3 sq. m.)
Scramble cafeteria	600 sq. ft. (55.7 sq. m.) of servery	12–14 (1.1–1.3 sq. m.)
Booth service	100 sq. ft. (9.3 sq. m.) of server station	12–14 (1.1–1.3 sq. m.)
Banquet (private dining)	25 sq. ft. (2.3 sq. m.) of storage and service area	10–12 (.93–1.1 sq. m.)
Fast food	50 sq. ft. (4.7 sq. m.) of counter area	9–11 (.84–1.0 sq. m.)

Notes: Service area is separate, not a part of the dining room. Square feet per chair includes space for aisles and general circulation.

Figure 4-20. Dining area space requirements.

The amount of space needed in a dining area is also influenced by the number of seats turned over per hour. For example, in a luxurious restaurant, the seats may turn over once every two hours, whereas a snack bar or fast-food restaurant may turn over seats three times per hour. The estimates of seat turnover for different segments of the foodservice industry in Figure 4-21 should be used as a guide.

The following is a typical calculation to determine the size of a dining area and support service area for a restaurant serving a moderately priced menu with 200 seats.

❑ Determine the size of the support area from the chart. A 200-seat restaurant would need 200 square feet (18.6 square meters) of server station space.

❑ Determine the size of the dining room. Multiply 200 seats by 13 square feet per chair, which equals 2,600 square feet (1.2 square meters per chair, equaling 240 square meters).

❑ Calculate the number of persons who could be served in one hour in this restaurant. Multiplying 200 seats by 1.5 turns equals 300 persons per hour.

Form of Service	Seat Turnover
Table service, moderate price	1.0–2.0
Table service, high price	0.75–1.0
Table service, luxury	0.5–0.75
Cafeteria service	2.2–3.0
Counter service	2.0–3.0
Booth service	2.0–3.0
Fast food	2.5–3.5

Figure 4-21. Table turnover rates for selected forms of service.

In this example the restaurant would make maximum use of the server station by keeping in the station as many of the accompaniments to the meal as possible. For instance, the station might contain:

- ❑ Silverware
- ❑ Linen (napkins)
- ❑ Condiments
- ❑ Coffee
- ❑ Soft drinks
- ❑ Ice
- ❑ Glasses
- ❑ Trash container
- ❑ Crackers
- ❑ Cups and saucers
- ❑ Bread
- ❑ Butter
- ❑ Cream
- ❑ Hot tea
- ❑ Cold tea
- ❑ Milk
- ❑ Point-of-sale terminal
- ❑ Soup

After determining the type of service, the amount of support space needed, and the seat turnover, the final consideration is the shape and size of the table. A dining room table in a fine restaurant might be shaped as shown in Figure 4-22a. This shape permits the service personnel to place side dishes, wineglasses, condiments, and other accompaniments to the meal on the table without crowding. This same shape for a cafeteria dining room would waste space and make it impossible for four people to place rectangular cafeteria trays on the table—note the black areas indicating where trays would overlap in Figure 4-22b. The wasted space in the example could be quite significant for a large cafeteria dining room. An estimate of

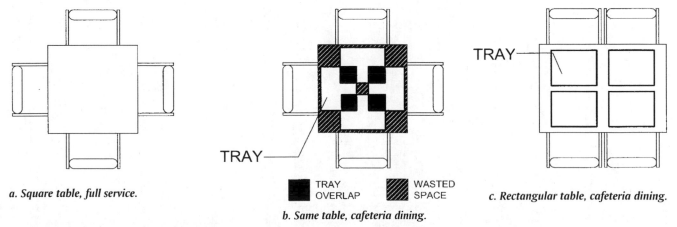

a. Square table, full service.

■ TRAY OVERLAP   ▨ WASTED SPACE

b. Same table, cafeteria dining.

TRAY

c. Rectangular table, cafeteria dining.

Figure 4-22. Saving space in a cafeteria or food court through properly designed dining tables.

the wasted space for a 400-seat cafeteria would be 4 square feet (.37 square meters) of wasted space per table times 100 tables, or 400 square feet (37 square meters). The extra amount spent in construction for this wasted space, if the cost was $200 a square foot ($2,153 a square meter), would come to $80,000. One solution to the problem is to choose a rectangular table on which four trays fit properly, arranged so that a natural aisle is created on the two short sides of the table, as shown in Figure 4-22c.

Special Design Features Two popular dining room styles that have been developed as alternatives to traditional table arrangements are fast-food or snack bar seating and booth seating.

Fast-food or snack bar seating. The special design features developed by the fast-food industry can be incorporated into any food operation in which space efficiency, ease of cleaning, and resistance to soiling is desirable. In these dining areas, table legs have been largely eliminated and seats are suspended from a table pedestal. The ease of sweeping and mopping the floors that this feature permits is important because of the large amount of food spillage and paper debris common in fast-food facilities. Another distinctive feature is the bevel or space that is often designed into the tabletop to encourage the sharing of the table with strangers. The division creates the impression of two tables when in fact there is only one.

Booth seating. The use of booths in foodservice establishments, which creates a visual break from traditional seating, is popular because of the sense of privacy that it provides. Early American and Victorian decor often featured booths with extremely high backs and side panels that almost completely enclosed the diners. Although booths are more expensive than traditional chairs and tables, they are extremely space-efficient; their higher cost is more than offset by a reduction in the size of the dining room. Space efficiency results from adjoining booths being placed back to back. Figure 4-23 illustrates a typical booth arrangement with standard dimensions.

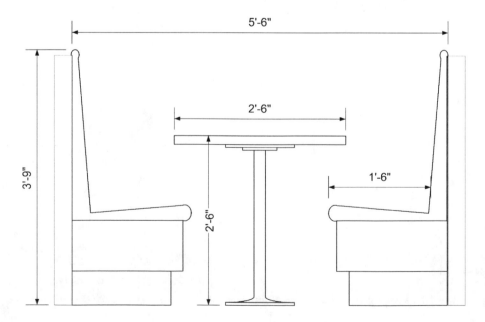

Figure 4-23. Booth seating.

BAR

The bar provides beverage service and bar and table seating for customers. Bars are of two basic types: customer bars and service bars. Customer bars provide beverage service to customers seated at the bar as well as to servers who take drinks to tables, whereas service bars are designed only for servers to pick up drinks. The major components of the bar space include the bar and bar equipment, the bar support area, and seating.

General Description of the Space

A bar consists of beverage service equipment that is enclosed in attractive finishes such as wood, brass, leather, decorative laminates, stone, and/or glass. The customer section of the bar provides high seating and a surface for beverage service. The employee's (bartender's) side of the bar provides the following:

THE BAR AND BAR EQUIPMENT

- ❏ Display and storage space for bottled spirits
- ❏ Refrigerated storage for bottled beers, wines, specialty soft drinks, and mixes
- ❏ Dispensers for tap beer and mixers
- ❏ Glass storage and glass washing
- ❏ Ice storage and dispensing
- ❏ Blenders for specialty drinks
- ❏ Coffee making and dispensing
- ❏ Sinks
- ❏ Cash registers/point of sale terminals

The back bar, or equipment behind the bartender, may also provide for some of the functions listed above. Bars traditionally are built in two separate steps by specialists. The bar equipment is first set in place. Then the bar is built around the equipment and finished by the bar builder or contractor to give it its distinctive features and appearance.

The bar support area provides storage for beverages. Spirits are stored in a locked storage room. Fine wines are stored horizontally in bins in a cool room (cellar); jug wines may be stored on storage shelves. Beer kegs and bottled or canned beers that need refrigeration may be stored in locked walk-in refrigerators. Beer taps (dispensers) may be mounted directly on a refrigerated unit in which the keg is placed once tapped. Or beer taps may be connected through a system of cooled tubes to a remote system located in the bar support area. Mix dispensers usually are supported by bag-in-a-box systems located in bar support areas. Carbon dioxide for mixes and soft drinks may be provided in interchangeable tanks or, in larger operations, by a single stationary tank that is filled directly from a supply truck. Ice makers also are located in the bar support area.

BAR SUPPORT AREA

Customer seating at the bar itself usually takes the form of stools or high chairs. Seating in the bar area also may be at tables where snacks or food can be served, or at small cocktail tables. Service bars, designed only for servers, do not have seating for customers.

SEATING

Relationship to Other Areas   When the bar is used as a waiting area for guests who will be dining, it should be located adjacent to the reception area. If the bar is a destination in itself, it should be located near the main entrance. If customers in the bar can order food, then the bar should be located adjacent to the final preparation area of the kitchen. The bar support area should be located adjacent to the bar, be easily secured, and be accessible from the receiving area.

Amount of Space Needed   The amount of space needed for the bar area is a combination of the space needed for the bar itself, the bar support area, and the seating areas to be located in the bar. A bar in a restaurant is often designed as a holding area so that diners have a place to sit while waiting for a table. Designing this holding area so that it can generate revenue (and profit) is highly desirable. Many restaurateurs and investors consider the combination of a cocktail lounge and restaurant to be the most profitable arrangement. In this combination, the emphasis is on the food as well as the marketing of before-dinner cocktails, wine with dinner, and after-dinner cordials.

THE BAR   The space required for the bar itself is determined by the number of customers who need to be accommodated by the bar. Each seat at the bar requires between 28 and 36 inches (711 and 914 millimeters) of linear distance, depending on the actual width of the seats. The depth of the bar is dictated by the seating space (24 to 30 inches/610 to 762 millimeters), the bar and underbar equipment (48 to 56 inches/1220 to 1422 millimeters), the aisle (42 to 54 inches/1067 to 1372 millimeters), and the back bar (30 to 36 inches/762 to 914 millimeters). Long bars often are configured in rectangular patterns to minimize the number of steps the bartender has to take.

BAR SUPPORT AREA   The space required by the bar support area is a function of the complexity of the beverage menu. Bars with a full complement of spirits, multiple beers on tap, and a collection of fine wines that need to be cellared require substantially more space than a bar that serves primarily beer and inexpensive wines.

SEATING   Additional seating (beyond that provided at the bar) will require between 10 square feet (.93 square meter) per person (at small cocktail tables) and 15 square feet (1.4 square meters) per person.

Figure 4-24 provides space estimates for several kinds of bars. These data are based on the assumption that the bar is an integral part of a restaurant operation. A bar in a cocktail lounge, brew pub, or other operation dedicated primarily to beverage service is likely to have a large bar. The data do not reflect an industry standard but do represent commonsense relationships.

Special Design Features   The visual characteristics of the bar are important in creating an atmosphere that supports the owner's concept for the facility. The guidelines suggested above for dining areas apply to bar seating as well.

From the functional perspective, the area behind the bar needs to be designed for ease of cleaning and sanitation, especially beneath equipment.

Restaurant Dining Room Size		Suggested Cocktail Lounge and Bar Size*			
				Bar Size†	
Seats	Square Feet (Square Meters)	Seats	Square Feet (Square Meters)	Length Feet (Meters)	Square Feet (Square Meters)
50	750 (69.7)	15	150 (13.9)	10 (3.0)	120 (11.1)
80	1,200 (111.5)	20	200 (18.6)	15 (4.6)	180 (16.7)
100	1,500 (139.4)	30	300 (27.9)	20 (6.1)	240 (22.3)
140	2,100 (195.0)	40	400 (37.2)	30 (9.1)	360 (33.4)
180	2,700 (250.8)	50	500 (46.5)	35 (10.7)	420 (39.0)
200	3,000 (278.7)	60	600 (55.7)	40 (12.2)	480 (44.6)

* A standard of 10 square feet (.93 sq. m) per seat (including bar stools) is used for this calculation.

† A bar with a 3' 6" (1.1 m) back bar, 4' 0" (1.2 m) aisle, and 4' 6" (1.4 m) front bar would have a total depth of 12' 0" (3.7 m). The length of the bar multiplied by 12' (3.7 m) thus determines the total square footage.

Figure 4-24. Space requirements for bars in restaurants.

Control of inventory and cash is an important issue with respect to bars. Secure storage of spirits, wines, and beer in the bar support area is crucial. The bar itself needs to be designed so that management can readily observe the activities of bartenders—particularly with respect to cash handling.

WAREWASHING

General Description of the Space

The one word that best describes the environment in the warewashing area is *wet*. With the exception of the hot-food preparation area, warewashing equipment and surrounding areas receive more wear and abuse than any other section of the food facility. Water on the floor, spilled food, steam and high humidity, and the striking of carts and utensils against the walls and equipment are often a common part of the warewashing environment. Food facilities designers, architects, and engineers should make every effort to eliminate the wet conditions while recognizing that the floor, walls, and ceiling must be constructed to withstand a large amount of moisture.

Health department standards for the equipment and interior of warewashing rooms have become increasingly stringent because of the potential for spreading food-borne diseases. In designing the warewashing area so that it is easy to sanitize and will withstand the wet conditions, the use of slip-resistant quarry tile floors, ceramic or structural glazed tile walls, and a moisture-resistant acoustic ceiling is recommended.

Relationship to Other Areas

The most important relationship of the warewashing space is to the dining room. The design should facilitate the movement of soiled dishes from the dining room to the warewashing area. In many institutions where self-busing of dishes is encouraged, the warewashing space must be located adjacent to the exit from the dining room. Without this convenient feature, customers are unlikely to cooperate in busing their own dishes. The primary problem with the close proximity of warewashing to the dining area is the noisiness of the former. Conveyor belts for soiled dishes, screening with masonry walls, or the use of double sets of doors to isolate the warewashing area are all common solutions to the noise problem.

Warewashing must also have a close working relationship with the main kitchen, especially if pots, pans, and utensils are cleaned in the warewashing area. The warewashing room may be designed with three-compartment pot sinks or potwashing machines, or it may be the practice of management to have most small and medium-sized utensils washed by the standard dish machine. If pots and utensils are to be washed in this area, the primary food production spaces and the warewashing unit should be reasonably close.

Amount of Space Needed

Warewashing machine ratings are usually based on the number of standard 20-by-20-inch racks or the number of dishes per hour that can be processed through the machine. Since neither the machine nor the machine operator can operate at 100 percent efficiency, an efficiency factor of 70 percent is normally used. Figure 4-25 provides a range of square footage requirements for several different styles of dishwashing systems. The data were determined under the assumption that a three-compartment pot sink with drain boards is included in the warewashing space.

Special Design Features

Nowhere in the design of a foodservice facility is an understanding of time and motion in the work environment more important than in warewashing. A dishwasher usually works in a restricted area with a minimum amount of walking. Good warewashing design must include a study of each move that the dishwasher makes so that the dishes can be handled in the most efficient way possible. The basic steps that are normally taken in washing dishes are:

❑ Separation of dishes from paper, trays, and so on
❑ Scraping (prerinsing may be done in combination with this step)
❑ Stacking or accumulating
❑ Racking
❑ Prerinsing (if not done earlier)

Type of Dish System	Dishes per Hour	Square Feet (Square Meters)
Single-tank dishwasher	1,500	250 (23.3)
Single-tank conveyor	4,000	400 (37.2)
Two-tank conveyor	6,000	500 (46.5)
Flight-type conveyor	12,000	700 (65.1)

Note: Figures given include space for dish carts, empty racks, and potwashing. The size of the space will vary significantly on the basis of the layout of the soiled- and clean-dish tables. For instance, a single-tank dishwasher located along a wall in a small restaurant might occupy only 125 sq. ft. (11.6 sq. m).

Figure 4-25. Warewashing area space requirements.

❑ Washing

❑ Air drying

❑ Removing clean dishes

The design principle of simplicity discussed earlier is important to keep in mind when designing warewashing systems. Elaborate conveyor and bridge systems for soiled-dish tables often add to the clutter and expense of the warewashing area and create barriers that are difficult to move around. At the other extreme, designs that do not provide sufficient space for soiled-dish accumulation or warewashing rooms that have insufficient cart storage space for clean dishes are to be avoided.

Sound-absorbing materials on the ceiling, a high level of lighting (80 to 100 foot-candles), and the use of bright colors on the walls and ceiling are desirable design features. One frequent mistake in the engineering of warewashing areas is to provide inadequate circulation of air. The vents and small hoods required by the health department on dish machines often are not sufficient for the removal of moist air from the space. Supply and exhaust equipment that will accomplish sixty air changes per hour is recommended.

SUMMARY

A general description of the primary spaces of a foodservice facility has been included to provide the food facilities planner with basic guidelines concerning the spaces needed. Each of the spaces should work in harmony with other functional areas so that a high level of efficiency is achieved. The penalty for ignoring space relationships is an increase in labor and other operating costs. Food facilities owners and managers are encouraged to visit existing operations to familiarize themselves with a variety of design alternatives and to see how others have dealt with spatial relationships.

The amount of space needed for each area will vary. Some spaces may be squeezed and others made larger, depending on the special circumstances of the design or the desires of the owner or manager. The special design features presented for each of the spaces reflect solutions to problems that are frequently encountered in the process of planning and designing foodservice operations.

CHAPTER 5

EQUIPMENT LAYOUT

THIS CHAPTER

☑ Describes the desirable relationships between the component parts of a work area in a food facility

☑ Develops the methods for analyzing a layout and lists the features that should be included in each work area

☑ Illustrates typical layouts for each functional area of a foodservice operation

EFFECTIVE LAYOUT

Layout is the arrangement of equipment to create efficient, safe, and ergonomically correct work areas. As was discussed in Chapter 3, design focuses on the arrangement of functional areas in the entire facility, whereas layout focuses on the way equipment is placed within individual work spaces. When work areas are logically arranged according to the principles of good design and the equipment is carefully selected to meet the specific criteria of the operation, the space will yield a high level of efficiency and employee productivity. Effective layout thus depends upon access to raw materials, attention to the flow of food and personnel in the production process, relationships to other departments, access to utensils and equipment, and ease of cleaning and sanitation.

Access to Raw Materials

In a typical factory setting, materials move down an assembly line past each employee's workstation. This is an ideal arrangement because the worker is not required to walk great distances, the raw materials are readily available, and the speed of the process (productivity) can be established by management. Often raw materials or parts are delivered to the factory at several points along the assembly line to eliminate double handling. The flow of materials in a factory assembly-line process is illustrated in Figure 5-1.

The idea of applying the factory assembly-line model to a foodservice operation has not had wide acceptance except in hospitals, where a conveyor belt is often used to move trays down an assembly line as food items

111

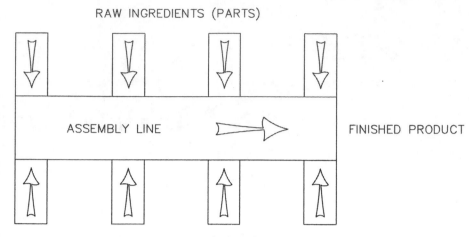

Figure 5-1. The assembly-line model.

are added. Although a conveyor belt would have limited usefulness for other types of foodservice facilities, the principles underlying the factory layout can be adapted to the needs of any foodservice design.

Raw or unprocessed materials in a foodservice operation are usually stored in walk-in refrigerators and freezers or in the dry-goods storeroom. The materials for the final assembly of the meal are usually found in or on:

❏ Walk-in refrigerators

❏ Reach-in refrigerators

❏ Dish storage cabinets or carts

❏ Steam tables

❏ Slicing machines

❏ Food-holding cabinets

❏ Portable food racks

❏ Beverage containers and dispensers

❏ Utility or receiving carts

The raw materials must be available to each work area so that a minimum number of steps are required for the worker to obtain the ingredients, process them, and transfer them to the next work area or to storage.

Figure 5-2 illustrates a cold-food preparation area designed to provide access to raw materials. This example is taken from a large facility that often prepares food for banquets. A walk-in cooler has been located adjacent to the preparation area, where it provides convenient access to the raw ingredients needed for cold food (salad and dessert) preparation. Notice that the walk-in refrigerator is available for storage of both raw ingredients and the finished product, thus serving a dual purpose. Designers frequently make the mistake of placing the walk-in refrigerators in a row, with little consideration of the workers' need for easy access to raw materials. Access doors in the side wall of the cooler are far more convenient for employees than doors that are placed at the front of the cooler. When salads are prepared in this area, employees remove the raw ingredients from the cooler; clean, cut, and chop them as needed; and assemble them on individual plates set on sheet pans. The plated salads then are covered with food wrap and set on

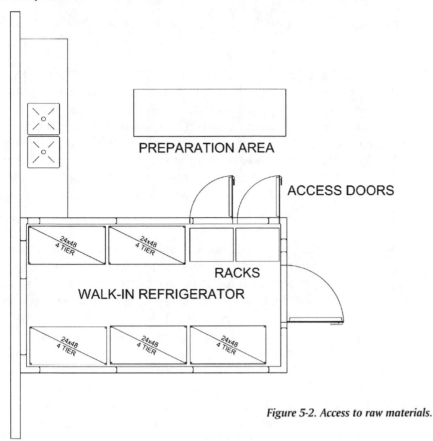

Figure 5-2. Access to raw materials.

racks in the cooler. When the time has come for the salads to be served, the racks are removed and taken to the banquet staging area, and the salads are brought to the guests.

Figure 5-3 illustrates how access to raw materials is supported in the layout of a final preparation area. A single-compartment reach-in freezer is located to the right of the fryers so that frozen french fries can easily be reached. To the left of the fryers is a grill, next to which is a single-compartment refrigerator where hamburger patties, chicken breasts, and other grill items are stored.

Convenient access to raw materials is especially important in the final preparation area. Without refrigerated storage at hand, the cooks are likely to bring an entire pan of steaks, seafood, or poultry and set it somewhere on the range section to save them from having to make multiple trips. The temperature of the food in the pan, exposed to the heat of the cooking

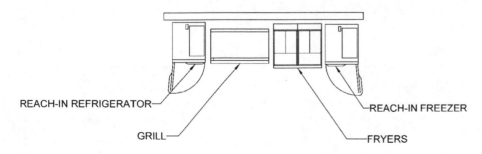

Figure 5-3. Access to raw materials in final preparation.

equipment, soon rises into the danger zone, increasing the risk of food poisoning.

Flow   In discussing the design sequence (Chapter 3), it was stressed that the layout of each part of the food operation should follow a logical progression. If the raw ingredients and/or the finished parts of the meal are arranged in the order in which they will be used (as on a factory assembly line; see Figure 5-1), the food operation is likely to be more efficient.

The flow relationship in each work area is most efficient if the movement is in a straight line or L shape. If workers are frequently required to move materials across an aisle or to work around another person, inefficiency and worker fatigue will result.

Relationship to Other Departments   Each part of a foodservice operation is closely related to the other parts. In design, the word *system* is often used to describe a functional part of the facility—a regularly interacting group of elements that form a whole. Dishwashing, for example, is described as a system, because each part of the process relates to every other part (see Figure 5-4). At the same time, dishwashing relates to other functions or systems within the facility. For instance, in a cafeteria the dishes might be moved in small dish carts from the dishwashing area to the cafeteria line. A good layout in the cafeteria area would permit the dish carts to roll under the steam tables, for use by the person who is dishing up the food. This feature of the service system eliminates double handling of dishes and decreases labor and dish breakage.

The layout of one department must be carefully considered to make sure that it works well with other departments. A helpful tool in under-

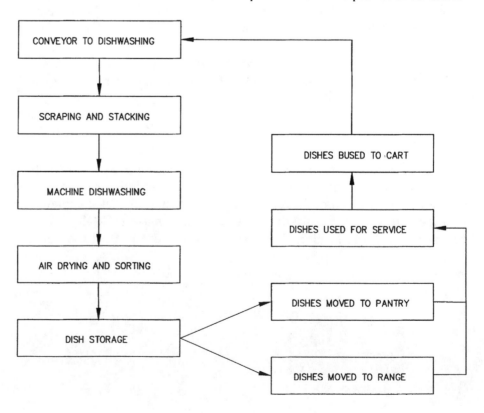

Figure 5.4. Dishwashing process flow.

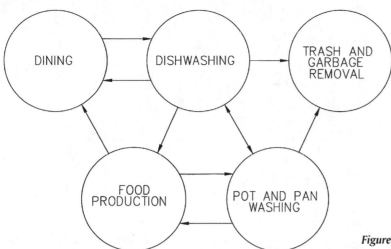

Figure 5-5. Relationship of diswashing to other functions.

standing how the departments interact is the bubble diagram (Figure 2-2) illustrating departmental relationships. The interaction of dishwashing to other departments is illustrated in Figure 5-5. Notice in the illustration that some functions have simple relationships with one or two other activities, while others have complex relationships with three or more departments.

Certain pieces of equipment are needed in each work area of a food facility. For instance, all food preparation and service areas should have a sink with hot and cold water and a utensil storage area. Pieces of equipment that are infrequently used or too expensive to duplicate, or both, cannot be located in each work area. A slicing machine, for example, is often placed on a portable stand so that it can easily be moved from one department to another to avoid unnecessary duplication. A mixer may be needed by the salad preparation workers for two hours a day and for three hours per day by the cooks in hot-food preparation. A single mixer could be located between the two departments, or each department could have its own high-speed food processor, since it is a small, inexpensive item.

Access to Utensils and Equipment

Another factor that needs to be considered in the location of equipment is the availability of cart-parking space, which is often a problem in small kitchens. Two parking areas are needed in the food production area: a place to temporarily place carts containing raw ingredients, and space for carts holding the finished product. A space 3 feet (.91 meter) deep by 4 feet (1.22 meters) wide will accommodate most portable carts. Parking spaces in a typical salad preparation area are shown in Figure 5-6.

Often the difference between an excellent layout and a mediocre one is the amount of attention given to detail in each work area. A checklist of utensil storage criteria (Figure 5-7) can be used to determine whether the layout of a food facility provides adequate working storage and access to utensils.

Careful attention to the details of equipment layout is necessary to create work areas that are easily cleaned and sanitized. Ease of cleaning and sanitation is a function of several factors. In manufactured equipment, ease of sanitation results from the following:

Ease of Cleaning and Sanitation

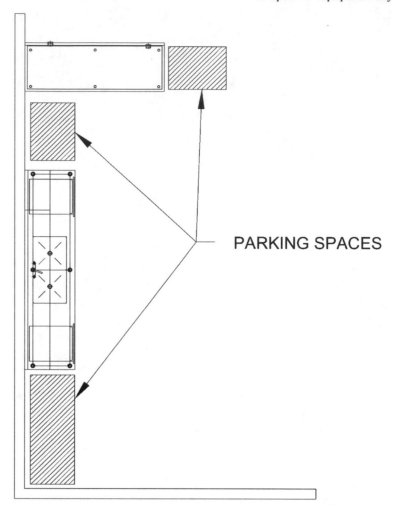

PARKING SPACES

Figure 5-6. Spaces for parking partially finished products during preparation.

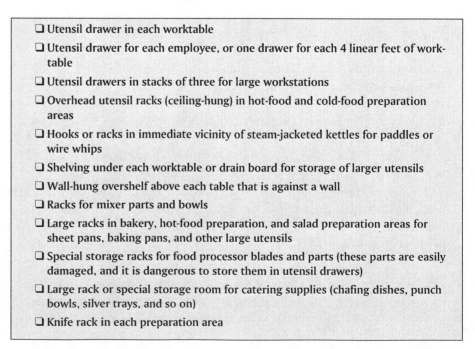

❏ Utensil drawer in each worktable

❏ Utensil drawer for each employee, or one drawer for each 4 linear feet of worktable

❏ Utensil drawers in stacks of three for large workstations

❏ Overhead utensil racks (ceiling-hung) in hot-food and cold-food preparation areas

❏ Hooks or racks in immediate vicinity of steam-jacketed kettles for paddles or wire whips

❏ Shelving under each worktable or drain board for storage of larger utensils

❏ Wall-hung overshelf above each table that is against a wall

❏ Racks for mixer parts and bowls

❏ Large racks in bakery, hot-food preparation, and salad preparation areas for sheet pans, baking pans, and other large utensils

❏ Special storage racks for food processor blades and parts (these parts are easily damaged, and it is dangerous to store them in utensil drawers)

❏ Large rack or special storage room for catering supplies (chafing dishes, punch bowls, silver trays, and so on)

❏ Knife rack in each preparation area

Figure 5-7. Working storage and utensil checklist.

❑ Use of easily cleaned materials, such as stainless steel

❑ Sealed food-contact compartments, so that food debris cannot fall into the inner workings of the equipment

❑ Construction without ledges, crevasses, joints, and other areas that trap food debris and breed bacteria

❑ Simple disassembly and reassembly on equipment that has to be broken down for cleaning and sanitizing (e.g., slicers)

❑ Ready access to catch pans for grease and food debris (e.g., on griddles)

❑ Removable components that can be run through the dish machine, such as grease extractor cartridges in the hood system

❑ Mounting on 6-inch (15-centimeter)-high legs or casters so that workers can clean under the equipment

❑ Enclosed and sealed controls that cannot be damaged by water in the cleaning and sanitizing process

Fabricated equipment, such as worktables and dish tables, also should be designed for ease of cleaning and sanitation. Important design features include the following:

❑ *Stainless-steel understructure.* Tables that are constructed with painted metal legs are less expensive than their stainless-steel competitors. However, painted legs have to be sanded and repainted regularly. Operators pay the small price difference of stainless-steel understructure many times over when employees have to sand and repaint the worktable legs every three years.

❑ *Backsplashes.* Where tables meet walls, stainless-steel backsplashes rising 10 inches (254 millimeters) above worktables and 16 inches (406 millimeters) above dish tables and pot sinks make work areas easy to clean (Figure 5-8).

❑ *Coved radius corners.* Wherever food contact surfaces make 90-degree corners or edges, a cove with a minimum radius of ¾ inch (20 millimeters) allows thorough cleaning and sanitizing. Otherwise, food debris will become trapped in a sharp corner and grow bacteria. On sink bowls and the edges of dish tables, the radius often is as much as 1½ inches (38 millimeters). Figure 5-9 shows examples of the edge profiles used in the construction of dish tables and worktables.

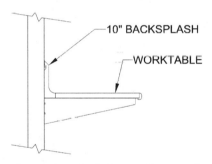

Figure 5-8. Backsplash on wall-mounted worktable.

❑ *Spreaders under fabricated tables.* Worktables are often constructed with a solid lower shelf for storage. However, solid shelves collect dust, dirt, and food debris, and are often overlooked during the cleaning and sanitizing of the kitchen. A more sanitary solution is to design worktables with spreaders (stainless-steel tubes) running lengthwise on 6-inch (152-millimeter) centers. Large pots and pans can be stored readily on spreaders, but the open design forces food debris, dirt, and dust to fall to the floor, where they are more likely to be mopped up. Figure 5-10 illustrates a worktable with spreaders rather than a solid undershelf.

Ease of cleaning and sanitation also is affected by the location of utility connections, discussed below.

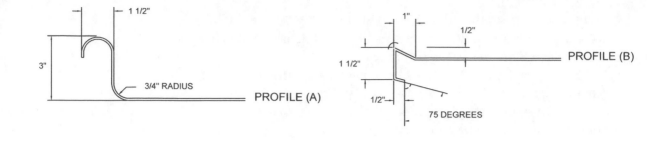

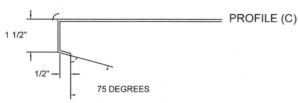

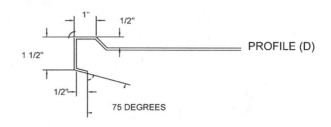

Figure 5-9. Edge profiles for stainless-steel tables and countertops.

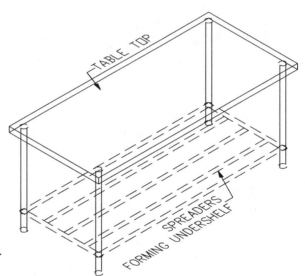

Figure 5-10. Worktable with spreaders.

PHYSICAL CHARACTERISTICS OF EQUIPMENT LAYOUT

The ability to assess a layout comes from experience as a food facility designer or from working for many years in a food operation. A layout can be planned in part on the basis of space allocation and desirable layout relationships, as already discussed in this text. There are other characteristics in equipment layout that are desirable if an efficient overall design is to be achieved. These characteristics are:

❏ Configuration (shape) of the layout
❏ Method for mounting the equipment
❏ Utility connection methods

The three most common shapes for work area layout are the straight line, the L, and the U. Each shape has advantages and disadvantages, but the straight line is usually considered the best arrangement from a time-and-motion-efficiency standpoint. Although warewashing layouts have been designed using every imaginable shape, more-elaborate (and expensive) layouts tend to be inefficient. A straight-line layout, in which the dishes are unloaded, scraped, stacked, and placed directly into the dish machine, is usually the most efficient one. An example of such a layout is illustrated in Figure 5-11. The disadvantage of this layout for a high-volume food operation would be the limited dish drop-off area. It might, therefore, be desirable to create an L in this instance, as shown in Figure 5-12.

These and similar layouts, each with its particular advantages, can be used for food preparation areas. Several examples are shown in Figure 5-13. The L-shaped arrangement uses a limited amount of space and provides a very convenient work surface. This arrangement also creates a workstation that is out of the traffic aisle, which is a desirable feature if other equipment is likely to be parked in the work area. The U-shaped layout offers a large amount of table surface area, but walking in and out of the U may add many steps to the employee's workday. The parallel and back-to-back parallel tables are very efficient as work areas and for this reason are frequently used in food production layouts. The tables shown are of a standard width, 2 feet 6 inches (762 millimeters), but, as can be seen in the illustrations, each shape uses a different amount of floor space.

Configuration of the Layout

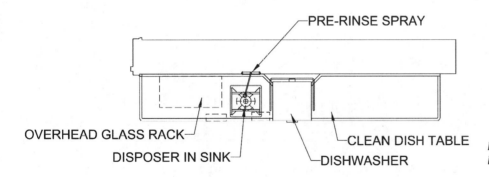

Figure 5-11. Straight-line dishwashing layout.

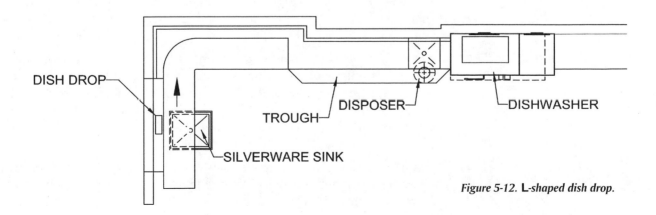

Figure 5-12. L-shaped dish drop.

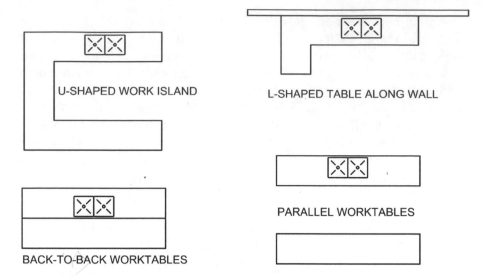

Figure 5-13. Work area layouts.

Methods for Mounting Equipment

To design the area for efficiency, the layout of a work space must be considered from a three-dimensional perspective. The effective use of space above and below the table surface must be carefully considered by the food facilities consultant. Below the table surface, the most important consideration is the method for mounting the equipment. The most common mounting arrangements are:

- ❏ Concrete bases
- ❏ Small steel legs
- ❏ Equipment stands
- ❏ Casters
- ❏ Wall-hung equipment
- ❏ Pedestals

Concrete Bases

Concrete bases are typically used under large pieces of equipment, such as refrigerators or broilers, as a means of eliminating difficult-to-clean areas under the equipment. Because of the inflexibility that a large concrete base creates in a kitchen, this mounting method is now used less frequently than in the past.

Small Steel Legs

The standard leg for kitchen equipment is 6 inches high. However, this height does not easily allow for thorough cleaning under the equipment. Six-inch legs on large pieces of equipment such as ranges or broilers make cleaning under the equipment especially difficult because of the distance from the front to the back of the equipment.

Equipment Stands

The range section of a foodservice facility is traditionally mounted in a bank or row of equipment, one piece beside the other. This arrangement creates several problems:

❏ The grease that flows into cracks between pieces of equipment cannot be easily removed.

❏ The short legs on which the equipment is mounted make cleaning underneath it difficult.

❏ Utilities are connected from behind the equipment, making cleaning and repair difficult.

❏ Ovens are located close to the floor in many pieces of equipment, making it difficult to load and unload food being cooked.

A good design solution to these problems is to place this equipment on an equipment stand. Since equipment stands are sized to accommodate modular equipment in the range sections, the designer can specify the proper stand to fit each piece. Figure 5-14 shows a typical range section mounted on equipment stands.

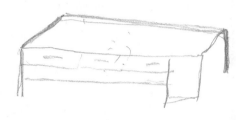

The use of casters is a popular option in mounting foodservice equipment. Portability is often a desirable feature because the equipment can be easily moved for cleaning or shifted from one part of the food operation to another, permitting better utilization. Casters can be used on virtually any piece of foodservice equipment except those that require permanent, rigid utility service connections, such as drains or ducts. Gas and water connections on caster-mounted equipment are made using flexible connectors (braided hoses) with quick-disconnect devices. A disadvantage of caster-mounted equipment is that employees may forget to disconnect the power cord, gas supply, or water hoses before rolling it away from the wall prior to cleaning. If so, the utility connection may be pulled right out of the wall by the inertia of, say, a double-stack convection oven. Restraining cables that are shorter than the utility connections should be installed on caster-mounted equipment to prevent this kind of damage.

Casters

Wall-Hung Equipment

The best but most expensive means for mounting equipment is to suspend it from the wall, creating an open area above the finished floor. The advantage of this method of installing equipment is ease of sanitation. A mop can be run along the floor under the equipment freely, without having to work around legs, stands, or bases. An example of wall-hung equipment is shown

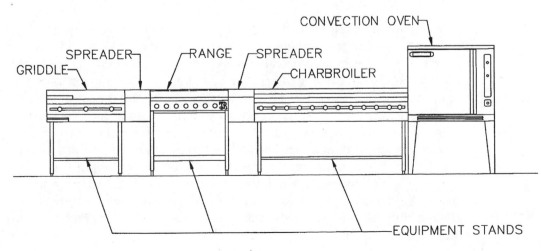

Figure 5-14. Range section on equipment stands.

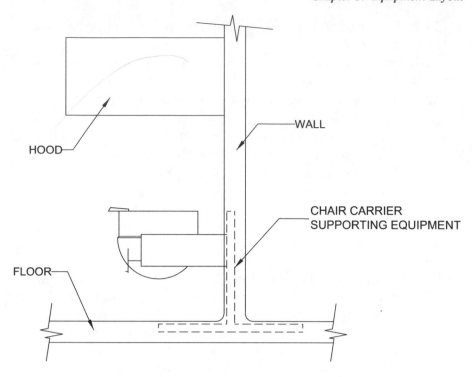

Figure 5-15. Wall-hung equipment.

in Figure 5-15. Notice that the wall mounting bracket is connected to a chair carrier, which has been built into the wall. The chair carrier transfers the weight of the kettle to the floor. Because the carrier must be built into the wall during the construction phase of the project, full coordination is necessary between the general contractor, kitchen equipment contractor, and design consultant to ensure that the chair carrier is installed properly and the utility connections are completed before the wall is closed and finished.

The cost of a wall-hung kettle is more than double the cost of the same size kettle mounted on legs. Most owners of a food facility cannot afford the luxury of hanging large, heavy pieces of equipment. However, many tables, shelves, and other smaller pieces of equipment can be hung using brackets attached securely to the wall.

Pedestals The mounting of equipment on tables supported by a pedestal base, rather than in enclosed cabinets, is a good method of solving a sanitation problem. This design approach provides a space for temporary storage of portable equipment under the counter. Figure 5-16 illustrates a cafeteria steam table mounted on two pedestals, with undercounter parking. Pedestals have the added advantage of providing a sanitary and convenient means of connecting the equipment to the appropriate utility. Water, gas, electric, steam, and drain lines can all be run through the pedestal, avoiding the problem of a conduit that protrudes through the floor or walls. The disadvantage of pedestals is that the equipment is difficult to move in the event of a change in layout. Because the pedestals rest on concrete curbs, changes in design require significant construction work to remove them and repair the floor.

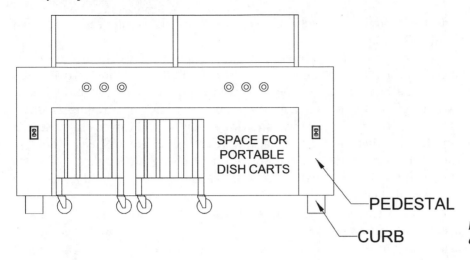

SPACE FOR
PORTABLE
DISH CARTS

PEDESTAL

CURB

Figure 5-16. Counter mounted on pedestals, creating space for dish carts

THE LAYOUT OF FUNCTIONAL AREAS

To create a efficient layout, each area of the food facility must be considered according to its function. The layouts of the major functional areas of a foodservice facility are discussed below. Because layout is closely related to space analysis and programming, the reader may find it helpful to review the corresponding sections in Chapter 4 for each of the primary functional areas in a foodservice facility.

Receiving

The primary components of the receiving area include the loading dock, access control (a locked door), space for staging food while it is being checked, a surface (worktable) on which cartons, lugs, flats, and other items can be set during inspection, and a scale. The primary considerations in the design and layout of a receiving area include the following:

❑ Providing adequate space for large trucks to maneuver while delivering products.

❑ Providing a large enough dock. The width of the dock determines how many trucks can be parked at one time. Small foodservice operations typically need space for only one truck. However, larger operations may need space for two trucks, particularly if they do catering by truck.

❑ If the loading dock is shared by other functions in the building, then foodservice needs a controlled entry.

❑ Adequate aisle width needs to be provided so that products can be checked and weighed without blocking access to the dock.

Storage

The optimal layout of storage areas is one that maximizes usable storage area and minimizes unnecessary aisle space. The specific layout depends upon the owner's operational priorities. If products are brought from receiving in cases or cartons on a hand truck, then standard shelving and dunnage racks separated by 3-to-4-foot (.91-to-1.22-meter) aisles will be adequate. If products are transported by forklift and stored on pallets, then industrial (warehouse) shelving may be used and aisles will need to be 6 to 8 feet (1.83 to 2.44 meters) wide.

The majority of foodservice operations use hand trucks and standard shelving. Standard shelving depth for storage should be 24 inches (610 millimeters) because it permits most product containers to be stored without extending into the aisle, where they could be struck by a rolling rack and knocked to the floor. Narrower shelving requires food cartons to be stored lengthwise rather than back to back, which is less efficient. Shelving heights vary, but for most foodservice operations shelving higher than 72 inches (1.83 meters) is rarely used except when storing cartons of light items, such as paper products.

Shelving should be laid out to minimize the amount of space used by aisles relative to actually storing products. Figure 5-17 shows two identically sized dry-storage rooms (interior dimensions 15 feet 3 inches by 14 feet 2 inches [4.65 meters by 4.32 meters]). Figure 5-17a shows 4-foot (1.22-meter)-wide aisles and a single row of center shelves, whereas Figure 5-17b shows 3-foot (.91-meter) aisles and a double set of center shelves. Using only the minimum necessary aisle width increases effective storage by 20 percent. Given the high cost of construction (often $150 or more per square foot [$1,615 per square meter]), efficient layout is a good investment.

In laying out the storage area for dry goods, the separation of cleaning supplies from food products is a health requirement in the United States. The reason for this requirement is to diminish the chances of accidentally mixing cleaning supplies with food. The separation of food products from paper supplies or uniforms is desirable in order to increase control over those products and to prevent employee pilferage. If a decision is made to issue partial cases of food to the kitchen, leaving the rest in the storeroom, then those partial cases would probably be stored in a separate section than the unbroken cases. Opened cases of foods require different types of shelving than whole cases, and they also invite pilferage. The separation of spices and broken cases into a special area of the storeroom equipped with solid shelving and secured by a special fence or "cage" is a common solution.

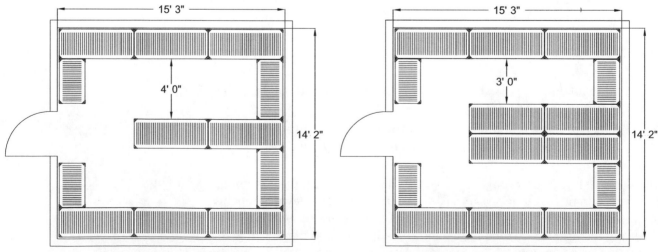

Figure 5-17a. Dry storage with 4-foot aisles.   *Figure 5-17b. Dry storage with 3-foot aisles.*

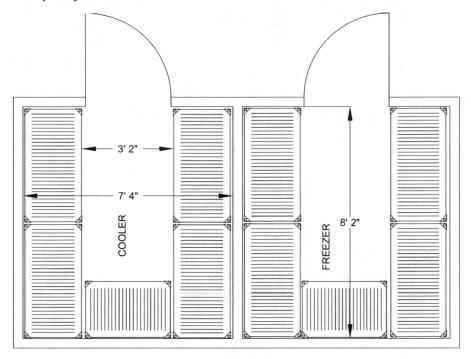

Figure 5-18. Minimum efficient size for a walk-in combination.

Maximizing shelving and minimizing aisle space is critical in the layout of walk-in coolers and freezers because of the high cost per square foot of these units. Figure 5-18 illustrates a minimum size for a combination (side-by-side) walk-in cooler and freezer unit. The interior width of the cooler and freezer sections is 7 feet 4 inches (2.24 meters), allowing for 24-inch (610-millimeter)-deep shelves and a 38-inch (965-millimeter) aisle (the remaining 2 inches [51 millimeters] provide clearance between the shelving and the walls).

Smaller walk-in units are available, but their space utilization is often very inefficient. For example, a walk-in that is wide enough for shelving only on one side—often called a step-in rather than a walk-in (Figure 5-19)—is functionally equivalent to a reach-in refrigerator but far more expensive because the operator is paying to refrigerate a 3-foot (.91-meter)-wide aisle.

Walk-ins are often designed so that the door to the freezer section opens from inside the cooler section on the belief that significant energy savings will result. Such savings are likely to be minuscule and not worth the loss of storage space in the cooler required to accommodate the door to the freezer. However, other design considerations may make that approach unavoidable.

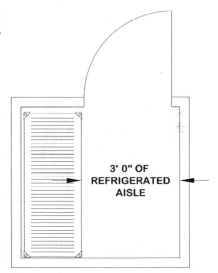

Figure 5-19. "Step-in" cooler (inefficient use of space).

Pre-preparation

Depending on the size and complexity of the foodservice operation, pre-preparation areas can be as simple as a worktable with sinks or as complex as an entire room dedicated to producing ingredients in the exact weights and measures necessary for final preparation. Pre-preparation areas typically include worktables with sinks and a disposer, utensil storage, mixers, food processors and choppers, and parking spaces for racks. Pre-preparation areas also may include kettles, ovens, and similar equipment.

Figure 5-20 shows the layout of a basic pre-preparation area for a restaurant. It is designed for use by two or three employees. Figure 5-21 shows the layout of a pre-preparation area for a large institutional foodservice operation.

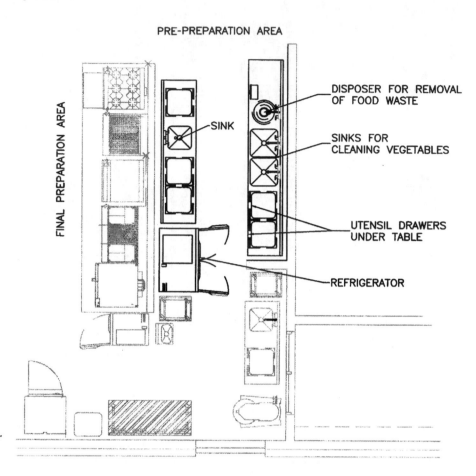

Figure 5-20. Preparation area (darker line areas) for a 160-seat restaurant.

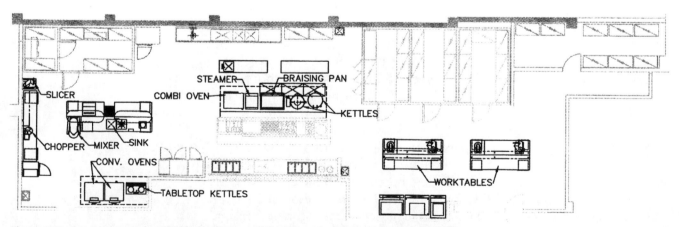

Figure 5-21. Preparation equipment (darker line areas) for a large institutional foodservice facility.

In restaurants, clubs, and similar facilities, the cold-food area or pantry is dedicated to the preparation, assembly, and service of cold foods such as salads, sandwiches, desserts, and cold appetizers. In table service operations, the pantry is located as near as is feasible to the front of the kitchen, convenient to servers. Alternatively, some pantry functions may be located in large server stations so that servers can obtain salads and desserts without going into the kitchen area proper (this design approach is discussed in a later section of this chapter). Foodservice operations that do not use table service often incorporate the cold-food preparation area with the final preparation area because both require access to raw materials stored in walk-in coolers.

Cold-Food Preparation (Pantry)

Pantries typically include worktables with sinks, refrigerated storage for raw materials as well as for finished items, a refrigerated makeup area with cold pans, and a pickup station for servers. Depending on how the production processes are divided between the pre-preparation area and the pantry, pantries may also include small mixers, food processors, and/or slicers.

The layout of the final preparation area is an especially critical part of the design and layout process in all foodservice concepts. This is so because errors in design, layout, and equipment selection in final preparation are most likely to have a direct impact on the satisfaction of the guest. Poorly laid-out final preparation areas may cause delays in service, over- or under-cooked entrees, unattractive presentation, and mistakes in fulfilling orders. Further, poor layout reduces the productivity of the highest-paid employees in the back of the house (the chefs).

Final (Hot-Food) Preparation

In restaurants, clubs, and other operations that feature cook-to-order food with table service, everything necessary to prepare the finished hot entrees must be immediately accessible to the chef and/or line cooks. For this reason, the owner and the foodservice consultant pay careful attention not only to the selection and layout of final preparation equipment but also to the design of the chef's table, where food is plated, garnished, and picked up by the server (or runner).

Customers in quick-service restaurants expect their food to be ready just a few minutes after placing their order. The layout of final preparation areas in these restaurants is critical for the success of the concept. Large chains carefully research the effects of even the smallest changes in the layout of the final preparation area and the design of each piece of equipment. Even the design of a utensil to scoop fries into a bag has been the focus of intense research and development.

A trend in institutional foodservices has been the shifting of final preparation from the back of the house to the servery, where the customer can see the food being prepared. Because institutional food facilities often feed large volumes of people in relatively short periods, the design of these final preparation areas is critical for operational efficiency and to prevent lengthy waits for menu items.

Equipment for the final preparation area should be selected for the desired cooking technique (e.g., sauté, charbroil, or steam) and should be sized to meet the anticipated demand for each item on the menu. Equip-

Menu Item	Preparation Technique	Equipment Required	Servings/Hour*
Strip steak	Broil	Charbroiler	36
Swordfish steak	Broil	Charbroiler	16
Chicken breast	Broil	Charbroiler	44
Shrimp	Sauté	Open-burner range	12
Scallops	Sauté	Open-burner range	8
Calamari	Sauté	Open-burner range	4
Lobster tail	Steam with heat	Combi oven	12
Fried chicken	Deep-fat fry	Fryer	12
Home fries	Deep-fat fry	Fryer	32
Asparagus	Steam	Combi oven	24

*Servings per hour are shown as exact values to illustrate the concept of relating equipment selection to the anticipated demand for each menu item. In actuality, a range of estimated servings would be used to select and size equipment.

Figure 5-22. Sample worksheet for determining final preparation equipment requirements based on menu.

ment that is specifically designed for the task is preferable to equipment that does many things but none of them well. Figure 5-22 is an example of a worksheet that can be used by the operator and the foodservice consultant to determine the kinds of equipment and capacities necessary for final preparation.

Figure 5-23 shows the final preparation line for a medium-sized table service restaurant. Each piece of equipment has a specific function dictated by the menu.

Service Areas   The layout of the service areas depends upon the concept of the food facility. Table service restaurants have far different requirements from quick-service restaurants, and quick-service restaurants are very different from institutional concepts.

The complexities of service areas in the dining room can range from a simple side stand to an elaborate server station. In a restaurant the labor cost will be directly affected by the distance between the final preparation

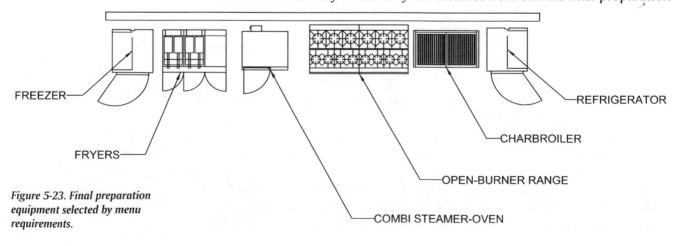

FREEZER

FRYERS

REFRIGERATOR

CHARBROILER

OPEN-BURNER RANGE

COMBI STEAMER-OVEN

Figure 5-23. Final preparation equipment selected by menu requirements.

and the service area. This distance can be altered significantly by the use of well-designed server stations. The importance of the server station for quick, efficient service cannot be overemphasized. If the service personnel must walk to the kitchen to pick up the typical table setup, this might result in the following trips:

First trip: Pick up linen, glasses, silverware, and condiments.
Second trip: Pick up water, ice, butter, crackers, and bread.

After the order is taken, the following additional trips might be necessary:

Third trip: Pick up cocktail or wine order from the service bar.
Fourth trip: Place appetizer order and salad order.
Fifth trip: Pick up appetizer and salad.

After the cocktail and appetizers are served, the following trips might occur:

Sixth trip: Place the entree order.
Seventh trip: Pick up the entree.
Eighth trip: Clear appetizer and cocktail (or combine this with the seventh trip).
Ninth trip: Clear entree and place dessert order.
Tenth trip: Clear dessert, soiled linen, and all glassware and silverware.

Three or four of these trips to the kitchen can be avoided with a well-designed and properly located server station. Figure 5-24 lists thirty items that may be kept at the server station.

Eliminating four trips to the kitchen will provide the following advantages:

❑ An increase in the speed of service

❑ Bread	❑ Hot tea and Sanka
❑ Butter	❑ Boiling water
❑ Butter plates	❑ Linen napkins and tablecloths
❑ Baskets for bread	❑ Receptacle for soiled linen
❑ Coffee machine	❑ Milk
❑ Coffee and filters	❑ Crackers
❑ Coffee cups and saucers	❑ Tray stand or shelf for trays
❑ Cream	❑ Condiments (salad dressings, sauces, seasonings)
❑ Cream pitchers	❑ Sour cream
❑ Sugar	❑ Soup
❑ Silverware	❑ Precheck machine and/or space for writing out checks
❑ Water and water pitcher	❑ Microwave oven
❑ Glasses	❑ Soft drinks
❑ Ice	❑ Trash container
❑ Cold tea	❑ Pickup control board

Figure 5-24. Potential items located in a server station.

❏ A possible reduction in service personnel

❏ A less crowded kitchen

❏ More attention to guests by the service personnel

One disadvantage of the use of well-designed server stations is some loss of control over the products that are located in the station. For this reason, the items listed are generally inexpensive and not the kind of food items that service personnel would steal or eat on the job. It would not be a good idea to place desserts, alcoholic beverages, or expensive appetizers on the server station. These items should be picked up from the cold-food area after being listed on the guest check.

An example of a redesigned kitchen in a country club, with a server station located near the dining area, can be seen in the before and after drawings of Figure 5-25. By exchanging the locations of the cooler and pantry areas in the before drawing, a server station could be created in the dining room that backs up to the pantry area of the kitchen. A pass-through refrigerator that opens to both areas is stocked by the pantry employees with salads and desserts so that servers can pick them up for guests without going into the kitchen itself.

Quick-service restaurants involve the customer in the service process of taking the food to the table (or picking it up at the drive-through window). Although there is a great deal of similarity among quick-service restaurants, there also are important differences. These differences are illustrated in Figures 5-26a and 5-26b, in which two service areas are contrasted. Figure 5-26a shows a counter with multiple service points where the customer receives his or her entree, side order, and beverage. In this layout, the customer places the order and then stands in place waiting for the salesperson to assemble and bag it. Figure 5-26b, in contrast, shows a service counter where the customer places his or her order, waits while the order is assembled, and then moves along the counter to a point where the food is delivered. While the effects of these differences on the speed of customer service may be slight, chain foodservice firms seek even the slightest advantage—real or perceived—in the convenience they offer their guests.

Cafeteria service designs have changed dramatically over the past two decades. The traditional straight-line design has been replaced by a family of closely related approaches: the scramble, the scatter system, or the food court. Figure 5-27 shows a schematic design for a scramble cafeteria design with multiple food stations and a convenience store intended for corporate dining.

The change from straight-line to scramble designs has occurred for several reasons:

❏ Faster service

❏ Greater menu variety through multiple food stations

❏ Better merchandising

The principle behind the scramble (or scatter) design is to provide multiple stations from which the customer can freely select. Unlike the straight-line cafeteria service layout, in which the speed through the line is only as fast as the slowest customer, the scramble system can be designed so that

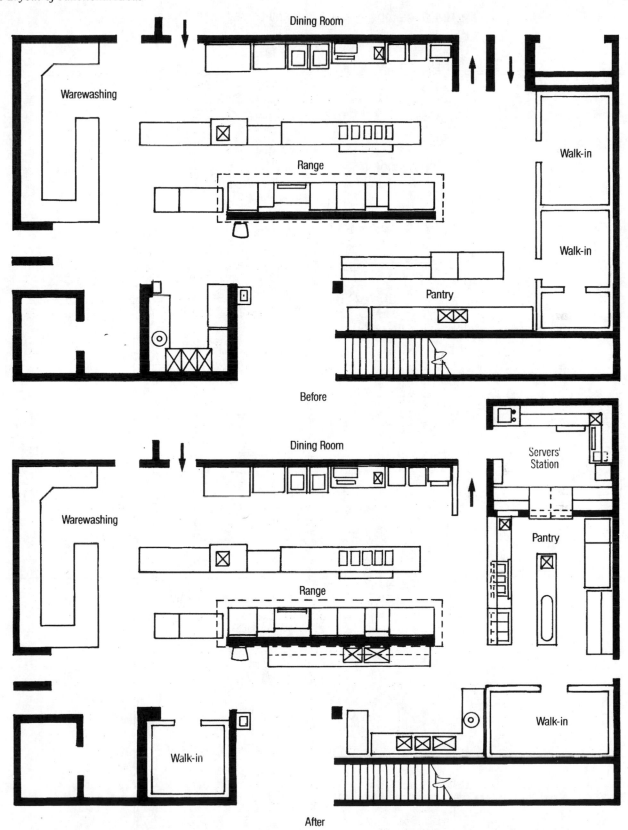

Before

After

Figure 5-25. Redesigned kitchen in a country club, with a server station located near the dining area (upper right corner).

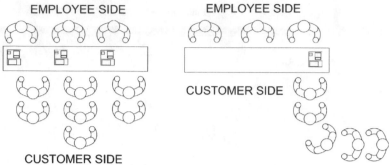

Figure 5-26a. Customers served simultaneously.

Figure 5-26b. Customers served one at a time.

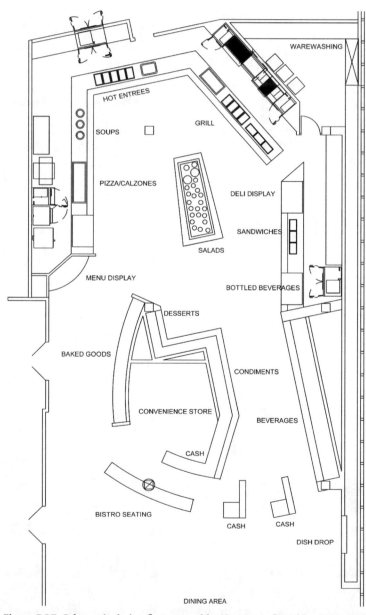

Figure 5-27. Schematic design for a scramble. (Courtesy of Maddox-NBD, Inc.)

each station serves at a predetermined rate. The only disadvantage of the scramble service layout is that it requires generous circulation space so that a large number of customers can move freely from station to station.

The overall approach taken to the layout of the dishwashing area is a function of the following factors:

❏ *The concept of the foodservice operation.* The concept affects the type and volume of dishes that need to be washed. Fine-dining establishments use far more dishes and silverware on a per-customer basis than a simple family restaurant. Similarly, health care facilities need to wash specialized trays and containers, whereas schools may need only to wash a single tray.

❏ *The size of the operation.* The number of customers has a direct effect on the layout of a warewashing area.

❏ *The timing.* A foodservice operation that serves six hundred covers in three hours places a different demand on the dish operation than an operation serving the same six hundred covers in forty-five minutes.

❏ *The operational approach to dishwashing.* There are several distinct approaches to organizing the warewashing process within the dishroom, especially in large operations. For example, a carousel dish machine requires a significantly different layout than does a flight-type machine serving the same demand.

A representative dishroom layout for a small foodservice operation is shown in Figure 5-28. This design utilizes a single-tank, door-type dish machine that fits in a corner. Figures 5-29, 5-30, 5-31, and 5-32 illustrate dishrooms using a two-tank dish machine, a flight machine, a circular (carousel) machine, and a corner dish machine with a tray accumulator, respectively.

The wash-down room is a space, usually located in the vicinity of the receiving dock, used for cleaning carts and trash cans. For a small or medium-sized food operation, the room needs to be large enough to accommodate a hose reel, a large floor drain, and one or two parked carts. A space 6 feet wide by 10 feet long (1.83 meters wide by 3.05 meters long) would be adequate. Large hotel or hospital foodservice facilities would need a larger wash-down room because of the extensive use of carts. Wash-down rooms may be equipped with steam cleaners and foot-operated can washers, but these are usually not necessary.

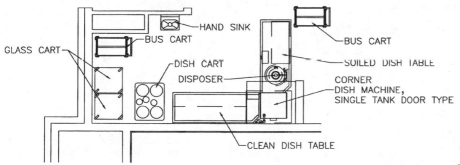

Figure 5-28. Dishroom for a small foodservice operation.

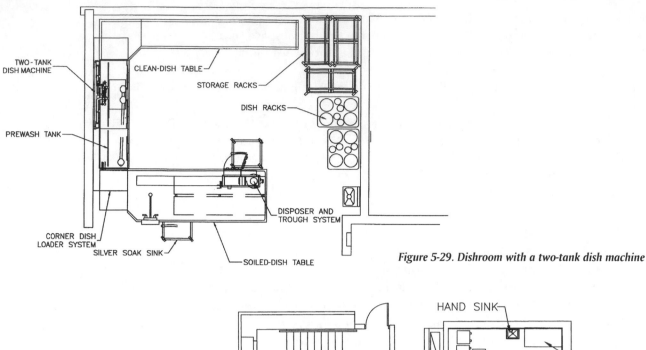

Figure 5-29. Dishroom with a two-tank dish machine

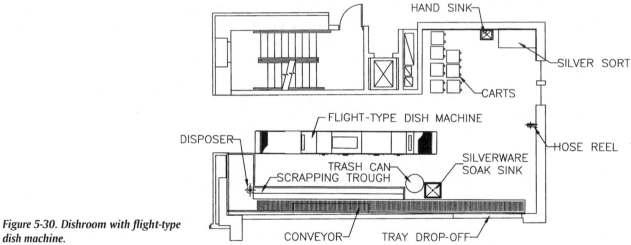

Figure 5-30. Dishroom with flight-type dish machine.

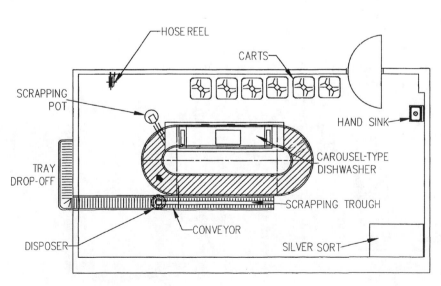

Figure 5-31. Carousel dish machine layout.

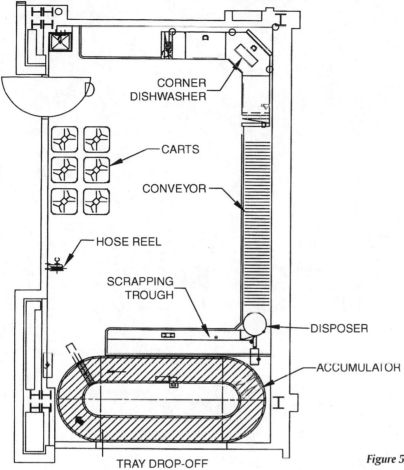

CORNER
DISHWASHER

CARTS

CONVEYOR

HOSE REEL

SCRAPPING
TROUGH

DISPOSER

ACCUMULATOR

TRAY DROP-OFF

Figure 5-32. Dishroom with tray accumulator.

Linen and Locker Room

Table linen is usually stored in a special storage space that is protected from moisture and convenient to the service personnel. Uniforms are usually issued to the employees on an exchange basis (each employee turns in a dirty uniform for a clean one). The use of a combination linen room/locker room/toilet is a good space-saving design for handling uniform exchange (Figure 5-33). Notice in the drawing that linen is placed in the back side of the locker by the linen rental company or the person responsible for linen. The employee places his or her soiled uniform in the locker in exchange for a clean uniform. Separate lockers are provided for coats and street clothes.

Service Kitchens

Banquet halls and private dining rooms can best be served if a space is provided for holding the food prior to service. Service kitchens are not usually needed, however, if the banquet hall or private dining room is near the kitchen.

The amount of space needed for a banquet service kitchen will vary with the number of seats being served. Figure 5-34 lists guidelines for the square footage requirements of service kitchens based on the number of seats in the adjacent dining area.

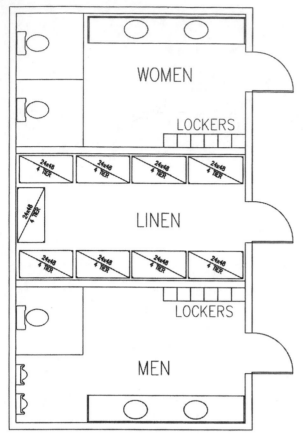

Figure 5-33. Restrooms with employee lockers and linen storage room.

Number of Seats in Dining Area	Size of Serving Kitchen (Net)
50–100 seats	75–100 square feet (6.97–9.29 square meters)
100– 250 seats	100–150 square feet (9.29–13.94 square meters)
250–500 seats	150–300 square feet (13.94–27.87 square meters)
500–1,000 seats	300–500 square feet (27.87–46.45 square meters)

Figure 5-34. Guidelines for serving kitchen area.

Necessary	May Be Desirable
Sink with hot and cold water	Dish machine
Ice machine	Refrigeration
Storage for china	Fryers, grills, or broilers
Table for holding service equipment	Steam table
Coffee urn	Storage for catering equipment
Electrical outlets for portable equipment	Heated cabinets
	Convection oven
	Three-compartment sink

Figure 5-35. Equipment recommendations for serving kitchens.

Service kitchens can be equipped with support cooking equipment and elaborate hot and cold holding cabinets. An empty room that can accommodate portable equipment will serve the same function. A simple service kitchen with a minimum amount of equipment is preferred by most food facility design consultants. Figure 5-35 identifies equipment that should be considered for the service kitchen. Figure 5-36 shows the layout for a fine-dining service kitchen.

If space is needed for the storage of tables and chairs, this should be added to the above space requirement figures. A formula that can be used as a guideline in calculating the space for storage of tables and chairs is to add 0.6 square foot (.056 square meter) per seat.

Health care facilities, such as congregate care and retirement villages, often use serving kitchens for resident dining areas on the units or floors. These facilities often require larger serving kitchens in relation to the number of seats. To ensure that the food served to residents is fresh, final preparation equipment such as a steamer to cook vegetables and a griddle for eggs, pancakes, and French toast are added to the design. A serving kitchen for a large long-term-care community is shown in Figure 5-37.

EQUIPMENT SCHEDULE

ITEM	QTY	DESCRIPTION			
K-01	2	HAND SINK, ELECTRONIC	K-20	1	COUNTER, PLATE PICK-UP
K-02	1	PREP TABLE	K-21	19	SHELVING UNIT
K-03	1	CUTTER-MIXER, VERTICAL	K-22	1	DISHWASHER, DOOR-TYPE
K-04	1	SLICER, AUTOMATIC FEED	K-23	1	BEVERAGE COUNTER
K-05	1	PREP TABLE	K-24	2	REFRIGERATOR, 1-SECTION
K-06	1	INGREDIENT BINS	K-25	3	DISPOSER, 2-HP
K-07	1	ICE MACHINE WITH BIN	K-26	1	COFFEE BREWER
K-08	1	POT WASH	K-27	1	MIXER, 20-QUART
K-09	1	REFRIGERATOR, 1 SECTION	K-31	1	DISHTABLE, SOILED
K-10	1	KETTLE, TILTING	K-32	1	DISHTABLE, CLEAN
K-11	1	FLOOR TROUGH, ANTI-SPILL	K-35	1	CART, HEATED
K-12	1	OVEN, COMBI	K-37	1	DISH DOLLY
K-13	1	RANGE, 6 BURNER WITH OVEN	K-38	1	TOASTER
K-14	1	CHARBROILER, MODULAR	K-39	1	WAFFLE IRON
K-15	1	GRIDDLE, MODULAR	K-40	2	SOUP WELLS
K-16	-	OPEN ITEM			
K-17	1	FRYER, DEEP FAT, GAS	R-01	1	WALK-IN REFRIGERATOR
K-18	1	CHEF'S COUNTER	R-02	1	WALK-IN FREEZER
K-19	1	BANQUET CABINET, HEATED	R-03	2	REFRIGERATION SYSTEMS

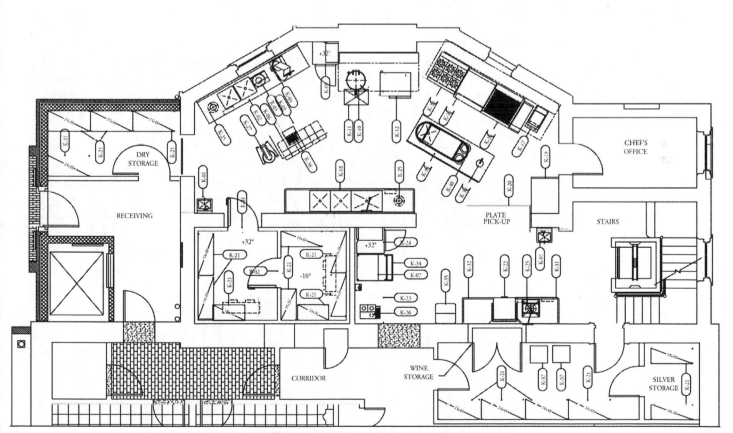

Figure 5-36. Service kitchen for catering in a fine-dining operation.

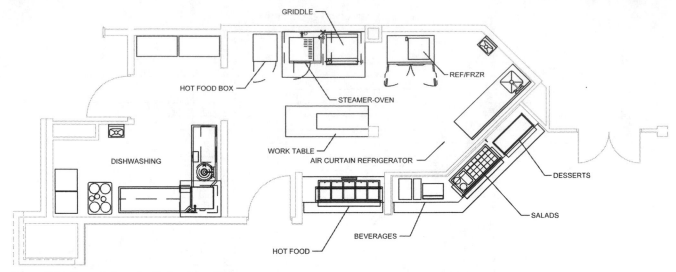

GRIDDLE

HOT FOOD BOX

STEAMER-OVEN

REF/FRZR

WORK TABLE

AIR CURTAIN REFRIGERATOR

DISHWASHING

DESSERTS

SALADS

BEVERAGES

HOT FOOD

Figure 5-37. Expanded service kitchen in retirement center.

SUMMARY

A foodservice facility must be designed with both space and function in mind. The workspace will function best if attention in design is given to the interface between the employee and the foodservice equipment. The equipment must be laid out with due consideration to access to raw materials, the flow of raw materials and people, the relationship to other departments in the facility, and access to needed utensils and equipment.

There are certain physical characteristics that are desirable in all work areas. To determine the best physical arrangement, the designer must consider the shape of the layout, the best method for mounting the equipment, and the best means for connecting the utilities to each piece of equipment.

Design considerations are different for each area of the food facility, and each area must therefore be considered according to its function. Storage spaces, preparation areas, service areas in the dining room, and special support areas must have special design features if they are to be efficient.

CHAPTER 6

FOODSERVICE EQUIPMENT, PART I

THIS CHAPTER

☑ Describes the basis for selecting foodservice equipment

☑ Outlines the standards of workmanship and common materials for constructing food-service equipment

☑ Provides an overview of the equipment specifications as they would appear in a set of contract documents

EQUIPMENT SELECTION

The purchase of a major piece of equipment is an important event for the manager or owner of a foodservice operation. A new piece of equipment may be selected for any of the following reasons:

❏ The equipment is a part of a new food facility.

❏ Existing equipment needs to be replaced.

❏ Changes in the menu or variations in volume of business require an addition to the food facility.

❏ The equipment will reduce labor costs.

❏ The equipment will reduce maintenance costs.

❏ The equipment will produce savings in energy.

Trade journals and equipment shows in the foodservice industry offer a smorgasbord of interesting equipment that can be tempting to a prospective buyer. A careful evaluation of available alternatives is important in order to select the correct piece of equipment at the lowest possible total cost of ownership.

The total cost of ownership for a piece of equipment is a function of the following factors:

❏ The initial purchase price

❏ The cost of installing the equipment

❏ The direct costs of operation

❏ The cost of maintenance and repair

❏ The labor costs required to operate the equipment

❏ The useful life of the equipment

Each of these factors is briefly discussed below.

Initial Purchase Price   Equipment purchasing decisions are often made strictly on the basis of the initial purchase price. For example, an oven costing $5,200 may be selected over one whose price is $6,500. Unfortunately, it is not always the case that the lower initial price represents the lowest total cost of ownership. An operation that serves three meals per day, 365 days per year, would probably be better off purchasing the more expensive oven—provided, of course, that the higher cost reflects better-quality components that will last substantially longer under heavy use. On the other hand, a facility that serves one meal per day only nine months of the year, such as an elementary-school kitchen, would probably be well served by the less expensive oven.

Foodservice equipment manufacturers recognize the tremendous variety of needs within the industry and offer products that are designed to address the full spectrum of operational requirements. Thus, the owner needs to clearly understand the specific requirements of his or her operation in order to select equipment that is appropriate. This knowledge is especially important because of the competitive nature of the foodservice equipment industry. Manufacturer's representatives are rewarded for selling their lines against the competition. Similarly, equipment dealers receive rebates for selling favored lines in quantity. These incentives can lead manufacturer's reps and dealers to push a favored product over a competitor's that may, in fact, be better for the application—especially when the product is less expensive. On the other hand, it also is true that many equipment manufacturers strive to bring products to market that genuinely offer higher quality at a lower price through new or improved technology.

How can the owner evaluate the relative merits of competitive brands of equipment? One important source of information is to talk to other people with similar operations regarding their experience with specific items. A second source of information is the foodservice facility design consultant, because of his or her experience specifying equipment and inspecting its operation when it has been installed. A third source of information is industry trade shows, such as the National Restaurant Association show, where the features of competing equipment can be evaluated virtually side by side.

Although the initial purchase price is relevant to equipment selection, it is only one factor in the equation. The most important initial consideration for any piece of equipment is not how much it costs but how well it fulfills the needs of the operation.

Installation Cost   For many foodservice equipment items, the installation cost is a minor factor. A replacement slicer, for example, simply needs to be removed from the box, set in place, cleaned and sanitized, and plugged into the wall.

Other equipment items can incur extraordinary installation costs. Consider the following examples:

❏ Adding a charbroiler could require expensive modifications to a ventilation system or even a new hood.

❏ Adding a steam-jacketed kettle could require cutting into the floor to install a trench drain.

❏ Adding a steamer with an electric steam generator could require additional power circuits.

❏ Replacing a hood could require additional ductwork running from the kitchen to the roof. If the kitchen is on a lower floor of the building and a new chase needs to be built running through each floor, the expense could be substantial.

In addition, large equipment (dish machines, hoods, serving counters, conveyors) could prove very expensive to install due to limited access—narrow doorways, small elevators, and so on.

The total investment required in new or replacement equipment includes both the purchase price and the cost of installation. Identifying the costs of installation prior to purchasing the equipment will prevent expensive surprises.

Direct Operating Costs

Direct operating costs include the expenses associated with utilities, such as gas, electricity, steam, and water. Methods for evaluating relative utility costs are discussed in detail in Chapter 8. Here it is important to note that gas-fired equipment, such as kettles, steamers, or tilting skillets, often is more expensive to purchase than its electric-powered counterparts. However, depending on the relative costs of electricity versus gas in any given area, the higher initial investment could be returned through lower direct operating costs. Dish machines represent another important example because of their use of hot water.

The direct operating costs of equipment can be estimated using information provided by manufacturers' catalog sheets, as well as local costs of electricity, gas, steam, and/or water.

Maintenance and Repair

The total cost of ownership of equipment also includes expenses associated with maintenance and repair. Maintenance requirements often can be determined by reading the operator's manual—for major equipment items, the owner should request copies of the maintenance sections of these manuals prior to making a final purchase decision. It is important to note whether the required maintenance can be done in-house or requires a service call from a service agency. In-house maintenance has a labor cost that should be estimated; similarly, the cost of a service call from an outside agency should be determined. Also important are the frequency and complexity of the maintenance required. A steamer with an enclosed, gas-fired steam boiler may seem to need relatively infrequent maintenance, but when it is time for it to be serviced, the boiler may need to be removed and partially disassembled. On the other hand, an electric steamer might need frequent maintenance, but all that is needed is to pour a de-liming solution into the tank and run the unit through a cycle. Of course, the cost of the de-liming solution for the electric steamer needs to be added to the estimated maintenance costs.

Repair costs are more difficult to estimate, simply because equipment breakdowns are difficult to predict with any degree of accuracy. However, for major equipment items, the owner can contact a service agency to ask for typical repair prices and relative repair frequencies for the equipment being considered.

Labor Costs of Operation

When replacing old equipment with new pieces, labor costs of operation generally are not an important factor in the total cost of ownership if the replacement is functionally identical to the original. Often, however, new equipment is purchased that is substantially different in terms of how it functions. For example, replacing a manual slicer with an automatic slicer potentially has an impact on labor costs. Similarly, replacing a standard pot sink with one that circulates water in the soak compartment will reduce the time employees need to spend washing pots. In these examples, the labor savings actually reduce the total cost of ownership.

The Useful Life of Equipment

How long will a piece of equipment last? When should an old piece of equipment be taken out in favor of a new piece? The answer to these questions depends mostly on the amount of maintenance given to the equipment and how heavily the equipment was used in the food operation. A steam-jacketed kettle that is well cared for and that does not have deep dents or scratches should last twenty-five years or more. The valves and piping to the kettle may need replacement before the useful life of this piece of equipment is over. On the other hand, a poorly maintained convection oven that is used continuously during the day for baking, roasting, and grilling might have a useful life of only five years. Figure 6-1 shows estimated useful lives of major pieces of equipment.

What Figure 6-1 does not show are differences in the useful life of equipment based on the quality and durability offered by competing manufacturers. Recall the example of deciding whether to purchase an oven for $5,200 or $6,500. If the less expensive oven lasts five years under heavy use but the more expensive oven lasts eight years, then the higher initial purchase price is justified (all other factors being equal). Hard data regarding the useful life of competing manufacturers' equipment are difficult to obtain. As suggested above, owners considering the purchase of major equipment items are well advised to check with operators in similar facilities and to contact a foodservice facilities design consultant..

The total cost of ownership of an equipment item thus is the sum of the purchase price, installation costs, direct operating costs, and labor costs or savings, divided by the useful lifetime of the equipment.*

---

* Our computation of total cost of ownership is a simplification. For large equipment purchases, the cost of capital and the time value of money should be taken into account. However, a treatment of capital budgeting goes beyond the scope of this text.

Item	Useful Life (Years)
Convection ovens	8–10
Deck ovens	10–15
Rotary ovens	12–20
Mixers	15–25
Ranges	10–15
Steam-jacketed kettles	15–25
Food choppers	10–15
Vertical cutter-mixers	12–15
Tilting skillets	12–20
Grills	8–12
Fryers	8–12
Broilers	8–12
Steamers—high and medium pressure	10–15
Steamers—convection	8–12
Walk-in refrigerators/freezers	12–20
Reach-in refrigerators/freezers	8–12
Coffee urns	8–12
Dish machines	10–15
Stainless–steel worktables, sinks	25–40
Shelving—stainless steel	25–40
Shelving—galvanized wire	8–12
Ice machines	5–8
Hoods/ventilation systems	10–15

Note: These estimates assume the following: (1) two to three meals per day, (2) ongoing maintenance, and (3) typical industry conditions.

Figure 6-1. Estimated useful life of foodservice equipment.

FOODSERVICE EQUIPMENT STANDARDS AND SPECIFICATIONS

Foodservice equipment is manufactured or fabricated according to industry standards governing safety. Appropriate standards are determined by organizations, such as the National Sanitation Foundation (NSF), Underwriters Laboratories (UL), the American Gas Association (AGA), and the American Society of Mechanical Engineers (ASME). In addition, governmental agencies formulate standards that affect the construction and installation of foodservice equipment. The standards and approval processes of the National Sanitation Foundation are particularly relevant because they address food safety and sanitation.

NSF Standards and Seal   The NSF seal of approval is a recognized standard of acceptance for many pieces of equipment. This seal assures the buyer that the equipment meets certain construction standards of sanitation and safety. NSF is an independent, nonprofit organization dedicated to the improvement of public health. Equipment manufacturers can write to the NSF testing laboratory to describe the equipment that is being developed and can learn whether it will meet NSF standards of construction. The manufacturer pays a fee to NSF to arrange for a representative to visit the manufacturing plant to inspect and test the equipment. (In some cases the equipment is shipped to the NSF testing laboratories for inspection.) If the equipment passes the inspection and tests, the manufacturer is given permission to display the NSF seal of approval. The continued use of the NSF seal requires ongoing communication between the manufacturer and NSF to ensure that changes in the equipment continue to meet the organization's standards.

NSF carries on a variety of activities in pursuit of its objectives. including:

❏ Providing liaison services to strengthen communications between industry, the public health professions, and the general public

❏ Conducting basic research and establishing standards on health-related equipment, processes, products, and services

❏ Disseminating research results to educate industry, regulatory agencies, and the general public regarding health hazards and means of eliminating them

❏ Issuing official NSF seals for display on equipment and products tested and found to meet NSF standards

The NSF seal of approval and the food facilities design consultant's specifications containing the statement "Equipment must be constructed to NSF standards" imply two different things. In the instance where the specifications state that the equipment must bear the NSF seal of approval, it is assumed that only those pieces of manufactured equipment that have been inspected and approved by NSF may bear this seal. For fabricated equipment, the consultant and fabricator follow the NSF handbooks containing the construction methods and standards that have been approved by NSF. In this case, the equipment will not bear the NSF seal but will be constructed in compliance with NSF standards.

Equipment Specification   Recall, from Chapter 2, that the role of equipment specifications in the overall design process is to ensure that the products have exactly the features required by the owner and are installed in complete accordance with governmental requirements and industry standards. The standards for the specification of equipment are derived from four primary sources:

❏ NSF, UL, ASME, AGA, and regulatory agencies such as health departments

❏ The standards of the manufacturers

❏ The functional capabilities and features desired by the buyer

❏ Industry standards, as reflected in the language of the consultant's specifications

Equipment specifications fall broadly into two categories: manufactured equipment, as selected from manufacturers' catalogs, and fabricated equipment, which is custom-built to meet the requirements of the project.

The specifications for equipment that is selected from a catalog are less complex than for fabricated equipment. The specifier—be it the owner or a foodservice design consultant—examines the catalogs of all the major manufacturers of the type of equipment desired, and, based on the functional needs of the operation, makes an equipment choice (many other factors, as discussed in the previous section, are also involved in the selection process). The specification is then carefully written to include all of the required features and characteristics yet remains sufficiently general to allow bids from several competing manufacturers. The specification of characteristics and features depends upon the kind of equipment being selected but often includes the following:

❑ The dimensions of the unit

❑ The quantity of units to be purchased

❑ The specific utility requirements of the equipment item

❑ The materials used in the construction of the equipment

❑ The specific construction techniques employed

❑ Any relevant performance criteria

❑ The desired features, accessories, and/or options

❑ The relevant industry, association, or governmental standards

Often the specifier also names a manufacturer and model number. The purpose of doing so is not to exclude other manufacturers with competitive products but to set a reference standard whereby other products can be judged. Also, naming a specific manufacturer and model typically is necessary to establish the utility requirements needed for the proper engineering of the project. If a bidder prefers to provide a competitor's product, he or she must demonstrate that it is equal to or better than the reference standard, and assume any cost involved in providing different utility services.

Chapter 7 discusses the major types of manufactured foodservice equipment.

MANUFACTURED EQUIPMENT

The buyer must write a complete and comprehensive specification for a piece of equipment that will be fabricated. Fabricated equipment, such as a soiled-dish table, must be described in complete detail so that the kitchen equipment contractor and the fabrication shop will know exactly how to build it. To assist the dealer and fabricator in understanding the appearance and general construction quality of the equipment, the food facilities consultant will prepare plan and elevation drawings. These drawings may also include detailed sections of the equipment so that the quality of the equipment and the way that it is constructed will be clearly understood. The fabrication shop will read the specification very carefully and prepare shop drawings, in large scale, showing all of the details of construction. The owner and/or foodservice design consultant will have an opportunity to approve the shop drawings before the equipment is actually built.

FABRICATED EQUIPMENT

EQUIPMENT CONSTRUCTION MATERIALS

The most common materials for constructing a piece of foodservice equipment are:

❑ Stainless steel
❑ Aluminum
❑ Galvanized iron
❑ Plastic
❑ Wood

Stainless Steel   Specifications for stainless steel in foodservice facilities are usually type 302 or 304, with a U.S. Standard 18.8 composition (18 percent chromium and 8 percent nickel). The stainless steel is polished to a number 4 finish, and the thickness is specified by gauge. The gauge (or thickness) has a great impact on cost, and the specifier should use the minimum thickness needed for each part of the equipment. Figure 6-2 indicates typical applications for various gauges of stainless steel.

Stainless steel is usually shaped under pressure at a fabrication shop and then welded and polished. The weld should be of the same metal as the material being welded; usually spot welding, soldering, or bolting is not acceptable. If equipment pieces are to be attached to each other, bolting is acceptable, and the pieces should be tight enough to form a hairline seam. The seam should be sealed with silicone to prevent grease or moisture from flowing into the crack.

Galvanized Iron   Galvanized iron and other types of galvanized sheet metal are frequently used in foodservice equipment construction. The obvious advantage of this material is that it has a significantly lower cost than stainless steel. A typical use of galvanized iron is a structure or underbracing for equipment; for example, iron is welded to the underside of stainless-steel tables and cafeteria lines.

Gauge	Typical Use
8 and 10	Support elements for heavy equipment or at stress points
12	Heavily used tabletops, pot sinks, or other surfaces that will receive a great amount of wear
14	Tabletops, sinks, overshelves, and brackets that will receive frequent use or that will carry heavy weights
16	Equipment tops and sides that are small and that will carry little weight; shelves under equipment and heavily used side panels
18	Side panels that are not exposed to wear, equipment doors, hoods, and partitions
20	Covers for supported or insulated panels, such as refrigerators or insulated doors

Figure 6-2. Stainless-steel applications by gauge (thickness).

Galvanized sheet metal is used for the construction of sinks, tables, and interior shelves in food facilities that have limited funds for kitchen equipment. Galvanized iron piping rather than stainless steel is frequently used for legs as an economy measure. Again, the advantage is lower cost, but the disadvantage is that a painted surface chips in a short period of time, and the legs and undershelving are difficult to clean and are not attractive.

Plastics

Thermoplastic cutting boards and tops have been approved by NSF because they do not warp or crack. Traditional maple cutting boards crack and separate in a short period of time, and the cracks harbor bacteria and soil. Thermoplastic tops and cutting boards should be used where cutting, chopping, or carving will occur. Typically, sandwich and salad makeup tables and occasionally the entire top surface of a worktable will be covered with this plastic material.

Plastic is now being used for the construction of carts and enclosed cabinets because of its strength, light weight, and ease of cleaning. Fiberglass, laminate tops, and cutting boards have also been used in place of wooden cutting surfaces.

Plastic laminates, which have been used for many years for dining room tables, are also frequently used to cover vertical and horizontal surfaces in foodservice equipment, particularly in serving areas. Cafeteria counters, server stations, snack bars, condiment stands, dish enclosures, and some worktables are all pieces of equipment that often are covered with plastic laminates. In addition to the cost advantage over stainless steel, the use of plastic laminates permits inexpensive changes to be made to the equipment. However, plastic laminates have a relatively thin wear surface that can easily become scratched and damaged through everyday use. Exposed corners and edges on serving counters are especially vulnerable because of frequent contact. "Solid surface" materials (such as Corian™) are a more durable alternative to plastic laminate for many high-wear surfaces.

Wood

Hard rock maple and pecan cutting tops are frequently used for dining room tables and bakery production tables in food operations. Many bakers prefer the maple top because the surface is easy to clean and dough and flour do not stick to it. Separation of the wooden top does not normally occur in a bakery because the fats from the dough keep the wood from being saturated with water. A well-cared-for maple table or countertop in a bakery should last for many years.

Wood finishes in service areas and on cafeteria counters are used primarily for decorative purposes. Wood may not be used in places where it can come into direct contact with food, but it is appropriate for cafeteria slides, decorative sneeze guards, edging for display shelves, and enclosures for dining room server stations.

Other Materials Used in Equipment Construction

Many different types of materials are used to build foodservice equipment. No list of materials can be considered complete, because imaginative designers are continually developing and experimenting with new surfaces and textures. The surfaces that need the most careful scrutiny, if they are to be built to NSF standards, are those that come in contact with the food or the food handler. These surfaces should be smooth and nonporous and should resist chipping and wear under frequent use. They should also be resistant to the corrosive effect of salt, food acids, and oils. Some alternative materials used in construction include:

- ❏ Glass
- ❏ Solid-surface materials, such as Corian
- ❏ Ceramic tile
- ❏ Stone, such as granite
- ❏ Rubber
- ❏ Copper
- ❏ Brass
- ❏ Cast iron

FOODSERVICE EQUIPMENT SPECIFICATIONS: AN OUTLINE

Following the standards of the design and construction process, foodservice equipment specifications for a new or renovated foodservice facility are contained in Section 11400 of the project manual. Equipment specifications follow a generally accepted outline. The three major divisions of Section 11400 are General, Products, and Execution.

Part 1—The General section of the foodservice equipment specifications typically includes the following provisions:

- ❏ Refers the bidder to other parts of the contract documents that are necessary for understanding all of the project requirements.
- ❏ Describes the specific responsibilities of the foodservice equipment contractor, as well as the electricians, plumbers, and other tradespeople, in connecting the equipment.
- ❏ Indicates who will provide the hardware necessary for plumbing connections—the plumber or the foodservice equipment contractor.
- ❏ Discusses how the foodservice equipment contractor is to deal with removal, storage, repair, and reinstallation of existing equipment that is to be used in the new or renovated facility.
- ❏ Establishes the requirements for submittals, such as shop drawings, catalog sheets, and samples, to be provided by the foodservice equipment contractor for review and approval.
- ❏ Instructs the foodservice equipment contractor how to handle deviations from the requirements of the contract documents. Such changes occur as a result of many factors. For example, a manufacturer might change the utility requirements for a piece of equipment. Such changes must be "conspicuously noted" in correspondence so that all members of the project team are aware of the new requirements.
- ❏ Sets standards designed to ensure a quality installation. Such standards are necessary to ensure that the bidder has the financial

resources, physical capabilities, and workforce necessary to complete a major equipment installation.

❏ Sets standards for the manufacture and installation of the foodservice equipment. A "reference standard" essentially means that by referring to the standard in the specifications, that standard becomes a part of the project requirements—just as if the entire text of the standard were typed into the project manual. Standards address sanitary construction techniques, approved electrical components and construction, fire protection, safe steam boiler construction, quality standards for architectural millwork, and installation that conforms to health department regulations.

❏ Provides information to the foodservice equipment contractor regarding storage, delivery, and handling of the foodservice equipment. These contract provisions are necessary to prevent complications during the installation of the equipment.

❏ Requires the foodservice equipment contractor to check that the utility services are appropriate before actually installing the equipment.

Part 2—The Products section of the foodservice equipment specifications typically includes the following provisions:

❏ Sets standards for the composition and quality of the stainless steel used in manufactured and fabricated equipment.

❏ Sets standards for other raw materials used in the construction of foodservice equipment.

❏ Describes the requirements for the components to be used in the foodservice equipment, including plumbing (faucets, drains) and electrical components (junction boxes, receptacles).

❏ Sets standards for workmanship in stainless-steel fabrication, such as how joints are to be made and the quality of the arc-welding.

❏ Sets standards for the fabrication and installation of stainless-steel sinks, drainboards, utensil drawers, work surfaces (table tops), legs, shelving, and other fabricated items.

❏ Sets standards for architectural millwork, including the grade and type of materials and specific construction techniques.

❏ Provides a brief description of each item of foodservice equipment to be provided.

Part 3—The Execution section of the foodservice equipment specifications typically includes the following provisions:

❏ Requires the foodservice equipment contractor to verify that the utility rough-in connections provided by the electricians and plumbers are located where required for the equipment.

❏ Requires the contractor to "field-measure" to determine that dimensions are as required for the equipment installation.

❏ Provides specific instructions for the installation of walk-in coolers and freezers.

❏ Describes how field joints in equipment are to be made. This is done because proper field joints enhance the quality and sanitation of the installation, whereas poor joints collect dirt and food waste, promote the growth of dangerous bacteria, and offer passageways for insects.

❏ Establishes the requirements and describes the procedures for ensuring the quality of the installation of the equipment in the field, including inspection—and rejection if necessary—of the work of the foodservice equipment contractor.

❏ Requires the foodservice equipment contractor to set up and test each item of equipment, adjust it as necessary, and replace equipment that is not functioning to specifications.

❏ Requires the foodservice equipment contractor to clean and sanitize the equipment prior to turning it over to the owner.

❏ Requires the foodservice equipment contractor to demonstrate the use of the equipment and clearly instruct the owner in proper maintenance procedures.

❏ Sets the requirements for product guarantees and warranties.

SUMMARY

This chapter discussed how foodservice equipment should be selected on the basis of many factors, including the overall cost of ownership. The total cost of ownership is a function of several factors, including the initial purchase price, the cost of installing the equipment, the direct cost of operation, the cost of maintenance and repair, the cost of the labor required to operate the equipment, and the useful life of the equipment.

It also introduced the importance of standards for the construction of foodservice equipment, especially with respect to sanitation. The function of the National Sanitation Foundation in promoting safe equipment construction materials and methods was described. The differences between manufactured and fabricated foodservice equipment were pointed out, and the primary materials used in the construction of foodservice equipment were identified. Finally, the chapter outlined the contents of a typical set of foodservice equipment specifications.

CHAPTER 7

FOODSERVICE EQUIPMENT, PART II: MANUFACTURED EQUIPMENT

THIS CHAPTER

☑ Introduces the major kinds of manufactured foodservice equipment, discussed below under six functional categories:
- ◆ Receiving and storage
- ◆ Pre-preparation
- ◆ Final preparation
- ◆ Service
- ◆ Warewashing
- ◆ Waste removal

☑ Each section of this chapter describes the characteristics of the equipment as well as its primary use in a foodservice operation.

RECEIVING AND STORAGE EQUIPMENT

Many foodservice operations use utility carts to transport foods from receiving to storage areas. Because utility carts are made of relatively light-gauge materials, using them to transport heavy cases of food causes the top shelf to bow and buckle. As a result, the utility cart loses its utility. A receiving cart made of heavy-gauge materials and designed to support heavy items is a good investment in a foodservice operation.

Receiving Carts

Shelving systems can be purchased to solve almost any food storage problem and to fit almost all types of spaces. (Figure 7-1 shows typical foodservice storage shelving.) The efficiency of a storage space is influenced by the efficiency of the storage shelves used in the space. The wooden

Shelving: Freestanding and Portable

151

homemade shelves that are often used in dry storerooms are difficult to clean and are not allowed by many health departments in the United States. The cost of heavy-duty (14- or 16-gauge) stainless-steel shelves with wheels is very high, but the great durability of the equipment, its ease of cleaning, and its portability may offset the initial investment.

Varieties of shelving include:

- ❑ Portable (on casters), freestanding (on posts), or wall-hung (cantilever)
- ❑ Multiple tiers (shelves), usually four or five for bulk storage
- ❑ Solid shelves with embossed, louvered, or flat shelf surfaces
- ❑ Shelves with removable plastic grids that can be cleaned in a dish machine
- ❑ Solid shelves constructed of stainless steel, galvanized steel, aluminum, high-impact plastic, or other materials
- ❑ Wire shelves constructed of stainless steel, galvanized steel, high-impact plastic, chrome-plated or epoxy-coated

The accessories that can be added are almost limitless, but the most common ones are:

- ❑ Casters
- ❑ Stainless-steel posts (uprights)
- ❑ Rotating bumpers on the uprights
- ❑ Strip or wraparound bumpers
- ❑ Extra bracing for heavy products
- ❑ Wall-mounting clamps
- ❑ Wire enclosures (for security)
- ❑ Drawers and baskets
- ❑ Labeling clip-ons

Dunnage racks are single-tier shelves designed to support stacks of heavy products, such as cases of canned goods, approximately 10 inches (250 millimeters) above the floor. They are frequently used in dry-storage and frozen-storage areas in large foodservice operations.

The sizes of shelving that are most often used in foodservice are as follows:

Width: 12 inches (305 millimeters), 18 inches (460 millimeters), 21 inches (535 millimeters), 24 inches (610 millimeters), and 27 inches (685 millimeters) are the most common widths for use in dry storerooms, for use in walk-in refrigerators and freezers, and for general kitchen utensil storage.

Length: 36 inches (915 millimeters), 42 inches (1,070 millimeters), 48 inches (1,220 millimeters), 54 inches (1,370 millimeters), and 60 inches (1,520 millimeters) are the most popular sizes. These lengths should not be exceeded because of the loss of strength and rigidity beyond the 60-inch (1,520-millimeter) length.

Height: The posts (uprights) can be purchased in many different heights. The most common are 36 inches (915 millimeters), 42

Figure 7-1. Shelving units. (Courtesy of InterMetro Industries.)

inches (1,070 millimeters), 72 inches (1,830 millimeters), 78 inches (1,980 millimeters), and 84 inches (2,135 millimeters).

General guidelines for shelving selection are as follows:

❏ *Walk-in refrigerators.* The 27-inch (685-millimeter) shelf with the maximum height possible is a good selection to maximize storage capacity. Narrow walk-in refrigeration (less than 7 feet 6 inches [2.3 meters] in width) will require narrow shelving.

❏ *Walk-in freezers.* Frozen foods are often shipped in boxes that are easily stacked. A combination of dunnage racks for case goods that can be stacked and four-shelf portable shelving units for odd-shaped items or small packages would be a good choice.

❏ *Dry storage.* Four- or five-shelf portable shelving units work well for spices, broken cases, or individual number 10 cans. For many larger foodservice facilities, the use of wooden pallets that are moved by forklift trucks may be appropriate, in combination with the standard shelving.

There are three kinds of attached shelving typically found in a foodservice facility: elevated shelving, undertable shelving, and cabinet shelving.

Elevated shelving is attached either to a wall above the equipment or directly to the piece of equipment by stainless-steel tubular uprights. Wall-mounted shelving is preferable because of the elimination of the uprights from the table surface of the equipment. For equipment that is placed away from the wall, however, the elevated shelving must be mounted onto the table or ceiling hung. The most sanitary means for accomplishing this is to mount the uprights into the backsplash of the table.

Undertable shelving consists of shelves located below the working surface of tables. This form of shelving is typically constructed of a sheet of 16-gauge stainless steel and is supported by the cross-members connecting the table legs. Pots, pans, bowls, and trays, as well as mixer attachments and small appliances, are often stored on undertable shelving where they can easily be reached by employees working at the table. However, solid shelving often accumulates dust, dirt, food scraps, and other unsanitary material. An alternative to solid shelving that accomplishes the same objective is to create a surface composed of 1–1¼-inch-diameter stainless-steel tubing running lengthwise on 4–6 inches under the table. The tubing supports larger pots, pans, and sheet trays, but dirt and food scraps fall between the tubes and are mopped from the floor.

Cabinet shelving refers to shelves within closed cabinets. Closed cabinets are often used for the storage of cleaning supplies and other items that require controlled access.

Shelving: Attached to Equipment

The refrigeration equipment found in the modern foodservice facility may include the following:

❏ Reach-in refrigerators and freezers

❏ Walk-in refrigerators and freezers

❏ Undercounter refrigerators and freezers

Refrigeration (Coolers and Freezers, Walk-in and Reach-in)

❏ Roll-in refrigerators and freezers
❏ Pass-through refrigerators and freezers
❏ Refrigerated cold pans
❏ Soft-serve machines and ice cream cabinets
❏ Display refrigerators, such as deli counters, refrigerated grocery display cases, and other merchandising devices
❏ Blast chillers and blast freezers
❏ Ice machines

The special features available for the many different types of refrigeration equipment are too varied to cover in this volume. This information can be found in any of the excellent reference books on foodservice equipment and refrigeration that are available. The most commonly used refrigeration systems are walk-in refrigerators and freezers and reach-in refrigerators and freezers. In recent years, blast chillers have become popular. Each is discussed below.

WALK-IN REFRIGERATORS AND FREEZERS

Currently, the two primary types of walk-in refrigerators and freezers are prefabricated and built-in. The prefabricated walk-in is usually constructed from a series of 4-inch (10-centimeter)-thick modular panels. Each panel is made with urethane insulation material that is foamed into place between two sheets of metal. The kinds of metal that can be specified for prefabricated walk-ins include:

❏ Galvanized steel
❏ Painted galvanized steel
❏ Aluminum (embossed or plain)
❏ Painted aluminum
❏ 18-, 20-, or 22-gauge stainless steel

Walk-ins are often specified with several different finishes, such as white painted aluminum for the interior walls and ceiling, stainless steel on the exposed exterior walls, galvanized steel on the unexposed interior walls, and galvanized steel on the interior floor so that quarry tile will be installed over it.

These panels are attached to each other (with a variety of latches and bolts) to form the outer walls, ceiling, partitions, and floor (optional) of the refrigerator. They can be purchased in many combinations of heights, lengths, and widths. A walk-in cooler is illustrated in Figure 7-2.

The specification of a prefabricated walk-in using the manufacturer's standard modular panels produces a refrigerator that is "nominal" in size. Each manufacturer determines the nominal widths, lengths, and heights of standard panels. A manufacturer's walk-in that is described as 8 feet by 12 feet (2.44 meters by 3.66 meters) may actually be 7 feet 6 inches by 11 feet 4 inches (2.32 meters by 3.45 meters) when built using standard panels of nominal size. Custom or full-size walk-in refrigerators are available and can be purchased, at an additional cost, in almost any size. The primary difference between nominal-size and full-size walk-ins is cost. Nominal-size units, because they use standard panels, are less expensive to manufacture than units requiring custom sizing of the panels. Knowing the difference

Figure 7-2. Walk-in refrigeration. (Courtesy of THERMO-KOOL/Mid-South Industries, Inc.)

between standard (nominal) and full-size walk-ins is critical when specifying these units.

Prefabricated walk-ins can be installed indoors using a number of different flooring systems, each with advantages and disadvantages:

❑ *Manufacturer's floor recessed into a pit*. A pit about 4 inches (100 millimeters) deep and slightly longer and wider than the walk-in is built into the concrete subfloor of the building. The walk-in's floor panels are set into the pit. Then quarry tile (or a similar flooring system) is run continuously from the kitchen into the walk-in. The primary advantage of this approach is that carts and racks can be taken in and out of the walk-in across a level surface. This approach is ideal in new construction where the concrete subfloor can be poured with a pit at little additional expense. The disadvantage of this approach is that it may be impractical in a renovation, where cutting a pit in the existing floor is prohibitively expensive.

❑ *Manufacturer's floor with ramps*. A ramp into the walk-in is necessary where the floor cannot be recessed. Ramps can be built either in the interior or the exterior of the walk-in. Interior ramps are furnished by the walk-in manufacturer. Exterior ramps often are built by the contractors who pour the floor and lay the tile. The disadvantage of this approach is that ramps can be steep enough to cause spillage as food items are carted up and down.

❑ *Installations without manufacturer's floor panels*. Prefabricated walk-ins can be installed without the manufacturer's floor panels. In this approach the walls are anchored to the building floor on screeds that seal and support the structure. This approach provides a level passage from the kitchen into the walk-in. However, this approach requires insulating the floor under freezers to prevent the concrete from cracking due to temperature differences.

For many years, the working surfaces of walk-in coolers were made of galvanized steel. Despite the galvanizing treatment, steel floors proved to be vulnerable to pitting and rusting due to the moist conditions in coolers. The floors often wore out long before the rest of the unit, creating unsanitary conditions. The National Sanitation Foundation now requires walk-in floors to meet substantially tougher standards for endurance. Stainless steel is an acceptable flooring material, as is aluminum tread plate provided that it is fully coved and integrated into the floor system. Galvanized steel can still be used in a walk-in cooler, but only if it is covered with another material that is acceptable as a working surface. Quarry tile is one such material.

A built-in refrigerator or freezer, which is more expensive than a prefab, is constructed of insulating foam walls, floors, and ceiling that are protected with structural glazed tile walls, quarry tile floors, and aluminum or stainless-steel ceilings. Large built-in refrigerators may also be constructed of fiberglass panels laid over the insulation. The built-in refrigerator has the advantage of lasting many years under conditions of heavy use but the disadvantage of being more expensive and more difficult to enlarge or move.

Walk-in refrigerators and freezers are usually specified with either self-contained (top- or side-mounted) or remote refrigeration systems. The self-contained units are usually hidden on top of the walk-ins by closure panels, but sufficient air space must be available to prevent the air-cooling units from building up heat in the space above the walk-in. If the large air mass in the space above the false ceiling is insufficient for removing the heat of the compressor, additional ventilation will be necessary. Remote refrigeration systems can be located some distance away, either inside or outside the building, but the farther the distance, the greater the heat (efficiency) loss. Remote refrigeration has the advantage of keeping noise and heat away from the food production area. Refrigeration systems can be either air-cooled or water-cooled, depending on environmental conditions and utility availability. Heat recovery equipment is an important accessory to refrigeration systems because of high energy costs and can be effective for preheating water or heating space in the building. Pre-engineered refrigeration systems with multiple compressors are often specified for large food operations, providing greater energy efficiency and longer compressor life.

Common accessories and features that may be added to the walk-in specifications are:

❑ Outdoor, protected refrigeration systems
❑ Freezer alarm system that activates when the temperature reaches 15°F (–9.4°C)
❑ Extra interior vaporproof lights
❑ Roof caps for walk-ins located outdoors
❑ Wall protectors to prevent damage from carts (interior or exterior)

❏ Ramps for walk-ins not level with the floor

❏ Locks for doors

❏ Windows for doors

❏ Closure panels and trim strips for improving the outside appearance

❏ Thermoplastic strip curtains to reduce loss of cold air when door is open

❏ Foot treadle openers for doors

❏ Air vent to relieve pressure when doors are opened or closed

❏ Glass access doors for placing foods in the walk-in without the necessity of walking in

REACH-IN REFRIGERATORS AND FREEZERS

The word *refrigeration* refers to mechanically cooled refrigerators and freezers, and *refrigerator* means a refrigeration unit that maintains a temperature of 36°F (2.2°C) to 40°F (4.4°C). The most frequently used refrigerators in all types and sizes of food facilities are the reach-ins. The versatility, reasonable cost, and storage efficiency explain why this kind of refrigeration is popular. Figure 7-3 illustrates a reach-in refrigerator.

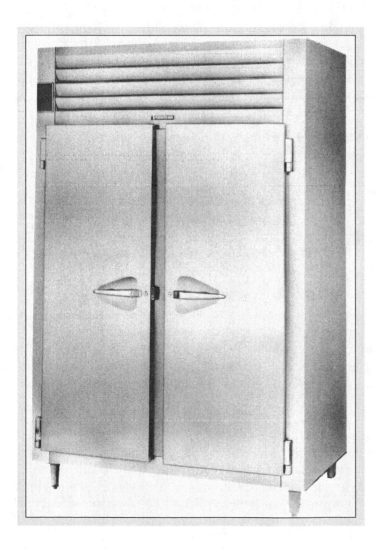

Figure 7-3. Reach-in refrigerator.
(Courtesy of Traulsen and Co., Inc.)

Reach-in refrigerators can be purchased with one, two, or three compartments and are available with many different options and accessories. In selecting this type of equipment, the questions to consider are the following:

- ❏ Will space and budget permit the installation of one, two, or three compartments?
- ❏ Will the refrigerator be used for general storage or for special products that would fit better on interior tray slides?
- ❏ Should the refrigerator be adapted for roll-in carts, which eliminate all interior shelving?
- ❏ What capacities of storage are needed for reach-in refrigerators and freezers in the food production area?
- ❏ Is this refrigeration the primary cold storage capacity for the food facility, or is the refrigeration being used to augment walk-in refrigerators and freezers?
- ❏ What special features would the owner like to have specified for this refrigeration?

Typical specifications might include:

- ❏ Automatic condensate evaporator, which eliminates the need for a floor drain
- ❏ Adjustable shelving or tray slides to accommodate trays that are standard in the foodservice industry, such as 18-by-26-inch sheet pans, 12-by-20-inch steam table pans, or 530-by-325 millimeter gastronorm pans.
- ❏ Cam lift on spring-loaded hinges that cause the doors to close automatically
- ❏ Stainless-steel interior and exterior, or a combination of anodized aluminum and stainless steel, or all anodized aluminum
- ❏ Exterior thermometer
- ❏ Interior lighting
- ❏ Full-size door or half doors
- ❏ Doors with glass windows
- ❏ Pass-through (doors on both sides)

In summary, there are many options available to the food facilities planner in choosing refrigeration for a food operation. An excellent source of information is an equipment catalog from one of the leading refrigeration manufacturers. These can be seen in the offices of the food facilities consultant or at a dealer's showroom or can be obtained directly from the manufacturer.

Primary Use in the Food Operation   Reach-in and walk-in refrigeration must be provided within easy access of the primary food production areas. Many restaurants, hotel dining facilities, and institutions use a combination of walk-ins and reach-in refrigerators. Walk-ins are usually used to store bulk foods, while reach-ins provide convenient cold storage near the production area.

Size of Food Facility (Seats)	Walk-In Refrigeration*				Reach-in Refrigeration†			
	Freezer		Refrigerator		Freezer		Refrigerator	
	Number	Size	Number	Size	Number	Size	Number	Size
Under 50	0	—	0	—	1	B	2	B
50–100	1	X	1	X	1	C	3	B
100–175	1	Y	2	X	2	B	3	C
175–250	1	Z	2	Y	2	B	3	C
250–500	1	Z	3	Y	2	C	4	C
500–750	2	Y	3	Z	2	C	5	C
More than 750	2	Z	4	Z	3	C	5	C

* Walk-in size key:

X: 9 by 12 feet (2.74 by 3.66 meters)

Y: 9 by 15 feet (2.74 by 4.57 meters)

Z: 9 by 20 feet (2.74 by 6.10 meters)

† Reach-in size key:

A: one-compartment

B: two-compartment

C: three-compartment

Figure 7-4. Refrigeration requirements based on facility size. (Courtesy of Sandra Ley, Foodservice Refrigeration *[New York: Van Nostrand Reinhold, 1980].)*

Determining Capacity and Size   The method of calculating the capacity of walk-in refrigeration is included in Chapter 4. Reach-in refrigeration capacities are usually listed as net capacity in cubic feet (or cubic meters). This designation should mean that the available interior space for storage is the net cubic footage. However, in many instances, the interior space is not totally available for storage because of evaporators, lights, tray slides, and so on, and the net cubic footage may be somewhat less. Typical interior capacities are:

    One compartment: 21.5 cubic feet (.6 cubic meters)

    Two compartments: 46.5 cubic feet (1.3 cubic meters)

    Three compartments: 70.0 cubic feet (2 cubic meters)

    One interesting variation on refrigeration is the "refrigerator" that heats rather than cools. These heated cabinet units are used to hold hot foods and are an excellent application in food operations that need a large holding capacity.

    The chart of capacities shown in Figure 7-4 may be useful in estimating the needed refrigeration.

Energy Usage and Utility Requirements   The efficiency of the refrigeration equipment will be determined in part by:

❏ The amount of insulation

❏ The number of doors and the frequency of opening

❏ The efficiency of the airflow within the cavity

❏ The distance between the compressor and the evaporator

❏ The level of humidity in the room

❏ The cleanliness of the compressor (if it is air-cooled)

❏ The temperature of the incoming water to the compressor (if it is water-cooled)

❏ Refrigerant level in the refrigeration system and type of refrigerant

❏ The condition and method of sealing the doors

The refrigeration system is usually rated by the horsepower of the motor and BTU (British thermal units per hour). Most reach-in refrigeration is connected to a 110-volt, 60-cycle, 1-phase power source. Walk-in refrigeration systems are also rated by horsepower and BTU, and may be connected to a 110-volt, 208-volt, 240-volt, or 460/480-volt power source.

Because the refrigeration equipment in a foodservice facility will be operating twenty-four hours a day, it is wise to do everything possible to reduce the loss of energy through the purchase of the best equipment possible. Refrigeration is not the place to cut corners or to omit energy-saving accessories. Heat recovery from water-cooled refrigeration systems is easy to engineer and will bring a quick return on the investment. Also, medium-size and larger operations are likely to benefit from installing a central refrigeration system that supplies walk-ins, reach-ins, display units, salad bars, ice machines, and all of the other refrigerated systems in the facility.

BLAST CHILLERS The blast chiller was developed to meet the challenge of food safety and to reduce the risk of food-borne illness. It certainly is not unusual for steam table pans pulled from the chef's table or cafeteria line to sit in the kitchen for hours before being put in the refrigerator. When this happens, the product stays for quite some time at a temperature that promotes rapid bacterial growth. A blast chiller is designed to prevent this problem by cooling food products rapidly. Figure 7-5 shows a blast chiller.

Figure 7-5. Blast chiller. (Courtesy of Traulsen and Co., Inc.)

The blast chiller has three basic components that make it different from a conventional refrigerator. These are:

❏ High-capacity refrigeration system

❏ High velocity of forced chilled air

❏ Microprocessor controls that gauge either chiller internal temperature or (with a probe) product internal temperature

The microprocessor can include many other features, such as the ability to download time/temperature data to a computer for later review and analysis, a dual temperature mode for automatically switching from blast chilling to normal temperature, and multibatch chilling for two or three different batches of food.

Recent emphasis on sanitation, brought about by HACCP (hazard analysis critical control point) regulations in which food handling and time/temperature considerations are emphasized, will undoubtedly create high levels of interest in blast chillers.

PRE-PREPARATION EQUIPMENT

A food facility's pre-preparation area is where foods are processed before the meal is finally prepared and served. Typically, foods are mixed, seasoned, chopped, roasted, or cleaned in this part of the kitchen. The designer must group only the equipment that will be used for pre-preparation in this area so that the highest level of efficiency can be achieved. The mixing of pre-preparation equipment with final preparation equipment is a frequent layout mistake made by inexperienced designers.

Desirable features of the pre-preparation area are sinks, worktables, utensil storage, access to refrigeration, and access to warewashing, as well as various kinds of food production equipment. The most commonly required equipment is discussed in some detail below.

The mixer is a very versatile piece of pre-preparation equipment that is found in nearly all kitchens. The specifier has many choices of sizes and accessories. Mixers are sized by bowl capacity, which ranges from 5 to 140 quarts (4.7 to 132.5 liters). The mixer bowl normally is stationary, and the mixer head rotates inside the bowl with a dual circular motion so that all parts of the bowl are covered in the mixing process. The mixer beaters usually furnished with the machine include a flat beater for general mixing, a wire whip for light products such as whipped cream, and a dough hook for heavy yeast doughs. Large mixers (80 quarts [75.7 liters] or larger) are usually constructed with power lifts to raise the heavy mixer bowls to the proper position. Most mixers are equipped with a power takeoff for attaching optional equipment. Typical foodservice mixers are shown in Figure 7-6.

Mixers

SPECIFICATIONS

Figure 7-6. Mixers. (Courtesy of Hobart Corporation.)

PRIMARY USE IN THE FOOD OPERATION   Mixers are used where large quantities of food are being mixed, where a variety of attachments are required, and where food processing is done.

DETERMINING CAPACITY AND SIZE   Figure 7-7 provides guidelines for determining the number and size of mixers necessary for a foodservice operation.

ENERGY USAGE AND UTILITY REQUIREMENTS   Mixers operate with an electric motor ranging in size from $\frac{1}{3}$ to 5 horsepower, and are available for a variety of electrical services (110-, 208-, 240-, or 460/480-volt, 1- or 3-phase). They use very little power compared with the heat-producing equipment in the kitchen. Mixers are usually well constructed and should last many years if they are reasonably well maintained.

ACCESSORIES   Vegetable slicers, meat grinders, bowl dollies, and special dough mixer attachments are typical of the accessories that can be purchased for a mixer.

Food Processors

SPECIFICATIONS   High-speed food processors, similar to the popular models designed for home use, have been used in the commercial foodservice industry for the past two decades. Prior to this, the most common food processors were the

Meals Served per Day	MIXERS Bakery Not Included		MIXERS Including Bakery	
	Quantity	Size	Quantity	Size
Less than 100	1	5 quarts (4.7 liters)	1	12 quarts (11.4 liters)
100–200	1	12 quarts (11.4 liters)	1	12 quarts (11.4 liters)
			1	20 quarts (18.9 liters)
200–400	1	12 quarts (11.4 liters)	1	20 quarts (18.9 liters)
	1	30 quarts (28.4 liters)	1	30 quarts (28.4 liters
400–600	1	20 quarts (18.9 liters)	1	30 quarts (28.4 liters)
	1	60 quarts (56.8 liters)	1	60 quarts (56.8 liters)
600–1,000	2	60 quarts (56.8 liters)	2	60 quarts (56.8 liters)
			1	80 quarts (75.7 liters)
1,000–1,500	1	60 quarts (56.8 liters)	2	60 quarts (56.8 liters)
	1	80 quarts (75.7 liters)	1	80 quarts (75.7 liters)
More than 1,5000	2	60 quarts (56.8 liters)	2	80 quarts (75.7 liters)
	1	80 quarts (75.7 liters)	1	140 quarts (132.5 liters)

Figure 7-7. Mixer requirements based on meals served per day.

buffalo chopper and the vertical cutter-mixer (VCM). VCMs are still very much in use in large commercial kitchens, and each has its advantages. Figure 7-8 shows a typical food processor.

Buffalo Chopper   The buffalo chopper is illustrated in Figure 7-9. The food is chopped by a semicircular blade that rotates rapidly under a protective cover. As the food moves around the outside edge of the revolving bowl, it is chopped hundreds of times. The more often the food travels around the bowl, the more finely it is chopped. Vegetables, meats, and many other foods can be processed in a buffalo chopper.

Vertical Cutter-Mixer   Similar to a blender except that it is much larger and more expensive, the vertical cutter-mixer will cut, mix, and blend foods in seconds, and is used primarily for chopping meats and vegetables (see Figure 7-10). It is also an excellent piece of equipment for the bakery and will blend most doughs and frostings in two or three minutes. The VCM uses a high-speed stainless-steel curved knife that rotates on the inside of the bowl. It should be located in the kitchen beside a floor drain and near a source of hot and cold water for ease in cleaning. The most common VCM bowl sizes range from 30 to 45 quarts (28.4 to 42.5 liters). Typical capacities used for frequently processed foods are found in Figure 7-11.

Figure 7-8. R2V food processor.
(Photograph by Liz Ware.)

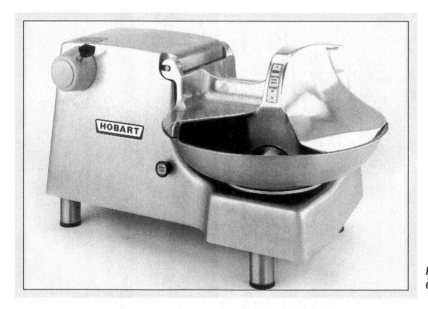

Figure 7-9. Buffalo chopper. (Courtesy of Hobart
Corporation.)

Other Types The variety of food-processing machines available is far too great to list or describe in this text. The manager or owner might want to see a demonstration before choosing any kind of processor. The new, smaller high-speed food processors are made by several companies, offering a wide number of choices. The use of a small model in combination with a buffalo chopper or VCM might be a wise choice for the large food operation, especially if a wide variety of salads is included in the menu.

Figure 7-10. Vertical Cutter Mixer (VCM). (Courtesy of Hobart Corporation.)

Product	Time	30-Quart VCM	45-Quart VCM
Bread crumbs	2 minutes	2–4 lb. (.91–1.81 kg.)	4–6 lb. (1.81–2.72 kg.)
Pie dough	1½–2½ minutes	2–6 lb. (.91–2.72 kg.)	3–8 lb. (1.36–3.63 kg.)
Hamburger	1–2 minutes	12–24 lb. (5.44–10.89 kg.)	18–36 lb. (8.16–16.33 kg.)
Lettuce	2–3 jogs of switch	4–6 heads	6–10 heads
Meat loaf	1–1½ minutes	12–25 lb. (5.44–11.34 kg.)	20–30 lb. (9.07–13.61 kg.)
Cake batter	2½–4 minutes	15–30 lb. (6.80–13.61 kg.)	25–60 lb. (11.34–27.22 kg.)

Figure 7-11. Vertical cutter-mixer capacities. (Courtesy of Hobart Corporation.)

Slicers

Slicers are motor-driven with a round carbon-steel or stainless-steel blade that is hollow- or bevel-ground. The blade and carrier are tilted at an angle of approximately 30 degrees from vertical so that gravity pulls the food product down the carrier into the path of the blade. A high-volume slicer can have a different configuration, with a horizontal cutting action and a device that stacks sliced product into portions with wax paper separators.

The diameter of the blade determines the size of the product that can be sliced. Most slicers have integral sharpeners to keep the blade in working condition. A wide variety of slicer sizes are available. Some, called automatic slicers, can be specified with a motor to move the carrier back and forth across the blade. As a safety device, most slicers have a hand grip and protective plate over the blade. Figure 7-12 shows a commercial slicer.

A wide variety of accessories are available for slicers, including:

❏ A food chute to hold different types of vegetables (tomatoes, cabbage, etc.) during slicing
❏ Variable speed control
❏ Gear-driven table adjustment for consistent slicing thickness
❏ Semi- or fully automatic slicing
❏ Removable or permanently mounted sharpener

A slicer often is mounted on a portable cart so that it can be used as needed in different areas of the kitchen. A cart with open shelves below the top and fold-down sides is ideal because it provides staging space for items to be sliced and short-term storage for finished products.

Slicers are dangerous pieces of equipment and should be used and cleaned only by trained employees. Although slicer manufacturers have done an excellent job of designing protective devices and safety features, accidents are still possible if the operator is careless.

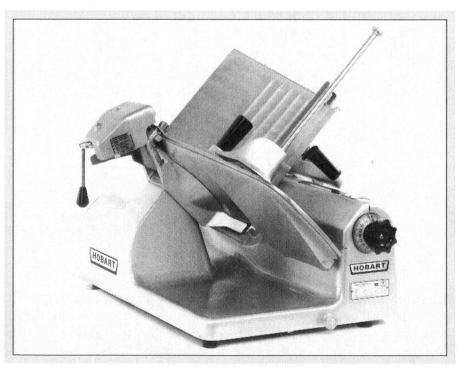

Figure 7-12. Slicer. (Courtesy of Hobart Corporation.)

There are many different types of ovens, and each has special advantages that must be carefully considered by the foodservice consultant or owner. The most popular ovens are classified as follows:

Ovens

❏ Standard (under the range)
❏ Convection
❏ Deck
❏ Rotary
❏ Conveyor
❏ Microwave (see "Final Preparation Equipment," below)
❏ Slow-roasting

Specifications The most widely used oven in the foodservice industry is the standard oven built into a hot-top, open-top, grill-top, or other heavy-duty piece of range equipment. These ovens are popular because they are inexpensive and are conveniently located in the range (hot-food preparation) section of the kitchen.

STANDARD OVENS

Standard ovens have some disadvantages that have caused specifiers of equipment to look for better types of ovens. The primary disadvantages are the following:

❏ The location under the range makes it difficult for the cook to see or reach into the oven.
❏ The ovens are poorly insulated and thus energy-inefficient.
❏ Under conditions of heavy usage, standard ovens require frequent maintenance and repair of door hinges and thermostats.
❏ Cleaning under and behind standard ovens is extremely difficult.
❏ The capacity of the standard oven is relatively small in comparison to other oven designs.

Primary Use in a Food Operation Standard ovens are used for roasting and baking in the small to medium-size foodservice operation. This type of oven should not be specified for a foodservice facility unless space and/or funds are severely limited. Other types of ovens discussed in this chapter offer superior choices for most foodservice operations.

Energy Usage and Utility Requirements Standard ovens are available using either gas or electricity. They lose much of their heat when the door is opened and are therefore very energy-inefficient.

Specifications The convection oven is energy-efficient and occupies a small amount of space in the kitchen—characteristics that make it highly desirable. Figure 7-13 shows a convection oven. Convection ovens can be purchased in either single- or double-cavity units. A double-cavity convection oven measures approximately 36 inches (915 millimeters) wide by 40 inches (100 millimeters) deep.

CONVECTION OVENS

In the convection oven, a fan circulates the heated air through the cooking cavity at a high rate. As the heat flows rapidly over the food product,

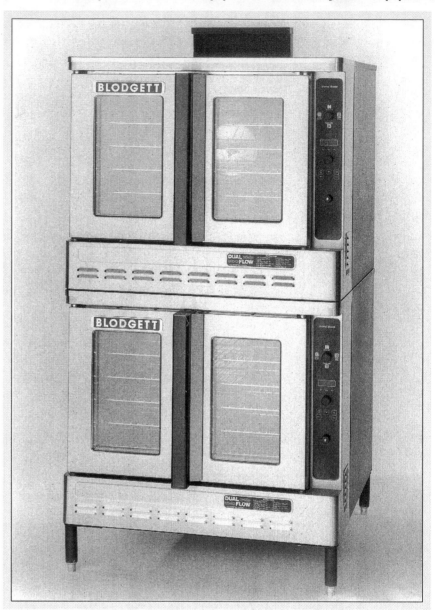

Figure 7-13. Convection oven. (Courtesy of Blodgett Oven Company.)

heat transfer occurs more quickly than in a conventional oven, and cooking time is reduced. Because the rapidly moving air reaches all parts of the oven chamber, the food can be placed in the convection oven on closely spaced shelves, thus increasing the capacity of the oven compartment.

The energy and space efficiency of the convection oven is primarily a result of rapid cooking and the utilization of almost all of the oven's interior space. Typical convection ovens will hold five full sheet pans of product in each of the oven chambers. Accessories for convection ovens include removable liners for ease of cleaning, automatic timing devices, and a variety of exterior finishes.

Primary Use in the Food Operation   Convection ovens are excellent for cooking many products that will fit on a standard 18-by-26-inch sheet pan,

Number of Meals Served per Day	Single-Compartment Oven(s)	Double-Compartment Oven(s)
Under 100	1	0
100–200	1	0
200–400	1	1
400–600	0	2
600–1,000	0	3
1,000–1,800	0	4
1,800–3,000	0	5

Figure 7-14. Convection oven requirements based on meals served per day.

or standard gastronorm pans. Meats, baked potatoes, bakery products, and small roasts are products that can be easily prepared in this oven. The roasting of large pieces of meat such as a whole turkey or ribs of beef can be done in a convection oven, but the space utilization is not as effective, because the size of the meat does not permit the use of closely spaced shelves.

Determining Capacity and Size   The oven capacity selected will depend on the number of items on the menu that are normally cooked in an oven and whether or not there is a bakery in the operation. Figure 7-14 illustrates typical convection oven capacity needs for foodservice operations.

Specifications   Often called a pizza oven because of its widespread use for making pizza, the deck oven is constructed of one, two, or three levels of oven space and can be either gas-fired or electric. A deck oven is illustrated in Figure 7-15. For many years, this was the most common oven in large res-

DECK OVENS

Figure 7-15. Deck oven. (Courtesy of Baker's Pride.)

taurants or institutions for doing all types of baking and roasting. Because of the variety of foods that were cooked in these devices, manufacturers developed different sizes and capacities to handle different food products. One variation of the deck oven is the roasting oven. This is the same as a conventional deck oven except that the cavity is higher to accommodate large standing rib roasts, whole turkeys, or steamship rounds of beef.

The typical specifications for deck ovens include:

❏ Gas or electric energy

❏ Exterior finish of stainless steel or galvanized steel with black lacquer finish

❏ Number of decks

❏ Height of the cooking cavities

❏ Steel or brick hearth (a baker may prefer a brick hearth for French bread)

❏ High heat levels for pizza baking

Primary Use in the Food Operation   The deck oven is a general-purpose piece of equipment that will handle a variety of roasting and baking needs. The deck oven's large footprint makes it impractical for the small food operation. A convection oven offers much greater cooking capacity with a smaller footprint. Many bakers continue to prefer the deck oven for the small to medium-size bakery, however. Deck ovens are excellent for pizza because the interior cavity is large, permitting easy peeling (removal of pizza with a large spatula), and the oven can be heated to high temperatures.

Determining Capacity and Size   A standard 42-by-32-inch (1,067-by-813-millimeter) deck in a deck oven would hold two standard roasting pans, two 18-by-26-inch sheet (bun) pans, twelve 10-inch pies, or four 1/1 (530-by-325-millimeter) gastronorm pans. Stacking the oven to three decks will increase these capacities accordingly.

Energy Usage and Utility Requirements   Gas-fired deck ovens will usually consume between 20,000 and 50,000 BTU per section, and a three-deck oven may consume 150,000 BTU. Electric deck ovens use approximately 10 kWh per section and are connected to a 208-, 240-, or 440/480-volt source. A three-deck oven would draw 30 kWh of electricity. Deck ovens are usually not well insulated, and when the door is opened, a large amount of heat flows out. These ovens are not energy-efficient when compared with a well-insulated convection or rotary oven.

ROTARY OVENS   *Specifications*   Rotary or revolving tray ovens are designed to increase air-flow over the food. Unlike convection ovens, which move the air across the food with a fan, rotary ovens move the food itself within the cooking cavity. Trays holding food are mounted to large "wheels" that rotate like a Ferris wheel. The food is cooked while it moves around in a circular motion in the large, heated chamber. This method of roasting or baking is excellent because the heated chamber can be well insulated and is therefore energy-efficient. Moreover, the food can be cooked more evenly as a result of the

Figure 7-16. Rotary oven. (Courtesy of Cutler Industries, LLC.)

airflow (convection) that is created when the food is in motion. Figure 7-16 illustrates a rotary oven.

The primary disadvantage of a rotary oven is its size. These ovens occupy a considerable amount of floor space as well as vertical space. The small rotary ovens of one leading manufacturer measure 81 inches wide by 44 inches from front to back and 82 inches high. Rotary ovens used for baking are much larger and are built on-site by the manufacturer.

Specifications that are typically used when purchasing this equipment include:

❏ Exterior finish (stainless steel or baked enamel on galvanized steel)

❏ Number of trays (capacity)

❏ Heating method (gas or electricity)

❏ Method of opening the door

❏ Insulation

❏ Adjustable revolving shelves

❏ Method of venting the oven cavity

❏ Temperature ranges

❏ Steam injection (for hard-crust breads)

Primary Use in the Food Operation　Rotary ovens are very popular with bakers because of the large capacity and even baking characteristics. These ovens often last many years under conditions of constant use, with only an occasional need for realignment or repair. Small rotary ovens are also excellent pieces of equipment for the production kitchen for roasting and are often used in conjunction with convection ovens.

Energy Usage and Utility Requirements　　The oven doors for rotary ovens are small, and each shelf is loaded or unloaded through the small opening. The small oven door, together with its well-insulated walls and ceiling, make this piece of equipment extremely energy-efficient. Either gas or electric models can be purchased.

REVOLVING RACK OVEN　　***Specifications***　　Like the rotary tray oven, the revolving rack oven moves the food product while baking or roasting. This oven uses a rack that can be rolled inside the heated chamber (see Figure 7-17). The baker loads the rack with items ready for baking and wheels it into the oven. The rack is lifted and rotated in the oven chamber during the baking period and then wheeled from the oven to cool. There are two advantages to the revolving rack oven over the rotary oven. First, the revolving rack oven can match the capacity of the rotary oven while using substantially less floor space. Second, the baker does not have to remove the bun pans from the rack to set them in the oven. Instead, he or she simply rolls the entire rack into the oven and back out when baking is complete.

　　Typical specifications for a rotating rack oven include the following:

- ❏ Size (capacity) in number of racks (one, two, or more)
- ❏ Energy source (gas, electric)
- ❏ Primary use (baking versus roasting)
- ❏ Steam injection for crusty breads

Primary Use in the Food Operation　　Rotating rack ovens are especially popular for baking breads, rolls, cakes, pies, cookies, and other items in large

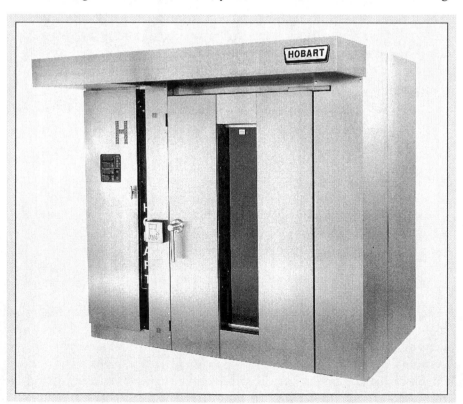

Figure 7-17. Rack oven. (Courtesy of Hobart Corporation.)

operations because of their high capacity. They also are used for roasting large quantities of meats and poultry. The primary advantages of rotating rack ovens are their ease of loading and unloading, as well as their high capacity within a relatively small footprint.

Energy Usage and Utility Requirements   Rotary rack ovens generate heat using gas or electricity. The motor that turns the rack, as well as the controls and lights, is electric-powered. Rotary rack ovens typically are too large to place under a common kitchen hood and so require separate powered ventilation.

Specifications   The conveying of foods through a heated chamber is becoming more and more popular, especially in food operations that employ semi-skilled and unskilled labor. A conveyor oven permits the food product to flow through the heated cavity at a predetermined speed while ensuring the same cooking time for each product prepared (see Figure 7-18). Conveyor ovens are in common usage in pizza operations.

   There are two techniques for heating the product. In one method, the heating elements are located above and below the metal conveyor belt, so that the product can be cooked on both sides at once as it passes through the oven cavity. The second cooking method, called impingement, involves blowing hot air from a heating chamber through small orifices located above and below the conveyor belt. This second method removes the cold air layer surrounding the food, cooking the product more evenly and without the danger of scorching or overcooking the surface of the food product.

Primary Use in the Food Operation   The conveyor ovens are best used in high-volume foodservice operations. Once the conveyor speed is set, products can be cooked in rapid succession with consistent results. Pizza, cookies, muffins, hamburgers, and other products that are not too thick or dense cook uniformly in the conveyor oven. These are excellent merchandising ovens because they can be located where the customer can watch and smell food such as pizza or cookies being prepared.

CONVEYOR OVENS

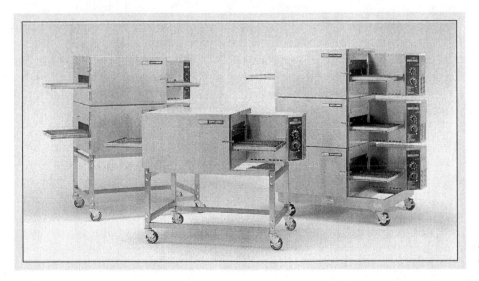

Figure 7-18. Conveyor oven. (Courtesy of Lincoln/Wearever, Inc.)

Baking Area (Square Feet/ Square Meters)	Belt Width (Inches/Millimeters)	Pizzas per Hour	Utility Requirements (BTUs per Hour)
8/.74	24/610	30	135,000
10.7/1.0	32/810	60	135,000
21.4/2.0 *	32/810	120	270,000
* The larger baking area and capacity are created by stacking two 32-inch-wide units.			

Figure 7-19. Conveyor oven capacities.

Determining Capacity and Size   Conveyor ovens are sized by length, width of the conveyor belt, and speed of the belt. The length will in part determine the amount of heat that is applied to the food product as it passes through the cavity of the oven. The width of the belt will determine the amount of food that can be placed on the conveyor at one time, and the speed of the belt will determine the degree of doneness and amount of heat applied. These factors, plus other engineering features, determine the capacity of the oven. Figure 7-19 shows typical production capacities for conveyor ovens.

SLOW-ROASTING OVENS   *Specifications*   Experiments with low-temperature roasting have been in progress for many years. High heat applied to protein hardens the surface, removes too much moisture and fat, caramelizes any sugar in the product, and results in shrinkage. Low-temperature roasting of meats reduces the shrinkage and decreases the browning effect on the outside of the product. Ovens that are specifically designed to cook at temperatures of approximately 200°F (104°C) to 240°F (116°C) and hold the moisture from the meat within the oven cavity are classified as slow-roasting ovens (see Figure 7-20). Manufacturers claim a 30 to 40 percent reduction in shrinkage, which translates into significant savings for food operators who serve large amounts of roast meats. Some operators have claimed a savings large enough to pay for equipment in only one year.

Specifications for slow-roasting ovens might include low power requirements, double stacked ovens, portability, and a hold feature. The hold feature automatically drops the temperature to approximately 140°F (60°C) at a certain time, so that the meat will remain at a proper serving temperature but will no longer cook. This is an important feature for foodservice operators who make a practice of cooking in the oven all night. (Ovens should not be set below 140°F because of the danger of bacterial growth.)

Primary Use in the Food Operation   The slow-roasting oven is primarily used for roasting meats. However, the oven can be very effective as a warming cabinet for holding hot foods and as a proof box for bakery products.

Determining Capacity and Size   A slow-roasting oven will hold between 80 and 120 pounds (36 to 54 kilograms) of raw meat per cavity. Where large food operations require additional capacity, these ovens can be stacked.

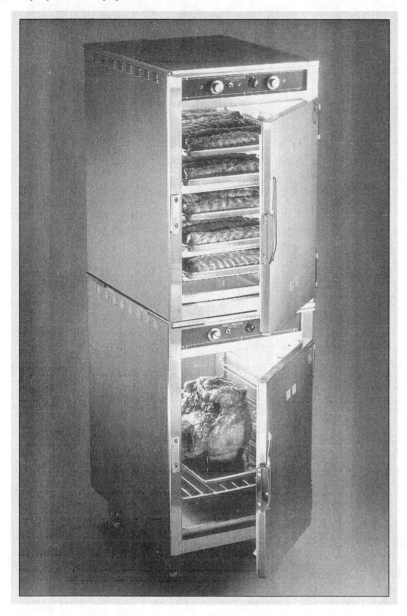

Figure 7-20. Slow-cook oven. (Photo furnished through the courtesy of Alto-Shaam, Inc., Menomonee Falls, Wisconsin, USA.)

The ovens are very space-efficient. For example, one leading manufacturer's slow-roasting oven takes up only 23 by 28 inches (560 by 750 millimeters) of floor space. The capacity of slow-roasting ovens is relatively less than similarly sized convection ovens because they require long roasting periods, typically between three and a half and six hours, depending on the size of the meat and the degree of doneness (internal temperature) desired. In the same period, a convection or conventional oven could roast several times the amount of food.

Energy Usage and Utility Requirements The energy savings using slow-roasting ovens are dramatic, for several reasons. First, even though the slow-roasting oven cooks over a longer period of time, a relatively small amount of energy is required to hold it at 220°F (104°C). For example, one manufacturer of these ovens requires a connected load of only 3 kilowatts, using a 110-volt power source. A convection oven, by comparison, may require 16 to 17 kilowatts and a 208- or 240-volt power source. Since electrical energy is charged to the customer by the utility company on the basis of connected load (demand) and usage, the low-temperature roasting oven scores exceedingly well. Second, energy savings are realized because of the excellent insulation that encloses the entire cooking cavity. Third, energy savings are achieved because the oven does not need to be placed under a ventilation hood. Very little heat or smoke is added to the food production area when these ovens are used.

COMBI OVEN/STEAMER   The combi oven brings together oven and steamer in a single unit (see Figure 7-21). The combi oven uses both convected heated air and steam as energy sources for cooking. This combination allows the cook to use the equipment as a convection oven, a steamer, or both at the same time. The result is a highly versatile piece of equipment that can prepare a wide variety of food with excellent quality. When both sources of energy are used

Figure 7-21. Combi oven-steamer.
(Courtesy of Blodgett Oven Company.)

together, the combi oven cooks very rapidly, without drying out or over-cooking the product. Other advantages of the combi oven are:

- ❏ Consistent flavor, color, and texture of the food item
- ❏ Ability to cook multiple food items at the same time without flavor transfer
- ❏ Reduced shrinkage when roasting
- ❏ Efficient use of kitchen space

Specifications   Specifications for combi ovens typically include a stainless-steel exterior and interior, a self-contained steam boiler, an attached hose (used to wash out the interior), and a computer-controlled cooking program.

Primary Use in the Food Operation   The versatility of this equipment permits the cook to steam, braise, roast, bake, defrost, or reheat a wide variety of food products. Because these pieces of equipment are expensive, many operators question the use of a single piece of equipment that would cost as much as or more than the combined prices of a separate convection oven and low-pressure steamer. If the food preparation staff is well trained in the use of a combi, then its many uses and space-saving feature seem to justify its high cost.

Determining Capacity and Size   The smallest combis hold six 12-by-20-inch steam table pans, and the largest hold forty pans (or more). The larger combis will also accommodate full-size 18-by-26-inch bun pans. European versions offer similar capacities for cooking in gastronorm pans. The smaller combis tend to limit the use of the oven for baking, while the larger ovens can be adjusted to receive transport carts for the quantities typical of large institutions. Figure 7-22 lists the capacities of combi ovens from one leading manufacturer.

Energy Usage and Utility Requirements   The combi oven is very energy-efficient because of a well-insulated cooking chamber and because both convection and steam cookery make excellent use of the heat. Small combis typically draw 9 kilowatts of electricity and large ovens up to 60 kilowatts. Gas models are also available and, depending on local utility costs, may be less expensive to operate than the electric versions.

Size	Capacity	Number of Steam Table Pans*
Counter model	75 to 100 servings	6
Small floor model	100 to 200 servings	10
Large floor model	200 to 400 servings	20
Mobile pan roll-in cart	400 to 600 servings	40

* 1/1 (325 by 530 millimeters) gastronorm pans have comparable capacities.

Figure 7-22. Combi oven capacities.

SPECIALTY OVENS

Wood-Burning Ovens   A popular trend for Italian or pizza restaurants is a custom-built wood-burning brick oven. These ovens are heated by a wood fire in a well-insulated brick-and-masonry enclosure with a stone or ceramic hearth. Pizzas and other dishes are placed inside the oven near the fire to give a pleasant smoky flavor to the food. These ovens require a skilled operator and a considerable amount of effort to build the fire, keep it burning, and clean it out. Other oven companies have simplified this process with a gas burner that is similar in appearance to the wood-burning model.

Barbecue Ovens   A variety of ovens are available that will cook pork, beef, or poultry and impart a smoky flavor from either hardwood chips or logs. Small units are simple aluminum or stainless-steel boxes on wheels with a heating and smoke-providing device in the bottom of the oven. Large units use either hardwood logs or logs plus gas as a source of smoke and heat. Capacities can range from 24 half chickens or 16 slabs of baby back ribs up to 270 whole chickens and 800 pounds of ribs.

Tilting Fry Pans (Braising Pans)

SPECIFICATIONS

The tilting fry pan is also called a tilting skillet or a tilting braising pan (see Figure 7-23). The advantage of this piece of equipment is versatility. Tilting fry pans can be used for grilling, steaming, braising, sautéing, or stewing. The piece of equipment has a long rectangular shape, with sides that are usually 6 to 10 inches (152 to 254 millimeters) high. The large, flat, inside surface is good for grilling, and the tall sides give the added advantage of holding a large volume of food. Typical sizes range from 20 to 40 gallons (76

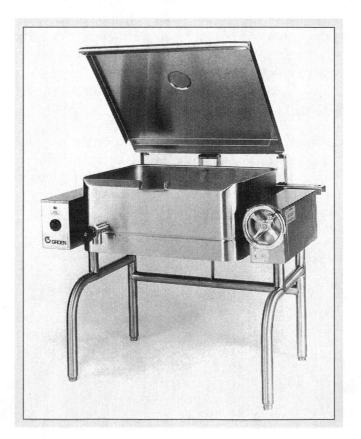

Figure 7-23. Tilting braising pan. (Photo courtesy of Groen, a Dover Industries Company.)

to 152 liters) and measure from approximately 36 inches wide by 30 inches deep (910 millimeters wide by 760 millimeters deep) up to 56 inches wide by 34 inches deep (1,420 millimeters wide by 860 millimeters deep). The fry pan tilts, as the name suggests, so that the liquids can be poured into a container. The tilting feature also permits easy cleaning if the pan is located over a floor drain. Accessories that are usually purchased with the equipment include a hot and cold filler faucet and/or spray rinse hose, as well as spreader plates for each side of the pan.

The tilting fry pan is very versatile, and can be used as:

❏ A bain-marie for holding foods in a hot-water bath

❏ A grill

❏ A braising pan

❏ A kettle for simmering or stewing

❏ A steamer with the lid in a closed position

❏ A fryer for foods cooked in small amounts of fat

❏ A poacher

PRIMARY USE IN THE FOOD OPERATION

The tilting fry pan should be purchased in the largest size that space and funds permit. The smaller fry pans are difficult to use for grilling because of the high sides. The equipment is most useful when it is installed beside a steam-jacketed kettle or grill. This arrangement permits the cooks to have a choice of equipment to use, depending on the menu and/or volume of food that must be prepared.

DETERMINING CAPACITY AND SIZE

Gas and electric fry pans can be purchased. The electric fry pan with an open, unobstructed stand is simple and easy to clean and might therefore be preferred. Energy efficiency is a strong selling point for the fry pan. The direct contact of the heated surface with the food, plus the large lid, contribute to its energy efficiency.

ENERGY USAGE AND UTILITY REQUIREMENTS

The kettle is often described as the workhorse of the kitchen because of its versatility and popularity among cooks and chefs. The steam-jacketed kettle is heated from an inner jacket that contains the steam. This double-walled construction is very efficient because the heat from the steam is transferred directly into the food through the stainless-steel wall of the kettle.

Steam-Jacketed Kettles

The American Society of Mechanical Engineers (ASME) has established safety codes that must be followed by manufacturers of steam equipment that is operated under pressure. The ASME requires that the inner jacket be able to handle from 5 to 50 pounds per square inch (psi) and that the kettle be constructed of heavy-gauge stainless steel. Steam-jacketed kettles should last many years in a kitchen unless they are dented or scratched through rough treatment. Most kettles use a simple steam valve that is opened slightly for simmering foods and more fully for cooking at higher temperatures.

Steam-jacketed kettles are usually furnished with a lid, and a large number of options are available to the equipment specifier. The most

SPECIFICATIONS

important of these is the selection of the method of mounting. Kettles can be mounted in a number of different ways:

❏ On legs
❏ On a pedestal base
❏ On a yoke (trunnion) for tilting
❏ Wall-hung
❏ Wall-hung and tilting
❏ On a tabletop

Figure 7-24 shows a kettle mounted on a pedestal; Figure 7-25 shows a wall-mounted kettle.

The price of the kettle increases dramatically as the mounting method becomes more complex. For example, a 40-gallon kettle mounted on legs will cost approximately one-third the price of the same capacity kettle wall-hung and tilting. The comparative advantages of the different mounting methods relate primarily to ease of cleaning and the convenience of pouring liquids from a tilting kettle.

Other accessories that are often specified to accompany a steam-jacketed kettle are the following:

❏ Hot- and cold-water flexible hoses for filling the kettles
❏ Spray rinse device for cleaning
❏ Water-metering device for measuring exact quantities to be added to the kettle
❏ Mixer attachments
❏ Cold-water attachments for rapid cooling of the product
❏ Large draw-off spigot

Figure 7-24 (left). Steam-jacketed kettle, pedestal-mounted. (Courtesy of Cleveland Range, Inc.)

Figure 7-25 (above). Steam-jacketed kettle, wall-mounted. (Photo courtesy of Groen, a Dover Industries Company.)

❑ Etched numbers on the inside of the kettle indicating the volume of liquid

❑ Self-contained gas or electric heaters that eliminate the necessity for a steam line

PRIMARY USE IN THE FOOD OPERATION

The steam-jacketed kettle is most often used for bringing any liquid product up to a boiling temperature. Soups, stews, vegetables, stocks, sauces, boiled meats—any food product cooked in a liquid—can be efficiently handled in a steam-jacketed kettle.

DETERMINING CAPACITY AND SIZE

The menu and cooking procedures will have a direct influence on the number and type of kettles needed. The table-mounted kettles are small in capacity, ranging between 6 and 40 quarts, while floor models range in size from 20 to 150 gallons. When considering the kettle capacity, allowance must be made for boil-over or foaming. Figure 7-26 may be used as a guideline for selecting kettles that will meet the needs of different types of food facilities.

ENERGY USAGE AND UTILITY REQUIREMENTS

Steam-jacketed kettles are very energy-efficient and operate best when they are directly connected to a source of steam. If a steam source is not available to the building, the kettle can be connected to smaller steam generators located in the kitchen. Steam cookers and other pieces of kitchen equipment are often hooked up to a small steam boiler that can supply the kettles as well. If it is impractical to provide a steam line, electric table-mounted kettles can be purchased.

Meals Served per Day	Quantity	Capacity
Under 100	1	10 quarts (9.5 liters), table-mounted
100–200	1	20 quarts (19 liters), table-mounted
200–400	1	20 quarts (19 liters)
	1	20 gallons (76 liters)
400–600	1	20 gallons (76 liters)
	1	40 gallons (151 liters)
600–1,000	1	20 gallons (76 liters)
	2	40 gallons (151 liters)
1,000–1,500	1	20 gallons (76 liters)
	1	40 gallons (151 liters)
	1	60 gallons (227 liters)
1,500–2,500	1	20 gallons (76 liters)
	2	40 gallons (151 liters)
	1	60 gallons (227 liters)
2,500 or more	1	20 gallons (76 liters)
	2	40 gallons (151 liters)
	2	60 gallons (227 liters)
	1	80 gallons (303 liters)

Figure 7-26. Kettle selection guidelines based on meals served per day.

Steam-jacketed kettles that are self-contained with either gas or electricity as a source of energy are large and expensive. Self-contained kettles are in common use, although the heating source increases the height and thickness of the kettle walls, making access to the kettle awkward for the cook.

FINAL PREPARATION EQUIPMENT

The final preparation area is physically located between pre-preparation and the service area of a food facility. In the final preparation area, foods are prepared immediately before and during the meal period. It should not contain pre-preparation equipment such as large kettles or food processors, which create confusion and many unnecessary steps for the kitchen personnel.

The final preparation area should include refrigeration for storing foods that have been processed and are ready to be prepared. Most final preparation equipment, such as grills and fryers, produces a large quantity of grease and soil and therefore should be installed in a manner that will permit easy cleaning. The final preparation area should be adjacent to the warewashing area for easy access to the pot sink and a supply of clean dishes.

The final preparation area should always include the following equipment for storing and handling:

❑ Worktables or spreader plates

❑ Utensil racks and storage drawers

❑ Sinks

❑ A pickup station

❑ Hot- and cold-food holding equipment

❑ A storage place for raw ingredients

The food preparation equipment for this area consists of:

❑ Low- and no-pressure steamers

❑ High-pressure steamers

❑ Bain-maries

❑ Broilers

❑ Microwave ovens

❑ Fryers

❑ Ranges

❑ Grills

❑ Grooved griddles

Low- and No-Pressure Steamers

SPECIFICATIONS

Steaming is an extremely efficient cooking method because of the quick heat transfer between the steam and the food product. Steamers can be purchased in high-, low-, and no-pressure models. The low- and no-pressure models may also be considered pre-preparation equipment because they can be used to prepare large quantities of food before the meal period begins. High-pressure steam cookers are used to prepare foods just before and during the meal period.

Low-pressure steamers (Figure 7-27), which have been in use in commercial kitchens for many years, operate under a pressure of 5 pounds per square inch. One-, two-, and three-compartment models are available. Each compartment has a large capacity and can be specified to hold two large (12 by 20 inches [530 by 325 millimeters gastronorm]) perforated pans for cooking such items as boiled potatoes. The compartments can also be fitted to accommodate six full-size steam table pans. The capacity of this equipment makes it best suited to large institutions or restaurants.

No-pressure "convection steamers" (Figure 7-28) have become popular in recent years because they are compact, will handle a large quantity of food, and are well liked by cooks and chefs. Since all steamers operate on the basis of convected heat, the term "convection steamer" is primarily a marketing device.

All steamers can be purchased with automatic timing devices, interior fittings to accommodate different sizes of pans, and special exterior finishes. Floor-mounted, wall-mounted, and modular units are available. The methods of producing steam and transferring the steam to the cooking cavity vary considerably from one model to the next. Many steamers are available with steam boilers located in a compartment under or beside the cooker.

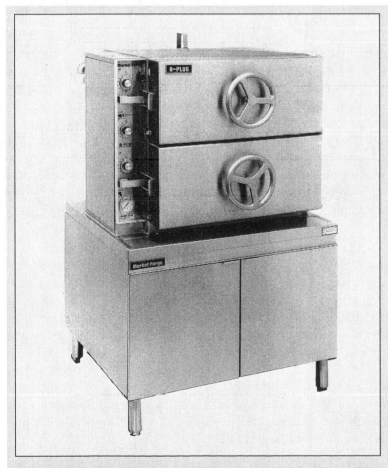

Figure 7-27. Pressure steamer. (Courtesy of the employee-owners of Market Forge Industries.)

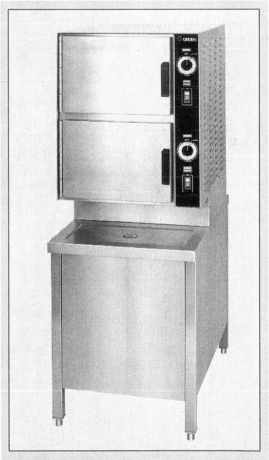

Figure 7-28. Convection steamer. (Photo courtesy of Groen, a Dover Industries Company.)

| | Cooking Time (Minutes) | |
Food Item	Fresh	Frozen
Chicken, 5–8 oz. pieces	18–20	
Ribs, 3 lbs. and under	20–26	
Halibut, 6–8 oz. portions	4–6	6–8
Asparagus, spears	4	6
Broccoli, spears	3	2–3

Figure 7-29. Convection steamer cooking times. (Courtesy of Cleveland Range, Inc.)

PRIMARY USE IN THE FOOD OPERATION

Low- and no-pressure steamers are used in the preparation of vegetables, starchy items, seafood, and eggs. They cook these items quickly and thus support the batch cookery concept.

DETERMINING CAPACITY AND SIZE

The standard for judging the size of a steamer is the cooking time and the steam table pan capacity. Low- and no-pressure steamers will cook most vegetables in eight to fifteen minutes. Rice, spaghetti, and potatoes will cook in twenty to thirty minutes.

ENERGY USAGE AND UTILITY REQUIREMENTS

The best way to operate steamers is through a direct connection to a steam source. Care must be taken to be sure that the steam is clean. Often steam boilers have chemicals added for reducing rust and foaming, which can contaminate the steam. If the steam is not clean, a steam-fired boiler can be used to produce clean steam. If direct steam is not available, gas or electric boilers located under the steam cooker can be used. Low- and no-pressure steamers are high in steam consumption, and the volume of steam provided must be carefully engineered in the food facility. In spite of the high steam consumption, however, steam cooking is more energy-efficient than other modes of cooking.

Bain-maries

SPECIFICATIONS

The bain-marie is a hot water bath usually located in the cook's table or in the range area. For many years, bain-maries were very popular in large hotel and institutional kitchens as a place to hold sauces, soups, and gravies at boiling temperature. The bain-maries were usually heated by a coil at the bottom of the bain-marie sink. As equipment manufacturers developed modern holding equipment, food facilities designers stopped specifying the bain-marie. In recent years, small bain-maries have become popular again because cooks find a double-boiler effect very convenient for making sauces without fear of scorching or burning.

Bain-maries can now be specified with small, attached water-circulating heating elements that connect to the side of the bain-marie sink. These heating devices maintain the water at 200° to 210°F (93.3° to 98.9°C).

PRIMARY USE IN THE FOOD OPERATION

The bain-marie is used for holding sauces, soups, and stock at near-boiling temperatures.

Electrically heated stainless-steel tables and holding cabinets with humidity control are both excellent pieces of equipment for keeping foods at the proper temperature. Kitchens, therefore, may not need large bain-maries. A bain-marie sink approximately 2 feet by 2 feet (610 millimeters by 610 millimeters) would be sufficient for most restaurant kitchens, and 4 feet by 2 feet (1,220 millimeters by 610 millimeters) would work well for a large institutional kitchen.

Steam and electricity are the primary energy sources available for the bain-marie. If steam is available in the building, it is usually less expensive to use than electricity. Bain-maries are energy-efficient except when they are allowed to boil rapidly for long periods of time unnecessarily.

A broiler is a final preparation piece of equipment that cooks rapidly from radiant or infrared heat. Most broilers cook either the top or the bottom of the food product, although some models cook the top and bottom at the same time. Broilers can be purchased as large freestanding pieces of equipment or can be table-mounted. There are four types of broilers that are typically used in the foodservice facility:

Broilers

SPECIFICATIONS

❑ Freestanding top-burner broilers, often called hotel-style broilers

❑ Charbroilers

❑ Salamanders

❑ Conveyor broilers

In broiling, the cooking time is usually controlled by the distance between the food and the source of heat. When using the heavy-duty hotel-style broiler (with heating elements above), as shown in Figure 7-30, the food is placed on a steel grate that can be adjusted up and down to control the temperature. The grate slides in and out also, so that food can be placed in or removed from the broiler.

Open-top charbroilers heat from below (Figure 7-31); the product is placed on the cooking surface and can be watched during the broiling process. The distance from the heat source to the food product is usually fixed in charbroilers; the time the food is exposed to the heat controls cooking.

Conveyor broilers are excellent cooking devices because they can be operated by semiskilled personnel. One well-known hamburger chain uses a conveyor broiler to cook the hamburger on both sides at once at a predetermined speed. In this application, the employee does not need to judge the cooking time for preparing the hamburger.

Salamanders are small broilers that cook from above and are located above the range. This type of broiler is used by cooks and chefs for last-minute heating, browning, or broiling of food products such as fish and other seafood and food items that are topped with cheese or bread crumbs.

Accessories for broilers are limited to the type of exterior finish and the inclusion of small ovens under the broiler opening.

Figure 7-30. Hotel broiler. (Courtesy of Southbend.)

Dry-heat cookery is used for steaks, chops, hamburgers, and other meat products. Foods that have been broiled are popular because the fat content

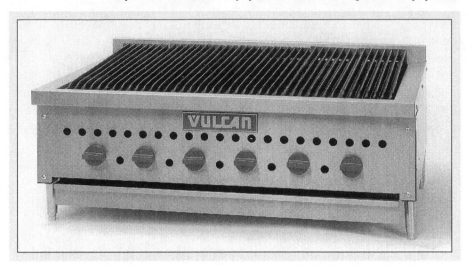

Figure 7-31. Charbroiler.
(Courtesy of Vulcan-Hart.)

is reduced and the caramelization of the sugars in the food gives it an appealing taste.

DETERMINING CAPACITY AND SIZE   Broilers are often rated for performance on the basis of the number of hamburgers or steaks that can be prepared in one hour. One well-known manufacturer of overfired broilers lists a range of production capacities, from a hundred 12-ounce T-bone steaks per hour for a small model to two hundred steaks per hour for a large double-section broiler. Determination of the correct size and number of broilers is based on estimates of the number of portions of each broiled item on the menu sold in a one-hour period.

ENERGY USAGE AND UTILITY
REQUIREMENTS   Broilers use either gas or electricity as a source of energy. Gas broilers are often preferred, especially in food operations where the broiler can be seen by the public, as a broiler with an open flame adds a touch of showmanship. Both hotel-style and open-top charbroilers generate large amounts of smoke and airborne grease, and both of these pieces of equipment use large quantities of energy. Unfortunately, most of the energy is removed from the kitchen through the hood. The energy waste associated with these pieces of equipment is further aggravated by the fact that cooks tend to leave the equipment turned on when food is not being prepared.

A specialty broiler is available that uses wood (such as mesquite) as a source of heat, so that the flavor of the wood smoke is transferred to the food product. These broilers are popular for restaurants specializing in steaks or ribs because of the unusual flavor produced by the burning wood.

Rotisseries

SPECIFICATIONS   Two styles of rotisseries are available, rotary and vertical. The rate of demand and the volume of cooked product needed would determine which of these two types is selected. Institutions and catering operations typically see most of their business during peak periods, while most restaurants require continuous service throughout the day.

Batch cooking versus continuous cooking dictates the type of rotisserie to use. For batch cooking, the rotary style is better. This rotisserie utilizes a rotary drum, in addition to rotary skewers, which creates a double rotation effect. As the product revolves, each piece is uniformly cooked and all are finished at the same time. The advantage is that a large volume of finished product is available at one time.

In vertical rotisseries (Figure 7-32), skewers are lined up one above the other in front of a heat source. Since the product at the top cooks first, the skewers are moved as cooking progresses, with uncooked items added at the bottom and completely cooked product removed from the top.

PRIMARY USE IN THE FOOD OPERATION

Rotisserie cookery is popular because it requires no added fat and offers the pleasant taste of chicken or other meats basted in their own juices. The appearance of rotating meats adds to the merchandising of the product, creating added sales.

DETERMINING CAPACITY AND SIZE

A variety of sizes are available, and most are designed for display cookery in clear view of the customer. Counter models with a total capacity of twelve to fifteen chickens are popular, but the serious rotisserie restaurant will need a capacity of approximately fifty chickens. Cooking time is typically

Figure 7-32. Vertical rotisserie. (Courtesy of Hardt.)

one hour for a 2½-pound chicken and seventy-five minutes for a 3½-pound chicken, so the total capacity needed is a function of determining the total needs for the peak meal and installing the number of units needed to handle the volume.

ENERGY USAGE AND UTILITY REQUIREMENTS

Both gas and electric models are available; for display models, gas is preferred. A large amount of energy is used in this equipment, and much of this energy is wasted to the ventilation hood. An output of 60,000 to 120,000 BTU is typical for gas-fired larger units, and an output of 20,000 BTU is usually required for a countertop unit.

Microwave Ovens

SPECIFICATIONS

Raytheon Corporation first manufactured the microwave oven in the early 1940s. The name of this oven is derived from the short wavelength of the energy that radiates from the oven into the food. Microwaves are a part of the electromagnetic spectrum and are similar to radio waves. The microwave oven converts 110 volts of electricity from an energy form with long wavelengths to one of short wavelengths, and transmits this energy through the cooking cavity. This energy source causes water and fat molecules to vibrate at very high speeds, thus generating heat. The food product heats most rapidly where moisture occurs and where the density or thickness is minimal. Thus a product that is thick in the middle will not cook as uniformly as a flat or thin food product, and a liquid will heat more quickly than a solid of the same dimensions. Uniform cooking is accomplished when small amounts of foods are cooked at one time and the oven is equipped with two emitters (magnetrons). The greater the amount of power from each magnetron, the faster the foods will cook. Ovens with a rating of over 1,000 watts are recommended for commercial use; microwave ovens rated between 400 and 800 watts are not recommended for commercial use.

PRIMARY USE IN THE FOOD OPERATION

Microwave ovens are widely used in restaurants to thaw and/or quickly cook small quantities of food. The chef can hold foods in the frozen or uncooked state until they are ordered and then prepare them rapidly. The oven has not been widely accepted for institutional use because it does not perform well for quantity cooking. As larger amounts of food are placed in the oven, cooking time increases.

Factors that affect cooking time are:

❏ Temperature of the food placed in the oven

❏ Amount of moisture in the food

❏ Density or thickness of the product

❏ Amount of food placed at one time in the oven

❏ Rated wattage of the oven

Typical uses of the microwave oven and the cooking times that can be expected from a 1,400-watt unit are found in Figure 7-33.

Fryers

SPECIFICATIONS

Fryers cook food by immersion in hot fat. Frying temperatures range between 300° and 450°F (148.9° and 232.2°C). Fryers can be purchased as freestanding (Figure 7-34), table-mounted, modular, or drop-in models. If

Food Item	Weight, Ounces (Grams)	Cooking Time
Roast beef	6 (170)	25 seconds
Steak (to be thawed)	12 (340)	20 seconds (each side)
Bowl of soup	8 (227)	45 seconds
Precooked bacon	2 (57)	15 seconds
Ham, sliced	3 (85)	30 seconds
Turkey, sliced	5 (142)	50 seconds
Meat loaf	5 (142)	50 seconds
Hot dog (2)	5 (142)	1 minute, 10 seconds
Stuffed lobster (thawed)	12 (340)	1 minute, 30 seconds
Fish fillet	5 (142)	30 seconds

Figure 7-33. Microwave oven cooking times.

the freestanding fryer is selected, gas can be used as an energy source. If the modular or drop-in method for mounting the fryer is chosen, electricity is likely to be used because so few manufacturers offer gas-fired drop-in units. The design of the gas-operated fryer requires a greater amount of

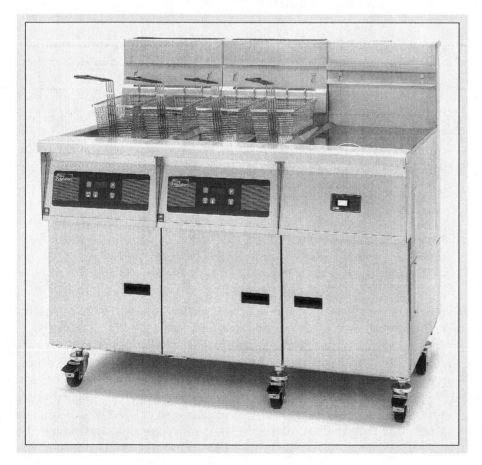

Figure 7-34. Fryer. (Courtesy of Pitco Frialator, Inc., a Blodgett Company.)

depth under the fat container, which must be enclosed in the floor-mounted cabinet.

Gas fryers are heated by a ring or straight "ribbon" burner located under the fat container or, in the newer high-capacity fryers, by a tube-fired system. Electric fryers are heated by resistance heaters enclosed in metal and immersed in the fat around the outside edges. Electric fryers are easy to clean because the immersion heaters can be raised out of the fat and the container can be removed and scrubbed in the pot sink. Gas fryers usually have a "cold" zone at the bottom of the fat container where crumbs and burned food particles can accumulate. Both types of fryers are popular, and neither type is recommended as more desirable than the other.

All fryers represent a safety hazard because the fat is kept at a very high temperature and can easily catch fire. Fire codes require that a fire extinguishing nozzle capable of automatically extinguishing a flash fire be located over each fryer. Fire codes also require a disconnect device that will cut off the source of energy from the device in the event that a fire does occur.

Accessories that are available for fryers include:

❑ Automatic fryer basket lifters

❑ Solid-state controls with timers

❑ Self-contained automatic fat-filtering device

❑ Stainless-steel frying chambers and exterior panels

❑ Semiautomatic loading systems

❑ Casters

Because of the extensive amount of grease that spills around fryers, sanitation is a major concern for the food facilities design consultant. Fryers that are portable or that are mounted in a modular bank and wall-hung are an excellent means of simplifying the sanitation problem. Both of these mounting methods permit frequent mopping under the fryer so that grease does not accumulate.

Pressure fryers seal the cooking cavity and introduce pressure. Pressurized frying results in a quicker cooking time. It takes more time, however, to load and seal products in a pressurized fryer than in a standard model.

PRIMARY USE IN THE FOOD OPERATION Fryers are popular pieces of equipment because the public demands foods that are cooked in hot fat to a golden brown appearance. French fries, breaded meats, batter-dipped meats and vegetables, and French toast are foods typically cooked in the deep-fat fryer or pressure fryer.

PASTA COOKERS The pasta cooker is included in the fryer section of this text because this piece of equipment is an adaptation of a fryer, using similar stainless-steel enclosures. Typically, two "fryer" units are placed side by side, and one side serves as the cooker and the second as a means of washing away excess starch. Automatic fryer lift baskets are used to lower and raise the baskets, so that cooking time is controlled. The basket of pasta is then placed in the second water bath for rinsing and holding, and a swing-away faucet is used to rinse away the starch. Cooking is stopped by the cold water, and the water drains into an overflow. Typically, 6 pounds (2.72 kilograms) of dry pasta become 15 pounds (6.80 kilograms) of cooked pasta, enough for about twenty-four servings. These cooked portions are placed in small containers, which can in turn be automatically lowered into the water that has been set for a warming mode.

Fryers are rated by the capacity of the fat container. Typical sizes range from 15 to 75 pounds (7 to 34 kilograms) of shortening or fat. Specifications are also often used in which pounds of french fries per hour are the standard of performance—typically, 30 to 100 pounds (13.6 to 45.3 kilograms) per hour. The number of fryers needed would depend on the variety of fried items on the menu and the volume of food to be prepared.

DETERMINING CAPACITY AND SIZE

Electricity and gas are the only sources of energy for deep-fat fryers. Fryers are energy-efficient unless they are left on needlessly. The number of BTUs required or the electrical load is determined by the size of the fryer and the speed of recovery. Fryers that have a quick recovery when the fat temperature drops are more expensive but are preferable because of the shorter cooking time. Fryers that permit the temperature of the fat to drop too low will produce a greasy, unpleasant food product. High-efficiency fryers using the tube-type burners may be a good investment because of the quick recovery, extended fat life, and high food output.

ENERGY USAGE AND UTILITY REQUIREMENTS

The range section of a foodservice facility is the most heavily used and often the most poorly designed section of the kitchen. Open-top (burner) and hot-top (solid) ranges are not energy-efficient to begin with, and they are usually turned on by the cooks when the operation opens and left on until it closes. Most food facilities would be better designed if the kitchen did not include open-top or hot-top ranges. The exception to this is the restaurant or club that includes a large number of sautéed foods or omelets on its menu. The open-top range is preferable for sautéing because the flame can be seen and adjusted. Figure 7-35 illustrates a range section with open burners.

Ranges

The types of ranges most often used in food-service facilities include:

SPECIFICATIONS

❑ Open top with burners for sautéing
❑ Grill (or griddle) top of polished steel plate on which food can be cooked (e.g., pancakes, hamburgers, chops, scrambled eggs, etc.)
❑ Hot top of solid steel, on which pans are placed but not food
❑ Radial fin top, for large stock pots

Ranges can be ordered in combinations of these styles, such as a grill section placed adjacent to a open-burner section.

The ranges are often placed in the hot-food section of the kitchen in a bank or line of equipment to form a continuous range section. Spreader plates can be placed between the equipment pieces to create convenient spaces for holding raw or cooked foods. The equipment can be specified with ovens under each piece or as modular with the equipment mounted on a stainless-steel stand. The modular version is much easier to clean but less space-efficient.

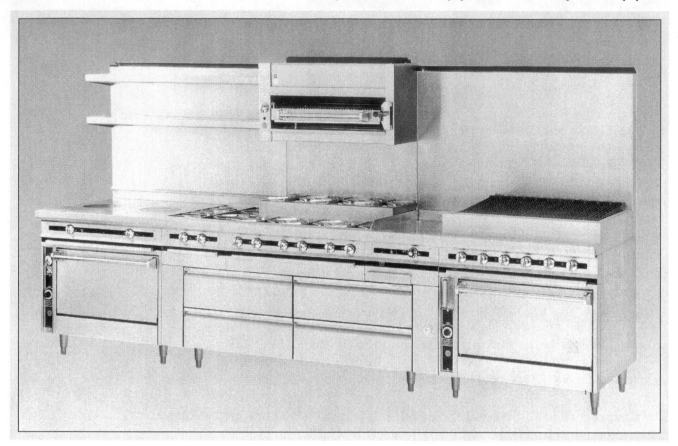

Figure 7-35. Range section.
(Courtesy of Jade Range.)

Ranges can be purchased that are only 1 foot (305 millimeters) wide with two hot-plate burners. These are very handy for small-volume range needs in a foodservice facility that does not have sautéed food items on the menu.

Many range manufacturers offer two (or more) lines of ranges, one described as being appropriate for restaurant use and the other for institutional or heavy-duty use. The nomenclature is not helpful to operators deciding which line of ranges to select because restaurants often place as many or more demands on their ranges than do institutional foodservice operations. The institutional line, though somewhat more expensive, generally is recommended for all commercial installations because it is more durable. In addition, restaurant ranges usually are offered in a limited number of configurations, whereas heavy-duty ranges can be custom configured to meet the exact needs of the operation. Restaurant ranges are appropriate in facilities where the demand is light, such as in a child-care center where one simple meal is produced each day.

PRIMARY USE IN THE FOOD OPERATION The small kitchen with a limited budget would probably include a range with an oven below it and an assortment of pots and pans for handling all of the cooking. The difficulty of cleaning, the inefficiency in energy usage, and the high labor costs in using and cleaning the pots and pans make the range an undesirable choice for a well-designed kitchen. The food facility that does a large amount of sautéing should include only one or two open-top ranges in combination with other, more efficient cooking equipment such as steamers, steam-jacketed kettles, and convection ovens.

The range ranks as one of the worst energy hogs in the entire kitchen equipment field. In a hot-top range, 91 to 94 percent of the energy is lost up the hood, with only 6 to 9 percent absorbed by the pot or pan; in an open-top range, 84 to 86 percent of the energy is lost up the hood, with 14 to 16 percent absorbed by the pot or pan.

ENERGY USAGE AND UTILITY
REQUIREMENTS

Utility connections for ranges include electricity, propane, and natural gas. Gas open-top ranges are usually preferred by cooks. The gas consumption by these pieces of equipment is typically between 40,000 and 120,000 BTUs.

Induction cooktop appliances are now appearing at equipment shows, but because of uncertainty among cooks and managers as to this technology, as well as high initial costs, only a limited number of these appliances are in use. The ceramic surface of the electric cooktop requires special cooking utensils, which is a disadvantage, but this technology offers interesting possibilities for the efficient use of electrical energy.

Grills

SPECIFICATIONS

A grill (often called a griddle) has a flat, heated surface that is used to cook foods quickly in short-order, institutional, and restaurant food facilities. A grill can be purchased as a freestanding unit, as a part of a range top, as a table model, or in a modular unit for mounting on an equipment stand. Recently, grills have been manufactured that can be dropped into a stainless-steel table, creating a smooth, easy-to-clean cooking area.

In institutions, grills are used to prepare a wide variety of food products, including steaks, chops, scrambled eggs, pancakes, and sautéed vegetables. The fast-food industry often uses a grill and a fryer for all of the hot-food preparation. Grills can be purchased for mounting on a stand with casters, permitting ease of cleaning after the grill is turned off at the end of the day. Fire regulations require automatic extinguishing devices because of the high temperature and the presence of flammable grease.

Accessories for grills are limited to the various methods for mounting the equipment, as discussed above. Grills that are purchased as part of a range section should be specified with spreader plates on each side so that raw ingredients and cooked products can be easily handled by the cook. Chrome-plated grills are popular because of the ease of cleaning the surface after the grill is turned off (Figure 7-36).

In the short-order restaurant, the grill is used for almost all breakfast menu items. At lunch, hamburgers, hot dogs, steaks, grilled sandwiches, and many other fast-food items are cooked quickly and efficiently on the grill. In all types of food facilities, the grill is an extremely valuable piece of equipment that can prepare many different types of food.

PRIMARY USE IN THE
FOOD OPERATION

Grills are usually purchased in widths of 2, 3, 4, 5, or 6 feet (610, 915, 1,220, 1,525, or 1,830 millimeters). The distance from front to back of the grill top

DETERMINING CAPACITY AND SIZE

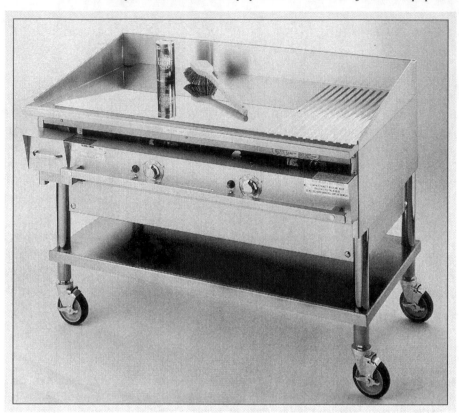

Figure 7-36. Chrome-plated griddle. (Courtesy of Keating of Chicago.)

is usually between 21 and 34 inches (530 and 860 millimeters), less the narrow trough that is located along the front or back edge for collecting grease. Grills are rated by the number of hamburgers per hour that can be prepared. This cooking performance standard usually falls within a range of 400 hamburgers per hour for a 24-inch (610-millimeter) grill to 2,400 hamburgers per hour for a 6-foot (1,830-millimeter) grill.

Large grills usually have one control dial and thermostat for each 12 inches (305 millimeters) of grill surface. This feature permits the cook to have different surface temperatures at several points across the grill, so that different foods can be cooked at the same time. For example, fried eggs, sausage, and pancakes could all be cooked at the same time on a 4- or 6-foot (1,220- or 1,830-millimeter) grill.

ENERGY USAGE AND UTILITY REQUIREMENTS

The grill is energy-efficient only if it is turned off when not in use. The common practice of keeping the grill on for many hours even though it is not being fully utilized makes this piece of equipment a high energy user. Grills can be preheated in six to eight minutes and should be either turned off or set at a very low temperature during the slow periods of the day. Gas and electric grills are both popular, and neither seems to have any advantage over the other. Special grills that significantly decrease cooking time are now manufactured by a few equipment companies. These grills use a hinged device that is placed over the food with infrared heaters that cook the product on the top while the grill surface cooks the bottom.

The grooved griddle (grill) is constructed in much the same way as a conventional grill. Deep grooves are molded into the cooking surface of the grill, which give a dark, striped appearance to the meat as it is cooked. The grooved griddle is an excellent alternative to the overfired or underfired broiler for several reasons:

❑ Less energy is consumed.

❑ The amount of smoke produced is greatly reduced.

❑ Grease from the product is easily collected.

❑ The quality of the food product is more easily controlled because the temperature can be precisely set.

❑ Meat products are marked attractively, and the caramelizing effect adds a pleasant taste.

This type of grill is an excellent substitute for the conventional broiler. In addition, grooved griddles can be used for almost all the same foods that are normally prepared on a grill, except for eggs and pancakes.

Grooved griddles consume significantly less energy than broilers and approximately the same amount of energy as grills. Gas and electricity are the two available sources of energy for this piece of equipment.

Grooved Griddle

SPECIFICATIONS

PRIMARY USE IN THE FOOD OPERATION

ENERGY USAGE AND UTILITY REQUIREMENTS

Bakery Equipment

Bakeries that are designed as a part of a restaurant or institution can range in size from a table in the corner with a small oven to a full-size production bakery to serve multiple dining halls at a university or large hospital complex. The size of the bakery and volume of product produced will determine the type of equipment needed. Bakery equipment is typically more automated because baked products are made in high volume with consistent processes. Automatic doughnut machines, roll dividers/rounders, and sheeter production tables are all highly specialized bakery equipment used for high-volume production.

As is the case with other preparation functions, the equipment selected for baking is determined by the menu. However, in selecting baking equipment, facility designers work closely with the owner to determine which items can be cost-justified. A family restaurant cannot bake sandwich bread (the usual white and wheat loaves) as inexpensively as it can be purchased from a large commercial bakery. But that same restaurant might be able to produce a signature sticky cinnamon bun at a cost that is justifiable. Similarly, a college that prepares 120 dozen cookies daily should invest in a cookie dropper, a machine that automates the process of forming balls of cookie dough on sheet pans.

Figure 7-37 compares the baking equipment that typically is used in small (restaurant) and medium (institutional) bakeries. The restaurant purchases bread, dinner rolls, and pies from a commercial bakery. It prepares breakfast muffins, sticky buns, and cakes from mixes. The institutional bakery purchases sandwich bread from a commercial bakery but makes dinner rolls, muffins, buns, cakes, pizza dough, and pies in its own bakery.

Equipment Item	Small Bakery (Restaurant)	Medium Bakery (Institution)
Maple-top baker's table	✓	✓
Bench scale	✓	✓
Mobile flour and sugar bins	✓	✓
Mixer for dough preparation	✓	✓
Proofer, simple	✓	
Proofer, complex		✓
Roll divider/rounder		✓
Dough sheeter		✓
Steam-jacketed kettle		✓
Convection oven(s)	✓	
Rotary or rack oven(s)		✓
Dough retarder		✓

Figure 7-37. Comparison of small (restaurant) and medium (institutional) bakeries.

Specialized baking equipment shown in Figure 7-37 includes the following:

❏ *Sheeter*. A sheeter (Figure 7-38) serves the function of a large metal rolling pin, driven by a motor. A small amount of flour falls onto the rolls to prevent the dough from sticking. Small pods of pie or pizza dough are placed between the rollers and stretched out into a large thin sheet. A pizza or pie crust is made quickly, saving a considerable amount of hand work.

❏ *Roll divider/rounder*. A divider/rounder is suitable for dividing and rounding soft roll doughs, kaiser rolls, hoagies, pizza, and French

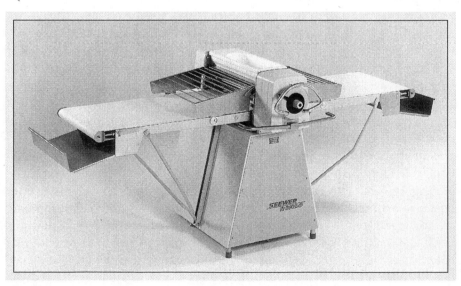

Figure 7-38. Sheeter. (Courtesy of Rondo.)

rolls. The machine compresses a round of dough (about the size of a dinner plate) and divides it into fifteen to thirty-six equal pieces. These pieces are then formed into round balls by a rotating action of the machine. A production capacity of five thousand to seven thousand rolls per hour is possible. Labor savings for a food operation serving over a thousand persons per meal would be significant.

❏ *Proofer*. A proofer is a heated cabinet with a means of maintaining moisture in which yeast doughs are placed to rise. The most common proofers are simple one-compartment portable cabinets with heating devices located in the bottom. The heating device has a container for water, which, when heated, distributes the steam through a small channel in the back of the cabinet to all of the shelves in the proofer. This type of proofer is inexpensive and will typically last for many years. For a medium to large restaurant or institutional bakery, a more complex proofer is desirable (Figure 7-39), in which full racks of rolls can be rolled into a one-, two-, or three-section proofer, with highly controlled steam (humidity) and temperature.

Figure 7-39. Proofer.
(Courtesy of Traulsen and Co., Inc.)

❑ *Retarder.* A dough retarder is nothing but a refrigerator. Cold temperatures slow the rising process by inhibiting the yeast's fermentation. Retarders are used to hold yeast-based doughs prior to baking.

SERVICE AND CAFETERIA EQUIPMENT

A wide variety of choices exist for the food facilities design consultant in developing the plans for service and cafeteria equipment. Service equipment usually includes those items that are located in or near the place where the food is presented to the customer. Typical kinds of equipment in these areas are:

❑ Cold-pan display (iced or mechanically chilled), such as salad bars

❑ Food warmers of various configurations

❑ Coffee urns and dispensers

❑ Ice machines and dispensers

❑ Refrigerators for holding dressings, butter, cream, and other perishables

❑ Beverage dispensing equipment

❑ Tray, silver, and napkin dispensers

❑ Condiment dispensing units

Information on some of these service items is included in other sections of this book. Certain kinds of equipment—cold beverage dispensers, for example—are furnished by vending companies and therefore not included in this text. Service equipment that should be carefully considered by the food facilities planner are food warmers, coffee urns, and ice machines and beverage dispensers.

Food Warmers

SPECIFICATIONS

As the name suggests, food warmers heat and/or hold foods to a temperature that is just below the cooking temperature with little loss of moisture. The thermostat setting for this equipment is usually between 100°F and 300°F (38° and 149°C). Because a wide variety of bread and food warmers are available, the capacities of this equipment can best be determined by reading the information available in equipment catalogs.

One common type of food warmer is the steam table. In the early part of the nineteenth century, steam tables were large steam-heated, water-filled compartments (bain-maries, in effect) that kept foods hot in deep pans from either a hot-water bath or the evaporating steam. A modern "steam" table is not heated by steam. Instead, the wells are heated using electric elements. Many steam tables can be operated "wet" (with water in the wells) or "dry" (without water in the wells). The water in the wells is heated by the electrical elements, creating heated water vapor and giving the customer the impression of "steam" heat.

Steam table wells (Figure 7-40) are designed for standard 12-by-20-inch pans. In countries using the metric system, steam tables are designed for standard sizes of gastronorm pans—e.g., 325 by 530 millimeters. The heat level is controlled by a thermostat. The capacity of this food warmer is a

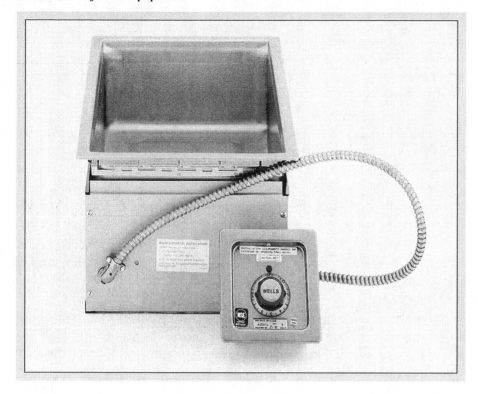

Figure 7-40. Hot-food insert. (Courtesy of Wells Manufacturing Company.)

function of the depth of the pans inserted into the wells. A hot food counter would be designed with enough wells to contain all the hot menu items.

The most popular bread warmers include one, two, or three stainless-steel drawers mounted in a cabinet. These warmers can be purchased as built-in or freestanding units. Capacities of the warmers vary with the height and width of the drawers and the number of drawers specified. Often, these bread warmers are located in the service area of a restaurant so that the service staff can provide rolls without making a trip to the kitchen.

Another popular form of food warmer is the heated cabinet. Some of these units are designed for countertop "grab-and-go" service, whereas others are designed to hold food for later service. Food warming and holding cabinets can be designed for portable use or for permanent installation. They include heated pass-through cabinets that are constructed to hold the standard 12-by-20-inch pan (325-by-530-millimeter gastronorm pan) and full-height pass-through warmers that are similar in appearance to a single-compartment refrigerator. Food-warming cabinets are available with a variety of options. Some simply heat the cabinet, while others introduce humidity and/or control the rate of evaporation within the cavity to preserve the quality and texture of sensitive foods such as eggs or biscuits.

The food facility design consultant should be conservative in specifying the number and capacity of food warmers because of the tendency of cooks to prepare food too early and then store it away in the food warmer well before the meal begins. To encourage last-minute and batch cookery, there should be enough food warmers to hold only a small proportion of the total food needed for the meal.

ENERGY USAGE AND UTILITY REQUIREMENTS

Thermostats and better insulation have dramatically increased the energy efficiency of bread and food warmers. Utility connections are usually 110 volts or 208/220 volts. Most hot-food inserts for steam tables are wired as a single bank of warmers. These food wells may be purchased with or without drains for wet or dry steam table operations.

Beverage Equipment

A wide variety of beverage-related equipment is available to the foodservice operator, and much of this equipment—especially coffee, juice, and soft-drink dispensing systems—is furnished by the beverage supplier. There are two reasons for this trend:

❏ The supplier wants the customer to use his/her product and to display the name of the product on the equipment. Providing the beverage equipment ensures an ongoing purchase of the product.

❏ The beverage supplier is concerned about the quality of the product and typically provides equipment that will dispense the best drink possible.

Soft-drink companies typically offer dispensing equipment to food-service operations as part of their contract to provide syrup and carbon dioxide (CO_2). Thus, many small to medium-size food operators simply call the local soft-drink company and ask for their assistance in designing and installing the proper beverage equipment. However, soft-drink firms may be reluctant to provide equipment if the volume to be served is very high or if the owner desires specialized dispensing equipment. In these situations, the soft-drink dispensing equipment would be purchased as part of the overall equipment package for the foodservice facility rather than furnished by the beverage vendor.

Two specialized equipment pieces that should be considered in many food operations are espresso machines and "bag-in-box" soft-drink systems.

ESPRESSO/CAPPUCCINO MACHINES AND COFFEE BEAN GRINDERS

The popularity of espresso and cappuccino has created a high demand for equipment that will produce these drinks in an authentic manner. Espresso is a thick, dark coffee made by forcing hot water through finely ground coffee under pressure. Good espresso has a strong, flavorful coffee taste and aroma and shows a foam called *crema* at the top. Cappuccino is a combination of espresso and hot steamed or frothed milk. Cinnamon, chocolate, and whipped cream are often added but are not part of the true Italian formula.

High-volume espresso machines (Figure 7-41) are expensive when compared to other coffee equipment, but the profit potential for a high-quality product may justify the expense. One-, two-, and three-unit brewing devices can be specified, and a variety of decorative domes and accessories are available.

Coffee grinders are usually sold by the same companies that sell the espresso machines and are available in a wide variety of sizes and appearances. Review of several manufacturers' products is recommended.

SOFT-DRINK SYSTEMS

There are two basic soft-drink systems: premix, in which the product is mixed and ready to drink and only needs to be chilled, and postmix, in

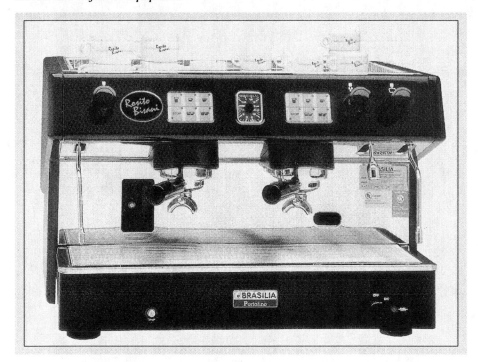

Figure 7-41. Espresso maker. (Courtesy of Rosito Bisani.)

which the product is shipped as a concentrate and water and carbon dioxide gas is added at the dispenser. Postmix systems are the most popular.

Depending on the volume, postmix systems can be as simple as a beverage-dispensing machine that is connected to a container of concentrate and a small tank of carbon dioxide (CO_2) plus cold water. The machine mixes, chills, and dispenses the beverage into a glass. The concentrate is typically held in a small (approximately five gallons) metal tank or in a cardboard-and-plastic "bag-in-a-box." Larger systems use a carbonator, a large CO_2 tank, a chiller, and plastic tubes that permit the beverage components to be located remote from the dispensing equipment. These larger systems permit the storage of the support equipment in a basement or nearby room, where cleaning and delivery access is simplified.

Coffee Urns

Although methods of brewing coffee have improved significantly over the chuck-wagon style of throwing a handful of grounds into a pot of boiling water, the basic method has been the same for many years. Boiling water is sprayed or poured over coffee grounds for a precise period of time so that the water carrying the coffee flavor and aroma drips through to the holding container. The coffee grounds are held in a cloth or stainless-steel basket, and the grounds are removed after the brewing process ends. This is done so that the bitter substance from the grounds does not continue to drip into the coffee. The formula for good coffee includes a clean urn, a good blend of coffee, and a fresh supply of water. The equipment is designed to hold the coffee at just below the boiling point by surrounding the coffee container with boiling water. This outer jacket of boiling water is used as the source of boiling water for the next batch of coffee and for making hot tea or other beverages. Figure 7-42 shows a commercial coffee urn system.

Figure 7-42. Coffee urns. (Courtesy of Grindmaster Corporation.)

SPECIFICATIONS   The most popular sizes are the 3-gallon urn, twin 3-gallon urns (6 gallons), 6-gallon urn, or twin 6-gallon urns (12 gallons). Automatic coffee urns do not require the operator to pour the boiling water over the grounds or to measure the water. These urns usually are provided with a mixing device that forces a small amount of steam through the brewed coffee to prevent "layering."

DETERMINING CAPACITY AND SIZE   The standard cup of coffee is 5 to 6 ounces, and the amount of coffee produced from one pound is usually 2½ to 3 gallons.

ENERGY USAGE AND UTILITY REQUIREMENTS   Coffee urns may be heated with gas, electricity, or steam. Gas-heated urns are economical but need a method for removing the gas fumes. Steam urns are energy-efficient and do not tend to "burn out," because they provide a more even supply of heat than do gas or electric urns. Electric urns are popular because they are less expensive to purchase, are easy to install, and can easily be relocated.

Although the coffee urn is frequently used in medium- and large-capacity foodservice facilities, one of the most popular coffee machines for restaurants, hotels, and small institutions is the automatic coffee brewer that deposits the coffee directly into a decanter. The principle of this coffee maker is that the water is heated as it flows through the device (rather than being stored) and is sprayed over a premeasured amount of coffee held in a paper filter. The coffee immediately pours in a small stream into a glass or stainless-steel container. The decanter can then be used by the server to pour coffee for the guests in the dining room. These units are less expensive than urns and produce an excellent quality of coffee. They are heated by electricity, and most can be plugged directly into a wall outlet.

A recent change to the popular automatic coffee brewer described above is the portable coffee brewing/serving unit (Figure 7-43). These coffeemakers heat the water as it flows from the plumbing connection (cold water), and the boiling water is sprayed over the grounds in a paper filter. The coffee then flows into two portable containers, which are well insulated and attractive in appearance. The insulated containers of coffee are popular because of the interest in different flavored coffees and the ease of moving the "shuttle" units to different locations—for example, a server station, a small employee cafeteria line, meeting rooms, and so on.

PORTABLE COFFEE BREWING/ SERVING SYSTEMS

Figure 7-43. Portable coffee brewers. (Courtesy of Bunn.)

Bar Equipment   Bar design has two distinct components. The front of the bar and the bar top are typically decorative. Wood, copper, plastic laminate, and vinyl or leather bar rails are all popular. The underside of the bar—the area used by the bartender—is where design efficiency is important. Several leading manufacturers have developed modular components in which the various parts fit together to form a sanitary and efficient work space. Typical components would include:

- ❑ Ice chest—an insulated storage area for ice (does not make ice)
- ❑ Drain board—both a work surface and a place to set glasses and utensils to air-dry
- ❑ Blender station—a space designed for blenders, including a small sink for sanitizing utensils
- ❑ Refrigerated storage chest—for holding condiments and cooling bottles
- ❑ Hand sink, including soap and towel dispensers—required by the health department
- ❑ Three-compartment sink—required by the health department for washing and sanitizing glassware
- ❑ Storage bins—a place to stack 20-by-20-inch racks of clean or dirty glasses
- ❑ Bottle rails, often called "speed rails"—used for storing open bottles of the bar liquor stock
- ❑ Fruit drawer—a special drawer to store fruit that will be used in mixed drinks

Although not widely used, small glass-washing machines are available for undercounter use. Storage cabinets for cooling bottles of beer and wine are often located on the wall behind the bar or out of sight under the bar. Figure 7-44 shows underbar units.

Figure 7-44. Bar units.
(Courtesy of Perlick.)

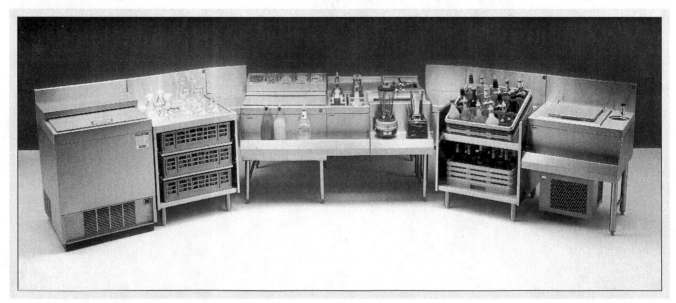

There are two methods for dispensing beer from a keg (actually three methods if the British system of pumping beer from the cellar is used). The direct-draw beer coolers are simple and highly recommended for the small to medium-size bar. These systems have a small undercounter refrigerated cabinet that keeps the keg cold and dispenses the beer through the top of the cabinet. The simplicity and ease of moving the beer to the glass is reason enough for recommending this piece of equipment. Remote systems are much more complex, requiring insulated beer lines for short distances or complex tube-within-a-tube systems. In these systems, circulated saline solution in the outer tube chills the beer in the inner tube and delivers the cold beer at a remote location. Obviously, remote systems are expensive and can only be cost-justified in large-volume operations that require the location of the keg some distance from the bar.

BEER SYSTEMS

Wine storage is fairly easy to handle in the food operation of restaurants, hotels, and country clubs. Red wines need to be stored in a cool area, with the bottles on their sides so that the cork stays moist. White wines need to be refrigerated prior to service, and there are many opinions as to the proper temperature. If the white wine is too cold, some of the subtle flavors are not fully realized. However, many white wines sit for some time and warm up considerably before they are consumed.

WINE STORAGE AND
DISPENSING EQUIPMENT

Equipment commonly used for the storage of white wines include small behind-the-bar refrigerators that merchandise the house wines very well or large single or double reach-in refrigerators with special racks for keeping the wine on its side. Another common wine display device permits the house wines to be opened and capped so that air does not destroy the flavors; this allows the bartender to save partially used bottles for several days.

Ice machines and dispensers have become commonplace in the United States because of the high demand by American consumers for ice in almost all beverages. Also, ice not only keeps food cold but adds aesthetic appeal to salad bars and other food displays. Automatic ice makers and dispensers facilitate the use of ice in institutional and commercial foodservice operations.

Ice Machines and Dispensers

SPECIFICATIONS

In the early days of automatic ice making, the machine and storage bin were housed in one cabinet. That concept, however, was not adequate for the large variety of production and storage requirements across the industry. Manufacturers then separated the ice maker and the storage bin, allowing operators greater flexibility in sizing their equipment. With separate production and storage units, an operation can have the production capacity it needs to store ice for peak demand periods, rather than producing it all at once. Today, the separate production and storage concept is the industry standard.

Another major trend has been toward increased customer self-service. Higher labor costs, more stringent sanitation requirements, and the overall convenience of self-service have made ice dispensers standard equipment in a growing number of food-service operations.

Ice dispensers are total systems comprising three major components: production, storage, and dispensing. With respect to production, ice makers can be divided into two general types: flakers and cubers. Cubers produce clear, solid forms of ice that melt more slowly than flakes. However, the equipment required to produce cubes in high volume is more complex and expensive than flake-producing machines. Flakers produce ice on a continuous basis and require fewer moving parts and less energy than cubers. Their major disadvantages are that the quality of the ice is difficult to control and it melts much faster than cubes.

Storage bins are available with varying capacities; 400 to 800 pounds is typical of one major manufacturer's line of dispensers. The bins can be refilled manually or automatically and are designed to stand on the floor or countertop or to be integrated into the service counter. Bins are insulated, equipped with a drain, and constructed of plastic, aluminum, galvanized steel, or stainless steel. A typical ice machine on a bin is shown in Figure 7-45.

Dispensing mechanisms consist of all the components necessary to move the ice from the storage bin into the customer's glass. The most common (and least expensive) dispensers are gravity-fed, with the ice stored above the dispensing device. Such dispensers may combine production, storage, and dispensing functions into a single unit, or they may only store and dispense. In other systems suitable for large-volume operations, the ice maker is located below the service counter and fills a storage bin located adjacent to it. Ice is mechanically drawn up from the bin by means of a rotating "sweep arm" or auger and dispensed into the customer's glass (Figure 7-46).

Figure 7-45. Ice machine. (Courtesy of Scotsman.)

Figure 7-46. Ice dispenser with under-counter ice maker. (Courtesy of Follett.)

Dispensers with storage bins located above the counter generally give a more consistent quality of ice than those with storage compartments below and are mechanically simpler in design. However, when large quantities of ice must be stored, it is generally preferable to build the storage compartment into the serving counter and out of the customers' view.

The ice machine or ice dispensing system is used to produce, store, and dispense ice for the various needs of the operation, such as beverage cooling and food displays.

PRIMARY USE IN THE FOOD OPERATION

In choosing equipment to meet the requirements for ice in a foodservice operation, a number of factors need to be taken into consideration. Ice requirements include the amount needed for beverages and for other cooling/holding purposes such as salad bars and seafood displays.

DETERMINING CAPACITY AND SIZE

Beverage ice requirements can be determined using a rule of thumb based on the capacity of the glass. A glass typically requires one-half its capacity in beverage volume (fluid ounces) and one-half in the weight of the ice. For example, a 10-ounce (296 milliliters) glass filled to capacity will have approximately 5 fluid ounces (158 milliliters) of beverage and 5 ounces (1.4 milligrams) by weight of ice. If it is typical in the operation to fill the glass only halfway with ice, then the weight of the ice required would be 25 percent of the capacity of the glass.

The main problem in determining the total ice required for beverage service is the varying demand for beverages experienced in almost all foodservice operations. During peak business hours, especially in the warmer months, the demand for ice is high; it drops off significantly at other times. Many operations experience peak demand for ice during lunch and dinner; hence the demand for ice is great between 11:30 A.M. and 9:00 P.M.

Ice machines are rated according to the amount of ice they can produce in a twenty-four-hour period; ice storage bins are rated by the amount they can contain. Although an ice machine may have the rated capacity to produce, for example, 384 pounds (174 kilograms) of ice per day, this does not necessarily mean that this amount of ice will be produced. If the storage bin holds 200 pounds (91 kilograms) of ice, the machine will shut itself off when the bin is full. When the peak demand hits, the 200 pounds (91 kilograms) of ice in the storage bin plus the amount of ice that the machine can produce during the peak period is the total amount of ice available. To obtain the full amount that the ice maker can produce, a storage bin must be selected that is slightly larger than the machine's rated production capacity. With a very large bin, however, there is the risk of ice melting at the bottom.

Figure 7-47 may be helpful in determining the capacity needed in ice production and storage to meet requirements for beverage service. For the sake of illustration, it is assumed that one peak period of demand occurs during the day and that the glasses contain 50 percent ice by weight. Each guest is expected to be served two servings of iced beverages. For example, if the operation serves 500 guests, each with two 8-ounce glasses, the minimum requirement would be 250 pounds of ice per day.

Meals per Day	Glasses per Meal	Total Glasses	Glass Size			
			4 oz	6 oz	8 oz	10 oz
250	2	500	63	94	125	156
	Plus 25%		78	117	156	195
500	2	1000	125	188	250	313
	Plus 25%		156	234	313	391
750	2	1500	188	281	375	469
	Plus 25%		234	352	469	586
1000	2	2000	250	375	500	625
	Plus 25%		313	469	625	781
1500	2	3000	375	563	750	938
	Plus 25%		469	703	938	1172
2000	2	4000	500	750	1000	1250
	Plus 25%		625	938	1250	1563
3000	2	6000	750	1125	1500	1875
	Plus 25%		938	1406	1875	2344

Figure 7-47. Ice requirements based on demand.

The production and storage capacity of the ice machine selected should exceed the amounts indicated on the chart by 25 percent or more, depending upon the operation, for the following reasons:

❏ Ice is used for other purposes, such as salad bars.

❏ Ice is wasted.

❏ The production capacity of the ice-making unit may decrease during the summer months, when the air (or water) used to cool the refrigeration system is warmer.

❏ Employees may take ice out of the bin because they assume it is "free."

Figure 7-47 shows the result of adding 25 percent to the ice requirements. In the example given above, the operation should select an ice machine capable of producing and storing a minimum of 313 pounds of ice per day.

ENERGY USAGE AND UTILITY REQUIREMENTS

Motors on ice machine compressors, which usually fall in the range of $\frac{1}{3}$ to 1 horsepower, consume small amounts of electricity. They are connected to a 110-volt or 208/240-volt power source, depending on motor size. Air-cooled ice machines do not use large amounts of water. If the ice maker is water-cooled, however, it uses a large amount of water because the machine typically operates for longer periods during the day. In a well-ventilated area where the heat released by the ice machine is not objectionable, air-cooled machines are preferable. In areas where ventilation is restricted or the release of heat into the environment is undesirable, then water-cooled ice-making equipment may be advisable. Careful thought must be given to a decision to use water-cooled refrigeration because of the waste of drinkable water.

A wide variety of soft-serve products can be made from a soft-serve machine (Figure 7-48). Frozen yogurt, frozen custard, sorbet (sherbet), and ice milk are all popular desserts. Sundaes, cones, cups, and mixed flavors of product, either served by an employee or self-served, are all possible and are typically very profitable.

Small countertop models have a refrigerated container at the top for the liquid mix, which flows by gravity down into a cylinder that has refrigeration coils around the outside. When the liquid mix comes into contact with the freezing walls of the cylinder, a dasher of stainless steel or hard plastic scrapes the frozen product off the walls, incorporates air, and breaks down ice crystals. This produces a smooth product with a significant increase of volume because of air and freezing. The product is then deposited into a dish or cone. Large machines often hold the liquid mix in a bottom container for ease in filling and pump the proper amount of product into the freezing chamber.

Typical output volume can be determined by the number of hours per day that the machine is operated, since the production of frozen product is

Soft-Serve Machines

*Figure 7-48. Soft-serve machine.
(Courtesy of Taylor.)*

continuous. The size and capacity of a machine is determined by the horsepower of the motor and the capacity of the hopper that holds the liquid mix. Soft-serve machines should be sized carefully in large foodservice operations where the demand likely peaks immediately after lunch or dinner. Heavy demand may result in the product being drawn from the machine faster than the freezing cylinders can do their work. Pump machines, although more expensive initially, are desirable in high-demand settings because they inject more air into the finished product than do gravity machines.

WAREWASHING EQUIPMENT

The warewashing machine in a foodservice facility usually represents the largest single cost of any piece of equipment. The purchase price of the machine plus the cost of the dish tables represents a substantial investment. In addition to the purchase price, the operating costs of the machine will include:

- ❑ Water
- ❑ Electricity for machine motors
- ❑ Electricity, steam, or gas for the wash/rinse tanks and water booster heater
- ❑ Ventilation
- ❑ Sewer charges
- ❑ Detergents
- ❑ Drying agents
- ❑ Labor
- ❑ Maintenance

Because of these costs, warewashing equipment is among the most expensive to operate in the foodservice facility. The dish machine must therefore be carefully selected, with consideration given both to the initial (capital) cost and to the ongoing cost of operation.

One common misconception is that the larger the warewashing machine, the higher the operating costs. In some instances the opposite is true. The smaller single-tank dish machine requires an employee to lift the doors and push the racks through manually, and it uses hot water and detergent far less efficiently. Moreover, since the low speed and small capacity require longer working hours, the cost per dish washed indeed might be higher.

The machine selected should wash the dishes at the lowest possible cost per dish, assuming that the needed funds and space are available.

For purposes of comparison, a university foodservice dining hall will be used as an example. The hall serves eight hundred students three meals per day with one-and-a-half-hour dining periods. The number of dishes to be washed per meal is estimated as follows:

800 persons × 6 dishes per person (includes glasses or cups)
= 4,800 dishes and glasses per meal

Because the dish operation cannot run continuously, an efficiency factor of 70 percent is assumed, so the rated capacity of any machine is multiplied by 0.7.

❑ A small single-tank door machine (rated capacity 1,500 dishes per hour) would wash these dishes in just over four and a half hours.

❑ A single-tank conveyor machine (rated capacity 4,000 dishes per hour) would wash them in under two hours.

❑ A two-tank conveyor machine (rated capacity of 6,500 dishes per hour) would complete the job in about one hour.

If employees working part time were used for the one-hour period needed to wash the dishes with the two-tank conveyor machine, then the economy of the largest machine, in comparison to machines that require a full-time dishwasher, is clear. In other words, by oversizing the machine, a significant labor savings is gained.

Warewashing machines all operate on the same principle. A spray of water is pumped over dishes and other utensils so that the soil is washed off by hot water and a detergent. The final rinse sanitizes the dishes either by spraying water at 180°F (82°C) or by using a chemical sanitizer. The dishes must be hot enough to dry without toweling when exposed to the air.

Dish Machines

TYPES OF DISH MACHINE

Single-Tank Door Machines   Single-tank door machines (Figure 7-49) consist of a tank containing hot wash water and a detergent dispenser. The

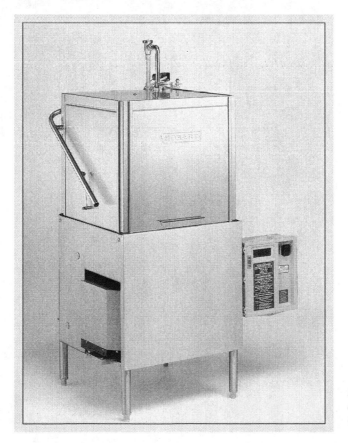

Figure 7-49. Single-tank door-type dish machine. (Courtesy of Hobart Corporation.)

machine is provided with stainless-steel doors. Scraping, loading, and unloading are done manually. The operator opens the doors, slides the loaded dish rack into the machine, closes the door, and initiates the wash cycle. Water and detergent are recirculated by an electric motor-driven pump that pushes water through spray arms or nozzles above and below the rack of dishes. The final rinse is sprayed onto the dishes at 180°F (82°C) after the wash cycle is complete. When the cycle is complete, the operator opens the door and slides the clean rack of dishes out of the machine and onto the clean-dish table for air drying.

Single-Tank Conveyor Machine   A single-tank conveyor machine (Figure 7-50) consists of a tank of hot wash water held at a temperature of 140°F (60°C) mixed with a detergent. After the dishes have been manually racked and prescraped, the operator pushes the rack to the load end of the machine. A conveyor with pawls catches the leading edge of the rack and pulls it through the dishwasher at a preset speed. The water and detergent are circulated by a motor-driven pump through spray arms above and below the dishes. The dishes pass through a final rinse at 180°F (82°C) and air-dry on a clean-dish table after they emerge from the machine.

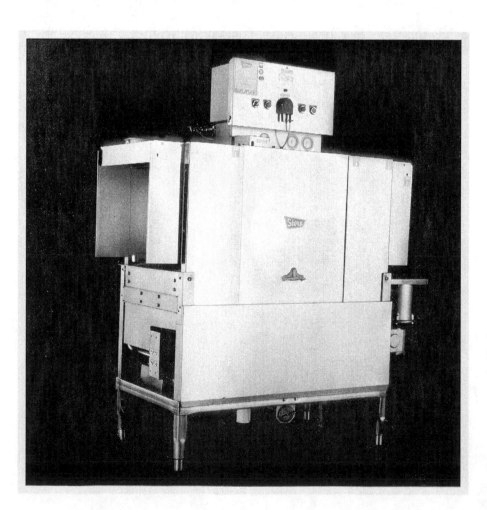

Figure 7-50. Single-tank conveyor dish machine. (Courtesy of Stero.)

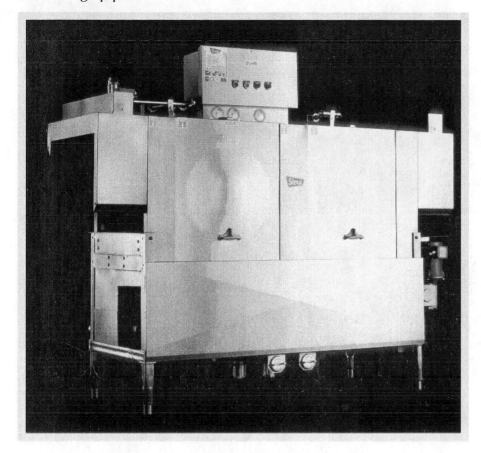

Figure 7-51. Two-tank conveyor dish machine. (Courtesy of Stero.)

Two-Tank Conveyor Machine   Two-tank conveyor-type dishwashing machines (Figure 7-51) are also available. The first tank contains hot wash water and detergent, and the second contains rinse water. The dishes go through a final rinse at 180°F (82°C). Motor-driven pumps circulate the wash water and spray rinse water over the dishes while they are carried through the machine by a conveyor. The addition of the extra rinse water tank permits dishes to be conveyed through the machine faster and results in a cleaner dish or utensil.

Flight, Rackless, or Peg-Type Machines   A flight-type dish machine (Figure 7-52) typically has two or three tanks. The two-tank machine consists of a wash tank and a rinse tank; the three-tank model has tanks for prewash, wash, and rinse. Both types provide a sanitizing final rinse. The flight machine uses a conveyor designed to hold most dishes and utensils without the need for racks. Dishes and trays are loaded directly onto the conveyor, which is equipped with rows of pegs approximately 4 inches high to hold trays and plates upright for proper washing, rinsing, and draining. The conveyor may be made of plastic and/or heavy-gauge stainless steel. Items such as cups, glasses, and silverware, however, must be racked in order to be conveyed through the machine.

Flight machines are frequently used in operations that wash dishes for six hundred or more persons per meal. Smaller flight machines with two

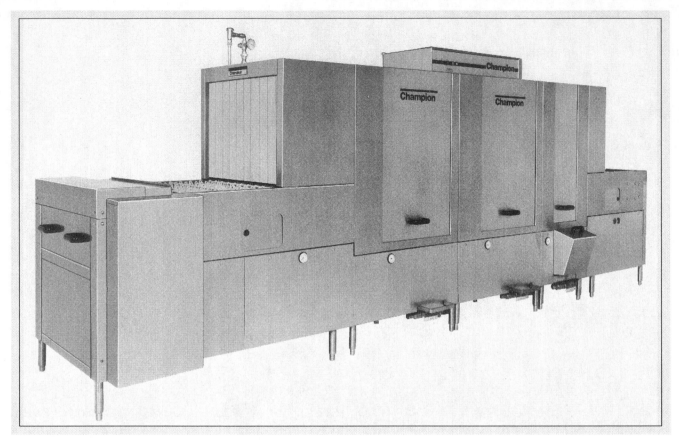

Figure 7-52. Flight-type dish machine. (Courtesy of Champion Industries.)

tanks may be economical for food facilities serving six hundred to nine hundred persons per meal. Food facilities that serve more than a thousand persons per meal would require a three-tank flight dish machine.

Circular Carousel or Continuous Conveyor Machine A circular dish machine (Figure 7-53) is a two- or three-tank machine attached to an oval-shaped dish table. The system uses a series of standard 20-by-20-inch (500-by-500-millimeter) dish racks that are conveyed around the oval. The circular dishwashing system is labor-efficient because the dishes are loaded directly onto the moving dish racks without first being stacked or accumulated. The second primary advantage is that the machine will continue to operate if left unattended for a few moments. (A flight-type machine will stop if a dish strikes the end of the conveyor without being removed.) The circular conveyor machine is especially labor-efficient in food operations that serve continuously over a long period of time or in high-volume foodservice operations.

SPECIFICATIONS Once the appropriate size and type of dish machine has been selected, a number of additional considerations must be addressed:

- ❏ *Tank heat energy source.* Options typically include steam coils, steam injectors, gas, and electricity.
- ❏ *Final rinse heat source.* Final rinse water is usually heated to 180°F (82°C) by a dedicated booster heater. Booster heaters traditionally

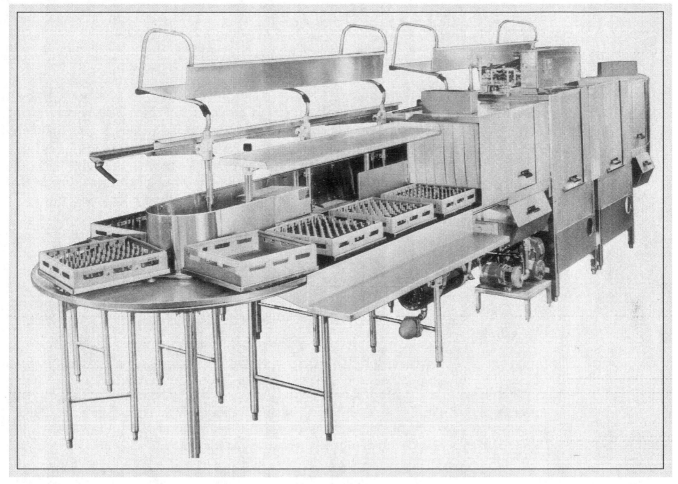

Figure 7-53. Carousel dish machine. (Courtesy of Adamation, Inc.)

have used steam (large machines) or electric (smaller machines) heat. Gas-fired booster heaters have recently become available and represent a potential operational savings where natural gas is less expensive than electricity.

❑ *Direction.* Dish machines are designed to operate either left to right or right to left, depending on the layout of the dish area.

Many accessories and options are available for all types of warewashing machines and of course add to their cost. Some of the options are:

❑ Blower dryer for rapid air drying of dishes and utensils

❑ Chemical sanitizing

❑ Vent hoods for each end of the machine

❑ Stainless-steel legs and frames (standard on some machines)

❑ Stainless-steel enclosure panels to cover the motors and plumbing

❑ Automatic fill

❑ Energy-saving features such as automatic shutoff after dishes (or racks) pass through the machine

❑ Common water, steam, and electrical connection points

PRIMARY USE IN THE
FOOD OPERATION

In addition to washing dishes, warewashing machines may be used to wash pots, pans, utensils, trays, sheet pans, and a variety of other items from the production areas. Unusual uses may include washing grease filters and ceiling tiles.

DETERMINING CAPACITY AND SIZE

Dish machines are rated by the number of dishes or racks per hour (at about twenty dishes per rack) that can be washed. Figure 7-54 illustrates the method for determining the dish machine size, assuming the standard efficiency factor of 70 percent. (It is always wise to err on the side of selecting a machine that is too large rather than too small.) Using Figure 7-54a, the volume of dishes for a 100-seat restaurant with an extensive menu that turns over the dining room one and a half times per hour would be:

$$100 \text{ seats} \times 1.5 = 150 \text{ persons per hour}$$

$$150 \text{ persons} \times 13 \text{ pieces of dinnerware per person} = 1,950 \text{ dishes per hour}$$

Figure 7-54b shows typical dish machine capacities taken from the catalog of a leading manufacturer. Continuing the example, 1,950 dishes per hour at 70 percent efficiency would require a machine that would handle:

$$1950 \div .70 = 2,786 \text{ dishes per hour}$$

Following Figure 7-54b, a two-tank conveyor machine would be the appropriate selection for this operation.

ENERGY USAGE AND UTILITY
REQUIREMENTS

To qualify for the NSF seal of approval, warewashing machines must have a preset time and volume of water for the dish to pass through the wash spray. The required volume of water for the final rinse for a single-tank machine is 74 gallons (280 liters) per hour, while for a flight machine the flow is 342 gallons (1,294 liters) per hour. This amount of water heated to 180°F (82°C) obviously consumes a large amount of energy. Added to this is the energy consumed by:

- ❏ Electric motors
- ❏ Tank heaters
- ❏ Electric controls
- ❏ Ventilation fans
- ❏ Heat for the blower dryer (if specified)
- ❏ Hot water that is used to fill the tanks

Type of Food Facility	Dishes and Glasses per Person*
Restaurant with limited menu	5–8
Restaurant with extensive menu	12–14
Cafeteria	7–10
Luxury hotel dining	12–16
* Does not include silverware or stainless eating utensils.	

Figure 7-54a. Dish utilization.

Dish Machine Type	Dishes per Hour	Racks per Hour
Single-tank door	1,550	62
Two-tank conveyor	5,850	234
Three-tank conveyor	6,650	265
Flight-type	12,000	

Figure 7-54b. Dish machine capacities.

Electrical connections are usually 208 volt, 220 volt, or 460/480 volt, and motors can be 1- or 3-phase. Since the energy and water bill for washing dishes is a very significant part of the total utility cost of operating the food facility, energy-saving accessories are certainly worth considering when purchasing a warewashing machine.

There are two primary differences between a potwashing machine (Figure 7-55) and a conventional dishwashing machine. First, the motor that pumps water under high pressure onto the pots and pans is larger than that normally installed on a dish machine. Dishwashing machines usually are manufactured with 2- or 3-horsepower motors, while potwashing machines are built with 5- to 10-horsepower motors that create a high-velocity water stream to strip off encrusted foods. Second, the internal size of the potwashing machine is large enough to accommodate large pots and standard 18-by-26-inch sheet pans, or standard gastronorm pans.

Potwashing Machines

SPECIFICATIONS

Figure 7-55. Pot and pan washer. (Courtesy of Insinger Machine Company.)

The specifications of a pot machine are determined primarily on the basis of the volume of pots and pans to be washed. Many large foodservice facilities do not use potwashing machines at all. Managers often feel that a standard three-compartment sink with a garbage disposal and hand-operated prerinse is sufficient for washing pots, pans, and utensils. Very large institutions and large restaurants with complex menus can justify the expense of these machines.

The construction of potwashing machines is usually extremely rugged, with frequent use of 12-gauge stainless steel. Some of the larger machines employ a complete self-contained system in which the pots and pans are washed and rinsed on a large carousel. Smaller machines are designed to fit between soiled and clean tables in a simple layout similar to that used for a single-tank dishwasher.

PRIMARY USE IN THE FOOD OPERATION

The use of pot and pan machines is very much a matter of personal preference among foodservice managers. Most management people feel that the pans must be washed before being placed in the machine and that the only purpose of the machine is to sanitize and remove any greasy film that might remain. Other managers feel that the machine does an excellent job if encrusted materials are prewashed or scraped off before putting the pots into the machine. Many steam table pans and sheet pans do not have hard, encrusted food particles and therefore are easily washed by the machine.

The primary use in a food operation, and the decision to use this type of warewashing machine, may be based on:

❏ The number of persons being fed
❏ The complexity of the menu
❏ The type of equipment used in food preparation (for instance, a steam-jacketed kettle eliminates the need for many pots)
❏ The amount of money and/or space available for equipment

DETERMINING CAPACITY AND SIZE

Only a few companies manufacture potwashing machines, and the types of machines that are available do not fall into any standard classification. Because each of the machines is very different in construction and design, the best way to determine the size and capacity is to determine the number of pots, pans, or standard 18-by-26-inch pans that can be washed per hour. These numbers should then be compared to the volume of such pans used each day in the food operation.

ENERGY USAGE AND UTILITY REQUIREMENTS

The amount of hot water, electricity, and steam used by this equipment is significant when compared with the amount of energy used in a three-compartment sink. For instance, the energy consumption of one medium-size machine from a manufacturer in the United States is 5 horsepower, 65 pounds of steam per hour, and 11 gallons of water per minute.

Power Pot Sinks

SPECIFICATIONS

A relatively new and innovative method of washing pots and pans is through the use of a power potwashing sink (Figure 7-56). These devices utilize continuous, soil-removing water turbulence in which 115°F (46°C) water is circulated at a high rate to loosen and remove soil from pots and pans. The

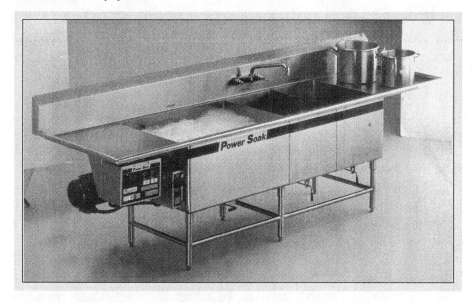

Figure 7-56. Power Pot Washing System. (Courtesy of Power Soak/Metcraft, Inc.)

operator typically prerinses the pot or pan and places it in a large sink containing a mild detergent and rapidly circulating water. The pot or pan is then placed in a large sanitizing sink, which also circulates the hot water. Specifications include 14-gauge stainless-steel construction, a variety of sink sizes, built-in dispensers, drain boards, and a wide variety of lengths and shapes.

PRIMARY USE IN THE FOOD OPERATION

The power pot sink cuts down on the effort required to wash pots and pans, which clearly is one of the most demanding jobs in a food operation. The significant reduction in cost, when compared to the purchase of a powerful potwashing machine, may be a good reason to consider this piece of equipment.

DETERMINING CAPACITY AND SIZE

The primary decisions regarding power pot sinks involve the size of the tanks and the lengths of the soiled-item and clean-item drain boards. A moderately sized restaurant or club will be well served by a large (36 to 42 inches [915 to 1,065 millimeters] long) soak/wash sink, with 24-by-30-inch (610-by-760-millimeter) rinse and sanitizing sinks so that sheet pans can be fully submerged. However, the cost of increasing the length of the soak/wash sink is money well spent because of the greater capacity for pots and pans.

ENERGY USAGE AND UTILITY REQUIREMENTS

The pumps and motors to operate the power do not consume a large amount of electrical energy. A control package that provides no heat with 208, 240, or 480, 3-phase service is available. A sink heater can be added if additional hot water is needed.

WASTE REMOVAL EQUIPMENT

The garbage can has long been the primary piece of equipment for removing waste from food production areas, and it continues to be used in modern kitchens, in spite of the development of sophisticated machines that have improved waste removal methods. However, waste removal through the use of garbage disposals and/or pulper/extractor systems has several advantages over the garbage can:

❏ The liquid part of the garbage is flushed into the sewer system, thus reducing the weight and volume of the garbage.

❏ The odors and vermin associated with garbage are greatly reduced.

❏ The waste material is transported through a soil pipe, eliminating the necessity of carrying a heavy can to a larger waste disposal container.

❏ Pulpers process paper-based products, thus speeding the decomposition process and reducing the impact on landfills.

The advantage of the garbage can is that it can handle metal and glass objects, while the mechanical systems cannot.

Disposals

SPECIFICATIONS

Commercial disposals (Figure 7-57) are specified primarily by motor size (see "Determining Capacity and Size," below). The following accessories and features are frequently specified for disposals:

❏ Prerinse sprays

❏ Cones to direct the water and garbage into the disposal

❏ Electrical control panels for switching the disposal and water on and off

❏ Electrical overload and reversing mechanisms

❏ Silverware saver devices to prevent metal objects from entering the disposal

❏ Stainless-steel covers

Figure 7-57. Disposer. (Courtesy of In-Sink-Erator, a division of Emerson Electric.)

Disposals grind food wastes and mix them with water so that they can be piped from the operation into the sewer system.

Garbage disposals are usually specified by horsepower, with typical ranges being between ½ and 7 horsepower. Many food facilities designers are of the opinion that the low-horsepower disposals are not a good buy. They do not have sufficient power to handle large quantities of refuse at one time, and therefore they often will cause clogging in the drain lines. Larger disposals, in the range of 2 to 3 horsepower, are recommended for general kitchen use. For dishwashing operations, particularly those that will require the disposal of both garbage and small quantities of paper, a 5-horsepower disposal is recommended. The installation of any type of disposal should provide adequate water intake to mix with solid particles, forming a slurry that will not clog the drain.

The primary cost of utilities for garbage disposals is water. Operating the motors and controls consumes a relatively small amount of electricity and therefore is not an important purchasing consideration.

Disposers often are built into soiled-dish tables to facilitate the scrapping of dishes. In smaller operations, the disposer is mounted in an 18-inch (460-millimeter)-diameter stainless-steel cone that is integrally welded to the dish table. This approach is functional for smaller operations. However, in larger operations, where several employees are involved in scrapping dishes, the soiled-dish table is fabricated with a trough (about 8 inches wide and 6 inches deep [200 millimeters wide and 150 millimeters deep]) through which water is circulated. The dish crew scrapes the waste from plates and dishes into the trough, where it is carried by the water flow to the disposer. The problem with this approach is high water consumption—as much as 9 gallons per minute goes through the disposer. A water recirculation system (Figure 7-58), integrated with a disposer, skims off the

Figure 7-58. Waste disposing system. (Courtesy of the Salvajor Company.)

waste and sends it through the disposer and returns most of the water back to the trough. This saves a significant amount of water and is far less detrimental to waste treatment systems.

Pulper and Extractor Systems

SPECIFICATIONS

The need for a waste disposal system that will not place large amounts of food or paper solids into the sewer system has increased dramatically. Many municipalities have ordinances against the use of commercial disposers because of the heavy load that they place upon the sewer system. A pulping and extracting waste system (Figure 7-59) is one of several alternatives available.

In a pulper, water and wastes are mixed together and ground into small particles (slurry). The grinding process is very similar to that of the conventional disposal, but the pulper does not wash the ground wastes into the sewer system. Instead, the water and slurry are piped to the extractor, where the solids are separated from the water. The water is returned to the pulper, mixed with fresh water, and reused in the grinding process. The

Figure 7-59. Pulper-extractor. (Courtesy of the Somat Corporation.)

solids from the extractor are conveyed to a conventional trash container. This material, which resembles wet sawdust or ground paper, is virtually odor-free.

Since much of the weight of garbage is the liquid, and the bulk of the garbage is reduced by grinding, the pulping and extracting process results in significantly less waste for a foodservice operation. However, the system costs considerably more than the conventional disposer and garbage can. The high initial cost of the pulper/extractor is offset by savings from:

❑ A reduction in waste handling resulting from a smaller volume of waste

❑ Reduced water consumption

❑ Labor simplification, as the garbage does not need to be physically carried from the kitchen

An additional, important advantage of the pulper/extractor system is the reduction in odor in the kitchen and around the trash container. The specifications for the equipment options and accessories are limited because only a few manufacturers make the equipment. Systems can be specified that will:

❑ Operate under a soiled-dish table

❑ Operate with the extractor connected to a remote location (the slurry is piped from the pulper to the extractor)

❑ Connect directly to the waste trough on a soiled-dish table

A foodservice facility with the kitchen and warewashing area located on the second floor is an ideal application for a pulper/extractor system. The pulper can be located on the second floor; the extractor is on the first floor near the garbage containers, and the slurry is piped from the pulper to the extractor downstairs. The need to carry heavy, smelly garbage down the stairs is eliminated.

The primary use of the pulper/extractor system is as an alternative method of garbage and paper disposal that does not place these waste materials into the sewer system.

PRIMARY USE IN THE FOOD OPERATION

Pulper/extractor systems handle from 600 to 1,000 pounds (272 to 454 kilograms) of typical food waste per hour; higher capacity is available if multiple pulpers and extractors are installed. A facility considering a pulper/extractor system will need to estimate the quantity of waste produced. This type of waste system, unlike a garbage disposal, requires a significant quantity of pulp—that is, paper products—to work effectively. Ideal applications are in large-volume facilities using Styrofoam and paper plates, cups, and other containers.

DETERMINING CAPACITY AND SIZE

The pulper/extractor systems use large motors (5, 7, and 10 horsepower) to grind the garbage and paper, and smaller motors to extract the solids. The engineering of these systems is complex because it involves plumbing for the slurry lines to the extractor and lines to return water to the pulper. The ideal time to install this equipment is when a building is new or is being renovated. If the distance from the warewashing area to the trash containers is

ENERGY USAGE AND UTILITY REQUIREMENTS

not too great, plumbing lines can frequently be run in existing buildings. The energy usage for the pulper/extractor is modest, particularly in view of the savings in water use.

Pulping and extracting systems are not cost-justified in the small restaurant or institution. A restaurant or institution serving under five hundred meals per day would probably not have the funds necessary to purchase this equipment and would probably not have adequate space to house it. For larger foodservice operations, municipal codes, the amount of paper used in the operation, and the relative costs of using a conventional disposer and trash removal system are important considerations in determining whether to adopt the pulper/extractor system.

Trash Compactors

SPECIFICATIONS

Trash compactors are mechanical devices that compress waste materials so that the volume is greatly reduced. Compactors also permit wastes to be more easily transported out of the food production areas in portable carts or containers.

In recent years, the sale of compactors has dropped off considerably because their cost is high and they are difficult to clean (thus often creating sanitation and odor problems). In addition, many of the early designs had poor repair and maintenance records. The advantages of compactors in certain applications may outweigh the disadvantages, however. Large compactors may be installed at the back dock of large foodservice facilities, from which the garbage can be removed by trucks especially designed to lift and empty the compacted garbage from waste containers. Smaller compactors are often used in facilities that have a large accumulation of paper cups, plates, glasses, and boxes, and other types of trash.

SUMMARY

Foodservice equipment should be selected based on necessity, the condition of present equipment, and the possibility of reducing energy and operating costs. The NSF (National Sanitation Foundation), which establishes sanitation and safety standards for equipment construction, is a good source of information. The NSF seal of approval is a recognized standard in the foodservice industry.

The types of equipment included in this chapter are the major pieces that foodservice consultants and their clients will consider purchasing. Comprehensive information about this equipment can be obtained from equipment catalogs, from manufacturer's representatives, or at any of the large equipment shows, such as those of the National Restaurant Association (NRA) or National Association of Foodservice Equipment Manufacturers (NAFEM). The foodservice consultant should be well versed in the many types of equipment available so that he or she can help the client make the best selection.

CHAPTER 8

FOODSERVICE FACILITIES ENGINEERING AND ARCHITECTURE

THIS CHAPTER

☑ Describes the primary considerations to be addressed by facilities planners to ensure the most economical use of energy in foodservice operations

☑ Provides a basic understanding of the primary utilities used in foodservice

☑ Describes the construction of hoods and ventilation systems in kitchens, dishwashing rooms, and service areas

☑ Lists the most commonly used finishes for floors, ceilings, and walls in foodservice operations

☑ Describes the methods for reducing sound in both public spaces and employee work areas

☑ Discusses the effects of lighting levels on productivity and safe food handling, and offers recommendations for minimum lighting levels in foodservice facilities

FOODSERVICE FACILITIES ENGINEERING

The engineering of a hotel dining facility, a complex restaurant, or a large institutional foodservice requires the expertise of both architects and professional engineers. The facility owner or manager who attempts to design and install electrical, plumbing, or heating, ventilation, and air-conditioning (HVAC) systems without professional assistance is courting disaster. Even the seemingly simple installation of a new warewashing system in a restaurant involves:

❏ Hot and cold water
❏ Floor drains
❏ Dish machine drains
❏ Electricity, steam, or natural gas
❏ Special ventilation to remove moist air
❏ Special floor, wall, and ceiling finishes
❏ Special lighting

The material in this chapter is not intended to be a do-it-yourself guide to complex engineering systems in foodservice facilities; rather, it is intended to offer a general overview and several useful ideas for resolving problems peculiar to the foodservice industry. For both students and foodservice planners, it will serve as a guide to the most accepted methods of engineering a foodservice construction or renovation project, as well as providing an understanding of the basic language of the technical trades involved in electrical, plumbing, and HVAC systems.

Water Systems

The preparation of and service of food are dependent on a source of sanitary hot or cold water. Without water, vegetables couldn't be cleaned, soups prepared, dishes washed, or ice made. Hot water consumes about 13 percent of a restaurant's energy budget. Water use has an economic impact on the bottom line of a foodservice operation through the costs of:

❏ Supply: the metered cost of cold water
❏ Heating: the energy to heat water
❏ Waste disposal: the sewage costs of disposing of water

Although some foodservice facilities rely on wells, water is usually supplied through a municipal water system. Under most circumstances, these water sources are frequently checked and carefully monitored to keep out pathogenic bacteria or other harmful materials. The supply cost of municipal water is computed on the basis of gallons of consumption during a period ranging from one month to three months. When the water meter is read, the cost is then computed and a bill sent to the end user. Figure 8-1 shows the approximate consumption of hot water for typical uses in foodservice facilities.

WATER SUPPLY LOCATION AND HARDWARE

Decisions about the location of water supply and drains are important considerations in the design and layout process. It is far less expensive to add a faucet during the design phase than after the facility has been opened. Supplying water to steam tables to fill the hot-food wells, to chef's tables, to kettles and tilting skillets, and to server stations is likely to save steps (and therefore labor costs).

A tremendous variety of faucets, drains, hoses, connections, and other hardware is available for foodservice applications. Taking the time to select the right hardware for the specific task is a smart idea, even though the hardware is only a small part of the overall equipment package for a new or renovated facility. As competitive pressures force fabricators and manufacturers to cut costs, operators and consultants who do not specify exactly what is needed are likely to be rudely surprised when inadequate hardware is delivered to the job.

Equipment Item	Hot-Water Consumption Gallons (Liters) per Hour	
	Low	High
Vegetable sink	15 (57)	15 (57)
Triple-compartment pot sink	45 (170)	60 (227)
Prerinse spray for dishes	45 (170)	45 (170)
Prescraper for dishes, conveyor type		250 (946)
Prescraper for dishes, Salvajor type		180 (681)
Bar sink (three-compartment)	—	20 (76)
Bar sink (four-compartment)	—	25 (95)
Lavatory	3 (11)	5 (19)
Utility sink	3 (11)	5 (19)
Bain-marie	6 (23)	10 (38)
Coffee urn	3 (11)	5 (19)
Single-tank dish machine	45 (170)	50 (189)

Source: Adapted from *Guidelines for Hot Water Generating Systems for Food Service Establishments* (East Lansing, MI: State of Michigan).

Figure 8-1. Water consumption in food-service facilities.

WATER HEATING

Water-heating systems heat water to temperatures appropriate for dishwashing, food preparation, and lavatories. A water heater provides hot water to faucets in one of two ways: heating water at the faucet to the temperature at which it will be used, or heating it to a higher temperature, then storing it and tempering it with cold water before it reaches the faucet. Some foodservice establishments maintain separate water-heating systems for kitchen and lavatory use. One system generates very hot water to be piped to the kitchen, and the other warms water for the lavatories, where moderate temperatures are adequate.

All forms of energy can be used to heat water. Most foodservice establishments use electric or gas water heaters, although a few use oil or steam. Electric water heaters are efficient at converting electrical energy to hot water. However, they generally heat water more slowly than do other kinds of heaters and require a larger tank to keep an adequate supply of water available.

ENERGY CONSERVATION AND WATER USE

Even while maintaining the necessary high standards of sanitation, energy can be saved in water heating and dishwashing. Energy-saving procedures can be simple or exotic. Some foodservice operations now use rooftop solar collectors. The captured solar energy is used to warm the water before it enters the water heater, thus significantly reducing the energy expended by the water-heating system. Another popular idea is to use the waste heat from refrigeration cooling systems to heat dishwashing water. The concept of heat recovery is discussed in greater detail in the next section.

Significant energy and dollar savings can be achieved by keeping two basic objectives in mind. The first is to reduce the amount of hot water used, especially the amount wasted—every time water is used, some of it is wasted. The second goal is to reduce the temperature of the water to the lowest temperature appropriate for the use. Not only does it cost less to heat the water to a lower temperature, but heat losses from distribution pipes are related directly to the difference between the temperature of the water in the pipes and that of the surrounding air.

Specific recommendations for the design of energy-efficient food-service facilities include the following:

❏ A water heater uses less energy than a range top to heat the same amount of water. Hot tap water should thus be used for cooking whenever possible (an exception would be in localities where the water contains heavy concentrations of minerals). Cold water should be used only when required by the cooking method. Both cold and hot water should be supplied to the preparation areas.

❏ Water should be heated only to the temperature needed. Heating the entire supply of kitchen water to 180°F (82°C) is highly inefficient when only the final rinse of the dish machine needs water at such a high temperature. Booster heaters can be used to bring water to 180°F (82°C) where required for sanitizing. Similarly, heating the entire building's supply of hot water to 140°F (60°C) and then cooling it to 110°F (43°C) for hand washing is inefficient.

❏ Hot-water boosters should be located within 5 feet of equipment that needs 180°F (82°C) water for sanitizing. Longer distances cause heat loss in the pipes.

❏ Spring-operated valves on the kitchen and rest room faucets save water. One type is attached to hand levers, and another operates with a foot treadle. For kitchen sinks, spring-operated foot treadles are most effective because they leave the operator's hands free for other tasks. For lavatory faucets, a 15-second delay-action valve is required to satisfy health standards.

Hot-water usage can easily be determined for dishwashers, glass washers, potwashers, and silverware washers, as calculated in gallons per hour. These figures are established by the National Sanitation Foundation (NSF) and the manufacturer of the particular piece of equipment.

WATER CONDITIONING SYSTEMS Hard water contains mineral deposits in solution that subsequently precipitate in water heaters, boilers, and water lines. These deposits can decrease energy efficiency, clog the water supply pipes, and cause valves and other controls to malfunction. In addition, mineral deposits can leave unattractive spots on glasses and silverware, giving the impression of an unsanitary condition. Hard water increases the amount of detergent needed for proper cleaning and degreasing in dishwashers and pot sinks.

The hardness of water is usually measured in grains, expressed in terms of the amount of minerals (calcium carbonate and others) per million parts of water. One grain of hardness is equal to approximately 17 parts per million (ppm). If water contains less than 4 grains of hardness, it may not need to be softened. Water containing between 4 and 6 grains will leave deposits on pipes and on the walls of water heaters unless the water is treated by a water softener. Water softeners most commonly use a zeolite process in which a chemical reaction occurs between salt and a catalyst in the water softener. These systems are effective but are occasionally objectionable because of the small amount of sodium that remains in the water. An alternative to the zeolite process is the use of magnetic water treatment. These systems keep the minerals in water in suspension by passing the water through a multifield magnet, which helps prevent crystallization of the mineral substance.

Dish machines, steamers, combi ovens, coffee and beverage systems, and ice machines all are affected by the quality of the water supplied to them. Manufacturers of this equipment typically provide data on minimum water quality standards. When a piece of equipment is supplied with water that does not meet the manufacturer's standards, severe and expensive maintenance problems are likely to occur. Although conditioning systems rarely are able to eliminate water quality problems completely, they can reduce maintenance and repair costs substantially.

Small conditioning systems can be installed to improve the quality of the water supplied to individual equipment items. Or a large system can be installed to condition all of the water supplied to the kitchen. Each approach has both advantages and disadvantages. Small systems condition only the water needed by a steamer, coffeemaker, or ice machine. They are easily installed and relocated as necessary. However, multiple small systems take more time to maintain. A single large conditioning system treating the water for the entire kitchen is relatively easy to maintain. The disadvantage is that the operation is paying to treat water that does not require conditioning. The decision about which approach is best depends upon the overall quality of the water supply, how much equipment there is that needs conditioned water, and the capabilities of the maintenance staff.

Foodservice manufacturers often recommend simple water filters—as opposed to complex conditioning systems—for single-equipment items, such as ice machines, coffee makers, and steamers. These units are cost effective and are able to remove particulates and impurities from the water supply.

Electrical Systems

Electrical energy is one of the primary sources of energy for foodservice equipment as well as for lighting, air-conditioning, and ventilation. The basic unit of electrical energy is the *watt*. Foodservice equipment is rated in terms of *kilowatt-hours,* the number of watts (in thousands) consumed in an hour, abbreviated as kW or kWh. Building supplies of electricity are available in specific voltages, such as 110 volts, 208 volts, 230 volts, or 480 volts, and 1- or 3-phase. Higher voltages (e.g., 208, 230, or 480) and 3-phase connections are used for equipment that demands greater electrical energy.

Foodservice equipment must be selected to match the voltage and phase available in the facility. A dish machine designed for use with 208-volt 3-phase electricity will not operate if connected to a 110-volt 1-phase circuit. General guidelines for selecting the electrical characteristics of foodservice equipment are as follows:

❏ Determine the electrical characteristics of the building through discussion with the electrical engineer or building maintenance staff. The answer will typically be 110/240 volts, 110/208 volts, or 110/240~460/480 volts.

❏ Select the piece of equipment desired and use the highest electrical voltage possible. This will usually reduce the size of the copper wires that are used in the building and so will reduce the cost of the installation.

❏ If electrical motors are involved, use the highest electrical voltage possible and 3-phase connections (which are more efficient).

❏ Select the method for connecting the electrical equipment to the power source. Equipment that will be permanently installed should be direct-wired. A male and female adapter (plug) can be used for equipment that will be moved or frequently disconnected.

❏ Ensure that the electrical characteristics and the type of connector appear on the mechanical drawing, in the equipment specification, and on the order for the equipment.

Adequate electrical connections for portable equipment such as slicers, toasters, food processors, hot-food warming carts, and coffee servers also should be provided. These items typically are designed to be connected to a duplex receptacle using a standard cord and plug. However, the standard electrical power supplied to a duplex receptacle may not be sufficient for commercial equipment—particularly if several pieces of equipment are plugged into the same circuit. For example, many of the hot-food holding carts used for banquets require more power than is available from a standard 15-amp circuit. The owner's representative should work carefully with the electrical engineer to ensure that adequate electrical power is available in all duplex receptacles.

ELECTRICAL ENERGY USE AND CONSERVATION

Electrical energy conservation requires an understanding of the rate structures employed by utility companies. Two basic rate structures are the step rate and the demand charge.

With step rates, utility rates are often based on a reduction in the cost per kilowatt-hour as the consumption increases. Recently, objections have been raised to this method of billing because it rewards the customer for excessive usage. However, the idea of getting a discount for the purchase of large quantities still exists in the business community, and electricity is usually no exception.

The step rate schedule is often controlled by a local or state regulatory agency and may change as the cost of energy rises. A typical step rate schedule is illustrated in Figure 8-2.

In demand charge systems, a relatively large consumer of energy will probably have two charges on the electric bill: one charge for energy used and one for demand. While the energy billing represents the number of kilowatt-hours actually used, the demand charge reflects the cost to the utility of maintaining sufficient generating capacity to supply large, short-term energy demands put on the utility lines by consumers. The charge is based on the maximum energy demand imposed on the utility lines during a short

Kilowatt Hours	Rate per Kilowatt-Hour
1–50	$0.150
51–100	$0.100
101–200	$0.050
201–300	$0.040
301–500	$0.030
Over 500	$0.025

If the meter reading for a one-month period indicated that 750 kilowatt hours were used, the cost would be:

50 kWh at 0.150	$7.50
50 kWh at 0.100	5.00
100 kWh at 0.050	5.00
100 kWh at 0.040	4.00
200 kWh at 0.030	6.00
250 kWh at 0.025	6.25
TOTAL	$33.75

Figure 8-2. Electrical energy step rate illustration.

interval, generally a fifteen-minute period, during the billing period. The maximum demand is measured by a demand meter and the bill is based on the maximum demand (kilowatt-hours) multiplied by the demand charge (cost per kilowatt-hour) for the billing period. If the peak usage for a given billing period is 50 kilowatt-hours and the demand charge is $5 per kilowatt-hour, the demand charge for that period will be $250, even if this peak is reached for only one fifteen-minute period during the month.

Demand charges may constitute a large percentage of the total electric utility bill. A serious energy management program needs to focus on demand as well as energy use because significant savings can be realized by lowering the peak demand. The food facilities consultant must be aware of the kilowatt-hour rating of each piece of equipment and give consideration to the total electrical demand created as a result of the kitchen design.

Gas

Natural gas, as well as other forms of refined fuels such as propane, are primary sources of energy for foodservice equipment. In fact, there are very few examples of preparation equipment that are not available with gas as the principal source of energy for cooking.

The decision to use gas-powered or electrical equipment often is based solely on the relative costs of operation for each energy source. In a later section of this chapter the procedure for comparing the cost of gas with alternative energy sources is discussed. However, there are several other factors that are important to consider in the selection and specification of gas-fired equipment:

❑ *Operational practices and preferences.* A key factor in the selection of gas-fired equipment is the preferences of the employees who will use the equipment on a regular basis. Most chefs, for example, prefer a gas-fired range for sautéing because it offers a high degree of control over the heat applied to the pan. Preferences may not play as large a role in the selection of a gas-fired fryer or convection oven versus electric models.

❏ *Durability and maintenance.* Depending on the piece of equipment, electric heat may be a more durable source of heat over time. For example, gas-heated dish machines tended to suffer breakdowns because the high heat from the burner eventually damaged the water tank. New dish machine burner designs are submerged in the water tank and are far more durable.

❏ *Initial cost.* The same equipment may be substantially more expensive in a gas-fired version than the electric version (or vice versa).

❏ *Ventilation requirements.* Gas-fired equipment uses a combustion process, and the waste gases must be exhausted from the room. If the selection of gas-fired equipment would necessitate a separate ventilation hood and/or ductwork, those costs should be factored into the decision.

GAS VERSUS ELECTRIC EQUIPMENT: ENERGY COSTS

The efficient use of energy is important to the manager of a foodservice operation not only because everyone has a responsibility to conserve energy, but also because conservation can save money and increase profits. The average cost of energy for a restaurant exceeds 5 percent of the total sales. Food and labor usually are the only costs that exceed the cost of energy.

For those engaged in planning food facilities, the selection of the most economical fuel is a complex matter. The use of steam, for instance, has previously been mentioned as an economical cooking source under certain circumstances of availability, because of its ability to transfer heat efficiently to food. Figure 8-3 reports estimates regarding the relative energy requirements of gas versus electric equipment. These data suggest that a strong case can be made for the use of electricity based on its efficiency.

The data presented in Figure 8-3 do not take into account two important considerations when comparing the cost and efficiency of natural gas versus electricity. First, the actual connected load and energy usage for a given type of equipment may vary significantly among manufacturers. Not all fryers, ovens, or grills require the same amount of electricity. Some are substantially more efficient than others.

Figure 8-3. Estimated energy requirements for foodservice equipment.

Equipment Item	Electrical BTUs Required	Gas BTUs Required
Kettle (40-qt.)	41,000	52,000
Fryer	72,000	110,000
Convection oven	38,000	55,000
Combi-oven	72,000	190,000
Steamer	61,000	90,000

Second, the data in Figure 8-3 do not reflect the amount of energy that is actually transferred to the food. Studies done by one of this book's authors at Michigan State University indicate that the type of equipment selected is often more important in energy savings than the source of the energy. Frozen vegetables cooked on a hot-top range (gas or electric) will require much more energy than the same package of vegetables cooked in a pressure steamer. The reason for the difference is obvious. With stovetop cookery, most of the energy goes up into the hood and is wasted, whereas the closed cooking chamber holds the energy inside the steamer and allows it to be absorbed into the product being cooked.

Most of the energy used in a typical restaurant is used to prepare and store food. Cooking equipment is the greatest consumer of energy for the following reasons:

❏ Heat-producing appliances require the highest consumption (flow of electricity or rate of use of gas).

❏ Cooking equipment is turned on for many hours during the day (often unnecessarily).

❏ Most of the heat produced is lost to the hood and is not recovered.

❏ The conversion of electricity or gas to heat is inefficient.

The answer to conservation is not easily found, but there are certain things that the foodservice operator can do to reduce cooking energy loss:

❏ *Select equipment that is enclosed and insulated.* Closed cooking vessels contain the energy and permit it to be absorbed by the food. Rotary ovens, convection ovens, convection steamers, steam-jacketed kettles with lids, and microwave ovens are good examples of closed cooking vessels.

❏ *Cook foods in the largest quantity possible.* This cannot be done for vegetables and other foods that are cooked in small batches as the meal progresses. However, energy savings can be realized when certain foods (chili, soups, and casseroles) are cooked in large quantities all at once.

❏ *Cook at the lowest temperature possible.* The savings in shrinkage for low-temperature roasting of meats has been known to the foodservice industry for years. However, cooks continue to roast meats at high temperatures (300° to 400°F) to "seal in the juices," though in fact this method serves only to dry out the product. Slow cooking means lower energy consumption even though the cooking time is longer.

❏ *Carefully monitor preheating time for each piece of equipment.* It is all too common for cooks to turn on the main battery of cooking equipment first thing in the morning and allow the ranges, fryers, and ovens to go full blast all day long. Most modern cooking appliances have a quick recovery time and can be brought up to proper cooking temperature in only a few minutes.

❏ *Monitor the demand curve for electricity.* Electricity is sold in part on the basis of peak demand for the day. Be sure that the equipment is not turned on all at once during the opening hours of the food facility.

Steam   Steam is a primary source of energy in many foodservice operations, particularly large institutional facilities that use it as an energy source for other purposes. Smaller foodservice facilities rarely have steam available as part of the building's utility services. However, small steam generators for use solely in foodservice are available.

Steam cookery has a number of important advantages:

❏ Steam transfers energy to food rapidly.

❏ For cooking vegetables, steam is highly desirable because it prevents much of the loss of nutrients, color, and texture that occurs when vegetables are boiled in a stock pot.

❏ Because steam always remains at 212°F (100°C) when not under pressure, and at up to 250° F (121° C) under pressure of 15 pounds per square inch, it is a moderate, uniform cooking medium.

❏ Steam equipment requires little or no warm-up time; thus preheat time losses are minimal.

❏ Cooking times are usually much shorter using steam equipment than they are using range-top cooking or boiling.

Steam can be used to cook foods in two ways. Direct steam cookery involves introducing steam into a cooking compartment, where it comes into direct contact with food. Examples of direct steam cooking equipment include steamers and combi ovens. Indirect steam cookery uses steam to heat the metal walls of the cooking vessel, as in the case of steam-jacketed kettles. A third use of steam in the commercial kitchen is as a heat source for other purposes. For example, steam coils can be used to provide heat for hot water in dish machines and pot sinks and to provide heated makeup air in ventilation systems.

Reduced to its barest elements, a steam-heating system consists of a means of converting water to steam (the boiler or converter), piping to conduct the steam to where it is to be used, a coil or other surface for condensing the steam and transferring the latent heat from the steam to the air, a trap to prevent the steam from passing through the coil before it is condensed, and return piping to conduct the condensate back to the boiler.

LATENT HEAT   Steam is an efficient cooking medium because it contains and then releases a tremendous amount of energy. Raising the temperature of 1 pound of water from room temperature (70°F [21°C]) to the boiling point (212°F [100°C]) requires about 142 BTUs. However, creating one pound of steam from boiling water demands almost an additional 1,000 BTUs. A pound of steam thus is highly charged with energy, which it quickly transfers to cooler surfaces when it condenses (cools back to liquid form).

Figure 8-4 shows how the temperature of 1 pound of water would vary with time if subjected to a constant rate of BTU input. Notice that it would stay at 32°F (0°C) and 212°F (100°C) at sea level until, in each case, the latent heat conversions had taken place for the entire pound of water.

SATURATION   If a container of water is heated sufficiently at a constant pressure, the water temperature will rise until the boiling point is reached. While the water is boiling, the temperature will remain constant until all the water has

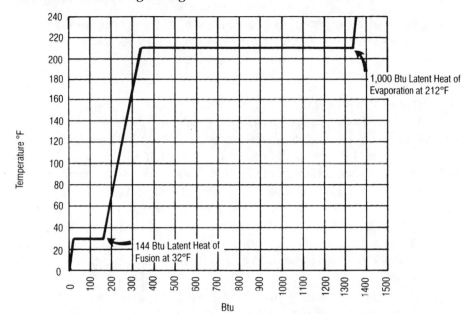

Figure 8-4. Latent heat of water when converted to steam.

been converted to steam. Then the temperature will rise again as the steam is further heated (see Figure 8-4). Steam at the temperature at which it coexists with water is called saturated steam, and the temperature is called the saturation temperature. The saturation temperature varies with the pressure. An increase in pressure increases the temperature at which the latent heat transfer takes place. The pressure at which the latent heat transfer takes place at a given temperature is called the saturation pressure.

STEAM PRESSURE

In the English-speaking world, steam pressures are measured in pounds per square inch (psi). There are, necessarily, two reference levels. One is the pressure above atmospheric pressure. This is the boiler's pressure, commonly called the gauge pressure and abbreviated *psi* or *psig*. Because of the variable nature of atmospheric pressure, steam pressures are more accurately described in terms of their absolute pressure, which is the total amount of their pressure above a perfect vacuum.

SUPERHEAT

As in the case of any gas, steam can be heated above the boiling point. Once steam has risen above the saturation temperature, each additional increase of 1°F (.56°C) requires only about half a BTU per pound. The increase in temperature above the saturation temperature is called superheat. Steam that has a small amount of superheat is called dry steam. If heated more than a few degrees above the saturation temperature, it is referred to as superheated steam.

Obviously, neither dry nor superheated steam can coexist with liquid water. Since steam is a gas, it tends to expand in direct relation to increased temperature. The increased volume and small amount of extra heat value make superheat a relatively worthless factor in steam heating. Its only real value is to ensure that there will be dry steam at the point where the steam is to be used. In other words, a few degrees of superheat at the boiler will minimize condensation in the supply lines to the steam coils.

CONDENSATION   When steam gives up its latent heat and changes from saturated steam to water at the same temperature, it condenses. The water is spoken of as condensate.

HEAT TRANSFER   Heat transfer usually occurs through a steam coil or by steam injectors. A steam coil is a heat exchanger, a metal tube into which steam is introduced and where it condenses, giving off its latent energy in the form of heat that radiates from metal tubes and/or fins on the outside of the coil. All steam coils are 100 percent efficient in the sense that the heat released by condensing steam within the coil has nowhere to go but into the air surrounding the coil. Tube and fin material, fin spacing, air velocity, and several other factors affect the rate at which the heat transfer (and therefore the condensation) takes place, but they cannot alter the fact that the steam's latent heat has only one place to go: into the coil, and from the coil into the surrounding air.

Steam injectors transfer heat by allowing the pressurized steam to escape into another medium, such as water or air. For example, steam injectors are sometimes used to heat the water in the wash tank of dish machines. The injectors are submerged in the tank and, when charged, expel steam directly into the water to heat it.

Steam coils generally are preferred over steam injectors for most heating purposes. Because coils are a closed system, there is no danger of contaminating food with "dirty" steam. Coils also are far quieter in operation than injectors.

SOURCES OF STEAM   Steam is generated for use in foodservice facilities in several ways. It can be:

❑ Purchased from a utility owned by a municipality or commercial company and piped to the kitchen

❑ Generated in a building boiler room and piped to the kitchen

❑ Generated in the kitchen by a small boiler located under or near the equipment

❑ Generated in the kitchen by a small boiler that is integral to the foodservice equipment

Of the four sources of steam, the installation of small boilers for each piece of equipment is the least satisfactory because of the high maintenance costs and additional kitchen heat that they create.

In foodservice facilities, steam is an economical energy source, especially under the following circumstances:

❑ The facility already has a source of steam.

❑ Several pieces of equipment are selected that are steam-heated. This helps to justify the cost of installing steam supply lines and condensate return lines.

❑ The steam source produces clean steam, with no unsafe impurities from rust inhibitors and antifoaming chemicals. Many hospitals must have a source of clean steam because of the frequent use of steam in autoclaves for sterilizing equipment. These clean steam systems use chemicals that are approved by the United States Department of Agriculture and are also safe for direct injection on food products.

If a new boiler is required to generate steam for the foodservice equipment, the size of the boiler is determined by the amount of steam needed by each piece of equipment. Steam is measured in terms of flow (pounds per hour) and pressure (pounds per square inch). Boilers typically are sized in terms of boiler horsepower (BHP), which equals approximately 34.5 pounds of steam per hour. Using data provided by the foodservice consultant, the mechanical engineer determines the BHP of the boiler required to supply the kitchen equipment. Because steam loses energy in pipes, boilers are located as close as feasible to the equipment they supply and are oversized to compensate for energy loss in the plumbing.

STEAM BOILER SIZING

Utility Costs and Energy Conservation in Selecting Foodservice Equipment

An effective approach for selecting the energy source to be used for heating, cooling, and cooking purposes should compare all of the available alternatives for achieving the desired result, rather than simply pitting electric equipment against gas. The following simple, step-by-step system can be used by any foodservice manager to determine the most economical fuel for heating, cooling, or cooking:

1. Identify the relevant equipment alternatives for achieving the desired result. For example, vegetable cookery can take place in a stock pot on a range, in a kettle, or in a steamer.
2. For each piece of equipment and each possible form of energy, determine the utility load. Electrical loads are rated in terms of kilowatt-hours (kW or kWh), gas loads in terms of cubic feet or BTUs, and steam loads in pounds per hour. This information can be obtained from the equipment manufacturer's catalog sheets or, where the equipment itself is available, from the manufacturer's identification plate.
3. Convert the energy demand (usage) for each equipment alternative to a common unit of measurement, the BTU, so that they can be compared. Use the following conversion values:
   Electricity: BTUs = 3,413 × kilowatt-hours
   Gas: BTUs = 1,000 × cubic feet
   Steam: BTUs = 1,000 × pounds per hour
4. Determine the cooking time for several typical products that would be prepared by the equipment. For example, a 5-pound (2.3-kilogram) box of green peas cooked on an open-top range might take 12 minutes to prepare but would take 6 minutes to cook in a convection steamer. Or a beef roast might take 4 hours to cook in a conventional deck oven but only 3 hours and 15 minutes in a convection oven.
5. Extend the cooking time to cover a meaningful period of time in the operation, such as a day or a week. This step is important to take account of variations in demand that occur by day part or by day of the week.

6. Multiply the preparation time for the period (in hours) by the BTU consumption for each piece of equipment. Be sure to take into account that employees run some kinds of equipment continuously even though they are only actually used for cooking intermittently (e.g., hot-top ranges). A steamer thus might be used for a total of twelve hours in a week, whereas a hot-top range might be consuming energy for seventy-two hours.

7. Determine the cost of each type of energy from the utility company rate sheet (or from recent bills). Multiply this cost by the consumption. A steamer using 96 kW of electrical energy per week will cost $4.32 to operate for a typical week if electricity is billed at the rate of $.045 per kW.

8. Convert to BTUs for comparison purposes. The steamer uses 27,304 BTUs (8 kW × 3,413) per hour at a rate of $.27 per hour (8 kW × $.045). Do this for each alternative piece of equipment and energy source.

9. Compare the projected energy consumption and utility costs.

Ventilation

FOODSERVICE EQUIPMENT VENTILATION SYSTEMS

The successful removal of heat and air that is laden with grease particles and food odors requires a well-designed hood exhaust system. Many energy-saving hoods are now available, and each hood manufacturer claims to have come up with the most effective design. The buyer cannot hope to make an intelligent choice without understanding the principles of hood exhaust operation, including both the action of thermal air currents and the functions of the component parts of a hood system. Because of the high initial cost of the hood and the high ongoing costs of operation for the life of the entire system, time spent in acquiring such knowledge is a worthwhile investment.

Hoods remove air, water vapor, grease, and food odors from the kitchen range area and air and water vapor from dishwashing rooms. Electric ovens, steamers, and steam-jacketed kettles require hoods that remove only air, heat, and water vapor. If large quantities of grease from a broiler, charbroiler, fryer, or grill are present, the hood system must extract this pollutant before the air is drawn by fans to the outside of the building. To understand the most effective and energy-efficient means of removing hot air and airborne grease, it is necessary to outline the function of a simple hood system.

The basic functions of a kitchen ventilation system are to *capture* the air heated by the cooking process, *remove* as much grease from it as possible, *exhaust* the heated air to the outside, and *resupply* or "make up" the air removed from the kitchen. Ventilation systems typically capture air from cooking in stainless-steel canopies hung over the cooking equipment. The air rises into the canopy by means of convection (hot air rises). A fan, usually located on the roof of the building, is connected to the canopy by ductwork. The negative pressure (vacuum) created by the exhaust fan pulls the heated, grease-laden air from the cooking surface through filters or extractors designed to capture the grease. Because many kitchen ventilation systems exhaust a large quantity of air, it is often necessary to return air to the kitchen from outside the building. When a large amount of air is exhausted in the kitchen, a negative pressure condition is created that causes air to flow from other parts of the building. Makeup air systems are designed to offset this problem by introducing air at or near the hood to replace some portion of the volume of air lost to the exhaust process. Ventilation systems are designed to exhaust and/or supply a specific volume of air, measured in cubic feet per minute (CFM).

The volume of air to be exhausted and supplied by a ventilation system ideally is determined by two factors: the amount of heat generated by the equipment below the hood, and the design of the hood itself. The amount of heat generated by cooking equipment varies tremendously. Ovens, steamers, and kettles generate relatively little heat because they enclose the cooking cavity; they produce approximately 20–25 CFM of thermal current per square foot of surface area. A hot-top range with a surface temperature approaching 800°F may generate 100 CFM of thermal current per square foot. A gas-fired charbroiler, because of its open-flame burners, may generate as much as 175 CFM of thermal current per square foot. Exhaust fans must be sized to capture all the heat generated by the equipment.

SIZING HOODS (COMPUTING EXHAUST VOLUME)

The design of the hood itself also affects the exhaust requirements. For example, hoods mounted against walls with closed ends that extend down to the surface of the equipment (side curtains) contain the flow of hot, grease-laden air relatively well, whereas island-style hoods, open on all four sides, will require 30–50 percent greater exhaust CFM to capture the air effectively. This is because the exhaust fan is effectively drawing air up from all four sides of an island hood, but from only one side of a wall hood with side curtains. Also, because a single hood may have equipment of varying exhaust requirements beneath it, it is common practice to size hoods according to basic guidelines. Figure 8-5 provides an example of a manufacturer's sizing guidelines.

In actual practice, the sizing of a hood system often deviates from the ideal process described above. The exhaust requirements for a hood system often are determined by looking to state and local building codes. Such building codes typically state the minimum requirements for ventilation quite conservatively in order to protect the public and the foodservice operator from the possibility of an unscrupulous "tin-knocker" building a hood system that isn't functional. Most state and municipal codes offer exceptions to the rule for hoods that have met stringent performance standards and that have been tested by independent organizations, such as Underwriters Laboratories. However, foodservice operators rarely are aware of these exceptions and so are not in a position to take advantage of them. In addition, engineers who lack experience in the design of mechanical systems for kitchens—as well as some local code compliance officials—may not be aware of the relevant exceptions or understand how to apply them. As a result, the operator may end up with a hood system that moves far more air than is necessary. One of

The following table shows typical exhaust requirements in cubic feet per minute for each linear foot of hood for kitchen ventilation systems. Where systems have a UL (Underwriters' Laboratories) listing, they are approved at the exhaust levels established by the manufacturer. Non-UL-listed hoods must comply with local building codes. Local codes typically adopt broader standards, such as those developed by NFPA (National Fire Protection Association) and BOCA (Building Officials and Code Administrators International). The exhaust requirements shown below are for wall-mounted hoods (island type hoods typically have higher exhaust requirements).

Type of Hood/Filter	Equipment	CFM per Linear Foot
High-velocity grease extractor	Steamers, ovens, kettles	150–200
	Ranges, griddles, fryers	200–250
	Charbroilers, hot-top ranges	250–300
Baffle filters (UL-listed)	Steamers, ovens, kettles	250
	Ranges, griddles, fryers	300
	Charbroilers, hot-top ranges	350
Non-UL-listed hoods	Varies by municipality	300–500

Figure 8-5. Exhaust requirements for various types of foodservice equipment.

the advantages of working with an experienced food facilities design consultant is his or her specialized knowledge and experience in the design and specification of kitchen ventilation systems.

CAPTURING GREASE PARTICLES: FILTERS AND EXTRACTORS

The two most commonly used devices for capturing grease from the air as it passes through the hood canopy are filters and extractors. In the past, filters were designed to trap grease in fine wire mesh (like steel wool) located in the path of the exhaust air. While these filters effectively captured grease, they retained it over the cooking surface and so represented a serious fire hazard. Contemporary filters force grease-laden air to move across baffles, changing direction rapidly, thus flinging grease particles onto the surface of the baffles. The baffles are designed to drain the grease into a trough for easy removal. Extractors operate on the same principle as baffle filters but force the air to make multiple reversals before entering the exhaust duct. Most baffles are 50–60 percent efficient, whereas extractors often remove more than 90 percent of the grease that passes through them. Figure 8-6 illustrates the difference between baffles and extractors.

The filters or extractors in most ventilation hoods need to be removed regularly and washed in the dish machine. However, systems are available that automatically wash the extractors and duct plenums, saving maintenance costs. These systems require a significantly greater initial investment because of the plumbing that must be built into the hood system.

MAKEUP AIR SYSTEMS

There are three basic approaches to introducing makeup air in a kitchen ventilation system (Figure 8-7).

Discharging air inside the hood. Makeup air can be discharged inside the canopy itself; this approach is often referred to as a "short-cycle" design

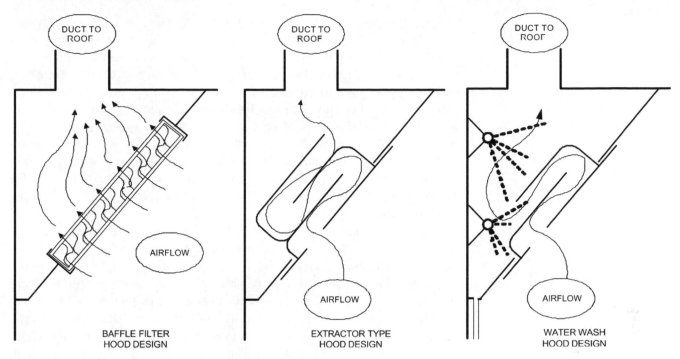

Figure 8-6. Baffle filters versus extractors in removing grease.

(Figure 8-7a). A system of ducts connects the makeup air discharge to a supply fan located on the roof. Because the supply air is introduced into the hood cavity itself, these systems are designed to use untempered air (air brought directly from the outside without any heating during the winter months). Although the short-cycle design does not require the expense of tempered makeup air, it has two disadvantages. First, the amount of air that can be introduced directly into the hood cavity is limited to between 40 and 60 percent of the exhaust volume in most systems. This means that a large

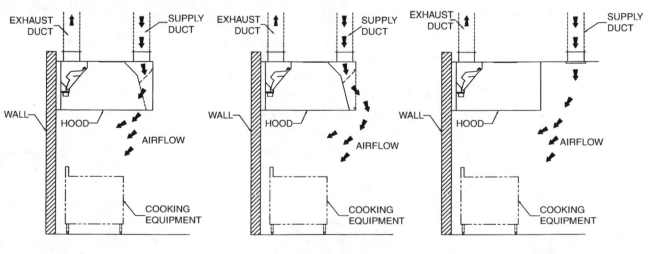

Figure 8-7a. Supply air discharged inside the canopy (short-cycle type).

Figure 8-7b. Supply air discharged from the face of the hood.

Figure 8-7c. Supply air discharged from a separate register in front of the hood.

volume of indoor air is lost to the outdoors. Second, on winter days, when the cold makeup air meets the moist heated air rising from the equipment, a tremendous amount of condensation is created under the hood.

Discharging air along the face of the hood. A second approach for introducing makeup air is to locate ducts and registers along the face of the hood (Figure 8-7b). This approach can handle a far greater volume of makeup air—as much as 90 percent of what is exhausted. However, the supply registers direct the air out and down from the face of the hood, where it blows across the head and shoulders of the chef. For this reason, the supply air in front-discharge systems must be tempered to a level that is comfortable for the cooks (typically 55°F). In addition, most manufacturers offer air registers that diffuse the high volumes of air over a relatively large surface area.

Discharging air from separate registers. Internal and front-discharge makeup air systems integrate the supply air registers and ductwork with the hood canopy. However, it is also feasible to use a completely separate duct and register system for introducing makeup air. Such systems tend to locate the registers in the ceiling just in front of the canopy (Figure 8-7c).

Makeup air requirements typically are determined in relation to the volume of air exhausted by the hood, as well as by the design of the makeup air system itself. In general, makeup air systems replace between 50 and 90 percent of the air removed by the exhaust system. The amount of air supply needed to make such a system effective is a matter of debate in the industry. The authors' experience is that negative pressure is necessary to keep cooking odors in the kitchen and out of the dining room. A hood system using 80 percent or less makeup air seems to create a good balance between energy savings and a reasonable amount of negative air pressure in the kitchen.

FIRE SUPPRESSION SYSTEMS

Kitchen ventilation hoods require fire suppression systems. Traditionally, such systems consist of a pressurized tank filled with an extinguishing chemical and a series of pipes that terminate over the cooking equipment. If a fire develops, sensors (fusible links) open and the chemical is discharged. Once the fire has been put out, the operator cleans up the remaining extinguishing chemical, repairs any damage, and sanitizes the equipment before reopening for business.

Although these chemical systems continue to be widely used, they have several distinct disadvantages:

❑ If the fire is not completely extinguished and flares up after the canister has been emptied, the operation has no remaining protection.

❑ The chemical agent used to extinguish the fire must be completely cleaned from the equipment and the work area before the operation can reopen.

❑ The system must be inspected and regularly maintained in addition to the maintenance of other building fire suppression systems.

Several ventilation system manufacturers now offer fire suppression systems that are connected to the building's main sprinkler system. Although it seems counterintuitive to put out a grease fire with water, these systems actually do an excellent job. Water is sprayed in a very fine mist from nozzles over the equipment, effectively suffocating the fire. In addition, these systems are not limited in capacity like the canister systems and require far less maintenance. Moreover, the installation cost of water-mist fire suppression systems often is competitive with the cost of traditional canister systems in larger hoods.

The primary disadvantages faced by the operator who wants to realize the advantages of a water-mist fire suppression system result from its relative newness in the design and construction industry. Unless the engineers have had substantial experience dealing with kitchen mechanical systems, they are unlikely to be familiar with water-mist systems. Also, state and local building codes may make it difficult to install such systems. Some municipalities require water-mist systems to have sprinkler heads throughout the ductwork leading all the way to the roof—even though the traditional systems are not expected to meet a similar requirement. In a properly designed and installed water-mist system, there is no need for sprinkler heads beyond the duct collar; however, not all codes have caught up with this fact. The operator who desires the greater protection and lower maintenance costs of the water-mist system may need to advocate with the design team or, if a food facilities consultant is involved in the project, rely on the consultant to guide the team in this area.

AIR AND HUMIDITY CONTROL FOR THE DISHWASHING ROOM

Since warm air will hold more moisture than cool air, when moist warm air is cooled, water vapor condenses. Cool air containing less moisture increases the amount of moisture that can evaporate from the skin, and therefore is more cooling and comfortable for customers and employees. In foodservice establishments, the concern is that the air seem fresh and that humidity be low enough for comfort while the customers are sitting quietly in the dining room. For the employees, who are more active, a work space is comfortable if the temperature and humidity are slightly lower than in the dining room and if the air is moving rapidly. Unfortunately, in the dishroom the air is often very moist and the temperature extremely high.

Food facilities planners must insist that architects and engineers design into the HVAC system a sufficient amount of air supply and exhaust to keep the moisture level as low as possible in the dishwashing and potwashing areas. Failure to create this condition will result in low productivity and high employee turnover among the warewashing personnel. A second problem arising from poor ventilation in the dishroom is a decrease in the effectiveness of air drying as the dishes emerge from the washer. Wet dishes encourage bacterial growth, make a poor impression on customers, and, if towel-dried, are likely to be contaminated with organisms that cause illness.

HVAC SYSTEMS FOR DINING

The heating, ventilating, and air-conditioning systems for the dining room and other public spaces in a foodservice facility are beyond the scope of this text. The best heating source, the complexities of humidity and temperature control, and the environmental treatment of all spaces in both the front and back of the facility are technical matters that should be left in the hands of licensed and trained engineers.

Conveyor Systems   Conveyors have been used for many years in the industrial and manufacturing industries for moving materials from one place to another, at a maximum speed and with a minimum effort. In foodservice facilities, conveyors not only move objects but also can be designed to improve food quality (as in hospital tray makeup systems) and provide aesthetically pleasing dish tray areas in cafeterias and other self-service operations.

Although many conveyor systems are fabricated especially for the needs of a particular food operation, conveyors designed for general use in a foodservice facility can be purchased from a manufacturer's catalog. The general construction features of conveyors are:

❏ Conveyor transport or belt—the medium that moves the material (many conveyors don't actually have belts; instead, they use different transport devices)

❏ Conveyor bed—the part of the conveyor along which the belt travels

❏ Drive mechanism (if the belt is powered)—to move the belt along the bed

❏ Drive enclosure—a closed space, such as a cabinet, in which the motor and drive system are housed

❏ Return track for belt, with limit switch and belt-washing system—typically located at the opposite end of the conveyor from the drive unit

❏ Drip pan—catches any liquids that fall from the conveyor belt

❏ Removable skirt panels—to enclose the structure of the conveyor bed

These parts vary, depending on the complexity of the conveyor system and the features desired by the foodservice owner or manager. Five transport systems are widely used in conveyors: belts, slats, rollers, pins, and links.

Flat, water-resistant conveyor belts were common during the early period of conveyor usage. Belts are still available, but are not as popular as slat conveyors because of their inability to "bend" around turns and corners.

Slat "belts" actually are composed of Delrin or other hard, flexible plastics. Each slat is 1 to 2 inches (25 to 50 millimeters) wide and 8 to 12 inches (200 to 305 millimeters) long. These slats are linked together at their centers to form a continuous flat transport surface. They are usually designed so that the belt can turn corners, and the slats overlap on the turns. Slat conveyor belts, with self-washing systems, are a clean and attractive solution for self-busing dish drop-off areas in cafeterias.

Roller conveyors may have "skate wheels" (about ½ inch [12.7 millimeters] wide and 2 inches [50.8 millimeters] in diameter) or rollers (as wide as the conveyor and about 2 inches [50.8 millimeters] in diameter). Roller conveyors are frequently used for gravity (nonpowered) conveyors or at the termination of a powered conveyor system. Gravity conveyors are less expensive and require little maintenance. However, in self-service applications they are not as attractive and can cause accidents or dish breakage.

Pin conveyors are constructed of metal links with small pins protruding upward. The pins ensure that the tray or container being conveyed does not slip.

Link conveyor belts, constructed of a series of links made from Delrin or other hard but flexible plastics, are an excellent solution for conveying cafeteria trays. Installed in parallel pairs, these conveyors can be designed to move trays around sharp turns. The links are very strong and have been successful in self-service applications because they are attractive and do not break easily.

Conveying systems offer the potential for reducing labor costs in large foodservice operations, particularly in busing and warewashing areas. In operations that use trays and china, a well-designed conveyor system offers a far more attractive and sanitary solution than placing aluminum kitchen racks in the dining area to accumulate soiled trays. However, the design of conveying systems requires attention to detail, such as:

❑ Ensuring that the rate of conveyor travel is appropriate to the needs of the operation at *both ends* of the process. A conveying system that brings trays into the dishroom at twice the rate at which the crew can break them down and load them into the dish machine is clearly a poor solution.

❑ Providing a buffer at the unload end of a tray conveyor that runs into the dishroom, such as a gravity roller conveyor and accumulating table.

❑ Coordinating with the architects to provide a noise barrier shielding the tray drop area from the noise of the dishroom.

❑ Providing access to the conveyor for cleaning and maintenance, particularly at each end.

❑ Avoiding—at all costs—conveyor runs that are anything but horizontal. Vertical conveying systems are extremely difficult to keep clean and in good repair.

Utility Distribution Systems

Large foodservice operations typically require multiple ovens, kettles, steamers, grills, and fryers set adjacent to one another along a common wall. Gas, water, electric, and steam connections must be carefully routed through the interior structure of the wall to multiple rough-in points. When equipment is designed in two work areas, located back to back along a common wall, all of the utility connections for the equipment on each side must come through the common wall. As the type and number of utility connections required in a single wall increase, so also do the coordination demands and overall construction costs. An alternative approach is to locate the utility services in a stainless-steel raceway that is custom fabricated according to the design of the facility. The raceway is nothing but a horizontal enclosure, 8 to 10 inches (203 to 254 millimeters) across and 12 to 18 inches (305 to 457 millimeters) high, that runs horizontally about 30 inches (762 millimeters) above the floor (see Figure 8-8). It contains pipes for hot and cold water, a gas supply pipe, an electrical conduit and "bus bars," and a steam supply (if needed). Connections to the equipment are made from the side or the bottom of the raceway.

Advantages of utility distribution systems include the following:

❑ Unlike connection points built into permanent walls, connections in the raceway can be added, removed, or relocated with relative ease should the equipment change.

❑ Connections from the raceway to the equipment are well above floor level, making the cooking areas easy to clean.

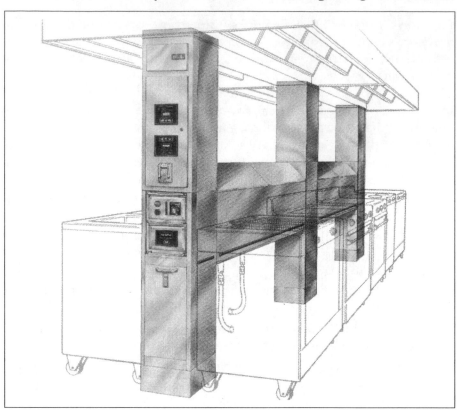

Figure 8-8. Utility distribution system. (Courtesy of AVTEC Industries.)

❏ Electrical and plumbing contractors at the job site need to make only one or two physical connections to the utility distribution system, rather than multiple connections for each piece of equipment.

Utility distribution systems generally are expensive. However, their cost needs to be weighed against the costs of engineering and constructing an array of complex utility services within a permanent wall. In large foodservice facilities, where sizable banks of equipment are required, a utility distribution system can prove to be a cost-effective alternative in comparison to traditional approaches.

Heat Recovery Systems

The cost of hot water is one of the biggest items on the foodservice energy bill. Hot water is used almost constantly during the normal operating hours of the facility, with peak usage when dishes are washed at breakfast, lunch, and dinner. Likewise, refrigeration equipment operates continuously during the normal operating hours of the foodservice facility. One way to save energy is to take the heat lost during refrigeration and use it for partial heating of dishwashing water.

Three common ways to remove heat are air cooling, water cooling, and use of a cooling tower. In all three methods, the heat is wasted unless it can be transported back to the food facility to be used for purposes such as heating water for kitchen or dishwashing use. With technology that has been in use for many years, heat from refrigeration can be easily transferred to water. Heat recovery systems were not widely used in the past only because fossil fuels were so cheap and abundant that such systems did not make sense economically.

The systems that are used to heat water as a by-product of refrigeration all operate on the same principle. Cold water that normally enters the hot-water heater first passes through the heat exchanger and removes the heat from the refrigeration system (water cooling of condensers). The formerly cold water is now slightly warm as it enters the water heater, and the cost of increasing the temperature of the water to acceptable levels (120°–140°F [49°–60°C]) is reduced. The equipment to accomplish the transfer of heat looks like a large domestic water heater. Figure 8-9 illustrates how this type of heat recovery system works.

Heat recovery systems can be designed for either an air-cooled heat exchanger, as described above, or for a water-cooled refrigeration system, in which the water absorbs heat from the refrigerant as it leaves the compressor. Both approaches accomplish similar savings. Water-preheating heat recovery systems reduce energy costs, and the return on investment can be very dramatic.

Important factors to consider before purchasing a heat recovery system are:

❏ The hot-water needs of your operation

❏ Energy costs in your area

❏ Hot-water storage needs

❏ The location and condition of existing refrigeration equipment

❏ The amount of refrigeration in use

The most logical application for heat recovery systems in foodservice facilities is the large refrigeration system used for walk-in coolers and freezers. The compressors for these units are by themselves large enough to justify the cost for many heat recovery systems. Lesser, though significant, energy cost savings may be realized by connecting compressors for smaller pieces of equipment to the recovery system. Typically, reach-in refrigera-

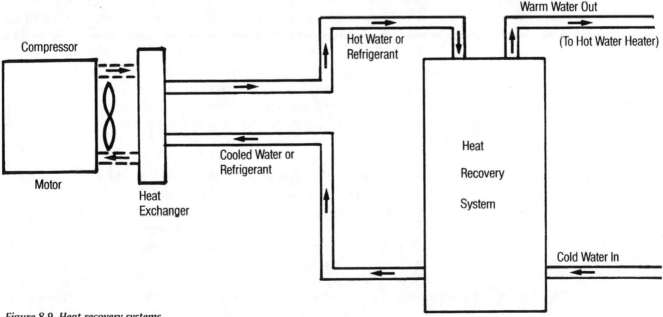

Figure 8-9. Heat recovery systems.

tors, display coolers, ice machines, and beverage dispensers are installed with self-contained refrigeration systems.

The compressors on these pieces are usually air-cooled, which means that the heat is dissipated into the kitchen, serving area, or dining room. If these areas are air-conditioned, each refrigeration unit adds to the air-conditioning load. Imagine the combined water-heating and air-conditioning savings that could be accrued by tying these smaller compressors into the heat recovery system. This is an excellent opportunity for energy savings that should not be overlooked when planning a new facility or renovating an existing one.

Other forms of heat recovery include solar heating and exhaust systems with heat exchangers. Systems for recovering heat from kitchen exhausts are designed to pull heat out of very hot air (from hoods over range sections and ovens) and recycle it into the water-heating system. Without some method of heat recovery, a tremendous amount of heat is lost "up the flue"; however, the air-to-water transfer that is used in these systems is much less efficient than other methods and requires a very large volume of hot exhaust air to justify the investment.

FOODSERVICE FACILITIES ARCHITECTURE

A complete treatment of architectural and interior design in relation to foodservice facilities lies beyond the scope of this text. However, there are several considerations in the architectural design of foodservice facilities that do need special attention because of their functional importance. These considerations include the construction of walls, floors, and ceilings; the provision of adequate lighting; and the control of noise.

The Construction of Walls, Floors, and Ceilings in Foodservice Facilities

The specification and construction of building surfaces are usually the responsibility of the architect in new or renovated foodservice facilities. However, the foodservice consultant and/or the owner are often asked by the architect for recommendations on the types of finishes that are desirable. The decision on the type of finish to be used may be based on budgetary limitations rather than the desirability of the surface. Ideally, the finishes that are recommended, especially for floors and walls, are chosen on the basis of ease in cleaning and resistance to damage or wear as well as aesthetics.

FLOORS The floor surface in the kitchen and service areas should be easy to maintain, wear-resistant, slip-resistant, and nonporous. The most universally accepted floor material is quarry tile, which has an excellent record in the foodservice industry for not being slippery and for resisting grease absorption. The grout between the tile is slightly porous at first but quickly becomes sealed from the dirt and grease of the typical food operation. Grout can also be coated with commercial floor sealers before use. These sealers need to be reapplied at appropriate intervals. The use of a colored or tinted grout creates a better appearance and eliminates the need for bleaching or cleaning the grout joint. Quarry tile with embedded Carborundum chips has greater slip resistance and is recommended for use in wet or high-grease conditions such as are found in range areas and potwashing and dishwashing areas.

Floor finishes in dining rooms and public places can be of any material that is wear-resistant and easily cleaned. Carpeting in dining rooms is popular because it absorbs sound and provides a feeling of luxury. Carpeting is not recommended in high-soil areas such as:

❑ Servers stations
❑ Tray and dish drop-off areas
❑ Beverage stations
❑ Condiment stations
❑ Major traffic aisles
❑ Cashier stations

Ceramic tile is an excellent floor finish for public rest rooms or high-soil areas. Unglazed tiles are the best choice because of their slip-resistant qualities.

Vinyl tile is not recommended in dining rooms or public areas because it usually requires a high level of maintenance, especially waxing and frequent machine buffing. The amount of labor required over a few years will exceed the extra costs of an easy-care quarry or ceramic tile floor. A vinyl tile floor wears out quickly in a commercial kitchen, is slippery when wet, and is not grease-resistant. Vinyl tile can be used as an inexpensive floor covering in employee dressing rooms, employee dining areas, or offices.

Figure 8-10 lists recommended floor finishes for foodservice facilities.

Foodservice Area	Recommended Floor Finishes
Kitchen	Quarry tile
Dishwashing	Quarry tile with Carborundum
Storerooms, dry stores	Sealed concrete
Wash-down rooms for carts and trash containers	Quarry tile with Carborundum; quarry tile; sealed concrete
Receiving	Quarry tile; sealed concrete
Offices	Quarry tile; vinyl tile; carpet; wood
Employee rest rooms	Quarry tile; vinyl tile; unglazed ceramic tile; terrazzo
Corridors, back of the house	Vinyl tile; unglazed ceramic tile; sealed concrete
Corridors, public	Vinyl tile; unglazed ceramic tile; carpet; terrazzo
Dining rooms	Quarry tile; unglazed ceramic tile; carpet; terrazzo
Public restrooms	Quarry tile; unglazed ceramic tile; terrazzo
Service areas	Quarry tile; unglazed ceramic tile; terrazzo

Figure 8-10. Recommended floor finishes for foodservice areas.

WALLS   Wall finishes used in food storage and preparation areas include structural glazed tile, ceramic glazed tile, concrete block with epoxy coating or paint, plaster, and painted drywall as well as special materials, such as Marlite. However, not all of these finishes are ideal for foodservice applications. Figure 8-11 lists recommended wall finishes for different areas in a foodservice facility.

Budget limitations may dictate a less expensive finish over the more desirable ones. Such substitutions can result in costly problems in the end. For example, one approach to reduce costs is to use concrete block with epoxy paint behind the equipment in the range section of a kitchen. However, the high heat generated by fryers, ovens, ranges, and charbroilers eventually causes the paint to discolor and flake off. Further, the grease generated by cooking is very difficult to remove from the small pits in the concrete block.* The ideal wall finishes in cooking areas are structural glazed tile or ceramic tile, either of which will resist damage from heat, grease, and frequent cleaning. The structural glazed tile is also highly resistant to impact when struck by a cart or other portable equipment.

CEILINGS   Ceilings in a foodservice facility are of two types: the structural ceiling, which supports the floors above, and the false ceiling, which may hide ducts

Foodservice Area	Recommended Wall Finishes
Kitchen, range section	Structural glazed tile; glazed ceramic tile
Kitchen, cold-food section	Structural glazed tile; glazed ceramic tile; concrete block with epoxy paint
Dishwashing	Structural glazed tile; glazed ceramic tile
Storerooms, dry stores	Concrete block with epoxy paint
Receiving	Concrete block with epoxy paint
Wash-down rooms for carts, etc.	Structural glazed tile; glazed ceramic tile
Offices	Painted drywall
Employee rest rooms	Glazed ceramic tile; concrete block with epoxy paint
Corridors, back of the house	Concrete block with epoxy paint; painted drywall
Corridors, public	Decorative wall selected by interior designer
Dining rooms	Decorative wall selected by interior designer
Public rest rooms	Glazed ceramic tile; decorative wall selected by interior designer
Service areas	Glazed ceramic tile; concrete block with epoxy

Figure 8-11. Recommended wall finishes for foodservice areas.

* Our illustration deals with the use of standard epoxy paints applied over concrete block. There are two-stage epoxy-based materials, such as Sanitile by Carboline, that can be applied effectively to concrete block in a foodservice application.

and other architectural features or serve mainly to enhance the room's attractiveness.

New materials for ceilings are introduced so frequently and ceiling materials vary so widely that any list would be outdated in a short period. The most common ceiling materials are:

❏ Acoustical tile

❏ Drywall, painted

❏ Plaster, painted

❏ Wood, sealed or painted

❏ Exposed concrete

❏ Fiberglass

❏ Aluminum or other metal

The acoustical ceiling is the most common of those listed, because of its low cost and excellent sound-absorbing qualities. Special acoustical tiles have been developed that do not easily absorb moisture or grease from the air. The health department or local building codes usually have specific recommendations for the type of ceiling material that is acceptable for foodservice operations. Aluminum panel ceilings with perforations are often used because they can be easily removed for cleaning. Some aluminum ceiling panels can actually be put through the dishwashing machine.

If the ceilings in work areas are sound-absorbent, grease-resistant, moisture-resistant, and light-reflective, they will probably be acceptable to health officials. Ceilings in dining rooms and other public areas can be constructed of or covered with many types of material as long as they do not create either a fire safety problem or a health hazard.

Controlling Noise

Excessive noise in the workplace is of concern to managers because it can cause fatigue, irritability, and low productivity among workers. Noise control in the dining room and public areas of a foodservice facility is a significant consideration in creating a pleasant dining experience. Stopping the transfer of sound from areas adjacent to a banquet hall or private dining room can mean the difference between a successful and an unsuccessful meeting or convention.

Architects, engineers, and foodservice consultants spend a significant amount of time seeking methods of creating a quiet environment. One of the problems with sound control in a typical foodservice operation is the nature of the operation itself. The activity and movement of workers, the noise of equipment, conversations between guests at the tables, the speech of servers taking food orders and communicating with the kitchen, the clatter of glasses and dishes, and background music (when present) add up to a very high sound level.

Sound level (loudness) is measured in decibels. Noise above 130 decibels is painful to the normal ear and would seldom be encountered in a foodservice operation. Another characteristic of sound is the number of vibrations per second created from the sound source. The average human ear can hear sound only in the range of 15 to 20,000 vibrations per second.

In the dining environment, it is desirable to keep the decibel level low and to introduce low-frequency background music. High-frequency music or sound is generally less pleasant to the ear, especially in an eating place where conversation is encouraged among the guests.

SOUND-ABSORBING MATERIALS   Carpeting and draperies absorb sound and can create a pleasant appearance in the dining room. Glass and hard-surface floors, walls, and ceilings reflect sound and create reverberations that make table conversation difficult.

A mixture of these materials in the public spaces of a foodservice establishment is the usual approach taken by the architect and interior designer to control sound. For example, glass, quarry tile, and terrazzo reflect 70 to 90 percent of sound, while carpet or cloth reflect only 40 to 65 percent (depending on the density and characteristics of the material). Generally, the use of some carpeting in the dining room and the selection of acoustical material for the ceiling will create the proper sound levels.

Noise in the kitchen and other support areas of a foodservice facility can be decreased but not eliminated. The use of quarry tile floors, ceramic tile, or other hard-surface walls and ceilings creates a sound-reflecting environment. Noises made by the use of dish machines, mixers, garbage disposers, metal pots and pans, stainless-steel tables, and other metal utensils add a considerable amount of sound to the kitchen. The following list of sound reduction ideas should be considered in the planning of the kitchen and other support areas:

- ❑ Acoustical ceilings
- ❑ Sound-deadening coatings on the underside of stainless-steel work surfaces
- ❑ Remote compressors for reach-in and especially for walk-in refrigerators and freezers
- ❑ Electronic transmittal of orders to display screens in the preparation areas, rather than by servers shouting out the orders to the cooks
- ❑ Low-volume background music in the workplace (such music tends to discourage radio owners from playing their sets full blast in the kitchen)
- ❑ Physical separation and/or enclosure of dishwashing and potwashing from other parts of the kitchen with walls designed to prevent sound transmission

Lighting   Well over 80 percent of our impressions are visual, and vision is essential to many elements of the foodservice business, such as preparation, service, and cash handling. When food workers cannot see accurately, errors and delays result, seriously affecting productivity.

Consider also the reasons people patronize foodservice operations: not only to eat, but also because of the quality of the physical environment. The difference between "eating" and "dining" depends upon the ambiance of the facility and the total experience—conscious and subconscious—of the customer. Properly directed light can help dissolve negative feelings and tensions. The goal is to provide guests with pleasant sensations designed to fit together into a complete dining experience. To create consistently positive experiences, control must be exerted over where the light goes, what its true color will be, and what effects it will have on the guests and workers, as well as the effects on the overall appearance of the interior design elements of the facility.

Each part of the eye sees a specific type of light. The cones of the retina allow one to see colors and details in bright sunlight. Studies have shown that cone color vision is improved by the stimulus of sound waves. The normal hustle and activity in a lunchroom therefore stimulate a keener perception of color. This may require the alignment of the color decor elements with the light levels and their direction to avoid assaulting the mind with a barrage of tension-producing stimuli. The effects work both ways. During evening dining, the sound waves from service activity will appear to warm up the colors in the room. This is an advantage, as the colors are otherwise perceived as being duller under the lower evening light levels. However, the efficiency of the retina rods, which allow one to see black and white under dim lighting conditions, is reduced by the stimulation of sound waves. Therefore, guests will experience greater difficulty in reading the black and white print of the menu, promotion cards, wine lists, charge slips, or checks. The room may appear to be well lighted to the manager when he or she sets the light levels during the quiet early evening hours. What happens is that the menu becomes harder to read as the *sound* in the dining room increases with the arrival of more guests. Ironically, unbalanced light levels can mean that when people are waiting to be seated and the operator wishes to turn the tables faster, the patrons already seated actually need more time to read printed materials and make a selection.

Although the eye can adapt to a wide range of lighting conditions, it doesn't always function with the same degree of efficiency. In order to establish light levels that can assist the eye in seeing more efficiently, five factors must be considered: time, size, contrast, brightness, and sound.

Time. One's level of comfort or discomfort, and therefore one's perception of time, are affected by the level and the tone of light. Waiting to be served and waiting for a check can be very tense experiences for a customer in a hurry. The degree of environmental comfort can mean the difference between the customer's being irritated or satisfied. Reading a menu under poor lighting conditions could take up too much time during a lunch or dinner rush and slow the turnover unnecessarily. Or if the customer is rushed into making a selection, he or she may not have time to read the entire menu.

Size. Light also affects space perception. Proper lighting can make a small room seem open and can make a large room feel cozy. In a darkened room, people seated a few feet apart feel much closer together than they would in a room with more light. On the menu, the size of the print has a direct relationship to the customer's ability to see efficiently at various light levels.

Contrast. The perceived difference between the detail of an object and its background is referred to as contrast. Spotlighting, in which light shines directly on a specific area, offers high contrast. On the other hand, the contrast between a coffee stain and a brown rug is low. Good contrast between the colors of the ink and paper can make a menu easier to read at any light level. In the kitchen, contrast comes into play when cooks work on highly reflective stainless-steel tables.

Brightness. The amount of light the eye sees on an object's surface is the brightness. This is the last controllable element of lighting, since time, size, contrast, and sound are often fixed before the acceptability of the light levels is evaluated. Putting more light on an object will improve the visibility of the object despite its small size, poor contrast, or the shortness of time allotted in which to distinguish the object.

Sound. As mentioned above, light levels should be readjusted as the sound levels vary in the room. This can be done quite effectively with a light dimmer switch.

HOW MUCH LIGHT IS ENOUGH?

If you were in a dark cave with only a book of matches to light your way, you would be amazed at how efficient such a small amount of light can be. There is a rapid increase in the efficiency of light when moving from darkness into light, using as little as 3 foot-candles of light. In fact, when a task is illuminated, the available light may be as much as 90 percent efficient at a very low level. However, to move to 95 percent efficiency may require three times as much light, and to be 100 percent efficient may require 10 to 100 times as much light. Close work involving very small objects, such as microcomputer chips, may require as much as 1,500 foot-candles of light, but only at the work surface.

Another factor in efficiency, similar in concept to contrast, is the reflective difference level of the task and the surrounding area. The comparative brightness of the light reflected off the object and off the background determines how easily the eye can distinguish the former. Ideal reflective levels would range from 40 to 60 percent at 40 foot-candles of light illuminating the task and the surrounding area. The surrounding area should reflect back 40–50 percent of the light, while the task should reflect back 50-60 percent. Except in a case such as reading, which normally requires a brighter background, there should be at least 10 percent more light reflected back from the task than from the surroundings. For example, as the illumination of a cash register keyboard is kept constant and the surrounding brightness of the countertop is raised gradually, the ability to see the keyboard improves. This improvement will be gradual and constant and will be at its maximum when the brightness of the surrounding counter is equal to or slightly less than the brightness of the keyboard. When the brightness of the surrounding counter exceeds the brightness of the keyboard, there is a radical falling off in the ability to see the keyboard without making computation errors.

Another example of reflectance difference would be a menu board on a bright wall. The bright wall competes for the eye's attention and would reduce the efficiency of reading the menu board.

One solution to this problem is found in the use of brightness ratios that mathematically compare the brightness of the task with the surrounding brightness. A 3 to 1 ratio is normal, 10 to 1 the high limit. However, brightness ratios can be misleading. A work area could have a favorable brightness ratio but abnormally high levels of reflected glare from the task.

If the brightness ratio of the menu board to the wall, for example, was 3 to 1 and the light on the menu board required to compete with the brightness of the stainless-steel wall was 1,000 watts, the excessive task light would reflect glare back into the customers' eyes and reduce their ability to see the board.

Glare is a common problem in poorly designed lighting systems. To reduce glare, one can reduce the reflectance of the surface or move the light out of the direct line of vision. Another solution is to build up a balanced intensity of brightness that absorbs and distributes the glare. For example, if the restaurant windows reflect glare from the perimeter lighting back into the eyes of the customer, shades may be hung in the windows, or the overall lighting level in the room may be increased so as to build a balanced intensity, which could be reduced as the sun sets. Figure 3-7 (Chapter 3) lists recommended light levels for various foodservice applications.

LIGHTING AND PRODUCTIVITY

Light is one of the many inputs that affect productivity. Its impact shows up most obviously in problems that can be traced to poor visibility. For example, low productivity may be revealed in sales figures that are not correctly transcribed, or by a server's check that cannot be read under kitchen illumination, resulting in the preparation of the wrong item. But light has less noticeable effects. The level and kind of light can influence the way we function, both physically and psychologically. How motivated do we feel, for instance, when the weather is gray and cloudy, or when lighting is subdued rather than bright and warm?

Providing more illumination, however, is not the whole answer. In fact, reduced productivity often occurs in operations with high light levels that are merely running up utility costs unnecessarily. Better lighting and higher productivity are the result of knowledgeable planning, not merely adding wattage.

Studies show that a small increase in light levels can raise productivity significantly. Increases of 5 to 33 percent in productivity have been achieved by the proper placing of as little as 25 foot-candles of light. Better lighting reduces the time required to see and act on the task to be done. When speed increases, confidence grows, which further increases speed. Too little light or an unbalanced distribution increases the rate of error and reduces output.

The reduction of error is as important as increasing output. In a Federal Energy Administration test conducted at Ohio State University, a 12 percent reduction in errors in handwritten numbers occurred when light levels were properly adjusted. This reduction could be significant for restaurateurs in many ways, not least at the cash register.

Motivation is influenced by the way people perceive their environment. Workers seldom consciously consider the light falling on their tasks until strain, a headache, or fatigue sets in, but it affects them nonetheless. With better task visibility, work can be accomplished and high standards achieved with less effort. The right lighting also helps to create the impression of a comfortable work environment, in which employees are likely to approach their day with a more consistently positive attitude.

LIGHTING DESIGN   People tend to orient themselves and their activities according to the brightness levels of their environment. This visual aesthetic sense has a significant effect on what activities people consider proper in different levels of light. Overall, brightness is appropriate for spaces in which physical activity takes place, such as washing areas, receiving areas, stockrooms, assembly areas, and refrigerators. Lower light levels would be suitable for accounting, cash handling, counter sales, waiting areas, expediting stations, and access corridors. In either case, light levels should remain within a moderate range. When areas are too bright, colors and shapes appear jarring or distorted, and workers' concentration is affected.

Brightness also influences the mind's perception of the apparent weight of objects. Tote boxes, cases, trash cans, and trays will seem easier to lift if they are white or painted a bright color. It is a pity that most cardboard cartons remain a standard dull brown. If more manufacturers bleached or painted their containers white, as Sexton does, the handling of cases of food off the truck and into storerooms would be perceived as an easier task than it is now. In any event, to achieve a good level of reflectance, light levels should be high in areas where lifting and handling must be done.

The color of uniforms is another factor in lighting design, because of its visual impact. Uniforms for physical work should be bright.

Bacterial strains, especially those that cause odors and food poisoning, respond to light as well. Research has shown that streptococci of various strains (the kind usually found in food poisoning cases traced to poor employee hygiene) are killed by natural daylight, either direct or filtered through glass. The possibility of killing or preventing the growth of bacteria during food preparation, or of destroying odors without having to cover them up with equally obnoxious fumes, should interest any foodservice manager. Ultraviolet light also benefits employee health directly. It has been found to increase the level of working capacity and resistance to infections, improve the stability of clear vision, and reduce respiratory infections.

SUMMARY

The owner, architect, foodservice consultant, and engineer must become involved in the engineering decisions affecting the foodservice facility. The quality of interior lighting, the HVAC system used, the energy efficiency of kitchen equipment, and the final cost of the project are all outcomes of engineering decisions.

A basic understanding of the types of energy sources available and the methods for designing high-energy-consumption equipment such as hoods and dishwashing machines is helpful in arriving at sound decisions regarding utility usage. Because floor, ceiling, and wall finishes have a great impact on the final cost of the project, the foodservice consultant must understand which ones will perform best. Trade journals, manufacturers' representatives, and professional engineers are good sources of information on foodservice facilities engineering.

APPENDIX 1

FOODSERVICE-RELATED PROFESSIONAL ASSOCIATIONS

L. Edwin Brown, Executive Director
American Culinary Federation
10 San Bartolla Road
P.O. Box 3466
St. Augustine, FL 32084
(904) 824-4336

Julian Haynes, Executive Director
American Dietetic Association
430 North Michigan Avenue
Chicago, IL 60611
(312) 280-5000

Robert L. Richards, Executive Vice President
American Hotel and Motel Association
888 Seventh Avenue
New York, NY 10019
(212) 265-4506

Ann G. Smith, Executive Director
American School Food Service Association
4101 East Cliff Avenue
Denver, CO 80222
(303) 757-8555

Kathleen Pontius, Director
American Society for Hospital Foodservice Administrators
840 North Lake Shore Drive
Chicago, IL 60611
(312) 280-6417

Horace G. Duncan, Executive Director
Club Managers Association of America
7615 Winterberry Place
Washington, DC 20034
(301) 229-3600

Jean Denwood, Executive Director
Dietary Managers Association
4410 West Roosevelt Road
Hillside, IL 60162
(312) 449-2770

Barbara Chalik, Executive Vice President
International Foodservice Executives Association
111 East Wacker Drive
Chicago, IL 60601
(312) 644-6610

APPENDIX 2

TYPICAL FOODSERVICE FACILITY DESIGNS

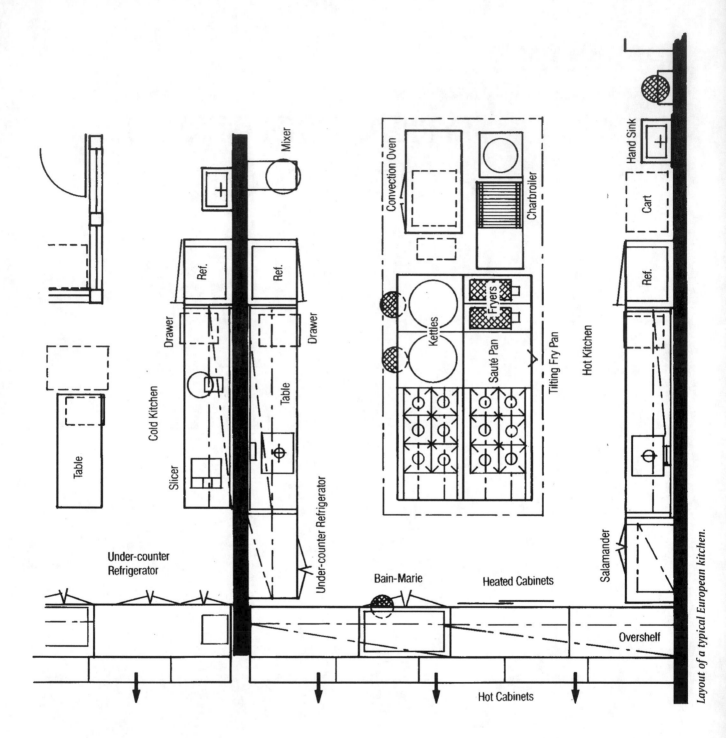

Layout of a typical European kitchen.

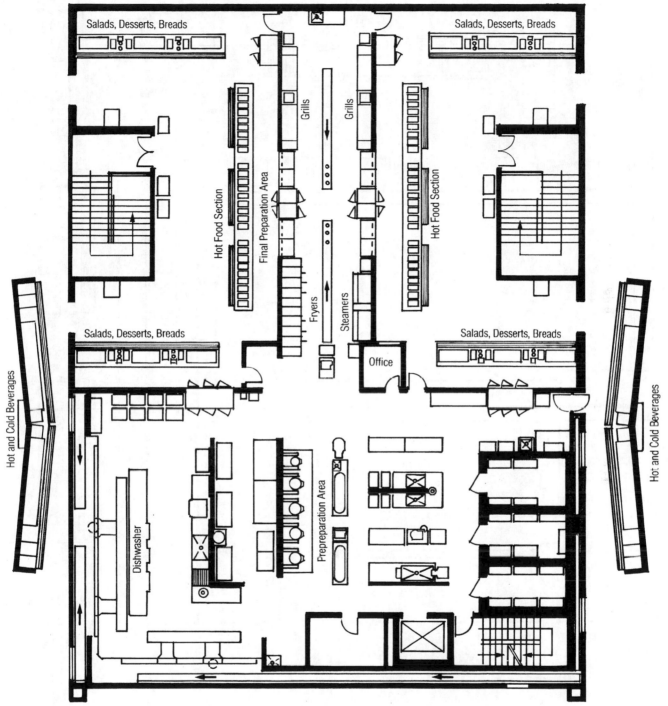

Salads, Desserts, Breads

Salads, Desserts, Breads

Grills

Grills

Hot Food Section

Hot Food Section

Final Preparation Area

Salads, Desserts, Breads

Salads, Desserts, Breads

Fryers

Steamers

Office

Hot and Cold Beverages

Hot and Cold Beverages

Prepreparation Area

Dishwasher

Dining hall (kitchen and servery) serving 6000 meals per day (University of Tennessee).

261

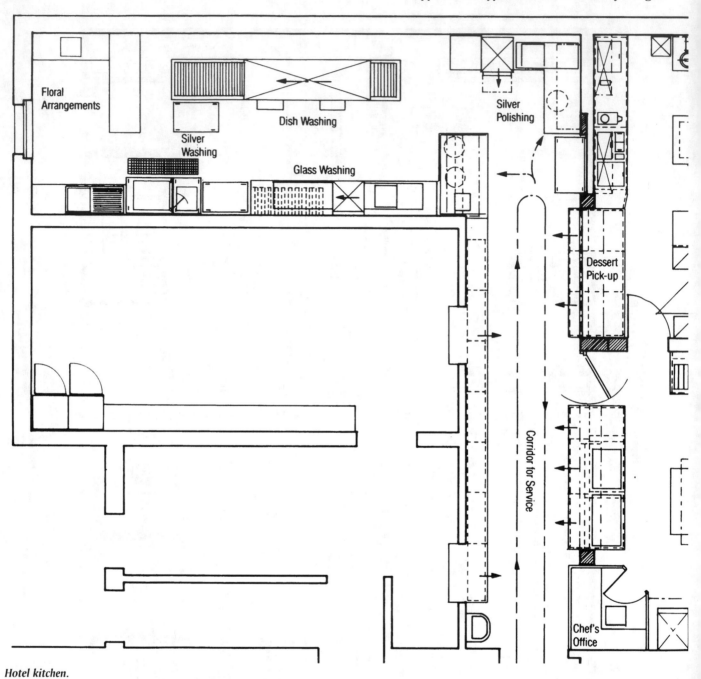

Floral
Arrangements

Silver
Washing

Dish Washing

Glass Washing

Silver
Polishing

Dessert
Pick-up

Corridor for Service

Chef's
Office

Hotel kitchen.

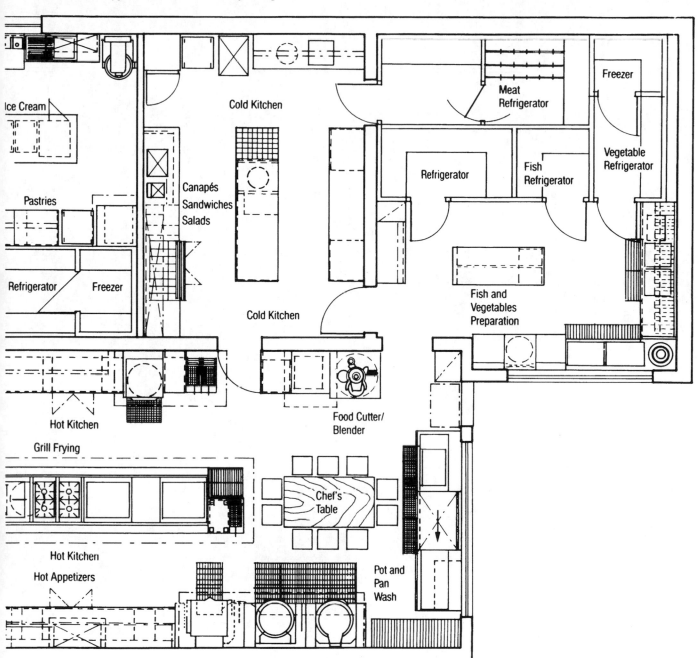

Ice Cream

Pastries

Refrigerator   Freezer

Hot Kitchen

Grill Frying

Hot Kitchen

Hot Appetizers

Canapés
Sandwiches
Salads

Cold Kitchen

Cold Kitchen

Food Cutter/
Blender

Chef's
Table

Meat
Refrigerator

Freezer

Refrigerator

Fish
Refrigerator

Vegetable
Refrigerator

Fish and
Vegetables
Preparation

Pot and
Pan
Wash

APPENDIX 3

COMMON FOODSERVICE FACILITY DESIGN SYMBOLS

Water rough-in	●
Water rough-in and connection	⊙⊙
Wastewater rough-in	○
Condensate drain or indirect waste	○ - - - IW
Wastewater rough-in and connection	○-○W
Gas supply rough-in	✪
Gas supply rough-in and connection	✪-○
Steam supply	■
Steam supply stab-out	▶
Steam return	◪
Steam return stub-out	▷
Floor sink—open	☐ FS
Floor sink—angle grate	▤
Floor sink—funnel grate	▦
Floor drain	☐ FD
Hose bib	⊤ HB
Hose rack	▭○ HR
Hot-water tank	○ HWT

265

Lavatories: wall, corner	L1, L2, etc. L1, L2, etc.
Grease trap	GT
Can washer	CW
Clean-out	CO
Dishwasher	DW
Sink	S-1, S-2, etc.
Water heater	WH

PIPING

Above grade soil or waste	
Below grade soil or waste	
Cold water	
Hot water	
Gas	

ABBREVIATIONS

HW	Hot water
HSW	Hot soft water
CW	Cold water
PRV	Pressure reducer valve
AFF	Above finished floor
KEC	Kitchen equipment contractor
PC	Plumbing contractor
EC	Electrical contractor
C&P	Cord and plug
EF	Exhaust fan
AC	Air-conditioning
FD	Floor drain

FS	Floor sink
D.S.	Dimmer switch
LV	Low voltage
V.A.	Vinyl asbestos
V.B.	4-inch vinyl base—cove type
E.C.	Exposed construction
E.PAINT	Epoxy paint
A.T.	Acoustical tile
C.T.	Ceramic tile
P.L.	Plastic laminate
Q.T.[1]	6×6 quarry tile
Q.T.B.	6-inch covered bull-nose quarry-tile base
G.C.B	Glazed concrete block
Q.T.[2]	Six-sided quarry
M.P.	Metal pan-ceiling system
ML	Marlite fiberglass
S.P.	Stucco paint on drywall
E.M.U.	Exposed masonary units
C.B.	Concrete block
PT.	Paint
GL. BR.	Glazed brick base, recess ½ inch
PART. BD.	Particleboard

ELECTRICAL SYMBOLS

Conduit stub flush couple with curb	▲
Flex tubing (36-inch minimum exposed)	♂
Waterproof conduit stub	●
Junction box, waterproof with final connection to equipment (36-inch minimum seal tight flex)	(J)$_{WP}$
Junction box at ceiling	(J)
Junction box at wall	—(J)
Junction box above floor	(J)
Junction box with final connection to equipment (36-inch minimum exposed)	(J)

Junction box installed in equipment	Ⓙ
Single convenience outlet (wattage as shown)	⊖
Duplex convenience outlet (wattage as shown)	⊜
Single convenience outlet w/switch	⊖⌒
Duplex convenience outlet (installed in equipment)	⊖
Single-purpose power outlet, 1 phase	◕
Single-purpose power outlet, 1 phase (installed in equipment)	⊙
Single-purpose power outlet, 3 phase	⊗
Single-purpose power outlet, 3 phase (installed in equipment)	⊗
Floor outlet, flush or pedestal	⊘
Floor junction box	⊙
Recessed convenience outlet, single (wattage as shown)	⊖$_s$
120V motor	◗
208–240 V 1-phase motor	○
208–240 V 3-phase motor	◔
Clock outlet	©
Ground connection	⟟
Buzzer	◻
Infrared warmer	▰
Heat lamp	◉
Incandescent light (number when scheduled)	⟡
Pull box (installed in equipment	⌐⌐
Switch	S
3-way switch	S$_3$
4-way switch	S$_4$
Switch with neon pilot	S$_p$
Vaporproof switch	S$_{vp}$
Automatic door switch	S$_D$
Double-pole waterproof switch	S$_{2wp}$
Pull switch	Ⓟ
Push button switch	▣

LIGHTING

Incandescent strip (number when scheduled)	⊲①⊳
Fluorescent fixture (number when scheduled)	🔲①
Fluorescent strip light (number when scheduled)	⊲①⊳
Wall-washer light (number when scheduled)	①◁
Neon tubing	- - - -
Exit light	⊗
Transformer	T
Lighting panel	▭
Power panel	▨

REFRIGERATION

Thermostat	⊣T
High-temperature alarm relay with red light and bell	⌂⌂
Safety alarm bell with red light	▢◖
Vaporproof light, 100 watts	◯
Evaporator (blower coil) with fan	⸤⟡⸣
Liquid line solenoid	Ⓢ$_L$
Conduit run for refrigerant, CO_2, gas, and carbonation lines	= = =
Pull box	▭

Reprinted from *News and Views,* Food Equipment Distributors Association, January 1977.

APPENDIX 4

SAMPLE DOCUMENTS

EXHIBIT A

SAMPLE
CONSULTANT PROPOSAL AND COVER LETTER TO THE
CONSULTANT/CLIENT AGREEMENT

(Note: Because of potential legal complexities which could involve this document, consultation with an attorney is suggested.)

Date

Addressee
Mr. John Smith
124 Central Avenue
Anytown, State, Zip

Re: Project Name:
    Location:
    Proposal No:

Dear:

Introductory Paragraph

1. Pleased about the opportunity to submit a proposal for (services) for (project) located at........

2. Brief description of project

Statement of Objectives
A brief statement of the work to be done on the project by the consultant.

Recommendation of Specific Services
(statement of scope of services pertinent to this project or requested by client)

Reference should be made to Exhibit B
Example: It is our opinion, based on your project objectives, that a phased proposal is the most prudent approach to accomplishing your goals. The phases are listed in the approximate chronological order they would be accomplished with a fee for each phase so that you can evaluate the overall project.

FOODSERVICE CONSULTANTS SOCIETY INTERNATIONAL

	Not to Exceed
Phase I - Programming and Preliminary Planning	$ _____
Phase II - Design Development & Engineering	$ _____
Phase III - Preparation of Bid Documents	$ _____
Phase IV - Coordination and Approval of Shop Drawings	$ _____
Phase V - Final Inspection and Training	
Total Fee	$ _____

This proposal and cover letter defines each of the phases in detail; it is upon the amount of work included in this detail that the fee has been computed. In addition to the fees set forth above, we will invoice for all reimbursable expenses incurred in the interest of the project as set forth in the Consultant/Client Agreement (Exhibit B) to which this proposal has been attached and made reference.

Additional Services Option
that can be provided by the Consultant (to be included unless specifically asked to omit)

Closing Paragraph
(assures follow-up)

1. Schedule follow-up or next step or arrange to call client at a certain time.

2. Tickler follow-up for a certain date to find out what is happening to proposal.

3. Thank client for consideration of our firm.

Respectfully submitted,

Writer's Name
Title

Initials: initials

Attached to this proposal and letter is:

Exhibit B: Consultant/Client Agreement

EXHIBIT B

SAMPLE
CONSULTANT/CLIENT AGREEMENT

(Note: Because of potential legal complexities which could involve this document, consultation with an attorney is suggested.)

Consultant: **(name and address of consultant)**

                           hereinafter called the CONSULTANT

Client: **(name and address of the client)**
                           (name of primary contact person, as designated by the client)

                           hereinafter called the CLIENT

Project: **(official name of project)**

                           hereinafter called PROJECT.

REFERENCE DOCUMENTS:

Exhibit A.   Consultant Proposal and Cover Letter attached to the Consultant/Client Agreement
Exhibit B.   Consultant/Client Agreement

WHEREAS, the CLIENT desires, in connection therewith, to engage the CONSULTANT and the CONSULTANT desires to be retained by the CLIENT to perform consulting services as described in Exhibit A all upon the terms and subject to the conditions hereinafter stated;

NOW, THEREFORE, in consideration of the covenants herein contained, the parties agree as follows:

1. AGREEMENT

The CONSULTANT agrees to perform the basic services hereinafter set forth. Pursuant to the payment schedule, the CLIENT agrees to pay the CONSULTANT for their services the fees as set forth in Exhibit A herein made a part of this Agreement.

2. THE CONSULTANT'S SERVICES

The CONSULTANT's basic services shall include all those services as set forth in Exhibit A.

FOODSERVICE CONSULTANTS SOCIETY INTERNATIONAL

3. REIMBURSABLE EXPENSES

The CLIENT will reimburse monthly to the CONSULTANT for all actual expenditures made in the interest of the PROJECT for the incidental expenses apart from the fee set forth in Exhibit A including:

- expense of transportation
- traveling in connection with the PROJECT at actual cost for automobile rental and public transportation and the current U.S. Government approved allowance for automobile travel
- long distance telephone calls, telegrams, postage, delivery charges
- reproduction of drawings, specifications, programs, reports and manuals
- other normal disbursements and obligations incurred on the CLIENT's account. The CONSULTANT will request, in advance, the CLIENT's authorization and approval for any unusual or extraordinary expense

4. PAYMENT SCHEDULE OF FEES

The CLIENT will compensate the CONSULTANT for services performed in accordance with the schedule set forth in Exhibit A. Invoices are due and payable upon presentation monthly and a late charge of ____% will be added to all balances unpaid ____days after date of invoice and each month thereafter cumulatively. In addition, should it become necessary that an unpaid invoice be referred to our attorneys for collection, the CLIENT agrees to pay their reasonable fee for such work as well as any costs of suit which may be incurred.

Fee Retainer: The CLIENT shall pay to the CONSULTANT upon execution of this Agreement a retainer in an amount equal to ____% of the Fee, either estimated or actual, unless specified otherwise in Exhibit A. Said retainer shall be held by the CONSULTANT until the completion of the PROJECT, at which time it will be applied against the final invoice on the PROJECT.

(Note: Fees may be paid in several ways including, but not necessarily limited to, the following. CONSULTANT/CLIENT terms to determine which applies.)

a. Hourly Fee Basis: Invoices will be used monthly for the total number of hours expended during the month in the interest of the PROJECT in accordance with the Hourly Rate Schedule that is a part of this Agreement. The current rate schedule will remain in effect for this Contract for ___years after the date of this Agreement. After ___years, the then current schedule will be reviewed with the CLIENT and will become the effective rate schedule.

b. Fixed Fee Basis: Invoices will be issued monthly in accordance with the schedule set forth in Exhibit A.

5. DEFERRAL OR TERMINATION

This Agreement may be terminated by either party upon ___ days written notice should the other party fail substantially to perform in accordance with its terms through no fault of the other.

In the event the PROJECT is deferred for a period of more than ___ months during any stage prior to completion of the Scope of Work outlined in Exhibit A or there is more than one delay or deferral of ___ months or more, each during any stage prior to completion of the Scope of Work outlined in Exhibit A or the PROJECT is terminated or the CLIENT ceases to require services for any reason beyond the CONSULTANT's control, the CLIENT agrees to pay the CONSULTANT within ___days, in addition to any amount which may have been paid pursuant to the terms of this Agreement the following:

a. all fees which may be payable to the CONSULTANT as previously identified herein but are unpaid at the date the CLIENT notifies the CONSULTANT in writing of such deferral or termination (the date of such notification being hereinafter referred to as the "deferral date" or the "termination date" – whichever shall apply)

b. all expenses due to the CONSULTANT as previously identified herein for which the CONSULTANT has not been reimbursed as at the deferral or termination date;

c. all amounts representing compensation for extra services as identified hereinafter which have not been paid as at the deferral or termination date; or

d. in the case of deferral, all work necessary to reactivate the PROJECT and to make adjustments in design, equipment selection drawings, and all other data made necessary or desirable due to the deferral; in addition, the CONSULTANT shall be compensated on the basis of the rate schedule in use at the time of the resumption of work, and all other fees shall be adjusted to suit the revised rate schedule and any other changes.

6. OWNERSHIP OF DOCUMENTS

Drawings, specifications, reports, manuals and programs as instruments of service are the property of the CONSULTANT whether the PROJECT for which they are made be executed or not and are not to be used on other projects except by agreement in writing with the CONSULTANT.

(Note: The CLIENT and the CONSULTANT are free to agree to the above, or that the documents may become the property of the CLIENT. This is suggested language favoring the CONSULTANT.)

7. SUCCESSORS AND ASSIGNS

The CLIENT and the CONSULTANT each binds himself, his partners, successors, assigns and legal representatives of such other party in respect to all covenants of this Agreement. Neither the CLIENT nor the CONSULTANT shall assign, sublet or transfer his interest in the Agreement without the written consent of the other.

8. EXTRA SERVICES

If the CONSULTANT is caused extra services or other expenses due to change orders or revisions to documents previously approved by the CLIENT, the CONSULTANT shall be paid for such extra expense or services in accordance with paragraph 4.a Hourly Fee Basis. Such extras or changes shall be requested or confirmed in writing.

For the purpose of carrying out any special project requested by the CLIENT, the CONSULTANT agrees to prepare a written proposal covering the scope of the special project, which proposal shall be accepted or rejected in writing by the CLIENT.

9. PROFESSIONAL RECOGNITION

The CLIENT agrees to acknowledge the professional services provided by the CONSULTANT in detailed press releases, magazine articles and the like where reference is made to the planning, design or management consulting services performed by the CONSULTANT relative to the Hospitality Facilities for the PROJECT.

10. INDEMNIFICATION

It is further agreed by the CLIENT that, except for breach of the terms of this Agreement by the CONSULTANT and for losses and damages due to the gross negligence or intentional torts of the CONSULTANT, its officers, agents and employees, the CLIENT shall defend, indemnify against and save harmless the CONSULTANT, its officers, agents and employees from all losses, expenses, liabilities, demands, suits and other actions of every nature and description (including attorneys' fees and any liability imposed by an applicable law, ordinance, code, rule or regulation) to which any of the aforesaid may be subjected by reason of any act or omission of the CONSULTANT or officers,

agents, employees, licensees or invitees of the CONSULTANT, where such loss, expense, liability, demand, suit or other detriment directly or indirectly arises out of or in connection with the CONSULTANT or its successors' and assigns' activities on the premises of CLIENT or with this proposed Agreement.

(Note: The above suggested language favors the CONSULTANT, and may have to be modified under certain contractual conditions imposed by the CLIENT in order to obtain the project.)

11. Where the CONSULTANT is requested by the CLIENT to engage the services of other Subconsultant(s) in connection with the PROJECT, or to select Subconsultant(s) to render services to the CLIENT, the CONSULTANT shall obtain the CLIENT's written approval of the selected Subconsultant(s). The CONSULTANT shall not be responsible to the CLIENT or other persons for any losses, damage or other expenses incurred as a result of the errors, omissions or negligent acts of the selected Subconsultant(s).

12. This contract, by agreement of the parties, has been made in _____(City, County, State)_____ and the laws of the State of _____(State)_____shall govern this contract. In any action by either party to enforce the terms of this agreement, at the option of ____(Consultant firm)____the venue thereof shall be In (City, County, State named above).

13. This agreement shall not be binding upon either party hereto until the agreement is signed by the CLIENT and returned to and accepted by the CONSULTANT within ____ days of date of proposal. Such acceptance by the CONSULTANT shall be evidenced by the signature of the CONSULTANT on this agreement.

In WITNESS WHEREOF the parties hereto have made and executed this Agreement, the day and year indicated in the acceptance area below.

ATTEST: _____   CLIENT: _____

_____   By: _____

Date: _____

_____   Title: _____   Date: _____

ACCEPTED AT (Location) _____   (Name of Consulting Firm) _____

ATTEST: _____   By: _____

Date: _____   Title: _____   Date: _____

FOODSERVICE EQUIPMENT GLOSSARY

Au Gratin Oven. Enclosure with hinged door mounted on top of a broiler. Also called finishing oven.

Bain-marie. Sinklike depression in a tabletop with a water bath heated by steam, gas, or electricity into which containers of food are placed to keep foods heated. Often used by chefs as a double boiler. Also called sandwich unit when used for refrigerated foods in sandwich preparation.

Baker's Stove. *See* Pot Stove.

Baker's Table. Table whose top has 4- to 6-inch-high curbing along the rear and sides to minimize spillage of flour onto floor during preparation. Often furnished with mobile or tilt-out ingredient bins under the top.

Banquet Cart. Insulated or noninsulated mobile cabinet with a series of interior shelves and/or racks to hold plates and/or platters of food. Usually equipped with an electric heating unit or refrigeration device.

Barbecue Grill. A live charcoal or gas-fired open-hearth horizontal grill having spits set across the top of the unit with rotisserie-type drive mechanism along the front working side.

Bar Workboard. Equipment below the top of a bar containing sinks, drain boards, cocktail mix stations, ice storage chests, beverage coolers, glass washers, etc. Also called sink workboard.

Beef Cart. Mobile unit, with or without bottled gas, alcohol, or electric heating unit. Used for display and slicing of roast beef in the dining room.

Beer Cooler. Cooler in which kegs, cans, or bottles of beer are refrigerated. The direct-draw cooler is a low-counter type with self-contained tapping equipment and dispensing head(s).

Beer Dispenser or **Tapping Cabinet.** Refrigerated or ice-cooled insulated cabinet with beer-, soda-, and/or water-dispensing heads, drainer plate, and pan recessed flush with the bar top and a drain trough under. Usually built into a liquor bar top, between workboards.

Beer System. A method for tapping beer from remotely located refrigerated kegs and transporting it through pressurized, refrigerated, and insulated lines to dispensing heads located at one or more stations in the bar and/or backbar.

Beverage Carrier. *See* Carrier.

Bin. Semienclosed rectangular or round container, open on top, with or without lift-off, sliding, or hinged cover. Floor-type bins are usually mobile, of height to roll under a table top. Bins under a baker's table may be mobile or built in to tilt out. An ingredient bin may be used for flour, sugar, salt, beans, dry peas, etc. A vegetable storage bin has a perforated or screened body. An ice storage bin is fully enclosed and insulated with hinged or sliding insulated door(s) at the front; it is normally stationary and set under an ice-making machine (head). A silverware (flatware) or cutlery bin is small and mounted in a holder set on or under countertop with other bins.

Blast Chiller. Quick-chill is the process of reducing the temperature of food rapidly to just above freezing (e.g. 34°F). Rapid cooling to low temperatures prevents the growth of microorganisms that cause food-borne illness. Blast chillers and quick-chill refrigerators have powerful cooling units that quickly bring food temperatures down.

Blender. Vertical mixing machine with removable cup or jar, having mixing and stirring blades in the bottom and mounted on a base with a drive motor. Normally set on a table or countertop. Used in preparing special diets in hospitals or in mixing cocktails in bars, as well as to whip or puree food generally at home.

Blower-Dryer. Motor-driven attachment with a blower and electric- or steam-heated coil, mounted on top of a dishwasher for quick drying of ware at the end of the final rinse cycle.

Blower (Evaporator) Coil. *See* Unit Cooler.

Board. A rectangular or round board, small for easy handling, set on a hard surface or countertop, to prevent dulling of the knife blade when cutting food. It can be made of laminated or solid hard rock maple or of rubber or thermal plastic material. Usually furnished with a handle or grip. Sandwich and steam table boards are rectangular and narrow; they are mounted on a sandwich unit or the corresponding section of a countertop. Also called workboard in preparation areas of a kitchen.

Boil-in Bag. A clear plastic waterproof pouch containing foods that are heated by immersing the package in boiling water.

Bone Saw. *See* Meat and Bone Saw.

Booster. *See* Hot-Water Booster.

Bottle Breaker. Motor-driven device with revolving, horizontal, open-top pan in which empty glass bottles are safely flogged with steel bars.

Bottle Chute. Flexible cylindrical tubing to convey empty bottles from bar to bottle storage bin or breaking or crushing device. Load end is usually located at the cocktail mix station.

Bottle Crusher. Motor-driven device with rollers or reciprocating plate(s) to crush bottles, plastic containers, and cans. The unit is mounted on a stand with a waste receptacle beneath to receive crushed and broken articles. The loading chute is provided with a spring-loaded or gravity-hinged door.

Bottle Disposer. System consisting of bottle chute and storage bin, bottle breaker, or bottle crusher.

Bottle Trough. Trough suspended along the front of a bar workboard, usually at the cocktail mix station, to hold various bottles of liquor or mixer used often. Also called speed rail.

Bowl. A round-bottomed container open at top for mixing food. The salad bowl is a shallow type for mixing and displaying leafy vegetables. A coffee bowl is the lower of a two-piece, siphon-type coffeemaker, used as a decanter.

Braising Pan, Tilting. *See* Fry Pan, Tilting.

Breading Machine. Horizontal rotating cylinder set on a base with a drive motor and filled with breading mix. Food is placed in one end, carried through the cylinder by an internally mounted auger, and discharged at the other end. Food is tumbled in breading mix.

Bread Molder. Machine with a series of rollers and conveyor belts to shape a ball of dough to pan bread, hearth bread, or long rolls of varied length.

Bread Slicer. (1) Motor-driven machine with a multiple set of reciprocating knives in a single frame through which bread is pushed, or vice versa. (2) Motor-driven or hand-operated machine with a single revolving knife to slice single slices while a bread loaf is moved along in a chute by a gear-driven plate. Slice thickness may vary.

Breath Guard. *See* Display Case.

Briquette. One of the coal-size pieces of permanent refractory material used in open-hearth gas-fired grills to provide radiant broiling heat.

Broiler, Backshelf. Broiler with gas-heated ceramic radiants or electric heating elements, having an adjustable sliding grill. The unit is normally mounted on a panel and brackets above the rear of the range. Also called salamander broiler.

Broiler, Charcoal. Horizontal-type unit with removable bottom pan containing glowing charcoals to radiate high heat into the bottom of foods set on a grill above. Mounted on stand or enclosed cabinet or masonry base.

Broiler, Char or Open-Hearth. (1) Horizontal-type unit with gas-heated briquettes under a grill at the top. (2) Horizontal-type unit with nonglowing electric strip heaters at the top. May also be equipped with an adjustable electric grill above the top grill to broil both sides at once.

Broiler, Conveyor. (1) Horizontal-type unit with openings at both ends, using a motor-driven grill-type conveyor to transport food between or under gas-fired ceramics or electric heaters. (2) Horizontal-type unit, open at both ends, using a motor-driven, revolving, heated griddle to transport food under gas-fired ceramics or electric heaters.

Broiler-Griddle, Combination. (1) Unit with front opening with griddle plate set into top, equipped with gas-heated radiants under the griddle. Radiants heat food and griddle simultaneously. (2) Unit with front-opening door(s) having gas-heated radiants at the top of the cavity and food placed on a sliding or swinging type griddle plate set below.

Broiler, Pop-up. Enclosed horizontal-type unit with a slotted opening in the top and gas-heated radiants on both sides of the cavity. Food is placed in an elevating mechanism and broiled on both sides at the same time. Similar to a pop-up toaster.

Broiler, Pork and Spare Rib, Chinese. Counter- or stand-mounted narrow-depth broiler with two or three decks, each having gas burners and radiants, for cooking pork slices and spare ribs in metal platters.

Broiler, Upright. Vertical-type unit with an opening at the front and gas-heated radiant ceramics or electric heating elements at the top of the cavity. Food is placed on a sliding adjustable grill set under the radiants. May be mounted on countertop, oven or cabinet base, or stand. Often aligns with ranges. May be equipped with removable charcoal pan.

Buffet Unit. One or more mobile or stationary counters having flat surfaces, with cold pans or heated wells at the top, on which chafing dishes, canapé trays, or other food displays can be placed for self-service.

Bun Divider. *See* Roll Divider.

Butcher Block. Rectangular or round shape—6, 10, 14, or 16 inches thick—consisting of hard rock maple strips, kiln dried, hydraulically pressed together, glued, and steel-doweled through. Work surface of block is smoothed surface of ends of strips. Block mounted on open-type wood or steel legs.

Butter Chip Dispenser. Enclosed insulated unit with mechanical refrigeration or ice to hold tiers of butter pats placed on chips and dispensed one at a time. Normally set on a countertop. Also called butter chip cooler.

Cafeteria Counter or **Serving Counter.** In a cafeteria, top that is usually provided with recessed cold pans, recessed pans for hot-foods section, display and protector cases, and drain troughs for beverages; set on legs or masonry base with enclosure panels, semi- or fully enclosed cabinets with refrigeration or warming units beneath; all as required to accommodate foods to be served. Unit may be equipped with tray slide.

Can Crusher. Motor-driven machine with rollers or reciprocating plates or arms to crush cans and break bottles. Unit mounts on stand with space under for refuse receptacle to receive crushed articles. Also called can and bottle crusher.

Can Opener. (1) Hand-operated or motor-driven device fastened to the top of a table, wall, cabinet, etc., to open individual cans. (2) Portable motor-driven device capable of opening cans while still in case.

Can Washer. (1) Enclosed cabinet with spray heads for washing the interior and exterior of a can, mounted on open legs. (2) Round platform with a rotating spray head at its center for washing the interior of a can, mounted on a stand with foot-operated water valves. (3) Rinse nozzle built into a floor drain and connected to a hand-operated quick-opening mixing valve.

Can Washer and Sterilizer. Enclosed cabinet with spray heads for washing the interiors and exteriors of cans, mounted on open legs, provided with detergent dispenser and 180°F hot-water rinse or steam-mixing valve for final rinse. *See* Pot and Pan Washer.

Carbonated Beverage System. *See* Soda System.

Carbonator. Motor-driven water pump, with tank and control valves, to combine cold water and CO_2 gas in a storage tank, producing soda water. Used for soda fountains, carbonated beverage dispensers, and dispensing systems.

Carrier. A unit for carrying food, beverages, and ware by hand for short distances, furnished with grip(s) or handle(s). Could be an enclosed cabinet, insulated, heated or refrigerated; or a wire basket or rack.

Cart. Mobile unit of varying structure: as an open shelf or shelves; a semi- or fully enclosed cabinet with single or multiple compartments that may be insulated. Used for transporting food or ware and for cleaning and storage.

Cash Drawer. Shallow drawer located under a countertop at the cashier end. Often provided with removable compartmented insert for currency and coins.

Cashier Counter. *See* Checkout Counter.

Cashier Stand. Mobile or stationary stand with solid top set on four legs, or semienclosed body open at bottom. May be provided with footrest, cash drawer, and tray rest on one or both sides.

Checkout Counter. Counter located between a cafeteria serving area or kitchen and a dining room, for use by checker and/or cashier. Also called cashier counter.

Chinese Range. Range with one or more large-diameter gas burners on an inclined top and a raised edge around each burner opening. Food is cooked in shallow bowls called woks. Range top is cooled by water flowing from a front manifold to a rear trough, with strainer basket at one end. A swing-spout faucet mounted on high splash guard at rear fills the bowl when the spout is turned 90 degrees.

Chopping or **Cutting Block.** *See* Butcher Block.

Clam Opener. Device with hand-operated, hinged knife and fixed, V-shaped block attached to a tabletop.

Cleaning Cart. Mobile unit with one or more compartments for soiled linen, waste, and water for mops and wringer.

Cocktail Mix Station. Section of bar workboard where drinks are poured or mixed. Usually includes open-top ice storage bin and wells for mixer bottles and condiments.

Coffee Filter. Perforated metal container or disposable paper or muslin bag in coffeemaker or urn to hold bed of coffee grounds.

Coffee Grinder. (1) Bench-mounted hand- or motor-driven machine with bean hopper at the top, grinding mechanism, and discharge chute with holder for container or filter beneath. (2) Coffee-grinding attachment for a food machine.

Coffeemaker. (1) Hand- or automatically operated electric-heated unit in which a measure of hot water at the proper temperature is poured over a measured bed of coffee grounds contained in a filtering unit. The extracted beverage is discharged into a container and/or serving unit. (2) Hand- or automatically operated electric-heated unit in which a measure of hot water at the proper temperature is combined with a measure of instant coffee mix and discharged into a container. (3) Unit consisting of one or more sets of upper and lower bowls set on gas- or electric-heated range. The measure of water boiled in the lower bowl is forced by pressure into the upper bowl containing measured coffee grounds. When the set is removed from the heat source, the cooling lower bowl creates a vacuum, causing the liquid to flow back down through a filter in the bottom of the upper bowl. The upper bowl is then removed to permit use of the lower bowl as a server or decanter.

Coffee Mill. *See* Coffee Grinder.

Coffee Percolator. Covered cylindrical container with up to 120-cup capacity, electric- or gas-heated. Percolating device in center causes heated water to flow over measured bed of coffee grounds contained in a filtering basket at top. Unit is normally hand-filled. Heating unit keeps coffee warm for serving. Bottom has draw-off faucet.

Coffee Range. Counter unit consisting of one to four low-rated gas or electric burners for making coffee with siphon-type coffeemakers.

Coffee Urn. Enclosed container of water with jar (liner) set into top. Urn water is heated by gas, electricity, or steam. A measure of hot water at proper temperature is poured over measured bed of coffee grounds contained in a filtering unit. Beverage collects in jar and is discharged through bottom connection to draw-off faucet. Urn water is not used for coffeemaking. Equipped with water inlet valve to fill urn body.

Coffee Urn Battery. Assembly of units consisting of one or more water boilers and one or more coffee urns heated by gas, electricity, or steam. Battery is complete with piping, fittings, and controls between boiler(s) and urn(s).

Coffee Urn, Combination. (1) Coffee urn with water inlet valve and additional draw-off faucet for hot water, to make tea and instant beverages. (2) Pressure siphon type has sealed water and hot-air chambers with piping control between water jacket and jar. (3) Twin type has two coffee jars set into top of single container. Urn body is usually rectangular in shape. (4) Automatic type has electrically operated device to pump and measure hot water at thermostatically controlled temperature.

Coffee Warmer. Countertop range with one or more gas, electric, or canned heaters to maintain coffee at serving temperature; each with coffee bowl or decanter. Also called coffee server.

Cold Beverage Dispenser or **Urn**. *See* Iced Coffee/Tea Urn.

Cold Pan. Insulated depressed pan set into a table or countertop; provided with waste outlet; may be refrigerated with crushed ice, refrigeration coil fastened to the underside of the lining, or a cold plate. A perforated false bottom is provided when ice is used.

Combination Steam Cooker and Kettle. *See* Cooker and Kettle, Combination.

Compressor, Refrigeration. *See* Condensing Unit, Refrigeration.

Condensate Evaporator. Finned coil through which compressed refrigerant flows, absorbing the heat inside refrigerator or freezer.

Condensing Unit, Refrigeration. Assembly consisting of mechanical compressor driven by electric-powered motor with either air- or water-cooling device. (1) Open-type unit has major components separate but mounted on same base. (2) Hermetic-type unit has major components enclosed in same sealed housing, with no external shaft, and motor operating in refrigerant atmosphere. (3) Semihermetic-type unit has hermetically sealed compressor whose housing is sealed and has means of access for servicing internal parts in field.

Condiment Cabinet. Semi- or fully enclosed cabinet, mobile or stationary, having several removable or intermediate shelves to store cook's or baker's condiments and spices in the cooking and preparation areas.

Condiment Shelf or **Rack.** Shelf or rack mounted above or under a tabletop to hold several condiment items for use by the cook or baker.

Condiment Stand. Standard-height mobile or stationary stand having a solid top with receptacle for holding condiment containers, and tray rest on one or both sides. May be open type with legs or enclosed type with cabinet base and shelves, or may have insulated cold pan and refrigerated base.

Confectioner's Stove. *See* Pot Stove.

Container, Food and Beverage. *See* Bin; Carrier.

Convection Oven. Gas- or electric-heated. Heat is circulated through the oven interior with fan or blower system. Interior may be equipped with racks and/or shelves. Ovens may be stacked or set on stand. Oven bottom may be constructed as part of the platform of a mobile basket rack cart.

Convenience Food. Any food item that has been processed by any method from the raw state and packaged for resale and/or further processing or use at later date.

Conveyor. A mechanized belt, often built into a stainless-steel cabinet, that transports materials from one location to another. In foodservice, conveyors are primarily used to move soiled trays from the dining area to the warewashing area. Conveyors can have a variety of types of belts. Usually they run horizontally, but they can also be designed to move trays vertically.

Cooker and Kettle, Combination. One or more steam-jacketed kettles with one or more steam cookers mounted in top of single cabinet base or tops of adjoining cabinet bases. May be for direct steam operation or provided with steam coil or gas- or electric-heated steam generator in the base under the steam cooker(s).

Cooker-Mixer. Direct steam-heated, gas-heated, or electric-heated steam-jacketed kettle, with hinged or removable agitator mounted to supporting frame or brackets.

Cookie Dropper. Motor- or hand-driven machine used to portion and shape drops of cookie dough using dies. Unbaked cookies are dropped onto baking sheet pans or conveyor belt. Also called cookie machine.

Cook's Table. Table located in the cooking area of kitchen for cook's use.

Corn Popper. Enclosed unit with transparent front and ends, transparent doors on the working side, electrically heated popcorn popper suspended from the top, and warming heaters for storage of finished popcorn. May be mounted on counter or enclosed base.

Cotton Candy Machine. Machine with round tub and spinning unit and electric heating unit for converting sugar into cotton candy. May be set on countertop or stand.

Creamer. (1) Insulated container for cream, having ice or mechanical refrigeration, and provided with adjustable draw-off faucet for each cream measure. Often anchored to counter or wall. Also called cream dispenser. (2) Soda fountain unit with self-contained ice cream cabinet.

Creamer Rack. Rectangular basket of wire or plastic with compartments to fit glass creamers. Used to wash, fill, and store creamers.

Crusher. *See* Bottle Crusher; Can Crusher; and Ice Crusher.

Cryogenic Freezer. *See* Freezer (3).

Cubing Machine. *See* Dicing Machine.

Cutlery Box. Unit consisting of one or more compartments for storage and dispensing of flatware (knives, forks, spoons). Often set on a counter or tabletop, and sometimes built into the front of a cabinet under the top, or as a drawer.

Cutting Board. *See* Board.

Deep Fat Fryer. *See* Fryer.

Defrost System. Refrigeration system for a freezer consisting of a blower evaporator coil, heating unit, and controls. Electric type employs heating elements; hot-gas type uses heat exchanger to remove frost from the coil and allow condensate to flow to the drain pan under the coil.

Dessert Cart. Cart with several shelves for display and serving of desserts. May be equipped with mechanical or ice-refrigerated cold pan or plate and with transparent domed cover.

Detergent Dispenser. Device mounted on a dishwasher or sink for storage and dispensing of liquid detergent or mixture of powdered detergent and water into the wash tank of the unit through the pump manifold or incoming water line. Some units are equipped with control device, electrically operated, to detect detergent strength in tank.

Dicing Machine. Bench-mounted hand- or motor-driven two-operation machine that first forces food through a grid network of knives in a square pattern and then slices the food the same length as the side of the square. May be attached to food mixing or cutting machine. Also called dicing attachment or cubing machine.

Dish Box. *See* Carrier.

Dish Cart. Cart for storage and dispensing of clean or soiled dishes. Usually of height to roll under counter or tabletop.

Dish Table. Work surface with raised sides and end(s) having its surface pitched to a built-in waste outlet, adjoining a sink or warewashing machine. There may be a soiled-dish table used for receiving, sorting, and racking ware, located at the load end of the sink or washing machine, and a clean-dish table at the unload end for draining of rinse water, drying, and stacking ware.

Dispenser. Unit for storage and dispensing of beverages, condiments, food, and ware. May be insulated and refrigerated or heated. May be provided with self-leveling device. May be counter- or floor-mounted, stationary or mobile.

Display Case. A semi- or fully enclosed case of one or more shelves, mounted on countertop or wall, for display of desserts. Semienclosed types have transparent end panels and sneeze guards along customers' side to protect uncovered foods. Refrigerated types have insulated transparent panels and doors. Heated types are usually provided with sliding doors and electric heating units, with or without humidifier.

Dolly. Solid platform or open framework mounted on a set of casters, for storage and transportation of heavy items. May be equipped with handle or push bar.

Dough Divider. Motor-driven floor-type machine to divide dough (usually for bread) into equally scaled pieces. Pieces are removed from work surface by conveyor to next operation. Normally used for bread dough. Also called bread divider.

Dough Mixer. (1) Motor-driven machine with vertical spindle to which various whips and beaters are attached. Bowl is raised to the agitator. Mixers of 5- to 20-quart capacity are bench-mounted. Mixers of 20- to 140-quart capacity are floor type. (2) Motor-driven, floor-type horizontal machine with tilting-type bowl and horizontal agitator(s) for a large dough batch. Also called kneading machine or mixer.

Dough Molder. *See* Bread Molder.

Doughnut Fryer. *See* Fryer.

Doughnut Machine. Unit consisting of hand- or motor-driven batter dropper and shallow fryer. Doughnuts are conveyed through heated cooking fat or oil bath, turned over, and discharged out of bath into drain pan.

Dough Proofer. *See* Proof Box or Cabinet.

Dough Retarder. May be upright reach-in, low-counter bench-type, or walk-in refrigerator with series of racks or tray slides and/or shelves, in which dough is kept cool, to retard rising.

Dough Rounder. Motor-driven floor-mounted machine into which a piece of dough is dropped and rounded to ball shape by means of a rotating cone and fixed spiral raceway running from top to bottom. *See* Roll Divider.

Dough Sheeter. Motor- or hand-driven machine with a series of adjustable rollers to roll dough to sheets of even thickness. Also called piecrust roller.

Dough Trough. Large tub with tapered sides, usually mounted on casters, for storing and transporting large batches of dough. Some troughs have gates at the ends for pouring dough when the trough is lifted above a divider and tilted.

Drainer. *See* Kettle Drainer.

Drink Mixer. Vertical counter-type unit with one or more spindles with motor at top. Switch is activated by drink cup when placed in correct position. Also called malted mixer.

Drop-in Unit. Any warming, cooling, cooking, or storage unit that is dropped into an opening in a counter or tabletop and is fitted with accompanying mounting brackets and sized flange.

Dunnage Rack. Mobile or stationary solid or louvered platform used to stack cased or bagged goods in a storeroom or walk-in refrigerator or freezer.

Egg Boiler. Electric-, steam-, or gas-heated unit with removable timed elevating device(s) to raise basket(s) or bucket(s) out of boiling water bath. Containers are lowered by hand. Ferris-wheel-type unit will automatically lower and raise baskets through water bath. Also called egg timer.

Egg Timer. *See* Egg Boiler.

Espresso Machine. A machine that heats and holds hot water and pumps it under pressure through coffee in a sieve to make espresso. Many espresso machines also produce steam that is discharged through a wand for heating and frothing milk to make cappuccino and latte.

Evaporator. *See* Condensate Evaporator; Unit Cooler.

Extractor. (1) *See* Juice Extractor. (2) *See* Grease Filter. (3) *See* Water Extractor.

Extruder. *See* French Fry Cutter.

Fat Filter. (1) Gravity type has disposable paper or muslin strainer set in holder on top of fat container. Unit is placed under drain valve of fat fryer. (2) Siphon type uses disposable paper or muslin strainer over fat container, attached to rigid siphon tube mounted on fat fryer, with other end of tube in fat tank. (3) Motor-driven pump type, portable or mobile, uses disposable paper strainer. Has flexible hose from fat tank to strainer. Strainer set on fat container.

Filter. (1) *See* Coffee Filter. (2) *See* Fat Filter. (3) *See* Grease Filter.

Finishing Oven. *See* Au Gratin Oven.

Fire Extinguisher. Hand-operated, sealed with chemical inside, most commonly wall-mounted and provided with control and directional hose, or horn.

Fire Suppression System (Kitchen Hood). A fire suppression system senses a fire in the cooking equipment under the hood and then opens nozzles that spray a fire-retardant chemical, extinguishing the fire. Some fire suppression systems spray a fine water mist that suffocates the fire rather than (or in addition to) fire retardant chemicals.

Fish and Chip Fryer. *See* Fryer.

Fish Box. (1) Ice-refrigerated insulated cabinet with counterbalanced hinged or sliding door(s) at the top, and drawer(s) at the bottom front. (2) Ice- or mechanically refrigerated cabinet with tier(s) of self-closing drawers with insulated fronts. Also called fish file.

Fish File. *See* Fish Box.

Flatware. Knife, spoon, and fork used by the diner.

Floor Scale. (1) Unit fixed in a pit, its platform flush with finished floor. May have dial or beam mounted on top of the housing at the rear of platform framing, plus tare beam. Used for weighing heavy objects on mobile carriers. (2) Mobile type. *See* Platform Scale.

Food Carrier. *See* Carrier.

Food Cutter. (1) Motor-driven bench- or floor-mounted machine with a rotating shallow bowl to carry food through a set of rotating horizontal knives whose axis is perpendicular to the radii of the bowl. Knives are set under hinged cover. (2) Motor-driven floor-mounted high-speed machine with vertical tilting bowl having a vertical shaft with rotating knife. Also called vertical cutter-mixer or sold under various brand names.

Food Freshener. Electrically operated unit that introduces live steam to the exterior or interior of food, heating it to serving temperature without loss of moisture. Cabinet type has a hinged cover or drawer for warming the exterior of foods. Hollow-pin type heats food interior through injection.

Food Merchandiser. Refrigerated, heated, or noninsulated case or cabinet with transparent doors and possibly transparent ends. Used for display and sometimes self-service of foods.

Food Processor. A food preparation appliance that chops, grates, and purees food into various sizes and shapes depending on the blade that is installed. Some food processors use a bowl that must be emptied into a pan when full; other are continuous-feed and empty directly through a chute into a pan.

Food Shaper. (1) Motor-driven unit with loading hopper, bench- or floor-mounted. Shapes food into rectangular or round patties of varying thickness. May be equipped with paper interleaving, removing, and conveying devices. (2) Attachment to meat chopper to shape ground food into rectangles of varied thickness. Also called food former.

Food Warmer. (1) Insulated mobile or stationary cabinet with shelves, racks, or tray slides, having insulated doors or drawers. May be electric, steam-heated, or gas-heated and provided with humidity control. (2) Infrared lamp or electric radiant heating element with or without a glass enclosure, mounted above the serving unit in a hot-food section.

French Fry Bagger. Motor-driven machine to convey, measure, and insert Fench-fried potatoes into paper bag blown open to receive product.

French Fry Cutter. Hand-operated or motor-driven machine or attachment to food machine that pushes potato through grid of knives set in square pattern in frame.

French Fryer. *See* Fryer.

Fryer. Floor- or bench-mounted unit heated by gas or electricity with tank of oil or fat into which foods are immersed. Common type has deep tank. Special types have shallow tanks for fish, chicken, doughnuts, etc., and basket-conveyor type has a shallow tank for draining with baskets, arms, mesh-type belt, or rotating auger to move foods through the bath. Pressure type has a lift-off or hinged cover to seal the top of the fryer tank.

Fry Pan, Tilting. Rectangular pan with gas- or electric-heated flat bottom, pouring lip, and hinged cover. Floor mounted on a tubular stand or wall mounted on brackets with in-wall steel carriers. A small electric pan may be table-mounted on legs. Also called braising pan, tilting griddle, or tilting skillet.

Fudge Warmer. Counter-mounted electrically heated insulated pot with hinged or lift-off cover and ladle.

Glass Washer. (1) Multitank horizontal machine with hand-activated rinse nozzle in one tank, revolving brushes in a second tank, and final rinse nozzles in a third. (2) Single- or double-tank door-type or rack-conveyor-type dishwasher.

Grater. (1) Bench-mounted hand- or motor-driven machine in which food is forced against the face of a revolving grater plate by a pusher or hopper plate. (2) Part of vegetable-slicing attachment to food machine.

Grease Filter or **Extractor.** (1) Removable rectangular or round frame having several layers of wire mesh or baffles and mounted in the exhaust equipment above or behind cooking units. (2) A series of baffles mounted in exhaust equipment, from whose surfaces grease deposits are flushed with wash water into a waste outlet. (3) Manifold-mounted water nozzles in exhaust equipment producing a fine spray mist that collects grease from laden air and drains through a waste outlet.

Griddle. Extra-thick steel plate with a ground and polished top surface, heated by gas or electricity. Surface edges are raised or provided with gutters and drain hole leading to catch trough or pan. May be set on countertop with legs, stand, or oven base.

Grill. Bench-mounted unit with fixed lower and hinged upper electrically heated plates. Plates have a waffle pattern for waffles and grooves for steaks, and are smooth for sandwiches.

Grill, Charcoal. *See* Broiler, Charcoal.

Grinder. (1) *See* Meat Chopper. (2) *See* Coffee Grinder.

Hamper. *See* Linen Hamper.

Heat Exchanger, Steam. Boiler with coils to generate clean steam with possibly contaminated house steam. Used for steam-cooking units.

High-Speed Cooker. *See* Steam Cooker.

Hors d'Oeuvre Cart. Cart with platforms on Ferris wheel having several food containers on each platform. Used for display and service.

Hot Chocolate Dispenser or **Maker.** (1) Counter-mounted electrically heated glass bowl with agitator or insulated tank with agitator for dispensing premixed hot chocolate. (2) Counter-mounted electrically heated unit that combines measure of heated water with measure of chocolate mix and dispenses mixture at touch of button.

Hot Dog and Hamburger Broiler. Semi- or fully enclosed cabinet with glass doors and panels for display. An electric heater under the top radiates onto hot dogs in baskets or on pins on wheel, or onto hamburgers laid on platforms mounted on motor-driven Ferris wheel. Food rotates while cooking.

Hot Dog Steamer. Counter-mounted cabinet with transparent display panels and hinged covers or doors. The unit is electrically heated with a water bath and immersion device to generate steam for heating hot dogs and dry heat for warming rolls.

Hot Dog Roller Grill. Counter-mounted unit with multiple steel rollers spaced about ¼ inch to ½ inch apart. Hot dogs are placed between the rollers; as they spin, the hot dogs turn over the heating elements.

Hot Food Cabinet. *See* Food Warmer; Carrier.

Hot Plate. Countertop or floor-mounted unit with one or more open gas or tubular electric burners arranged left to right and/or front to rear. French hot plates are round or square solid steel plates, gas or electrically heated.

Hot-Water Booster. Electric-, steam-, or gas-heated insulated tank or coil used to raise the incoming hot water from house temperature to sanitizing temperature, as required by code. Booster may be mounted inside housing or at end of warewashing machine, under warewashing table, or remotely located.

Housekeeping Cart. Cart with one or more semi- or fully enclosed compartments for clean linen, a compartmented tray at the top for supplies, a cloth hamper for soiled linen, and a waste receptacle.

Humidifier. Electric-, steam-, or gas-heated unit used to evaporate and distribute water inside proofing equipment and hot food warmers. May be fixed or removable attachment.

Ice Breaker. *See* Ice Crusher.

Ice Chest. *See* Ice Storage Bin.

Ice Cream Cabinet. (1) Mechanically refrigerated low-type chest with removable hinged flip-flop covers, used for storage and dispensing of ice cream. (2) Mechanically refrigerated upright cabinet with hinged door(s), for storage of ice cream.

Ice Cream Display Cabinet. Ice cream cabinet with sliding or hinged transparent doors or covers. Mostly used in self-service stores.

Ice Cream Freezer. Floor- or counter-mounted machine with mechanically refrigerated cylinder, having a dasher to mix and refrigerate an air and ice cream mix to flowing ice cream. The product is then placed inside a hardening cabinet.

Ice Cream Hardening Cabinet. Low cabinet with a lid(s) or upright cabinet with hinged door(s), insulated and refrigerated at a very low temperature to set ice cream hard.

Ice Crusher. (1) Motor-driven or hand-operated floor- or counter-mounted machine with spiked rollers, to crush large pieces of ice or ice cubes. (2) Attachment mounted between an ice-cube-making machine and an ice storage bin, having a damper for directing cubed ice to motor-driven rollers with spikes to crush ice as required.

Ice Cuber. *See* Ice Maker.

Iced Coffee/Tea Urn. Urn with stainless-steel or transparent glass jar and draw-off faucet. Stainless-steel type may be insulated. Glass jar may be equipped with ice compartment suspended from cover. Also called iced tea/coffee dispenser.

Ice Dispenser. A floor-, counter-, or wall-mounted stationary ice storage bin with motor-driven agitator and conveyor mechanism or gravity feed that dispenses a measure of ice (cubed or crushed) through a discharge chute into a container at working level.

Ice Maker. Floor-, counter-, or wall-mounted unit containing refrigeration machinery for making cubed, flaked, and crushed ice. Maker may have integral ice storage bin. Larger-capacity machines generally have a separate bin in which ice is received via a connecting chute. Capacity is rated in pounds of ice per twenty-four-hour day.

Ice Maker and Dispenser. Floor-, counter-, or wall-mounted ice maker with storage bin and dispensing mechanism. *See* Ice Maker; Ice Dispenser.

Ice Pan, Display. *See* Cold Pan.

Ice Plant. (1) An assembly consisting of a large-capacity ice maker that empties into a walk-in freezer or ice storage bin(s) on the floor below via directional chute(s). (2) A large-capacity, floor-mounted ice maker, having a small-capacity bin connected to vertical and horizontal conveyors with insulated sleeves for transporting ice to large-capacity bin(s).

Ice Shaver. Hand-operated or motor-driven floor- or bench-mounted machine whose rotating plate or wheel has a sharp knife that produces icelike snow when forced against the face of a cake of ice. Also called snow-cone machine.

Ice Storage Bin. Insulated mobile or stationary cabinet of one or more compartments with hinged or sliding door(s) or cover(s). It is commonly mounted under an ice-making machine, with opening(s) in the top to receive product(s), and is fitted with a waste outlet in the bottom. Ice is normally scooped out of bin. Unit may be built into counter.

Ice Vendor. Floor-mounted, mechanically refrigerated freezer with a coin-operated mechanism to release a measure of loose or bagged ice cubes at working level.

Infrared Heater or **Warmer.** Unit consisting of one or more lamps or electric strip heaters, with or without protective covering or reflector, mounted in a bracket or housing. Usually set over hot-food serving and display areas or inside enclosed displays. Unit produces infrared heat to keep food warm.

Infrared Oven. Oven having heat generated and radiated from electric infrared heating elements encased in a glass tube or from an exposed quartz infrared plate.

Injector, Rinse. *See* Rinse Injector.

Insert. Rectangular pan or round pot set into the top of a steam or hot-food table.

Juice Extractor. (1) Counter-mounted motor-driven ribbed cone having base with drain hole for juice. Half of fruit is pressed by hand, down onto cone. (2) Bench- or floor-mounted motor-driven machine that slices fruit in half and squeezes halves between nesting cones. (3) Hand-operated bench-type machine that squeezes fruit halves between inverted cones. Also called juicer.

Kettle Drainer. Mobile sink with screen or strainer basket, waste outlet with adjustable tailpiece, and push handle.

Kettle, Electric-heated. (1) Stationary or tilting two-thirds steam-jacketed, or stationary fully steam-jacketed kettle with electric immersion heater in water between shells. Kettle is floor mounted inside housing or attached to housing with tilting mechanism. Tilting device may be hand- or power-operated. Stationary unit is provided with water filler, hinged cover, and draw-off valve. Tilting type has pouring lip and may have draw-off valve, hinged cover, and water filler. (2) Stationary or tilting two-thirds steam-jacketed kettle set into top of cabinet base with remote electric-heated steam generator adjoining kettle. Kettle provided with hinged cover, water filler, and draw-off valve.

Kettle, Flat-bottom. Rectangular pan with flat bottom having inner and outer shells. Live steam is introduced between shells, heating inner shell for cooking. Kettle is tilting type, floor-mounted on tubular stand or wall-mounted with brackets and in-wall steel chair carriers. Kettle front has pouring lip. Top has hinged cover.

Kettle, Gas-heated. (1) Stationary fully or two-thirds steam-jacketed kettle with a gas burner under the bottom of its outer shell to heat water between shells. The kettle is floor-mounted inside housing and provided with a water filler and hinged cover. (2) Stationary or tilting two-thirds steam-jacketed kettle set into the top of a cabinet base with remote gas-heated steam generator adjoining the kettle. The kettle is provided with hinged cover, water filler, and draw-off valve. (3) Stationary floor-type direct-fired kettle with a single shell, mounted inside insulated housing, with a gas burner under bottom of shell, draw-off valve, and hinged cover.

Kettle, Steam-jacketed. Kettle having live steam introduced between the inner and outer shells to heat the inner shell for cooking. Deep-type kettle generally is two-thirds jacketed. Shallow-type kettle generally is fully jacketed. May be mounted to the floor with tubular legs or pedestal base, or mounted to the wall with brackets and in-wall steel chair carriers. Tilting or trunnion type may be floor- or wall-mounted, having a worm gear device for hand operation. The stationary kettle has a draw-off valve. The tilting kettle has a pouring lip and may have a draw-off valve. The kettle may be equipped with lift-off or hinged cover, filling faucet, water-cooling system, thermostat, etc.

Kettle, Tabletop. Two-thirds steam-jacketed kettle, tilting type, with operating lever up to 20-quart capacity, or tilting worm gear device for 40-quart capacity; all direct-steam, electric-heated. All kettles have a pouring lip. Tilting types have 20- and 40-quart capacity with a lever handle. Oyster stewing kettle is shallow tilting-type kettle.

Kettle, Tilting or **Trunnion.** *See* Kettle, Steam-jacketed; Kettle, Flat-bottom.

Kneading Machine or **Mixer.** *See* Dough Mixer.

Knife Rack. Slotted wood or stainless-steel bar set away and attached to edge of tabletop or butcher block. This forms a slot into which cutlery blades are inserted and held up by handles of same while the handles protrude at the top.

Knife Sharpener. (1) Bench-mounted motor-driven machine with rotating stones forming a V to grind edges on both sides of a blade. (2) Attachment to slicing machine. (3) Grinding-wheel attachment to food machine, having an attachment hub.

Linen Cart. Cart with several compartments for storage of clean linen. May be semi- or fully enclosed.

Linen Hamper. (1) Stationary or mobile metal cabinet with hinged metal cover. (2) Stationary or mobile framework with round cloth bag or cloth sides, ends, and bottom.

Lobster Tank. Transparent tank open at the top and with a water wheel at one end. Tank bottom is lined with special salt. Mounted on a stationary or mobile enclosed base with a filtering and mechanical refrigeration system for tank water. Also called trout tank, with salt omitted.

Machine Stand. Mobile or stationary stand with solid or open-frame top, mounted on open legs or cabinet base, with adjustable dimensions to suit a specific machine or device.

Malted Mix Dispenser. Counter- or wall-mounted unit with a transparent covered hopper, having a lever for dispensing a measure of malted mix powder.

Meat and Bone Saw Floor-mounted motor-driven band saw with upper and lower pulleys, stationary cutting table with gauge plate, and movable carriage.

Meat Chopper. Table- or floor-mounted hand- or motor-driven horizontal machine. Food placed in top-mounted hopper is fed by a stomper into cylinder with tight-fitting auger to drive food against rotating knife and perforated plate. Also called meat grinder.

Meat Grinder. *See* Meat Chopper.

Meat Hook Rack. One or more wood or metal bars mounted on a wall or floor stand, with fixed or removable sharp pointed metal hooks. Also called meat rail.

Meat Roaster, Steam-jacketed. Shallow steam-jacketed kettle with cover and draw-off valve.

Meat Tenderizer. Counter-mounted machine having two sets of round knives with spaced cutting edges, set apart on slow-speed rollers. Meats are inserted into a slot in the top, pass through the rollers, and are discharged at the bottom front.

Menu Board. Sign with fixed or changeable letters or removable lines listing the food items and prices.

Mexican Food Machine. Device used to hold a V-shaped tortilla when filling it to make a taco.

Microwave Oven. Stand- or counter-mounted oven in which foods are heated and/or cooked when they absorb microwave energy (short electromagnetic waves) generated by magnetron(s).

Milk Cooler. (1) Low insulated chest with mechanical or ice refrigeration, for storing and dispensing ½-pint to 2-quart containers of milk. (2) Counter- or stand-mounted refrigerator with one or more 2- to 10-gallon containers equipped with sanitary tube connections that extend through flow-control handles for dispensing loose or bulk milk.

Milkshake Machine. *See* Drink Mixer; Shake Mixer.

Mix Cabinet. Low counter-type or upright reach-in refrigerator in which the mix for frozen shakes or ice cream is stored.

Mixer, Dough. *See* Dough Mixer.

Mixer, Drink. *See* Drink Mixer.

Mixer, Food. Motor-driven machine with vertical spindle having several speeds on which various whips and beaters are mounted. Bowl is raised up to agitator. Mixers of 5- to 20-quart capacity are bench type. Mixers of 20- to 140-quart capacity are floor type.

Mixer Stand. Low-height stationary or mobile stand with four legs and a solid top to support a mixer up to 20-quart size. May be provided with undershelf and vertical rack for mixer parts.

Mixer, Vertical Cutter. *See* Vertical Cutter-Mixer.

Mixing Tank. Vertical type has center-, bottom-, or side-mounted agitator assembly. Horizontal type has end-agitator assembly. All are floor-mounted and provided with removable or hinged cover and draw-off valve. Tank may be provided with recirculating pump and filtering system.

Modular Stand. Low-height open stationary stand with four or more legs, having an open framework top, to support heavy-duty modular cooking equipment.

Molder, Food. *See* Food Shaper.

Napkin Dispenser. Countertop unit for storage and dispensing of folded paper napkins. Napkins forced to headplate by spring.

Order Wheel. Metal- or wood-spoked wheel with clips or hooks on its perimeter, located between cooks' and servers' areas, on which order slips are placed to maintain rotation and visibility.

Oven. Fully enclosed insulated chamber with gas-, electric-, or oil-fired heat, provided with thermostatic control. Deck-type units have chambers or sections stacked one above the other. Bake-type decks are approximately 7 inches high inside. Roast-type decks are 12 to 14 inches high inside.

Oyster Opener. *See* Clam Opener.

Pan and Utensil Rack. (1) One or more bars and braces suspended from a ceiling or mounted on posts or a wall, housing fixed or removable hooks for hanging pots, pans, and utensils. (2) Upright mobile or stationary unit, open or semienclosed, with tiers of angle- or channel-shaped slides to support pans. (3) Heavy-duty rectangular wire basket to hold pans and utensils upright in a pot washer.

Pan Washer. *See* Pot and Utensil Washer.

Pass-through Window or **Opening.** Trimmed opening between kitchen and serving areas having a shelf for a sill. May be equipped with hinged or sliding door or shutter.

Peanut Roaster. Electrically heated enclosed display case with hinged cover at the top.

Peeler. Floor- or bench-mounted machine having a vertical, stationary, abrasive-lined cylinder open at the top, a motor-driven agitator bottom plate, and an over-the-rim water supply. Product discharged through door in cylinder side. Wastewater is discharged at bottom. May be equipped with a peel trap basket that can be hung on a pipe over sink or set inside a cabinet base under the peeler. May also be equipped with garbage disposal unit.

Peeler Stand. (1) Special-height mobile stand, open type, with four legs. (2) Special-height enclosed cabinet with adjustable legs, a door designed to house a trap basket, and a waste outlet.

Pellet Heater. Counter-mounted electric-heated, insulated cabinet having one or more vertical cylinders in which metallic discs, inserted at the top, are heated. Discs are dispensed at the bottom through drawer-type device.

Pie and Pastry Case. *See* Display Case.

Pizza Oven. Baking-type oven of one or more decks, gas-, electric-, or oil-fired, having temperature range from 350° to 700°F. Deck(s) are of heat-retaining masonry material.

Pizza Sheeter. *See* Dough Sheeter.

Platform Scale. Mobile unit with a dial or beam, for weights up to 1,500 pounds. May be floor- or stand-mounted.

Platform Skid. *See* Dunnage Rack.

Popcorn Machine. *See* Corn Popper.

Pot and Utensil Washer or **Potwashing Machine.** Machine of one or more tanks with hood or wash chamber above, inside which large ware is washed, using very big, high-pressure pumps. Water is pumped from tanks and sprayed over ware placed in racks or set on a conveyor or platform. One or more final fresh-water rinses sanitize ware. Machine has a

34- to 36-inch working height. (1) Door-type single-tank machine has power wash and final rinse only. (2) Door-type two-tank machine has power wash and power rinse tanks and final rinse. (3) Belt-conveyor machine is straight-through-type machine having one to three tanks plus final rinse. Ware is set directly on a belt. (4) Revolving tray-table type has two to three tanks plus final rinse. Ware is set directly on turntable platform.

Pot Filler. Faucet or valve with a hose mounted at a range, pot stove, or kettle to fill a vessel directly.

Pot Sink, Powered. A powered pot sink circulates heated water around the pots and pans in the soak compartment, loosening food waste.

Pot Stove. Low, floor-mounted single-burner stove with high BTU or kW rating for use with large stock pots.

Prefabricated Cooler. Walk-in refrigerator or freezer having insulated walls, ceiling, and floor fabricated in a shop and assembled on the job site. The insulated floor and base of the walls may be constructed as part of the building.

Preparation Table or **Counter.** Unit located in the preparation area of a kitchen, for cutting, slicing, peeling, and other preparation of foods.

Prerinse or **Prewash Sink.** Sink constructed as an integral part of a soiled-dish table, located near a dishwashing machine, and furnished with removable perforated scrap basket(s) and spray hose.

Pressure Cooker. *See* Steam Cooker.

Pressure Fryer. *See* Fryer.

Prewash. Separate machine or built-in section of a warewashing machine with tank and pump or fresh-water supply. Pump recirculates water over ware; fresh-water type sprays over ware; before pumped-wash section of machine.

Proof Box or **Cabinet.** Fully enclosed cabinet with gas, steam, or electric heater and humidifier. Sometimes unit may be insulated and have thermostatic and humidity controls. Box may be mobile. Traveling-type proofer has a conveying mechanism inside the overhead cabinet, as in large commercial bread bakery.

Protector Case. A single shelf mounted on posts with transparent shield at the front or at front and ends. Mounted over a countertop at hot-food or sandwich sections to protect uncovered food.

Pulper. Floor-mounted garbage and waste disposal machine with a vertical cylinder, grinder plate, knives, and sump compartment for nongrindable matter. Waste material is ground in a deep-water bath to form a slurry that is piped to a water extractor. Water from the extractor is recirculated to the pulper.

Quartz Oven. Oven that employs an electrically heated quartz plate or infrared quartz element inside a glass tube to generate heat. Also called infrared oven.

Quick Chiller. *See* Blast Chiller.

Rack: Cup, Dish, Glass, Plate, or Tray. (1) Rectangular or round basket of wire or plastic construction, with or without compartments or intermediate lateral supports, used for washing and/or storage of small ware. Racks are self-stacking for cups and glassware. (2) *See* Tray Rack for upright unit.

Rack Pan. *See* Pan and Utensil Rack.

Rack Washer. Machine of one or two tanks with hood or wash chamber over, with one or two doors, using large-size high-pressure pumps and final sanitizing rinse. Steam- or electric-heated water is pumped from tanks and sprayed over racks wheeled onto tracks inside washer. Machine is made to recess into floor to have tracks set flush with finished floor.

Range. Unit with heated top surface or burners that heat utensils in which foods are cooked, or cook foods directly. Some ranges are equipped with an insulated oven base. Hot or even-heat tops and fry or griddle tops are gas- or oil- fired or electrically heated. Open or hot-plate tops have electric or gas burners.

Reel Oven. *See* Revolving Tray Oven.

Refrigerated Table. Tabletop mounted on counter-type refrigerated base.

Refrigerator Shelves. Shelves of wire, solid, embossed, or slotted material with reinforced hemmed edges, mounted on tubular posts with adjustable sanitary brackets. May be in stationary or mobile sections.

Rethermalizer. A rethermalizing unit is a heated cabinet that brings food that has been quick-chilled up to serving temperature.

Revolving Tray Oven. Gas-, electric-, or oil-heated oven with a motor-driven Ferris wheel device inside having four or more balanced trays. Bake or roast pans are loaded and unloaded from a single opening with a hinged-down door. Steam may be added.

Rinse Injector. Device mounted to top or side of washing machine for storage and automatic dispensing of liquid water softener into the final rinse manifold.

Roaster, Meat, Steam-jacketed. *See* Meat Roaster, Steam-jacketed.

Roast Oven. *See* Convection Oven; Oven; Revolving Tray Oven.

Roll Divider. Hand- or motor-operated machine that divides a ball of dough into equal pieces. Hand-operated unit is stand or table mounted. Motor-driven unit is floor mounted with a cabinet base and may be combined with a rounding device. Also called bun divider.

Roll Warmer. (1) Enclosed cabinet with a telescoping cover, heated by pellet or glowing charcoal under a false bottom. (2) Enclosed insulated cabinet with electric heating elements and humidity controls. The unit is provided with one or more drawers in a tier at the front; it sits on a countertop, legs, or a stand, or is built into a counter. Also called bun warmer.

Rotisserie. (1) Upright enclosed cabinet with a vertical grill having gas-fired ceramics or electric heating elements. A side-mounted motor drives revolving spits set in a tier in front of the heaters. The unit has hinged or sliding glass doors. (2) Upright enclosed cabinet containing a motor-driven Ferris wheel provided with food cradles or baskets passing under gas-fired ceramics or electric heating elements. (3) Enclosed, square, upright cabinet with meat suspended from top in center revolving motor-driven cradle, heated by four infrared lamps radiating from the corners. (4) *See* Hot Dog and Hamburger Broiler.

Salad Case. Unit consisting of a refrigerated counter with refrigerated food pans set into the top, and a refrigerated or nonrefrigerated display case mounted on the countertop.

Salamander. A backshelf or cabinet mounted over the rear of a range or steam table, absorbing the heat to keep foods on it warm.

Salamander Broiler. *See* Broiler, Backshelf.

Saw, Meat and Bone. *See* Meat and Bone Saw.

Scale. *See* Floor Scale; Platform Scale.

Self-Leveling Dispenser. *See* Dispenser.

Service Stand. A stationary cabinet with a solid top at a working height used in a restaurant; may have shelves, bins, drawers, and refrigerated section for storage of linen, flatware, glassware, china, condiments, water, and ice.

Settee Bench. Bench with upholstered seat and upholstered back.

Shake Maker. Floor- or counter-mounted machine with one or two mechanically refrigerated cylinders, having dashers to mix and refrigerate an air and milk mixture to a flowing frozen dessert beverage. Unit may be equipped with syrup tanks and pumps, and mixing spindle to blend various flavors in shakes.

Shrimp Peeler and Deveiner. Bench-mounted, motor-driven machine that removes vein and shell from shrimp and prawns.

Silver Burnisher, Holloware and Flatware. Machine with a tumbling barrel or vibrating open-top tub filled with steel balls and compound, in which silver-plated utensils are placed. Tumbling or vibrating action causes steel balls to rub tarnish from the surface of the utensils, exposing the base metal. Units may be bench- or floor-mounted or made mobile to roll under a tabletop.

Silver Washer and Dryer. Floor-mounted machine with a fixed or removable tumbling drum set inside a wash chamber with a hinged cover for washing, sterilizing, and electrically drying flatware. The removable drum has a perforated bottom and top cover. The fixed drum has a hinged cover and perforated ends. Machine has wash, rinse, and final sterilization rinse cycles. Electrically heated air is blown through wash chamber and drum to dry flatware.

Sink. (1) Preparation, cook's or utility: one- or two-compartment type with drain board on one or both sides, each compartment averaging 24 inches square. (2) Pot and pan or scullery: two-, three-, or four-compartment type with drain board on one or both sides, and possibly between, compartments. Each compartment should be minimum 27 inches left to right, and average 24 inches front to rear.

Slaw Cutter. Floor- or bench-mounted machine with revolving slicer plate and hopper. Cored and quartered cabbage heads inserted in hopper are forced against slicer plate and discharged through chute below.

Slicer. Bench- or stand-mounted machine with a stationary motor-driven round knife and slice-thickness gauge plate, and reciprocating feed trough or carriage. Flat trough may have hand- and/or spring-pressure feed plate. Gravity trough may have hand- or automatic-feed plate. Trough may be hand-operated or motor-driven. Slicer can be equipped with automatic stacking and conveying device.

Slicer, Bread. *See* Bread Slicer.

Slicer, Vegetable. *See* Vegetable Slicer.

Slush Maker. Floor- or counter-mounted machine with one or two mechanically refrigerated cylinders having dashers to mix and refrigerate a water mixture to a flowing frozen dessert beverage.

Smokehouse, Chinese. Floor-mounted, enclosed, insulated roasting cabinet with gas burners and baffle plates, hinged door(s), duct connection, and flue at top, and removable grease pan inside the bottom. Meat, fish, and poultry are mounted on skewers inside. Interior walls and door have deflector plates to direct drippings into the grease pan.

Sneeze Guard. *See* Display Case.

Snowcone Machine. *See* Ice Shaver.

Soda Dispenser. (1) Part of soda-making and refrigeration system: dispensing head attachment for mounting on a soda fountain, bar, counter, or at a server station, complete with drainer. (2) Enclosed cabinet, ice or mechanically refrigerated, to dispense premixed soda or combine soda water and syrup stored in a cabinet or remote tanks. (3) Floor- or counter-mounted cabinet with a self-contained soda and refrigeration system having remote or self-contained syrup tanks.

Soda Maker. Unit consisting of mechanical refrigeration system, carbonator, and soda storage tank.

Soda System. Assembly consisting of soda maker, syrup tanks, syrup, soda and refrigeration tubing, and soda-dispensing head(s) and/or cabinet(s). Also known as carbonated beverage system.

Soft Ice Cream Maker. Floor- or counter-mounted machine with one or two mechanically refrigerated cylinders having dashers to mix and refrigerate air and ice cream mix to a flowing frozen dessert. Unit is equipped with hand- or foot-operated dispensing head or control.

Soiled-Dish Pass Window. Trimmed opening in a partition between dishwashing and serving areas, having the soiled-dish table as a sill. The opening may be equipped with hinged or sliding door or shutter.

Soup Station. Section of cook's table or cafeteria counter with a hot-food receptacle, rectangular or round, set into the top.

Speed Rail. *See* Bottle Trough.

Spice Bench. Table with stationary cabinet above rear or below top, or mobile cabinet(s) under the top. Cabinet(s) have two or more spice drawers or bins.

Squeezer, Juice. *See* Juice Extractor.

Steam Cooker. Enclosed cabinet with one or more sealed compartments having individual controls into which clean steam is introduced for cooking or heating. Cooker may be direct-connected or equipped with gas-fired, electric, or steam coil generator in the base. (1) A cooker with compartments in tiers cooks with low-pressure steam. Each compartment has a hinged door with a floating inner panel and a sealing gasket made tight with a wheel screw. Unit is floor-mounted or if direct-connected, may be wall-mounted. (2) Cooker with high pressure has self-sealing door(s) with a gasket made tight by interior steam pressure. May be floor-, counter-, or-wall mounted. Also called high-speed cooker.

Steamer, Dry. *See* Food Freshener.

Steamer, Hot Dog. *See* Hot Dog Steamer; Steam Cooker.

Steam-jacketed Kettle. *See* Kettle, Steam-jacketed.

Stock Pot Stove. *See* Pot Stove.

Storage Rack. Unit consisting of one or more shelves mounted on angle, channel, or tubular posts, for storage of goods or ware.

Stove. Floor- or counter-mounted unit with one or more open gas or electric burners. Also called hot plate.

Swill Trough. (1) Depression in dish table approximately 6 to 9 inches wide and 2 to 6 inches deep, equipped with waste outlet, strainer basket, and perforated cover. (2) Extra sink compartment of shallow depth located between compartments of potwashing sink, equipped with strainer basket.

Table. Top with solid flat surface, mounted on floor with legs, on wall with brackets and legs, or on semi- or fully enclosed cabinet. May be stationary or mobile. May have shelves under, shelves over, and tool drawer(s).

Tea Maker or Dispenser. (1) *See* Coffee Urn. Same as coffee urn with tea laid in strainer. (2) Counter-mounted unit used to combine instant tea mix with heated water for hot tea or cold water for ice tea.

Tenderizer. *See* Meat Tenderizer.

Timer, Egg. *See* Egg Timer.

Toaster. (1) Counter-mounted pop-up type has two- or four-slice capacity. Electric only. (2) Counter-mounted conveyor type with a motor-driven conveyor carries the product between electric or gas-fired radiants. (3) Sandwich type: *See* Grill.

Tray Makeup or **Assembly Conveyor**. Motor-driven or gravity-type horizontal conveyor used to transport trays between various food loading stations.

Tray Rack. Upright mobile or stationary unit, open or semienclosed, having angle, channel, or tubular posts and one or more tiers of angle- or channel-shaped slides to support trays or pans. Rack may be built into cabinets or suspended from under tabletops.

Tray Slide or **Rail**. Horizontal surface that accommodates the width of a tray, extended out from, and running the length of, cafeteria countertop. May be constructed of solid material with or without raised edges and V beads, or of several tubular or solid rails or bars. Mounted on and fastened to brackets secured to countertop and/or counter body. Also called tray rest.

Tray Stand. Low-height, mobile or stationary four-legged stand with solid top. Top may have raised back and sides to prevent tray stacks from falling over.

Trough, Swill. *See* Swill Trough.

Trout Tank. *See* Lobster Tank.

Truck. *See* Cart.

Undercounter Sink Workboard. *See* Bar Workboard.

Unit Cooler. Semi-enclosed cabinet open at front and rear or top and bottom, depending on airflow, with a motor-driven fan blowing air through a mechanically refrigerated finned coil. Device is normally suspended inside a refrigerator or freezer. Also called blower (evaporator) coil.

Urn, Coffee/Tea. *See* Coffee Urn.

Urn Stand. Stationary stand with a solid top having raised edges all around, recessed drain trough(s) with waste outlet, and a drainer plate flush with the top. Raised, die-stamped openings are used to connect lines to an urn. Top set on open base with shelf, semi-enclosed cabinet with bottom (and intermediate) shelf, or enclosed cabinet with bottom (and intermediate) shelf and door(s). May also be equipped with fold-down step.

Vegetable Peeler. *See* Peeler.

Vegetable Slicer or Cutter. (1) Hand- or motor-driven counter-mounted machine having rotating removable plates with varied knives. Product is forced against plates and knives for slicing, dicing, grating, shredding, etc. (2) Similar attachment to a food machine with rotating removable plates and knife arrangements.

Vegetable Steamer. *See* Steam Cooker.

Vertical Cutter-Mixer. Floor-type machine with a vertical tilting mixing bowl having a 25- to 80-quart capacity. The bowl is equipped with a two-speed motor and a high-speed agitator shaft at bowl bottom with cutting-mixing knife. A hand- or motor-driven stirring and mixing shaft is fixed to the bowl's cover. A strainer basket may be included.

Waffle Baker. *See* Grill.

Water Boiler. (1) One or more urns of coffee urn battery, heated by gas, steam, or electricity, to bring water to boil for making beverages. Usually connected to other urns with water piping and controls. Can be used separately. (2) Gas-, electric-, steam-, or oil-fired unit to heat water for use in kitchen.

Water Extractor. Floor-mounted machine located at the terminal of a waste pulping system. The device augers pulp in a slurry out of the tank to a pressure head at the top, extracting water that is then recirculated into the system. The pulp is discharged into a chute to a waste receptacle.

Water Heater. Counter-mounted instant electric heating device with faucet for making tea and hot chocolate drinks.

Water Station. Section of a counter or stand with a glass and/or pitcher-filling faucet and drain trough.

Window, Soiled-Dish Pass. *See* Soiled-Dish Pass Window.

Wine Rack. Fixed or portable folding unit with alternating stacked compartments open at front and rear to support wine bottles in a horizontal position for storage and display.

Wok. *See* Chinese Range.

Wood Top. Tabletop constructed of kiln-dried laminated hard rock maple strips, hydraulically pressed together, glued, and steel-doweled through.

Workboard. *See* Bar Workboard.

Worktable. *See* Preparation Table.

BIBLIOGRAPHY

Allar, Bruce. (2000). California Gold: CPK's Founders Have Made Millions. Now It's the Chain's Turn. *Pizza Today*, Volume 18/6, Page 22+.

Arey, Donna. (1995). FE&SS Layout and Design: A Renovation to Maintain Tradition. *Foodservice Equipment and Supplies*, Volume 48/9, Pages 83–86.

———. (1995). FE&SS Layout and Design: Campus Cafeteria Serves up Flexibility. *Foodservice Equipment and Supplies*, Volume 48/11, Pages 53–56.

———. (1995). FE&SS Layout and Design: College Cafeteria Becomes a Keeper. *Foodservice Equipment and Supplies*, Volume 48/5, Pages 63–66.

———. (1995). FE&SS Product Knowledge: Food/Equipment Applications #45: Steaks and Chops: Taking Steak to Heart. *Foodservice Equipment and Supplies*, Volume 48/1, Pages 80–82.

———. (1995). FE&SS Product Knowledge: Product Focus #123: Griddles and Grills: Dressed to Grill. *Foodservice Equipment and Supplies*, Volume 48/7, Pages 59–60.

———. (1995). FE&SS Product Knowledge: Supplies Side: Cutting Boards: Below the Surface. *Foodservice Equipment and Supplies*, Volume 48/8, Page 77.

———. (1995). FE&SS Product Knowledge: Supplies Side: Steam Table Pans: Pans with the Proper Fit. *Foodservice Equipment and Supplies*, Volume 48/12, Page 65.

———. (1996). FE&SS Layout and Design: Steam Power Produces for NY Psych Centers. *Foodservice Equipment and Supplies*, Volume 49/9, Pages 51–54.

Attrino, Tony. (1999). Galley Design: Technology Meets Needs. *Cruise Industry News*, Volume 9/36, Pages 134–135.

Award for Excellence in Design. (2000). *The Consultant*, Volume 33/3, Pages 52–54+.

Bean, Russell. (1996). FE&SS Product Focus: That Old Versatility Champ. *Foodservice Equipment and Supplies*, Volume 49/13, Pages 53–54.

Bensky, Gary. (1999). Emerging Technologies Are Now Compatible with Every Kitchen. *Nation's Restaurant News*, Volume 33/40, Page 21+.

———. (2000). Chill Out: What to Look for with Reach-In Refrigerators. *Nation's Restaurant News*, Volume 34/26, Page 28.

———. (2000). Kitchen Topography 101: How to Bring Kitchens into the Future. *Nation's Restaurant News*, Volume 34/3, Page 22+.

———. (2000). Suite Success: No Kitchen Is Just an Island. *Nation's Restaurant News*, Volume 34/14, Page 26.

———. (2001). Equipment/Operations: Home on the Range, Where Chefs Produce Best, Most. *Nation's Restaurant News,* Volume 35/22, Page 26.

———. (2001). Time and Space: Early Expert Planning Can Counter Kitchen Limitations. *Nation's Restaurant News,* Volume 35/14, Page 28.

Bertagnoli, Lisa. (1995). Breakfast Is Served. *Restaurants and Institutions,* Volume 105/15, Page 132+.

———. (1995). FE&SS Product Knowledge: Product Focus #124: Carts and Kiosks: New Meaning for Meals on Wheels. *Foodservice Equipment and Supplies,* Volume 48/9, Pages 167–168.

———. (1995). New Styles for Steam Tables: Designers Like Steam-Table Technology, So They're Dressing It up with Wood, Stone and Marble. *Restaurants and Institutions,* Volume 105/11, Page 166.

———. (1995). Style on a Shoestring: Budget-Conscious Kitchen Designs Caught the Attention—and the Honors—at This Year's Food Facilities Design Awards. *Restaurants and Institutions,* Volume 105/21, Page 88+.

———. (1996). Espresso Concerns: Consider Labor, Timing and Cost Before You Buy an Espresso or Cappuccino Machine. *Restaurants and Institutions,* Volume 106/7, Page 88.

———. (1996). FE&SS Layout and Design: Harlequin's Marche Works. *Foodservice Equipment and Supplies,* Volume 49/7, Pages 55–58.

———. (1996). FE&SS Product Knowledge: Product Focus #129: Scales: Weighing Your Scale Options. *Foodservice Equipment and Supplies,* Volume 49/1, Pages 69–70.

———. (1996). FE&SS Product Knowledge: Product Focus #130: Fryers: Fry, Fry Again. *Foodservice Equipment and Supplies,* Volume 49/3, Pages 59–60.

———. (1996). Food/Equipment Applications: F&S for Asian Menus: The Orient Express. *Foodservice Equipment and Supplies,* Volume 49/8, Pages 46–48.

———. (1996). Friendly by Design: Comfortable Interiors and Display Kitchens Help Customers Feel Like They're Eating in When They're Eating Out. *Restaurants and Institutions,* Volume 106/1, Page 80+.

The Best Things in Life Are 3: Fine Cuisine Served in a Chic Setting Is the Order of the Day at Melbourne Central's Food on 3. (2000). *The Consultant,* Volume 33/1, Page 93+.

Bruns, Rick. (1999). Trying on Euro Style. *Lodging,* Volume 24/6, Pages 78–82 (Supplement).

Centralizing Production in California. (1995). *Food Management,* Volume 30/8, Page 82.

Charlie Trotter's. (1995). *Restaurant Business,* Volume 94/12, Pages 33–34 (Supplement).

CIA at Greystone. (1995). *Restaurant Business,* Volume 94/12, Page 24 (Supplement).

The Consultants' Forum. (1995). *The Consultant,* Volume 28/1, Pages 11–13+.

Cook, Lou. (2000). Cooking up a Storm. *Lodging F&B,* Pages 13–14.

Cooking Equipment: Charbroilers and Charcoal Grills: Charbroiler Checkpoints. (1996). *Foodservice Equipment and Supplies,* Volume 49/10, Pages 37–38.

Cooking Equipment: Coffee Equipment: A Perfect Cup of Joe. (1996). *Foodservice Equipment and Supplies,* Volume 49/10, Pages 41–42.

Cooking Equipment: Combination Oven-Steamers: The Right Combination. (1996). *Foodservice Equipment and Supplies,* Volume 49/10, Pages 49–50.

Cooking Equipment: Conveyor Ovens: Conveying Ideas. (1996). *Foodservice Equipment and Supplies,* Volume 49/10, Pages 53–54.

Cooking Equipment: Fryers: Fond of Fried Foods. (1996). *Foodservice Equipment and Supplies,* Volume 49/10, Pages 43–44.

Cooking Equipment: Griddles and Grills: The Grill of It. (1996). *Foodservice Equipment and Supplies,* Volume 49/10, Pages 45–46.

Cooking Equipment: Microwave Ovens: Catch the Wave. (1996). *Foodservice Equipment and Supplies,* Volume 49/10, Pages 55–56.

Cooking Equipment: Ranges: It's All the Range. (1996). *Foodservice Equipment and Supplies,* Volume 49/10, Pages 62–63.

Cooking Equipment: Rotisserie Ovens: As the Rotisserie Turns. (1996). *Foodservice Equipment and Supplies,* Volume 49/10, Pages 58–59.

Cooking Equipment: Steamers: Picking up Steam. (1996). *Foodservice Equipment and Supplies,* Volume 49/10, Pages 65–66.

Coomes, Steve. (1995). American Baking Boom Cooking up Fresh-Baked Profits. *The Consultant,* Volume 28/1, Page 32+.

Correll, John. (1996). Equipment: Cutting to the Quick: The Author Makes His Case for the Vertical Cutter Mixer. *Pizza Today,* Volume 14/9, Pages 54–56.

———. (1996). Mixers in Orbit: Reliable, Versatile and Easy to Operate, Planetary Mixers Are Perfect Dough-Makers for Many Pizza Operations—But They Do Have Limitations. *Pizza Today,* Volume 14/7, Pages 44–46.

Doty, Laura; Schechter, Mitchell. (1999). International Market Perspectives: United States: Building for the New Millennium. *The Consultant,* Volume 32/2, Pages 13–16.

———. (2000). International Market Perspectives: United States: College Foodservices Bloom in Spring. *The Consultant,* Volume 33/1, Pages 11–13+.

———. (2000). United States: Popularity Spurs Museum Foodservice Improvements. *The Consultant,* Volume 33/2, Pages 13–15+.

Excellence in Design: Pfizer Ltd. (1997). *The Consultant,* Volume 30/1, Pages 36–42.

FE&SS Product Knowledge: Product Knowledge: Product Focus: #127: Combination Oven-Steamers: Cooking with Dual Technology. (1995). *Foodservice Equipment and Supplies,* Volume 48/12, Pages 61–62.

FE&SS Supplies Side: Spice up Sales with Condiment Dispensers. (1996). *Foodservice Equipment and Supplies,* Volume 49/13, Page 55.

Frable, Foster, Jr. (1995). Operations: Steam Hisses Back into Kitchens—for More than Cooking. *Nation's Restaurant News,* Volume 29/37, Page 64+.

———. (1996). Operations: Enhance Operational Efficiencies with Improved Ergonomics. *Nation's Restaurant News,* Volume 30/32, Page 92+.

———. (1996). Operations: European Shows Offer Preview of What's Coming to N. America. *Nation's Restaurant News,* Volume 30/15, Page 22+.

———. (1996). Operations: Extractor Hoods a Bargain vs. Water Wash or Filter Hoods. *Nation's Restaurant News,* Volume 30/3, Page 49+.

———. (1996). Operations: Fabricated Equipment Is Long-Term Investment; Select Carefully. *Nation's Restaurant News,* Volume 30/45, Page 22+.

———. (1996). Operations: New, Low-Cost Pulpers Merit a Rethinking of Waste Disposal. *Nation's Restaurant News,* Volume 30/5, Page 39+.

———. (1996). Operations: Remote Refrigeration Takes the Heat out of Your Kitchen. *Nation's Restaurant News,* Volume 30/7, Page 28+.

———. (2000). Coming Soon to a Facility Near You—the Intelligent Kitchen. *Nation's Restaurant News,* Volume 34/22, Page 26+.

———. (2000). Features and Options to Look for When Evaluating Upright and Counter Refrigerators. *Nation's Restaurant News,* Volume 34/8, Page 19+.

———. (2000). Off the Wall: Improve Kitchen Cleanability by Eliminating Legs and Bases on Equipment. *Nation's Restaurant News,* Volume 34/26, Page 28+.

———. (2000). What to Look Forward to in 2000 When You're Planning a New or Renovated Kitchen. *Nation's Restaurant News,* Volume 34/1, Page 22+.

———. (2001). Innovative Heating, Refrigeration, Floor Protection: Top Kitchen Product Launches. *Nation's Restaurant News,* Volume 35/14, Page 28+.

———. (2001). Case Study: Display Cases Need Close Scrutiny to Optimize Their Functionality. *Nation's Restaurant News,* Volume 35/12, Page 34+.

Freddies: Making the Daily Routine Exceptional. (2000). *The Consultant,* Volume 33/3, Pages 68–69+.

Friedland, Ann. (1996). Kitchen Systems: Under Budget, Over-sized. *Food Management,* Volume 31/9, Page 38+.

Gallo-Torres, Julia M. (1996). FE&SS Layout and Design: Students Cook in Working Kitchen. *Foodservice Equipment and Supplies,* Volume 49/11, Pages 47–50.

Gaspar, Lesley; Schechter, Mitchell. (2001). Some D's Make the Grade on Campus. *The Consultant,* Volume 34/2, Pages 13–15+.

Goldstein, Joyce. (1996). Forum: Don't Be a Restaurant Slumlord. *Restaurant Hospitality,* Volume 80/5, Page 18.

Grimshaw, Heather Reese. (1998). Super Models: Today's High-Tech Espresso Machines Are Spawning a Generation of "Hands-Off" Baristas. *Cheers,* Volume 8/4, Page 52+.

Gunner, Emma. (1996). Restaurants: Tiger Feat. *Caterer and Hotelkeeper,* Volume 3946, Pages 74–75.

Hensdill, Cherie. (1996). 3 Case Studies in Kitchen Technology. *Hotels,* Volume 30/9, Pages 71–72+.

———. (1996). Form Meets Function in Kitchen Design. *Hotels,* Volume 30/1, Page 53+.

———. (1997). New Kitchens Show off Latest. *Hotels,* Volume 31/1, Pages 65–66+.

Hickey, Matt. (1996). Denver International Airport. *The Consultant,* Volume 29/2, Pages 33–38+.

———. (2000). Topz Trims the Fat, Not the Taste: Two FCSI Consultants Teamed to Help Create Topz, a Burgers-And-Fries Concept with a Focus on Healthy Food, Not Health Food. *The Consultant,* Volume 33/3, Pages 76–78+.

Hicks, Jennifer. (1995). FE&SS Layout and Design: Cook-Chill Fuels Washington School District. *Foodservice Equipment and Supplies,* Volume 48/10, Pages 61–64.

———. (1995). FE&SS Layout and Design: Healthcare Commissary Excels with Cook-Chill. *Foodservice Equipment and Supplies,* Volume 48/12, Pages 53–56+.

———. (1995). FE&SS Layout and Design: Traditional Kitchens Update Their Ways. *Foodservice Equipment and Supplies,* Volume 48/6, Page 71+.

———. (1995). FE&SS Special Feature: Design Winners Reduce, Reuse and Redo. *Foodservice Equipment and Supplies,* Volume 48/9, Pages 62–64+.

———. (1996). FE&SS Layout and Design: Temple Redesigns for the '90s. *Foodservice Equipment and Supplies,* Volume 49/6, Pages 47–50.

Huie, Nancy. (1998). The Evolving Cruise Ship Galleys. *Cruise Industry News,* Volume 8/33, Pages 56–57.

Hutchcraft, Chuck. (2001). Equipped for Labor's Pains: Tech-Driven Kitchen Innovations Appeal to Operators Hungry to Cut Labor Costs. *Restaurants and Institutions,* Volume 111/5, Pages 59–60+.

Johnson, Min. (2001). Black Magic. *Restaurants and Institutions,* Volume 111/9, Page 137.

Konopka, Carmen. (1996). My New Kitchen: On the Home Front. *Caterer and Hotelkeeper,* Volume 3934, Pages 64–66.

———. (1996). My New Kitchen: Smooth Operation. *Caterer and Hotelkeeper,* Volume 3943, Pages 72–74.

LaVallee, James. (1996). Excellence in Design. *The Consultant,* Volume 29/4, Pages 23–26.

Legato, Frank. (1996). To Dine for: In Restaurant Planning, Design and Supply, What Counts Is What Happens Behind the Scenes. *Casino Journal,* Volume 9/3, Pages 87–88+.

Liberson, Judy. (1998). More with Less. *Lodging,* Volume 23/8, Page 105+.

Liddle, Alan. (1996). Technology: McD, Utilities and Equipment Vendors "TEEM" to Test the Newest Technology. *Nation's Restaurant News,* Volume 30/36, Page 25+.

Lorenzini, Beth. (1995). Design Portfolio: Charlie Trotter Builds a Dream Kitchen. *Restaurants and Institutions,* Volume 105/15 (Independents Edition), Page 26.

———. (1995). Display Play: What's New in Exhibition Cooking? Induction Buffet Ranges and Insulated Crocks. *Restaurants and Institutions,* Volume 105/5, Page 126.

———. (1995). Form and Function. *Restaurants and Institutions,* Volume 105/6, Page 153.

———. (1995). Introduction to Induction: Electric Induction Ranges Need to Be Tried to Be Believed. *Restaurants and Institutions,* Volume 105/3, Page 128.

———. (1995). Soft-Serve Made Easy: New Equipment Simplifies Maintenance and Reduces Waste. *Restaurants and Institutions,* Volume 105/7, Page 130.

Marsan, Joan. (2001). Kitchens in Paradise: Sun International's Paradise Island Properties Celebrate Cooking Exhibition-Style. *Hotels,* Volume 35/2, Pages 64–66.

Martin, Richard. (1995). Dining Shares Center Stage at High-Tech Mall Prototype. *Nation's Restaurant News,* Volume 29/50, Page 116.

Matsumoto, Janice. (1999). The Great Campus Makeover: Campus Remodeling Turns Old Cafeterias into Cutting Edge—and Profitable—Retail Spaces. *Restaurants and Institutions,* Volume 109/22, Pages 73–74+.

———. (2000). Blade Runners: Sharp Operators Pay Attention to Advances in Slicers That Offer Safer, Easier-to-Clean Options. *Restaurants and Institutions,* Volume 110/32, Pages 59–60.

———. (2000). Fit to Be Fried: With No-Oil Fryers, Operators Can Serve "Fried" Foods Even When the Kitchen Is Closed. *Restaurants and Institutions,* Volume 110/11, Pages 81–82.

———. (2000). Heat Waves: Sophisticated Rethermers Deliver Hot Food Hot and Cold Food Cold. *Restaurants and Institutions,* Volume 110/9, Page 116+.

———. (2000). Hot Now! a Razor-Thin Labor Market and Heightened Food-Safety Awareness Put Central Kitchens Back into the Spotlight. *Restaurants and Institutions,* Volume 110/9, Pages 89–90+.

———. (2000). King Crimson: Teamwork Drives Harvard University Dining Services in 10-Year Renovation Plan. *Restaurants and Institutions,* Volume 110/29, Pages 89–90.

Meal Prep Flies at Megakitchen. (1995). *Restaurants and Institutions,* Volume 105/14 (Institutions Edition), Page 22.

New Central Kitchen to Improve Service to "Fighting Irish." (1996). *Nation's Restaurant News,* Volume 30/31, Page 18.

Niemi, Wayne. (1995). FE&SS Product Knowledge: Product Focus #121: Pulpers and Compactors: Refuge from Refuse. *Foodservice Equipment and Supplies,* Volume 48/2, Pages 49–50.

———. (1995). FE&SS Product Knowledge: Product Focus #125: Quick-Chillers: The Thrill of Quick-Chill. *Foodservice Equipment and Supplies,* Volume 48/10, Pages 67–68.

Niemi, Wayne; Ward, Brian. (1996). Food Safety and the Surge in Blast Chilling. *Foodservice Equipment and Supplies,* Volume 49/7, Page 40+.

Perlik, Allison. (2001). Waste Not, Want Not: Food-Waste Disposers Offer a Clean, Efficient Way to Address a Messy Problem. *Restaurants and Institutions,* Volume 111/10, Pages 59–60.

Planning a Sustainable Kitchen: Breakout 6. (2000). *The Consultant,* Volume 33/4, Pages 50–53.

Ponchio, Mary. (1996). Cruise Line Supplier Goes Ship to Shore. *Air, Ship, and Catering Onboard Services,* Volume 28/1, Page 46.

Popolillo, Melissa C. (1995). Marché-Style Dining at the University of Guelph, Ontario, Canada. *Food Management,* Volume 30/7, Pages 52–53.

Preparation Equipment: Electric Slicers: Any Way You Slice It. (1996). *Foodservice Equipment and Supplies,* Volume 49/10, Pages 110–111.

Preparation Equipment: Food Blenders and Processors: Not Just for Beverages Anymore. (1996). *Foodservice Equipment and Supplies,* Volume 49/10, Pages 105–106.

Preparation Equipment: Food Mixers and Cutters/Mixers: All Mixed Up. (1996). *Foodservice Equipment and Supplies,* Volume 49/10, Pages 108–109.

Regan, Kelley. (1995). First Glimpse. *Food Arts,* Volume 8/1, Pages 84–85.

Regan, Mardee Haidin. (1995). Kitchen Spy: Round-the-Clock Cooking in Boston. *Food Arts,* Volume 8/4, Pages 68–72.

———. (1996). Kitchen Spy: Osteria Del Circo. *Food Arts,* Volume 9/4, Pages 110–115.

Riell, Howard. (1999). Van Andel Arena: Boosting Grand Rapids: In Working on the Van Andel Arena in Grand Rapids, Mich., the Task for the Consultant Was Simple—Help Resurrect the City. *The Consultant,* Volume 32/2, Page 37+.

Rogers, Monica. (1996). FE&SS Product Knowledge: Product Focus #132: Toasters: A Toast to You. *Foodservice Equipment and Supplies,* Volume 49/9, Pages 57–58.

———. (1996). FE&SS Product Knowledge: Product Focus #133: Food Blenders and Processors. *Foodservice Equipment and Supplies,* Volume 49/11, Page 59+.

———. (1996). Getting Steamed: Vacuum-Pump Steamer Cooks Food with Low-Temperature Steam for a Higher Product Yield. *Restaurants and Institutions,* Volume 106/13, Page 144.

———. (2000). Chic NoMI: Petite But Powerful Is the Kitchen Equipment Motif at Hyatt's New Chicago Flagship. *Hotels,* Volume 34/9, Pages 74–76+.

Rousseau, Rita. (1996). The Backless Restaurant. *Restaurants and Institutions,* Volume 106/22, Page 68+.

Sanitation and Safety Equipment: Pulpers and Compactors: The Dirt on Disposal. (1996). *Foodservice Equipment and Supplies,* Volume 49/10, Pages 112–113.

Sanitation and Safety Equipment: Ventilation Systems. (1996). *Foodservice Equipment and Supplies,* Volume 49/10, Pages 117–118.

Sanitation and Safety Equipment: Warewashers: Somebody's Got to Clean It Up. (1996). *Foodservice Equipment and Supplies,* Volume 49/10, Page 116.

Sanson, Michael. (1996). A Blueprint for Safety. *Food Management,* Volume 31/8, Page 65+.

―――. (1996). A Blueprint for Safety. *Restaurant Hospitality,* Volume 80/8, Page 65+.

Scarpa, James. (1996). Foodservice Equipment. *Restaurant Business,* Volume 95/12, Pages 1–54 (Supplement).

Seigler, Linda. (1997). Back to Basics: What Consultants Should Know When Specifying Foodservice Fittings. *The Consultant,* Volume 30/1, Page 54+.

Serving Equipment: Carbonated Beverage Dispensers: Dispensers for Hire. (1996). *Foodservice Equipment and Supplies,* Volume 49/10, Pages 67–68.

Serving Equipment: Carts and Kiosks: Carting It Around. (1996). *Foodservice Equipment and Supplies,* Volume 49/10, Pages 71–72.

Serving Equipment: Display Cases: Mighty Merchandisers. (1996). *Foodservice Equipment and Supplies,* Volume 49/10, Pages 74–75.

Serving Equipment: Food, Soup and Drawer Warmers: From the Warming Front. (1996). *Foodservice Equipment and Supplies,* Volume 49/10, Pages 76–77.

Serving Equipment: Salad Bars and Cold Buffets. (1996). *Foodservice Equipment and Supplies,* Volume 49/10, Pages 81–82.

Serving Equipment: Steam and Hot Food Tables: How the Steam Table Turns. (1996). *Foodservice Equipment and Supplies,* Volume 49/10, Pages 79–80.

Sherer, Michael. (1995). Centennial Center, Malone College, Canton, OH. *Food Management,* Volume 30/3, Page 46.

Sheridan, Margaret. (2001). Dry Ideas: Warm Air, Paper Compete for Drying Business. *Restaurants and Institutions,* Volume 111/1, Pages 73–74.

Sherratt, Patti. (1996). Cool Move. *Caterer and Hotelkeeper,* Volume 188/3930, Page 70–73.

―――. (1996). Expert Imports. *Caterer and Hotelkeeper,* Volume 188/3912, Page 76–78.

―――. (1996). The Fab Floor-Plan. *Caterer and Hotelkeeper,* Volume 188/3916, Page 72–74.

Slomon, Evelyne. (1996). Wood to Gas: These New-Technology Ovens Match the Look and Taste of Wood-Burning Units with the Convenience of a Gas-Fired Appliance. *Pizza Today,* Volume 14/9, Page 62–65.

Smith, Margi. (1995). Fists of Fury Meet the Machine: You Don't Need Bruce Lee or Steven Segal to Pound the Dough if You Have the Right Dividing and Rounding Equipment. *Pizza Today,* Volume 13/6, Page 62–65.

Sodexho Restores Order in Food Court at Law School. (1996). *Nation's Restaurant News,* Volume 30/16, Page 18.

Stephenson, Susie. (1995). Design: Step Right up in a Dazzling New Servery. *Restaurants and Institutions,* Volume 105/8 (Institutions Edition), Page 30.

Storage and Handling Equipment: Ice Machines and Dispensers: Ice, Ice, Baby. (1996). *Foodservice Equipment and Supplies,* Volume 49/10, Pages 89–90.

Storage and Handling Equipment: Ingredient and Storage Bins: Stored with Freshness. (1996). *Foodservice Equipment and Supplies,* Volume 49/10, Page 93.

Storage and Handling Equipment: Mobile Cabinets: Cabinets That Move. (1996). *Foodservice Equipment and Supplies,* Volume 49/10, Pages 94–95.

Storage and Handling Equipment: Quick-Chillers: Just Chillin' Out. (1996). *Foodservice Equipment and Supplies,* Volume 49/10, Pages 85–87.

Storage and Handling Equipment: Reach-in Refrigeration: The Art of Staying Cool. (1996). *Foodservice Equipment and Supplies,* Volume 49/10, Pages 97–98.

Storage and Handling Equipment: Walk-in Refrigeration: Walking in the Cold. (1996). *Foodservice Equipment and Supplies,* Volume 49/10, Pages 101–102.

Taco Bells Adding $5,000 Grills for Menu Upgrades, New Product Rollouts. (2001). *Nation's Restaurant News,* Volume 35/9, Page 3.

Tansey, Geoff. (1996). Airline Catering: Catering on a High. *Caterer and Hotelkeeper,* Volume 3946, Pages 64–66.

Topp, Barbara. (1995). The Fastest Way to Roll Out Dough. *Pizza Today,* Volume 13/8, Pages 32–34.

Townsend, Rob. (1995). FE&SS Layout and Design: Flexible Design Draws Crowd at Sierra's Employee Cafeteria. *Foodservice Equipment and Supplies,* Volume 48/8, Pages 43–46.

———. (1995). FE&SS Product Knowledge: Product Focus #126: Shelving: Shelf Discovery. *Foodservice Equipment and Supplies,* Volume 48/11, Pages 67–68.

———. (1995). FE&SS Product Knowledge: Product Focus #128: Ranges: A Range of Possibilities. *Foodservice Equipment and Supplies,* Volume 48/13, Pages 59–60.

University of Notre Dame South Dining Hall. (2000). *The Consultant,* Volume 33/1, Pages 42–45.

Ward, Brian. (1995). FE&SS Layout and Design: Creelman Goes to Market. *Foodservice Equipment and Supplies,* Volume 48/8, Pages 61–64.

Webb, Ben. (2001). Building a Dream: Neighbor's Mill Bakery and Café. *The Consultant,* Volume 34/1, Pages 102–103+.

Wheeler, Phyllis H. (1995). Some Like It Hot, Some Like It Cold . . . *Club Management,* Volume 74/4, Pages 75–76+Jul/.

Whitehall, Bruce. (1996). Equipment: Counter Intelligence. *Caterer and Hotelkeeper,* Volume 3939, Pages 81–84.

———. (1996). Ice-Makers: Freeze Frames. *Caterer and Hotelkeeper,* Volume 3934, Pages 68–69.

———. (2000). Europe: Ventilation Issues Move to Center Stage. *The Consultant,* Volume 33/1, Page 17+.

Woodward, Mary Alan. (1996). Division of Labor. *Pizza Today,* Volume 14/6, Pages 68–70.

———. (1996). Equipment: Rolling in the Dough. *Pizza Today,* Volume 14/8, Pages 44–48.

———. (1996). Pizza Prep Course: What You Need to Know to Pass the Final Exam When Purchasing a New Prep Table. *Pizza Today,* Volume 14/7, Page 38+.

Zoffranieri, Dominic. (1997). Equipped for the Future. *Foodservice Hospitality,* Volume 29/11, Page 42+.

INDEX